Language Teacher Supervision:
A Case-Based Approach

CAMBRIDGE LANGUAGE TEACHING LIBRARY

A series covering central issues in language teaching and learning, by authors who have expert knowledge in their field.

In this series:

Affect in Language Learning *edited by Jane Arnold*

Approaches and Methods in Language Teaching second edition *by Jack C. Richards and Theodore S. Rodgers*

Beyond Training *by Jack C. Richards*

Classroom Decision-Making *edited by Michael Breen and Andrew Littlejohn*

Collaborative Action Research for English Language Teachers *by Anne Burns*

Collaborative Language Learning and Teaching *edited by David Nunan*

Communicative Language Teaching *by William Littlewood*

Developing Reading Skills *by Françoise Grellet*

Developments in English for Specific Purposes *by Tony Dudley-Evans and Maggie Jo St John*

Discourse Analysis for Language Teachers *by Michael McCarthy*

Discourse and Language Education *by Evelyn Hatch*

The Dynamics of the Language Classroom *by Ian Tudor*

English for Academic Purposes *by R. R. Jordan*

English for Specific Purposes *by Tom Hutchinson and Alan Waters*

Establishing Self-Access *by David Gardner and Lindsay Miller*

Foreign and Second Language Learning *by William Littlewood*

Group Dynamics in the Language Classroom *by Zoltán Dörnyei and Tim Murphey*

Language Learning in Distance Education *by Cynthia White*

Language Learning in Intercultural Perspective *edited by Michael Byram and Michael Fleming*

The Language Teaching Matrix *by Jack C. Richards*

Language Test Construction and Evaluation *by J. Charles Alderson, Caroline Clapham and Dianne Wall*

Learner-Centredness as Language Education *by Ian Tudor*

Managing Curricular Innovation *by Numa Markee*

Materials Development in Language Teaching *edited by Brian Tomlinson*

Motivational Strategies in the Language Classroom *by Zoltán Dörnyei*

Psychology for Language Teachers *by Marion Williams and Robert L. Burden*

Research Methods in Language Learning *by David Nunan*

Rules, Patterns and Words: Grammar and Lexis in English Language Teaching *by Dave Willis*

Second Language Teacher Education *edited by Jack C. Richards and David Nunan*

Society and the Language Classroom *edited by Hywel Coleman*

Teaching Languages to Young Learners *by Lynne Cameron*

Teacher Learning in Language Teaching *edited by Donald Freeman and Jack C. Richards*

Testing for Language Teachers second edition *by Arthur Hughes*

Understanding Research in Second Language Learning *by James Dean Brown*

Using Surveys in Language Programs *by James Dean Brown*

Vocabulary: Description, Acquisition and Pedagogy *edited by Norbert Schmitt and Michael McCarthy*

Vocabulary, Semantics and Language Education *by Evelyn Hatch and Cheryl Brown*

Voices from the Language Classroom *edited by Kathleen M. Bailey and David Nunan*

Language Teacher Supervision

A Case-Based Approach

Kathleen M. Bailey

Graduate School of Languages and Educational Linguistics
Monterey Institute of International Studies

CAMBRIDGE
UNIVERSITY PRESS

CAMBRIDGE UNIVERSITY PRESS
Cambridge, New York, Melbourne, Madrid, Cape Town, Singapore, São Paulo

Cambridge University Press
32 Avenue of the Americas, New York, NY 10013-2473, USA

www.cambridge.org
Information on this title: www.cambridge.org/9780521838689

© Cambridge University Press 2006

First published 2006

Printed in the United States of America

A catalog record for this publication is available from the British Library.

Library of Congress Cataloging in Publication Data

Bailey, Kathleen M.
Language teacher supervision : a case-based approach / Kathleen M. Bailey.
   p.   cm. – (Cambridge language teaching library)
Includes bibliographical references and index.
ISBN-13: 978-0-521-83868-9
ISBN-10: 0-521-83868-1
ISBN-13: 978-0-521-54745-1 (pbk.)
ISBN-10: 0-521-54745-8 (pbk.)
1. Language teachers – Training of.   2. Observation (educational method)
I. Title.   II. Series.
P53.85.B35   2006
418.0071'1 – dc22   2006043858

ISBN-13   978 0 521 83868 9 hardback
ISBN-10   0 521 83868 1 hardback

ISBN-13   978 0 521 54745 1 paperback
ISBN-10   0 521 54745 8 paperback

To
Richard K. McMillan
(1951–2001)

First brother.
First friend.
First person I ever thought I supervised.

Contents

Contents

Preface

This book is about language teacher supervision – a profession that many teachers enter almost by accident. Teachers can be promoted into supervisory positions for many reasons: they are excellent teachers, they have experience, they have "people skills," they are seen as loyal to the administration, they have seniority, and so on. Seldom are teachers made supervisors because they have had specific professional preparation for the role.

Sometimes teacher supervision feels like a tug-of-war, a power struggle between the supervisor and the supervisee. At other times, supervision can be a very rewarding profession, full of teamwork. As I look back upon my own career, it appears that I have been working between the tug-of-war and the teamwork for more than 30 years.

This book is a combination literature review and casebook. It is not a memoir, although some of my experiences are woven into it. My first supervisory job was in Korea in the summer of 1973. I was hired to teach and coordinate a remedial reading component of an education program for American soldiers. The only requirement for teaching in this program was a bachelor's degree in any field. With my teaching credential and limited experience, I was seen as one of the best-prepared reading teachers in the region, so I was asked to be a supervising teacher for the program. A motley assortment of people taught these remedial reading classes, most with no preparation and all with no support except the textbooks and whatever advice I could give them. Some teachers were book-bound, droning on and on, telling the students to turn to the next page, complete the exercise, raise their hands when they were done. When I gave these teachers feedback, some complained about my lack of skills or training as a supervisor, just as I complained about their lack of skills or training as reading teachers.

In August 1976, I completed my master's degree at UCLA. My thesis was a small experiment about observation systems in language teacher education. Then, one month after I finished my degree, I was hired as the coordinator of the ESL program at UCLA. I found myself observing teachers (many who were more experienced than I), giving them feedback, and writing evaluations. Anxiety permeated my days, but gradually I developed a modicum of professionalism as a supervisor, although it was a slow and painful process.

I completed my doctoral coursework and started teaching in the new master's degree program in TESOL at the Monterey Institute of International Studies in September 1981. In five years, the department grew to a full-time faculty of five, plus some adjunct professors. I became department chair and was expected to observe and evaluate professors whose skills and knowledge bases were different from mine. Thanks to their professionalism and cooperative spirit, there were no supervisorial crises.

In September 1988, I became the director of the intensive English program at the Monterey Institute. For two years, during times of declining enrollment and tight budgets, I tried to keep the program alive. Watching the ESL teachers work with the students, I was constantly reminded of how many creative ways there are to accomplish instructional goals. The classroom observations and evaluations directly affected decisions as to which teachers would receive contracts during the next session, so it was very important for me to do a good job.

At the Monterey Institute, we began offering a Certificate in Language Program Administration in September 1993. For this program, a 30-hour seminar I had been teaching on language teacher education and supervision was split into two courses. At that point, I realized that about 70 percent of the former course had been on teacher education and only about 30 percent addressed teacher supervision. So I started reading, combing the literature for information about language teacher supervision. Such literature was very limited, and I turned to the work on supervision in business and industry as well as in general education. For six years, I taught the supervision course from a compilation of photocopied articles and not-quite-appropriate textbooks that were borrowed from other disciplines. A sense of coherence in language teacher supervision continued to elude me.

In September 1999, in an attempt to impose some order on the chaos, I began to write a manuscript on language teacher supervision. This book – a combination literature review and casebook – is the result. The cases came easily, born of experiences (mine, my colleagues', my MA students'). However, reviewing the literature was a daunting task because the books and articles about supervision come from such diverse fields. The literature includes research and opinion pieces from general education, psychotherapy, foreign language education, business and industry, and social work.

Now that the manuscript is done, a real, bound book, I hope you will enjoy and benefit from the results of this work. Perhaps for you, gaining knowledge about supervision and developing skills as a professional language teacher supervisor will be more purposeful and straightforward than the largely haphazard endeavor it has been for me and many others like me.

Acknowledgments

This book on language teacher supervision was written with the support of many helpful individuals. I am very grateful to all of them for their input and encouragement.

My colleagues at the Monterey Institute of International Studies contributed both explicitly and implicitly to the volume's production. In particular I want to thank the teachers in the TESOL-TFL Program, the English Studies Program, the language courses, and the Intensive English Program, who graciously allowed my graduate students and me to observe their classes and discuss their teaching with them over the years.

The graduate students in the Monterey Institute's seminar on language teacher supervision helped me refine the ideas presented in this book. I especially want to thank the members of the fall semester 2000 class, who read and discussed the draft cases with me. The students in the fall semester 2001 class read the entire book in draft form. Various iterations of the revised manuscript were used by the students in fall semesters of 2002, 2003, and 2004.

In the Monterey Institute library, Zooey Lober patiently processed hundreds of interlibrary loan requests, with assistance from Joan Ryan and Jennifer Waterson.

The writing of this book was supported by the Mark Award for Faculty Development, a grant from Joseph and Sheila Mark, who have helped many Monterey Institute professors over the years. I gratefully acknowledge both their financial assistance and their moral support.

The text as it emerged was word processed by my incredibly capable student helpers: Angela Dadak, Steven Hales, Sarah Springer, Bethany Alling, and Britt Johnson. Britt's key role as my editorial assistant was made possible by the Marks' generous donation. Her responsibilities during the time we worked on this volume ranged from word processing to library and Web-based research, to pointing out problems of clarity in the text and keeping me sane. When Britt graduated, Sarah Springer continued, with grace, patience, and skill. Then Melanie Anderson and Jessica Massie came back from their Peace Corps assignments (in Russia and Guinea, respectively) to help with the final manuscript preparation.

Toward the end of the revision process, three anonymous reviewers provided detailed suggestions for improving the manuscript. While I have not incorporated all their suggestions, I hope that each of them will recognize evidence of their ideas in these chapters. I expect that all three are excellent supervisors, since their feedback was clear and supportive, striking a fine balance between criticism and encouragement. At Cambridge University Press, the book was guided into print by Angela Castro, Kayo Taguchi, and Kathleen Corley.

The work of many scholars, teachers, and teacher educators has shaped this book. In particular, the publications of Ruth Wajnryb, Michael Wallace, Jerry Gebhard, and Karen Johnson have influenced my thinking considerably. Reading the work of Donald Freeman, David Nunan, Bob Oprandy, and Leo van Lier, and talking directly with these authors, has been both challenging and fruitful.

And, as always, Les endured patiently while photocopied articles, sketchy figures, and books about language teacher supervision littered our home and our lives. I'm sorry you couldn't wait until it was done, sweetheart. The dining room table is cleared off now.

1 Doing supervision: Roles and skills

This book is intended for people who might become language teacher supervisors, as well as for those who already have supervisory responsibilities. It reviews literature on supervision in a variety of settings, including applied linguistics, business and industry, psychotherapy, general education, social work, and an emerging body of work in language teacher supervision itself. The majority of the literature cited here comes from North American contexts, but I have indicated those parts of the text that draw on research and practice from other regions.

Writing this book as a traditional literature review would be like using only the physics of motion and gravity to explain the art of Olympic pairs figure skating. Theory and research alone cannot capture the complicated dynamics of a masterly performance. Nor would a literature review about ice-skating greatly help inexperienced skaters with buckling ankles and unsteady balance increase their skills.

While language teacher supervision is not as physically demanding as pairs figure skating, it is dynamic, emotionally charged, and interactive, and there are many trials involved in supervising well. For these reasons this book combines a literature review with the case approach; and since supervision involves interaction, the cases are designed to put you, the reader, into situations requiring communication.

Because this book is in part based on my experiences and those of my students and colleagues, it is necessarily personal, and full of my own opinions and recommendations. I have tried to flag the parts of the text that are opinion and those that result from research or theory. For instance, *I* and *me* indicate my opinion or personal experience. And *we* is not the royal or the editorial *we*; rather, it marks my shared experiences with readers (you), either as teachers or as supervisors.

Finally, because the purpose of this book is to help supervisors (or future supervisors) do their work better and more confidently, each chapter contains activities to help you apply the concepts presented. These activities consist of the Case Discussion (about the specific case presented in the chapter), Tasks and Discussion (related to broader supervisory contexts), and Suggestions for Further Reading (to help you pursue your interest in the topic).

This chapter begins with a case that is based on a true story. The chapter then discusses supervision as a profession, focusing specifically on language teacher supervision. It reviews the roles of supervisors in various professional contexts, including education, before discussing the particular skills supervisors need. A rationale is also provided for using the case approach for learning about language teacher supervision. We will begin with a case to contextualize the issues raised in this chapter.

Case for analysis: Your new job as a language teacher supervisor

You have just completed your postgraduate work in applied linguistics and language teaching at a university that provides both language instruction and teacher education. During your studies you had a teaching assistantship (TA-ship), which enabled you to make money and to gain experience by teaching language classes as you completed your degree.

Upon finishing your degree, you are hired on a part-time basis to teach and to assist the professor who will supervise the teaching assistants (TAs) in the coming year. You will observe classes, help the new TAs learn about the curriculum, hold office hours, and administer the final examinations. You feel well prepared for the language classes you will teach, but you view your supervisory role with some trepidation, as you have had only a little prior experience in observing teachers, and it was not entirely positive. Nevertheless, you feel that you may gain some skills that will be beneficial to you by assisting the professor in charge of the teaching assistants.

Three weeks before the semester begins, that professor resigns. The teacher education professors in the department don't want to supervise the TAs; they feel this job consumes time that they should devote to research and publishing. The department chair therefore appoints you to serve as the TA supervisor for the coming year. There is no formal job description, but you are given a temporary faculty appointment, including benefits and a reasonable salary. That's the good news. The bad news is that you will be supervising and evaluating some of your closest friends, as well as some language teachers who are older and more experienced than you are.

Supervision as a profession

The status of supervision as a specific profession has been discussed in many fields, including business and industry, psychology, social work, and education. Writing about supervision in general education, Alfonso, Firth, and Neville have said:

> A major deterrent to full professional status of educational supervisors is an ill-defined knowledge base and a lack of an agreed-upon set of professional skills. Every profession equips its members with a conceptual and intellectual base from which skills are derived and expressed in practice. The skills of instructional supervision, however, have remained remarkably undefined and random, partly because the theoretical base is so thin. Moreover, the skills that are used are generally acquired on the job, rather than during professional preparation and internship. (1984:16)

Bernard has noted a similar situation in the preparation of clinical psychologists. She says that "unlike the literature that addresses counselor training, little has been said about the training of supervisors" (1979:60). Indeed, this lack of preparation for supervisors is a repeated theme in the literature of various professions. In recent years, however, publications in general education have suggested this situation is changing.

During the later decades of the past century, teacher supervision emerged as a career track in language education. Perhaps this trend developed because language teaching has become a commercial enterprise, and supervisors are needed to make sure that customers get what they pay for. Or maybe, in aspiring to establish language teaching as a profession, teachers have chosen to monitor their own programs' instructional practices (Nunan, 1999a, 1999b). On the other hand, perhaps so much language teaching around the world is done by people without professional preparation that there is a need for quality control mechanisms. Maybe language educators have simply adopted general education's traditional bureaucratic structures, including having certain employees be responsible for ensuring the quality of others' work.

Whatever the reasons, many language teachers find themselves working as supervisors. Their duties include visiting and evaluating other teachers, discussing their lessons with them, and making recommendations to them about what to continue and what to change.

Unfortunately, very few language teachers ever receive any formal preparation for carrying out supervisors' responsibilities. It is often assumed that teachers who are promoted to supervisorial positions will automatically know how to supervise because they have seniority or because they have displayed leadership qualities. Some are appointed as supervisors because they are stable, cooperative employees. Still others attain teacher supervision positions because they are recognized as effective teachers. If they continue to teach while in their supervisory positions, presumably they will serve as good role models. If their new duties mean they no longer teach, then they are expected to convey to

3

others, through description and discussion, what they themselves know about teaching.

This book is meant to fill a gap in the professional preparation literature of applied linguistics. We will begin by considering some definitions of supervision.

What is language teacher supervision?

What is supervision? The term has many possible definitions, which vary across contexts and over time. Most definitions come from general education or from business and industry rather than from language teaching itself.

The hierarchical contexts of language teacher supervision

One complication in defining supervision is that being a supervisor is usually a middle-management position in the organizational chart, meaning that the supervisor is answerable to both the teachers and the administration. Daughtrey and Ricks point out that industrial supervisors are also called first-line managers, referring to the first line above the workers on the organizational chart – those people who "work with the operating personnel who actually produce the product or service that the firm provides" (1989:13).

Like first-line managers, language teaching supervisors frequently work side by side with teachers. Some teach language courses themselves and supervise other teachers as one of many responsibilities. Others, such as program directors, department chairpersons, coordinators, or headmistresses or headmasters, may not have teaching responsibilities. Their roles typically include other administrative responsibilities in addition to supervising language teachers.

Definitions of supervision

Defining *supervision* is not a simple task. The field has "a variety of sometimes incompatible definitions, a very low level of popular acceptance, and many perplexing and challenging problems" (Anderson, 1982:181). Anderson notes that "even the terminology of supervision causes discomfort and weakens allegiance" (ibid.).

In some situations, supervision has been defined for legal and contractual purposes. For example, according to Hazi (1994:199), New Jersey law defines a supervisor as "any appropriately certified individual assigned with the responsibility for the direction and guidance of the work of teaching staff members." In that context, supervision is defined by the administrative code and is "legally synonymous with evaluation" (ibid.).

A broader definition comes from Daresh (2001:25), a general education author, who says that "supervision is a process of overseeing the ability of people to meet the goals of the organization in which they work." He stresses that supervision should be seen as a process rather than as a professional role.

Goldsberry defines supervision as "an organizational responsibility and function focused upon the assessment and refinement of current practices" (1988:1). He also notes the hierarchical nature of supervision: "Because it is an organizational responsibility, it necessarily involves interaction between an organizational superordinate and a subordinate – meaning that legitimate authority for decision-making resides with the supervisor" (ibid.:1–2).

In the context of the U.S. child welfare system, Gambrill and Stein (1983) say effective supervisors are those "who help their staff help their clients in a manner that maximizes positive consequences for all" (p. 7). In a similar way, effective language teacher supervisors help language teachers help students in order to maximize learning and positive attitudes.

Almost everyone in language teaching has folk wisdom about what it means to be a supervisor because so many of us have been supervised at some time. There are some specific definitions in our field, however. For instance, Wallace states that a supervisor is "anyone who has . . . the duty of monitoring and improving the quality of teaching done by other colleagues in an educational situation" (1991:107). Gebhard says that "language teacher supervision is an ongoing process of teacher education in which the supervisor observes what goes on in the teacher's classroom with an eye toward the goal of improved instruction" (1990a:1).

However, teacher supervision is not just concerned with the creative and positive aspects of helping language teachers achieve their full potential. If it were, the job title might be "teacher developer" instead. Supervision also includes less rewarding and rather unpleasant responsibilities, such as providing negative feedback, ensuring that teachers adhere to program policy, and even firing employees if the need arises.

Tensions in the supervisor-teacher relationship

The negative side of supervision has earned it some colorful nicknames, such as the "reluctant profession" (Mosher and Purpel, 1972). Supervision has also been referred to as "snoopervision" and as "managing messes" (Schön, 1983:14). The ongoing relationship between teachers and supervisors has even been called a "private cold war" (Blumberg, 1980).

In general education, where surprise evaluation visits are common, teachers have resorted to signals to alert one another about unannounced observations. Black documented teachers using the code warning "the ghost walks" to communicate that the school principal was making surprise classroom visits (1993:38). In another context, she says a note reading "Stand and deliver!" was passed along the corridors to spread the word that supervisory visits were imminent (ibid.). Clearly these phrases indicate a certain level of tension in the relationship between teachers and supervisors.

Supervisors' varied roles in professional contexts

The following literature review will discuss the varied roles and challenges of language teacher supervisors. Let me acknowledge at the outset that this literature is predominantly from North America, although it is drawn from a variety of professions. How language teacher supervision is depicted depends on the treatment of the subject by the author(s). Some incorporate ideas from supervision in business and industry, others discuss supervision in general education contexts, and still others focus almost entirely on language teacher supervision.

Historically, the assembly-line model in industry has influenced educational supervision. Hoy and Woolfolk (1989) say, "unfortunately, supervision has its roots in the industrial literature of bureaucracy. Close supervision was a classic response to production problems; it was management's attempt to control subordinates" (p. 113). These authors note that the terms *evaluation, assessment, appraisal,* and *rating* are "consistent with the industrial notion of overseeing, directing and controlling workers" (ibid.).

In some parts of the world, the development of the language teacher supervisor's role has paralleled a trend toward increasing individualization in education. Supervisors' responsibilities have moved from being largely judgmental and evaluative to being more developmental in focus. In 1984, Alfonso et al. summarized this change as follows: "[T]he task of supervision now is to refine the process of teaching and improve the effectiveness of the results of schooling" (p. 17).

As professional language teacher supervisors, particularly if we supervise teachers from different cultures or work in a different culture ourselves, we must remember that changes in language teacher supervisors' roles do not occur at the same pace or move in the same direction everywhere. The supervisor's role is, in part, culturally defined and conceptually located in the educational and political history of a particular region.

Over time, many alternatives have emerged as to how to enact the supervisor's role. Sometimes these options create confusion about supervisors' responsibilities. In general education, "although supervision has been a normal school-based activity for as long as there have been public schools in America, no real consensus has ever been reached concerning what supervision should be or what educational supervisors should do" (Daresh, 2001:3). This statement is true in many non-U.S. contexts as well.

Some authors lament the many roles that supervisors must perform. Goldsberry (1988:2) notes that many organizational roles (e.g., principal, reading supervisor, curriculum coordinator) involve several different important functions. He suggests separating the supervisorial role from these other functions so that supervisors can focus on improving instruction.

In general education, supervisors have many tasks: "They are expected to be instructional experts, diagnosticians, curriculum developers, instructional planners, problem solvers, innovators, clinical observation specialists, and managers of the processes of teaching and learning" (Alfonso et al., 1984:16–17). These various responsibilities are more or less inherently supervisory in nature: Curriculum development and instructional planning are often done by teachers and other professionals who are not supervisors, but supervisors' responsibilities often focus on more than teachers' classroom performance. Much of the literature has discussed "the 'role' of supervision, yet it has given too little attention to the identification and development of the skills needed to make supervision effective" (ibid.). Teacher supervisors seldom receive training to perform their roles, and perhaps for this reason "the major concept of current supervisory behavior is its undue emphasis on reactive performance – doing things as a result of a crisis orientation – rather than through careful, logical planning and preparation" (Daresh, 2001:25).

In child welfare work, Gambrill and Stein (1983:8) say evaluation of staff members must include both positive monitoring, or "attending to achievements and assets," and negative monitoring, or "attending to mistakes and deficiencies." They emphasize the former over the latter.

In psychotherapy, Bernard (1979:64) identified three key roles for supervisors working with counselor-trainees: the teacher-student approach, the counselor-client approach, and the consultant approach. She defined these roles in terms of their goals:

> The supervisor as teacher focuses on some knowledge or expertise that he or she wishes to transmit to the counselor. The supervisor as counselor places priority on the [trainee] counselor's personal needs, with the belief that this focus will allow the [trainee] counselor to overcome the nervousness or self-doubt that impedes natural development. The supervisor as consultant focuses on a relationship with the [trainee] counselor that

> is explorative in nature and assumes that the [trainee] has the ability to express his or her supervision needs. (ibid.)

Very few language teacher supervisors have formal training, so they may work "at an instinctive level . . . or at the level of folk models about what supervisors do" (Wajnryb, 1995a:73).

Roles of teacher supervisors in general education

The roles of educational supervisors vary greatly across time and place. For example, in 1967, Wiles portrayed supervisors in general education somewhat idealistically. In his view, supervisors "serve as liaisons to get people into contact with resource people who can help" (Wiles, 1967:11, cited in Daresh, 2001:11):

> They stimulate staff members to look at the extent to which ideas and resources are being shared, and the degree to which persons are encouraged and supported as they try new things. They make it easier to carry out the agreements that emerge from evaluation sessions. They listen to individuals discuss their problems and recommend other resources that may help in the search for solutions. They bring to individual teachers, whose confidence they possess, appropriate suggestions and materials. They serve, as far as they are able, the feelings that teachers have about the system and its policies, and they recommend that the administration examine irritations among staff members.

Wiles was a proponent of the human relations school of supervision. In some ways he was a man ahead of his time.

Abrell's humanistic supervision

Eventually, humanistic supervision did become a trend in general education. A humanistic supervisor "possesses and develops characteristics that enable him / her to consistently affirm a constructive other-centered action that leads to the growth of others, to the improvement of instruction, and to his / her own self-improvement" (Abrell, 1974:213). A humanistic supervisor needs to cultivate "those skills, attitudes and understandings essential to carrying out the multi-faceted role of person-centered supervision" (ibid.). By "person-centered supervision" Abrell meant that the supervisor would attempt to utilize "the aspirations, needs, and talents of the person(s) with whom he / she cooperatively works" (ibid.:214).

Abrell spelled out 10 key characteristics that effective humanistic supervisors need. The first three include the beliefs that all human beings

"(1) possess the power...of solving their own problems; (2) possess genuine freedom of creative choice and action, and are, within certain objective limits, the masters of their own destiny; [and] (3) achieve the good life by harmoniously combining personal satisfactions and continuous self-development with significant work and other activities that contribute to the welfare of those with whom one relates" (ibid.:215).

In addition, according to Abrell, humanistic supervisors must also exhibit the following characteristics:

4. a commitment to democratic procedures when working with others;
5. a willingness to question others' and one's own basic assumptions and convictions;
6. a deep commitment and capacity to make others feel worthwhile, important, and uplifted;
7. a willingness and ability to establish warm and empathetic relationships with all persons, regardless of their racial, religious, ethnic, or educational backgrounds;
8. an ability to listen and a desire to utilize the experience of others as a resource for planning and achieving goals;
9. an enthusiasm for and belief in supervision as a viable process for contributing to human growth and progress;
10. a commitment to upgrade oneself as a whole human being and the desire to carry on a continuing inquiry in the field of supervision.

Abrell concludes that the humanistic supervisor's frame of reference "is characterized by his / her compassionate concern for fellow workers" (ibid.).

Goldsberry's three models of teacher supervision

Goldsberry (1988) distinguishes three important models of educational supervision by the purpose of each. First, nominal supervision has the "primary purpose of maintaining a façade that supervision is being practiced" (p. 2). Second, the prescriptive model is "based upon the notion that the supervisor needs to correct deficiencies in teaching and has a primary purpose of surfacing these flaws and correcting them" (ibid.). This model is a long-lived view of supervision that has influenced language teaching as well (Freeman, 1982, 1989a; Gebhard, 1984; Wallace, 1991). Third, the reflective model assumes that "teachers need skilled support to refine their own efforts" (Goldsberry, 1988:2). This model's primary purpose is "the stimulation of guided reflection based upon disciplined inquiry into the ends and means of teaching" (ibid.). Goldsberry's key contrasts among these three models are summarized in Table 1.1.

Table 1.1 *Three models of supervision in general education (adapted from Goldsberry, 1988:3)*

	Nominal model	Prescriptive model	Reflective model
Purposes	To maintain status quo To protect "insiders" To provide a façade	To promote uniform practices To maximize benefits of expertise	To promote reflective adaptation To develop expertise
Reasons to observe	To comply with legal requirements To "keep in touch"	To identify weaknesses or deficiencies To check for standard practices To collect data germane to standards	To collect descriptive information To provide a second perspective
Reasons to confer	To comply with legal requirements To "keep in touch"	To prescribe needed changes To reinforce standard practices To recognize excellence	To promote reflection To surface puzzlement To formulate hypotheses of effect
Aim	Appearance of accountability	Widespread use of standards	Reasoned experimentation

Goldsberry calls nominal supervision a "void posing as supervision" and "lip-service supervision" (ibid.:4). He adds, "When there is inadequate time to do the job, when the supervisor lacks the preparation or skill to do it well, nominal supervision is preferred to trying to do too much in too little time and thus doing it badly" (ibid.:5). He concludes that "until supervisors are provided with adequate preparation and time to do the job, nominal supervision is all the organization can expect" (ibid.).

The prescriptive model, in contrast, is supervision taken seriously, Goldsberry says. Because the supervisor's diagnostic skills are assumed to be superior to the teachers' (ibid.:5),

> the supervisor's job is to prescribe treatment. If the problems are cured, then the teacher as patient simply goes on until another symptom appears or until time for the next regular check-up. If the problems persist, then the supervisor as physician proceeds with a battery of tests, increases dosages of treatments, calls in

specialists, or simply advises the patient teacher to wait and see what happens, hoping for the best. (ibid.)

Goldsberry sees the prescriptive model as applicable in three contexts: in working with teachers "who know (and admit they know) considerably less about teaching than the supervisor" (ibid.:6); when it is appropriate to promote uniformity or consistency across teachers; and when there is a need "to correct deficient teaching" (ibid.). However, Goldsberry acknowledges that this model is not appropriate in many contexts.

Goldsberry contrasts prescriptive supervision with the reflective model, which "focuses on the teacher's thinking about teaching as much as his actual teaching behavior." (ibid.:7):

> Where prescriptive approaches focus on the standards which undergird the commonalities among teaching practices, a reflective approach focuses on the idiosyncratic mix of values, purposes, learners, skills, settings and dispositions which distinguish the efforts of one good teacher from another. Where prescriptive approaches aim to strengthen teaching performance by working toward endorsed standards of practice, reflective approaches tend to examine the standards in relation to the peculiarities of the particular setting, people and time. Where a prescriptive method is based upon using the perceived superior expertise of the supervisor to enhance the teacher's performance, a reflective method is based upon using and developing the expertise of the teacher to examine ideal purposes and procedures for teaching, and to refine present performance accordingly. (ibid.)

Unfortunately, Goldsberry says the reflective approach to supervision is used less often than either the nominal model or the prescriptive model.

Clark's six roles of preservice teacher supervisors

Clark (1990) describes six roles supervisors of preservice teachers perform in general education. First is administrative supervision, which he describes as "judgmental supervision, mainly resulting in summative evaluation of student [teachers]" (p. 40). Clark says trainees' professional development is not a particularly important goal in this model (ibid.). A second role is to provide casual or informal supervision, described as "non-judgmental acceptance of teaching or learning behaviors" (ibid.). In this model, "development only occurs on an *ad hoc* basis and tension can result if students or supervisors are given conflicting or unobtainable goals" (ibid.). The third role is that of clerical supervision, which emphasizes the maintenance "of records of teaching such as aims and objectives, programs, student records and assessment results" (ibid.). According to Clark, clerical supervision involves maintaining school management records rather than focusing on effective teaching (ibid.). In a fourth role, cooperative supervision, student teachers supervise themselves. Skills development, cooperative supervision's main goal, is "encouraged and supported by the group" (ibid.). The fifth role, individualized or responsive supervision, "relates teaching and professional development directly to the personal psychological or social needs of the individual in the classroom rather than the teaching process" (ibid.). Finally, clinical supervision "can be related to all stages of teacher growth from the student teacher through neophyte and experienced teachers" (ibid.). The latter three roles are the ones that really promote the professional development of novice teachers, in Clark's view. They also fit with Wiles's (1967) somewhat idealistic concept of human relations oriented supervision.

Acheson and Gall's six types of teacher supervision

Acheson and Gall (1997) describe six broad categories of teacher supervision in general education: counselor, coach, consultant, inspector, mentor, and cooperating teacher. Of the counselor role, Acheson and Gall say, "Provided that personal counsel is not given at the expense of feedback on teaching, it can be a helpful adjunct. The line between teaching concerns and personal problems is often a fine one" (p. 242).

A second supervisory role is that of coach – someone who "observes closely the performance of others over time and gives advice for improvement" (ibid.). The term *coach* suggests appropriate activities in the context of instructional leadership and "explicit, focused feedback" (ibid.). (*Coach* here is not synonymous with *peer coaching*; see Chapter 15.)

A third supervisory role, that of consultant, implies voluntary rather than imposed contacts between the teachers and supervisors, according to Acheson and Gall. They add that many teachers "prefer the label 'peer consultant' over 'peer coach' because it connotes a collaborative relationship rather than a directive one" (ibid.).

Acheson and Gall note that "a role that has been associated with supervision in the past and is still used as an official title in some parts of the world is that of inspector" (ibid.). However, the "inspector" label has serious negative connotations. The authors maintain that "quality control is a function of supervision or instructional leadership, but it can be achieved without the pejorative overtones we tend to associate with 'inspection'" (ibid.).

A fifth and somewhat more benign role, according to these authors, is that of mentor. The mentor role fits Acheson and Gall's idea of an ideal supervisor, but as the field has evolved, the formal role of the mentor has been intentionally separated from that of the supervisor. Typically, a mentor does not have evaluative responsibilities, whereas a supervisor does. This distinction is purposeful. Because the mentor does not evaluate their work, novices can express concerns and admit weaknesses that they might not wish to share with a supervisor.

The final role that Acheson and Gall describe is that of cooperating teacher. A *cooperating teacher* is the teacher-of-record in a class where a trainee teacher gains practical experience. The more experienced teacher is "cooperating" with the training program. In the past, a teacher serving as a role model for novices was called a master teacher, but because the term has unintentional yet unfortunate connotations of a master-slave relationship, people in this role are now often called cooperating teachers instead.

Supervisory roles in language education contexts

Articles about supervision in language teaching began to appear in the 1980s. In an early publication, Knop (1980) discusses three approaches to language teacher supervision: the scientific approach, which involves competency-based education and the use of interaction analysis; the democratic approach, which views supervision as therapy and as ego counseling; and clinical supervision, in which the supervisor and teacher determine the goals of the observation. Concepts from all three approaches remain useful, though clinical supervision has had the greatest impact. (Clinical supervision is further addressed in Chapter 15.) The next section reviews other influential approaches in our field.

Freeman's three options for observers' roles

Freeman (1982, 1989a) describes three approaches to observing teachers and giving them feedback: the supervisory option, the nondirective option, and the alternatives option. The supervisory option is the traditional directive model, in which the supervisor is viewed as the expert and gives prescriptive advice. The nondirective option is just the opposite. In this role, the supervisor listens nonjudgmentally as teachers describe their work and interpret their actions. In the alternatives option, the supervisor's responsibility is to suggest, or help teachers discover, alternatives to their current ways of doing things (Freeman, 1982). Table 1.2 contrasts these three options in terms of observational procedures and the post-observation conferences.

A key factor that distinguishes the three approaches is power (see Chapter 3). In the supervisory option, the teacher has little power to determine the issues under discussion. In the nondirective option, the teacher has extensive opportunities to direct the discussion and make decisions. In the alternatives option, the teacher and the supervisor jointly negotiate what actions to implement.

Table 1.2 *Three options for language teacher supervision (adapted from Freeman, 1989a)*

Option	Procedures
Supervisory option	1. The observer establishes his or her purpose. 2. The observer determines the point(s) to be raised with the teacher. 3. In the conference, the observer "stands," making a brief statement to the teacher on the point. 4. The teacher may or may not respond during the conference. 5. The observer may make further statements.
Nondirective option	1. Before observing, the observer asks the teacher for background on the class. (This must come from a genuine desire to know. The observer "understands" but doesn't comment or react.) 2. After observing, the observer makes statements in the post-observation conference about the class that corroborate the teacher's background information. (The observer raises supportive examples but does not deal with inconsistencies.) 3. The teacher responds to the observer's statements during the conference. The observer reflects these comments so as to "understand" them as fully as possible. 4. The observer indicates a transition, or change of structure – he or she will offer input based on what the teacher has said. 5. The observer "stands," offering input and perspective. (The observer simply offers another point of view at this stage, *not* suggestions or advice.) 6. The teacher decides what to do next.
Alternatives option	1. The observer determines the points (and the activity) to be raised with the teacher. 2. During the conference, the observer states observations of what the teacher did in the activity. 3. The observer lists two to four specific alternatives to the teacher's actions without implying what the teacher "should have done." (The alternatives must be workable; however, they need not be consistent with either the teacher's or the observer's teaching philosophy.) 4. The teacher reacts to the alternatives, choosing one or another during the conference. 5. The observer asks the teacher to explain *why* he or she chose that alternative. 6. The observer plays devil's advocate, drawing out the teacher's reasons.

Additional descriptions of language teacher supervisors' roles

Freeman's work influenced Gebhard (1984), who describes five supervisory models: traditional directive supervision, alternatives supervision, collaborative supervision, nondirective supervision, and creative supervision. We have discussed three of these, but the other two bear some examination.

In a collaborative model, the supervisor's role is "to work with teachers but not to direct them. The supervisor actively participates with the teacher in any decisions that are made and attempts to establish a sharing relationship" (Gebhard, 1984:505). Gebhard equates collaborative supervision with clinical supervision, but he notes that this model may not always be appropriate. First, although "equality and sharing ideas in a problem-solving process can be appealing, the ideal and real are sometimes far apart" (ibid.:506). Second, this enactment may not be appropriate in all cultures. Gebhard says a colleague from the Middle East said teachers would think he wasn't a good supervisor if he used the collaborative approach there.

Gebhard's fifth model, creative supervision, is a selective combination of the other models. It is useful because an effective supervisor might need to switch roles during a conference, depending on the teacher's needs. For example, a conference might proceed with the nondirective option until it reaches an issue where the teacher has no experience and requests explicit guidance. At that point, the supervision could shift to the alternatives option.

The supervisor's traditional role has been "to prescribe the best way to teach and to model teaching; to direct or guide the teacher's teaching; and to evaluate progress" (Gebhard, 1990a:1). However, he notes that the following responsibilities are now central: "to train new teachers to go from their actual to ideal teaching behavior; to provide the means for teachers to reflect on and work through problems in their teaching; to furnish opportunities for teachers to explore new teaching possibilities; and to afford teachers chances to acquire knowledge about teaching and to develop their own theory of teaching" (ibid.).

Chamberlin says that over time the supervisor's role has shifted from that of a distant expert "to that of an engaged colleague who encourages teachers to talk about their work and reflect on their practice" (2000:656).

> The supervisor, once viewed mainly as an expert evaluator, is now charged with the responsibility of gaining teachers' trust and creating an environment that cultivates reflection, exploration, and change. This new role requires greater attention to the relationship between the teacher and the supervisor. (ibid.)

Table 1.3   *Approaches to clinical supervision (from Wallace, 1991:110, after Sergiovanni, 1977)*

Classic prescriptive approach	Classic collaborative approach
1. Supervisor as authority figure	1. Supervisor as colleague
2. Supervisor as only source of expertise	2. Supervisor and trainee or teacher as cosharers of expertise
3. Supervisor judges	3. Supervisor understands
4. Supervisor applies a "blueprint" of how lesson ought to be taught	4. Supervisor has no blueprint: accepts lesson in terms of what trainee or teacher is attempting to do
5. Supervisor talks; trainee listens	5. Supervisor considers listening as important as talking
6. Supervisor attempts to preserve authority and mystique	6. Supervisor attempts to help trainee or teacher develop autonomy, through practice in reflection and self-evaluation

Chamberlin concludes that the changing role of supervisors "reflects a reconceptualized vision of teaching" (ibid.:654). She also suggests that the relationship between language teachers and supervisors requires communication styles that create a positive, collaborative environment (ibid.) – an idea that is diametrically opposed to the view of supervision as "snoopervision."

The classic prescriptive approach versus the classic collaborative approach

These multiple descriptions of the supervisor's role focus on different responsibilities. The various roles can also be positioned along a continuum that locates decision-making power either with the supervisor or with the teacher. Along these lines, Wallace (1991) compares the classic prescriptive approach and the classic collaborative approach to teacher supervision. The contrasts between these two major approaches are summarized in Table 1.3.

The classic prescriptive and classic collaborative approaches are opposite views of the supervisor's role. Murdoch (1998, Conflicting Discourses section, paragraph 5) summarizes a conflict inherent in the two approaches. Two contrasting discourses result from language teacher supervisors' roles "as, on the one hand, facilitators of professional development, and on the other hand, as assessors of the quality of teachers' work." But according to Murdoch, these two roles, "and the discourses which they spring from, do not need to be constructed so oppositionally and problematically" (ibid.) as they usually are.

In summary, there are many ways to realize the language teacher supervisor's role. A general trend is away from the inspector's role and toward a more collegial role. However, the extent of this change depends on the culture; the trend is by no means universal.

Supervisory skills

As supervisorial roles have changed, so have the skills of effective supervisors. This section reviews the literature about the skills that teacher supervisors need today. Keep in mind that such skills may vary with the supervisory approach that you choose in your context.

Skills of teacher supervisors in general education

The general education literature on supervision became polarized in the 1970s and 1980s, with one faction of authors advocating a holistic, person-centered orientation and another faction espousing a more technical, scientifically based orientation. The supervisory skills perceived as valuable depended in part on how the supervisor's role was envisioned and defined. For example, Abrell's humanistic supervision (1974:213–214) entailed six key functions:

1. *Assessing-diagnosing function.* Helping coworkers assess and diagnose their needs for the specific situation in which they are working.
2. *Planning function.* Assisting colleagues in planning goals, objectives, and experiences that will produce maximum results.
3. *Motivating function.* Helping coworkers establish and maintain a climate that will precipitate the best in all parties.
4. *Strategic function.* Choosing and using those strategies which will produce intended outcomes.
5. *Resource function.* Making available those resource persons and materials needed to accomplish objectives and carry out experiences.
6. *Appraising or Progress Reporting function.* Helping those with whom one works to appraise and evaluate the results of their efforts to achieve goals . . . to assess the outcomes of a given set of experiences.

Abrell saw these six functions as central to humanistic supervision's goals.

According to Alfonso et al. (1984), supervisors need three types of skills: technical, human relations, and managerial. The authors define *technical skill* as the "specialized knowledge and ability required to perform the primary tasks inherent in a particular supervisory position" (p. 17). As an example, they cite using an observation system to analyze teaching. *Human relations skill* is the "ability to work with people and motivate them so they will desire good performance" (ibid.:18), such as getting teachers to commit to certain goals or to clarify their values. *Managerial skill* is "the ability to make decisions and see relationships that are crucial to the organization or unit goals for which the supervisor is responsible" (ibid.), such as conducting a needs assessment with a group of teachers. It is in part the supervisor's managerial skills that generate conditions necessary "for a teacher or staff to be effective" (ibid.).

More than two decades ago, Anderson claimed that educational supervisors should have "excellent and comprehensive theoretical and practical training with a strong clinical emphasis, plus demonstrated supervisory skill at a substantial level of mastery" (1982:185). Some research has investigated excellence, but mostly in general education.

Researchers at the University of Georgia reviewed supervision and identified 12 variables related to instructional improvement or professional growth (quoted from Pajak, 1990:xx):

1. Communication: ensuring open and clear communication among individuals and groups throughout the organization
2. Staff Development: developing and facilitating meaningful opportunities for professional growth
3. Instructional Program: supporting and coordinating efforts to improve the instructional program
4. Planning and Change: initiating and implementing collaboratively developed strategies for continuous improvement
5. Motivating and Organizing: helping people to develop a shared vision and achieve collected aims
6. Observation and Conferencing: providing feedback to teachers based on classroom observation
7. Curriculum: coordinating and integrating the process of curriculum development and implementation
8. Problem Solving and Decision Making: using a variety of strategies to clarify and analyze problems and to make decisions
9. Service to Teachers: providing materials, resources, and assistance to support teaching and learning
10. Personal Development: recognizing and reflecting upon one's personal and professional beliefs, abilities, and actions

11. Community Relations: establishing and maintaining open and productive relations between the school and its community
12. Research and Program Evaluation: encouraging experimentation and assessing outcomes

None of these qualities is surprising, but many are based on how supervisors relate to their constituencies – teachers and learners. Pajak's list is more closely aligned with the classic collaborative approach than with the classic prescriptive approach to supervision.

The Georgia researchers were writing about general education, but these skills are applicable to language teacher supervision. Before turning to our field, an examination of some literature from psychotherapy and social work might provide insights. As this information comes largely from publications in English-speaking countries, we must be careful in applying it in other cultural contexts.

Supervisory skills in psychotherapy and social welfare work

In research on supervisory roles in the training of clinical therapists, Bernard defines three skills that a counselor must possess. First, process skills "differentiate the counseling contact from a social contact" (1979:62). Second, conceptualization skills "reflect deliberate thinking and case analysis by the counselor" (ibid.). Bernard suggests that conceptualization skills include two types of thinking: "the conceptualization done *in the counseling session*, and the conceptualization done *between sessions*" (ibid.: italics in the original). These concepts parallel Schön's (1983) reflection-in-action (i.e., teachers' thinking during lessons) and reflection-on-action (teachers' reflection before or after lessons), respectively. Third, personalization skills are clearly related to what Wiles (1967) describes as the human relations approach to supervision. Personalization skills include the following:

> (a) [trainee] counselor's comfort in assuming some authority in the counseling relationship and taking responsibility for his or her specialized knowledge and skills, (b) the ability of the [trainee] counselor to hear challenges by the client or feedback from the supervisor without becoming overly defensive, (c) the ability to be comfortable with the [trainee] counselor's own feelings, values and attitudes, as well as those of the client, and (d) the ability to have a fundamental respect for the client. (Bernard, 1979:63)

We can recast these personalization subskills in the language teaching context as follows: Teachers must develop (a) authority and responsibility in teaching, (b) a nondefensive attitude toward negative input about their

19

teaching, (c) comfort with a variety of affective issues, and (d) respect for the program participants.

Extrapolating from this analogy, language teacher supervisors must develop (a) authority and responsibility in supervision (as well as in teaching); (b) a nondefensive attitude toward negative input from students, teachers, and administrators; (c) comfort with a variety of affective issues (raised by teachers and learners), and (d) respect for all the program participants.

According to Bernard, these three skills (process, conceptualization, and personalization) "can be used to delineate the abilities of a competent counselor, thus serving as an outline for supervision with the counselor-trainee" (ibid.). She also notes that such an outline has two purposes: "(a) it gives the [trainee] counselor an outline of behaviors necessary for successful completion of [the counseling] practicum, and (b) it serves as a guide for the supervisor in establishing training priorities for supervision sessions" (ibid.). By implication then, a description of competent language teachers must be used in guiding language teacher supervisors. In our field, however, this understanding is not as straightforward as it sounds – an issue that will be further discussed in Chapter 10.

In the field of child welfare work, Gambrill and Stein (1983:153) assert that effective supervisors of welfare workers

> offer rewarding feedback, handle emotional outbursts and complaints effectively, mediate conflicts that arise, respond to criticism, make and refuse requests, help workers find solutions to work-related interpersonal dilemmas, delegate responsibility, be persistent in the face of resistance, persuade others, build consensus, conduct effective meetings, anticipate and remove obstacles to communication, handle difficult people, and offer clear instructions.

Although Gambrill and Stein were writing about the child welfare context, this list of supervisory skills also pertains to language teacher supervisors.

Gambrill and Stein articulate eight problem-solving skills for effective supervisors. They include "(1) clear description of the situation; (2) description of alternatives; (3) selection of criteria to use to evaluate alternatives; (4) using these criteria to weigh the advantages and disadvantages of each alternative; (5) choosing the best alternative; (6) trying this out; (7) evaluating the results; and (8) changing what you do in similar situations in the future" (1983:154). These authors emphasize *rewardingness* – the extent to which supervisors support others' behavior and "how much they show liking rather than dislike of others" (ibid.:155).

Supervisory skills in language education contexts

What is the connection between these various supervisory skills in other fields and the supervision of language teachers? Bernard's personalization skills (1979) and Alfonso et al.'s human relations skills (1984) are related to the affective connection between supervisors and language teachers. Gebhard (1984) says that supervisors are told they should establish rapport with teachers, but they are rarely given guidance about how to do so. Rapport, he notes, is equated with harmony, empathy, or creating "a sympathetic relationship" (ibid.). To generate rapport, Gebhard says, the supervisor should match his or her communicative representational system with that of the teacher, in terms of both nonverbal behaviors and verbal predicates (such as *see, feel, sense*). He states that by "consciously and unconsciously matching verbal and nonverbal behavior with the other person" (ibid.), one can develop rapport.

Being an effective language teacher supervisor entails more than establishing rapport, however. Murdoch (1998, Figure 1) has identified the following 10 features of effective supervision in language programs:

1. Encourages the teacher to identify a particular issue to focus on during an observation.
2. Collects data from the lesson that can be analyzed by both teacher and supervisor.
3. Restricts feedback to agreed areas of focus and carefully selected teaching patterns that might be usefully examined during future observations.
4. Links classroom teaching events to wider ELT and educational issues.
5. Allows the teacher to try out his / her own teaching strategies and limits criticisms or suggestions before the observation conference.
6. Adopts a perspective on the lesson during observation which takes into account the situation of the teacher and / or the students.
7. Judges the quantity and depth of feedback in relation to the experience of the teacher and his / her ability to benefit from and / or act upon the analysis of . . . teaching.
8. Reinforces effective practices via positive comments so such practices are more likely to become an established part of a teacher's repertoire.
9. Uses the lesson as a text to engage in a dialogue with the teacher about pedagogical issues and to explore classroom teaching options.

10. Sets the agenda and analyzes data collaboratively at all stages in order to develop teachers' confidence and ability to reflect on their classroom practice.

How language teacher supervisors implement these behaviors depends on the approach chosen. For example, item 9 above would produce different discursive patterns depending on whether the supervisor used the supervisory, the nondirective, or the alternatives approach (Freeman, 1982).

Two experienced ESL program administrators, Geddes and Marks, recommend several procedures for effective supervision (1997:209). First, a supervisor should identify program components (e.g., instruction, office support) that require supervision. Next, the person in charge should assign supervisory responsibilities to staff members. The authors advise reviewing current research literature to select an appropriate supervisory model and "identify related approaches, procedures, and techniques" (ibid.). After these steps, program administrators should "establish a plan for the implementation of formal and informal supervisory activities" (ibid.). It is "vital to provide honest and meaningful feedback" (ibid.). In addition, effective administrators will determine the relationship among supervision, evaluation, and faculty development activities and decide how and when to link these three types of activities (ibid.).

Geddes and Marks were discussing program administration in general, rather than teacher supervision, so they address the supervision of support staff as well. Writing from their experience (rather than from research findings), they emphasize the importance of establishing systematic administrative procedures that will ensure fair treatment of employees.

The case approach to teaching and learning

The approach to supervisor preparation that I will present in this book combines a traditional literature review with the examination and discussion of several cases based on critical incidents that my students, my colleagues, and I have experienced as language teachers, teacher educators, and teacher supervisors. The use of case studies as teaching tools is widespread in such fields as law, business, and teacher training in general education (Ackerman, Maslin-Ostrowski, and Christensen, 1996; Carter, 1993; Clandinin and Connelly, 1991; Cooper, 1995; Shulman, 1992). In fact, Wallace (2000:13) says that in the study of both law and management, "the consideration of the individual case is the most favoured method of professional study." Recently, the case approach has been utilized in language teacher education as well. (See Jackson, 1997, 1998; Plaister, 1993; and Richards, 1998.)

Definitions of some key terms in the case approach

In teacher education, Shulman says that a case has "a narrative, a story, a set of events that unfolds over time in a particular place" (1992:21). A case is not just a report of an event.

> To call something a case is to make a theoretical claim. It argues that the story, event, or text is an instance of a larger class, an example of a broader category. In a word, it is a "case-of-something" and therefore merits more serious consideration than a simple anecdote or vignette. It implies an underlying taxonomy or typology, however intuitive or informal, to which a given case belongs. . . . To call something a case, therefore, is to treat it as a member of a class of events and to call our attention to its value in helping us appreciate more than the particularities of the case narrative itself. (ibid.)

Shulman also notes that cases can be either "documented (or portrayed) occasions or sets of occasions with their boundaries marked off, their borders drawn" (ibid.:12). (*Documented* refers to actual cases that have been written or recorded, whereas *portrayed* means the case is fictional or partly fictional.) In Shulman's terms, then, this book contains cases based on both documented and portrayed events.

Several key terms are associated with the case-based approach in teacher education. Here are some of the most important ones:

- **Case materials** are the raw data from which cases are constructed, whether by the original author or by a third party. They are diaries, personal letters, student work samples, videotapes, observers' notes, and so on (ibid.:19).
- **Case studies** are third-person accounts – the anthropologist's write-up of a native ritual, the psychologist's portrayal of a classroom episode, the teacher's presentation of the story of a child (ibid).
- **Case reports** are first-person accounts, reports written by someone who is reporting her own experiences, activities, and interpretations. When the author is the protagonist of the narrative, we are reading a case report (ibid).
- **Teaching cases** are original accounts, case reports, or case studies that have been written or edited for teaching purposes (ibid).
- **Casebooks** are collections of case reports, case studies, or teaching cases selected, sequenced, organized, and glossed for particular educational purposes (ibid.: 20).
- **Decision cases** are "cases which focus on dilemmas or critical incidents in teaching and are most often presented from the perspectives of individuals or organizations that must make decisions related to

those dilemmas" (Jackson, 1997:4). Decision cases are typically open-ended and the trainees are supposed to "make their own decisions while providing analyses and rationales to support their positions" (ibid.).

- **Personal case studies** are written by practitioners for their own development but are "not intended for general use" (Wallace, 2000:17).
- **Authored case studies**, according to Wallace (ibid.), are public "ready made" case studies that can be used for discussion (e.g., by an in-service training group).

Given these definitions, this volume is, in part, a casebook. It contains a number of teaching cases that focus on critical incidents in language teaching and supervision and are presented from the perspective of the supervisor who must deal with the issues at hand.

Rationale for using the case approach

Cases can be used "to teach (1) principles or concepts of a theoretical nature, (2) precedents for practice, (3) morals or ethics, (4) strategies, dispositions, and habits of mind, and (5) visions or images of the possible" (Shulman, 1992:2). Cases also help by increasing motivation to learn and by "serving as the instructional material around which participants can form communities for discussion" (ibid.:2–3). The cases in this book present contextualized topics for discussion by language teachers, trainees, supervisors, administrators, and teacher educators. However, in the language teacher development literature, teachers' own accounts of how they resolve teaching issues have not often been published (Richards, 1998: xi). Cases have not been widely used for professional development purposes in our field (Wallace, 2000:17), and even less of the available case-based material deals with language teacher supervision.

Cases (and particularly case reports) are helpful because they yield insiders' insights. Case studies are useful precisely because they provide both descriptive and reflective teacher-generated information (Richards, 1998: xii). Cases written by teachers illustrate the daily issues teachers face and explain "how teachers deal with problems such as classroom management, student motivation and attitudes, and teaching strategies" (ibid.). Richards adds that case accounts "allow access not only to accounts of the problems teachers encounter but to the principles and thinking they bring to bear on their resolution" (ibid.). The same can be said of supervision cases.

In the field of education, cases are stories about teaching and learning, including learning by teachers, teacher educators, and supervisors. Shulman (1992:21) finds that such narratives share a number of characteristics:

- Narratives have a plot – a beginning, middle, and end. They may well include a dramatic tension that must be relieved in some fashion.
- Narratives are particular and specific. They are not statements of what generally or for the most part is or has been.
- Narratives place events in a frame of time and place. They are, quite literally, local – that is, located or situated.
- Narratives of action or inquiry reveal the working of human hands, minds, motives, conceptions, needs, misconceptions, frustrations, jealousies, faults. Human agency and intention are central to those accounts.
- Narratives reflect the social and cultural contexts within which the events occur.

Narratives come from ordinary, everyday teaching experiences and from dramatic critical events. Both mundane and important turning points are useful as case materials.

The connection of experience with narrative gives cases instructional power. As Shulman explains, "cases instantiate and contextualize principles through embedding them in vividly told stories" (ibid.:5). Cases can also be useful in supervisors' development because they

> show little respect for disciplinary boundaries. They are messy and recalcitrant. They rarely admit of a single right answer. They are therefore ideal for inducting the neophyte into those worlds of thought and work that are themselves characterized by unpredictability, uncertainty, and judgment. (ibid.:8)

Language teacher supervision certainly is such a field. The unpredictability and the open-ended nature of *decision cases* make them ideal for the preparation of supervisors: "[T]hrough various twists and turns to some final situation... narratives... nearly always contain an evocative element that... allows them to experience something of what being in this sort of situation would feel like if they were actually there" (Mattingly, 1991:248). When we read or hear a case, we begin to wonder, "What would I have done? What would I do, faced with a similar situation?" These apparently imaginary situations provide us with safe contexts for thinking out alternative solutions to the problems raised before we ourselves become teacher supervisors. Or if we are already working as teacher supervisors, we can think through our possible reactions to various problems before they actually arise. This preparation is important because many situations that language teacher supervisors must deal with are time-sensitive and fraught with problems demanding quick action. Indeed, supervisory practice often places "undue emphasis on reactive performance – doing things as a result of crisis orientation – rather than through careful, logical planning and preparation" (Daresh, 2001:25).

Narratives not only give meaning to our experiences, but they "also provide us a forward glance, helping us anticipate meaningful shapes for situations even before we enter them, allowing us to envision endings from the very beginning" (Mattingly, 1991:237). It is my hope that the cases provided in this book will offer new language teacher supervisors (and language teachers who might become supervisors) that kind of forward glance.

In Richards's book of cases written by language teachers from 20 countries (Richards, 1998), each case includes a description of the context, a statement of the problem, the teacher's solution, and brief comments by a teacher educator. These examples of teaching incidents and the teachers' responses to them can be used to explore alternative reactions to the problems.

Telling stories allows us "to impose order and coherence on the unpredictable classroom reality where there are always alternative solutions to cope with similar problems" (Olshtain and Kupferberg, 1998:187). These authors continue, "This process of reflection constitutes a re-understanding of these events in the present circumstances" (ibid.). Carter says that "stories are especially useful devices for dealing with situation, conflict or obstacle, motive, and causality" (1993:7). The field of teacher preparation now has a "growing understanding . . . of the conditions needed for the development of cognitive flexibility to cope with unpredictable and fluid domains" (Shulman, 1992:26). Language teacher supervision is just such a domain.

Reviewing and interpreting cases with classmates or colleagues can lead to fruitful (and even heated) discussion. Shulman (ibid.:15) notes that such discussion entails two layers of discourse. At one level of discussion, the group focuses on the text or case itself as the object of inquiry. In the process, several alternative readings and solutions emerge. At the second level, however, the learners working with the cases begin to examine their own ideas and solutions. People analyzing a case "alternate between cognition and metacognition, between addressing the case and analyzing their own processes of analysis and review" (ibid.). Although Shulman refers specifically to "students" (teachers in training), his statement also holds true for in-service teachers, teacher supervisors, and future teacher supervisors working in discussion groups. In fact, Bliss and Mazur (1998: vii) assert that for new teachers, "narratives offer an opportunity to be better prepared for the demands of change, whether planned or unplanned." They add that narratives provide experienced teachers with "opportunities for focused reflection and networking" (ibid.). McCabe (2002) states that by analyzing what "conflicts with our expectations, we can come to a greater understanding of the expectations themselves – what our beliefs, philosophies, understandings, conceptions (of the classroom, of the language, of the students, of ourselves) actually are" (ibid.:83).

Concluding comments

This chapter has examined the status of supervision as a profession. We have noted that many supervisors receive no training for their roles and responsibilities, and we have considered some definitions of supervision, both from within language teaching and from other fields. We also saw that several negative views are associated with supervision.

Next, we saw that supervisory roles range from highly directive to very "hands-off," depending on how much autonomy the teachers have and how much power the supervisor exerts. We then considered the skills needed by language teacher supervisors, which vary considerably from one context to another and depend on the supervisor's chosen role. We examined how the roles and skills of supervisors have been discussed in business and industry, social work, psychotherapy, and general education.

We also saw that the case approach to teaching and learning has been used extensively in preparation for business, law, and general education, but less widely in language teacher development, and even less in the preparation of language teacher supervisors. Finally, several reasons were cited for using the case approach in this context.

The following chapters expand on the ideas introduced here, present other cases, and review pertinent literature. Chapters 2 and 3 provide the theoretical background we need for understanding supervisors' work. Chapter 2 discusses awareness and attitude in the context of sociocultural theory. The topics of autonomy and authority are addressed in Chapter 3, against the backdrop of the types of power at work in organizations.

Chapters 4, 5, and 6 are all related to observing teachers. Chapter 4 raises several controversial issues in classroom observation. Chapters 5 and 6 review manual and electronic data collection procedures, respectively.

Chapters 7 and 8 discuss the post-observation conference as a speech event. The former reviews the literature on how to conduct supervisory conferences. Chapter 8 draws on microanalyses of the discourse in such conferences.

Chapter 9 focuses on purposes, participants, and principles of language teacher evaluation. These issues lead us to the topic of Chapter 10: the criteria for language teacher evaluation. We will see that language teacher evaluation is fraught with problems, but that some helpful information is available.

The next four chapters address specific audiences language teacher supervisors work with: preservice teachers (Chapter 11), teaching assistants (Chapter 12), in-service teachers (Chapter 13), and non-native speaking teachers (Chapter 14). Finally, Chapter 15 discusses alternatives to language teacher supervision in the context of professionalism and paradigm shifts. It also reviews reflective teaching and research on excellence in supervision.

First, however, we will consider the case at the beginning of this chapter – the situation in which you suddenly find yourself unexpectedly working as a language teacher supervisor.

Case discussion

1. Regarding language teacher education, Jackson (1997) has suggested posing seven questions to focus the analyses of decision cases. These questions, which "are intended to encourage creative and critical thinking, rather than suggest predetermined views about the case" (p. 7), are also appropriate to ask about cases in language teacher supervision. Please answer these seven questions (quoted from Jackson, 1997:7) about the case in this chapter.
   A. Why is this case a dilemma?
   B. Who are the key players?
   C. What are the main issues or problems?
   D. What, if anything, should X [here, the new supervisor] do to resolve the dilemma?
   E. What would the consequences be of each solution?
   F. What would you do if you were the decision maker?
   G. What did you learn from this case?
   Are there other questions you would want to pose, either as additions or alternatives?
2. In the context of this case, what supervisorial role(s) do you think you should adopt? Why?
3. Imagine your first staff meeting with the teaching assistants (TAs). How would you explain your approach to supervision? Role-play your explanation to the TAs, using either Freeman's supervisory option, the alternatives option, or the nondirective option as your approach.
4. List at least five skills you already have that would be helpful to you in this new position as a TA supervisor. What additional skills would you need to develop to be effective in this role? List three to five skills, and prioritize the one(s) you would want to work on first.

5. Which of the following skills (from Gambrill and Stein, 1983:153) would be most important in your new role as the TA supervisor? Put *1*, *2*, and *3* next to the three most important skills, and *X*, *Y*, and *Z* beside the three least important:

_____ A. offer rewarding feedback

_____ B. handle emotional outbursts effectively

_____ C. handle complaints effectively

_____ D. help TAs find solutions to work-related interpersonal dilemmas

_____ E. respond to criticism

_____ F. make and refuse requests

_____ G. mediate conflicts that arise

_____ H. delegate responsibility

_____ I. be persistent in the face of resistance

_____ J. conduct effective meetings

_____ K. anticipate and remove obstacles to communication

_____ L. handle difficult people

_____ M. offer clear instructions

6. Bernard (1979:63) described four components, or subskills, of personalization skills. How might each of these be a factor in your new role as a TA supervisor?

A. developing authority and responsibility

B. developing a nondefensive attitude toward negative criticism

C. developing comfort with a variety of affective issues

D. developing respect for the participants in the program

How do these skills relate to Abrell's (1974) humanistic supervision?

7. In working with these TAs, when would the supervisory, the nondirective, or the alternatives approach (Freeman, 1982) be appropriate? Under what circumstances would each of these options be inappropriate for you to use as the TA supervisor?

Tasks and discussion

1. Why has supervision been called "snoopervision," the "reluctant profession," and a "private cold war"? Why do the teachers described by Black (1993) pass along a secret warning about unscheduled observations? Have you ever had a similar experience?

2. Several authors have described different ways in which supervisors enact their roles:

Goldsberry (1988): nominal model, prescriptive model, reflective model

Knop (1980): scientific approach, democratic approach, clinical supervision

Clark (1990): judgmental supervision, casual or informal supervision, clerical supervision, cooperative supervision, individualized or responsive supervision, clinical supervision

Abrell (1974): humanistic supervision

Bernard (1979): teacher-student approach, counselor-client approach, consultant approach

Acheson and Gall (1997): counselor, coach, consultant, inspector, mentor, and cooperating teacher

Freeman (1982): supervisory option, nondirective option, alternative option

Gebhard (1984): traditional directive supervision, alternative supervision, collaborative supervision, nondirective supervision, creative supervision

Place these role labels along a continuum whose poles are Wallace's classic prescriptive approach and the classic collaborative approach. Are there any roles that clearly do not fall neatly on this continuum? If so, why don't they fit?

3. Bernard (1979) identifies three kinds of skills – process skills, conceptualization skills, and personalization skills – for supervising psychotherapists in training. How important is each skill for language teacher supervisors? Rate each type, using a scale of 1 to 5, where 1 equals "not at all important" and 5 equals "extremely important." Discuss your ratings with a colleague.

4. Alfonso et al. (1984) discuss three types of supervisory skills: technical skills, human relations skills, and managerial skills. If you are a supervisor or in-service teacher, identify an instance when each of these skills has been needed in your context. If you are a preservice teacher, when might these skills be needed in the context where you plan to work?

5. Characterize the Geddes and Marks (1997) supervisory procedures as either technical skills, human relations skills, or managerial skills (as described by Alfonso et al., 1984).

6. Acheson and Gall (1997) described six supervisory roles, while Bernard (1979) described three roles in the supervision of trainee psychotherapists. What are the similarities and differences between Acheson and Gall's six categories and Bernard's three roles?

7. Which of the supervisory roles described in this chapter best suit your style, personality, and philosophy? Which one(s) do you find least suitable?

8. Imagine you are an experienced language teacher supervisor working in a new program. Once you begin your duties, the director says

your model of supervision (approach X) is not appropriate and that you will need to adopt approach Y. With a colleague, role-play a conversation with the director in which you explain why you prefer X to Y.

9. Here's a job announcement for a supervisory position in a refugee camp. Which language teacher supervisor's role would be appropriate in this context? What factors influenced your choice? What information are you lacking to make an informed choice?

Job Announcement: Teacher Supervisor

To provide training and supervision in theory and methodology to a team of up to eight teachers as they implement a comprehensive program to prepare elementary children for U.S. school integration. Responsibilities include the following:

A. To supervise and train a team of up to eight teachers on a daily basis
B. To convene regular team meetings as scheduled within the training design
C. To provide regular classroom observation of teacher instruction (to also include model and demonstration teaching as necessary)
D. To present formal and informal training sessions as determined by the training schedule
E. To document teacher performance and conduct performance evaluations for each teacher
F. To monitor and coordinate classroom materials use and needs of teachers
G. To assist in writing curriculum if requested
H. To report in writing monthly to the training specialist and more frequently as requested

---

How do the responsibilities listed here match those listed by Gebhard (1984)? Is this a job you would like to have? Why or why not?

10. Gambrill and Stein (1983) identify rewardingness as an important supervisory skill. They stress positive monitoring over negative monitoring. Think of an example of rewardingness in the work of a supervisor you have known (or in your own supervisory experience). Next, think of an instance when rewardingness could have been used but wasn't.

11. Pajak's (1990) review of the general education literature on teacher supervision identifies 12 variables related to instructional improvement and teachers' professional growth. Think of an effective

supervisor you have known. Which characteristics were apparent in that person's work? Were any of them absent?

12. Think about your own experience as a teacher, teacher educator, or supervisor. Identify two experiences that you have had that would serve as a basis for case materials, case studies, or case reports. If you are working with colleagues, tell a professional story to one of them. If you are working alone, write or tape-record the narrative that you have in mind. When you have done so, in Shulman's (1992) terms, you will have a case report.

13. Shulman (1992:2) says cases can be used "to teach (1) principles or concepts of a theoretical nature, (2) precedents for practice, (3) morals or ethics, (4) strategies, dispositions, and habits of mind, and (5) visions or images of the possible." Think of an example for each concept from your own experience.

Suggestions for further reading

Bolin (1987) discusses how supervision has been defined in the United States, beginning in 1876. See also Ebmeier and Nicklaus (1999).

Gambrill and Stein (1983) discuss supervisory skills in child welfare work. Bernard (1979), Hackney (1971), and Walz and Roeber (1962) discuss the supervision of psychotherapists in training.

Many general education supervision textbooks grapple with role definition and supervisory skills. See Acheson and Gall (1997); Glickman, Gordon, and Ross-Gordon (1998); and Goldsberry (1988). In Glanz and Neville (1997), each chapter contains a question that one author answers with *yes* arguments and another answers with *no* arguments.

The articles by Freeman (1982) and Gebhard (1984) have been widely cited in discussions of language teacher supervision. Gebhard's work influenced Sachs, Cheung, Pang, and Wong (1998), who wrote about the use of various supervisory models in Hong Kong. Harrison (1996) includes quotes from supervisors in Oman whose roles are that of "inspector." See also Gebhard and Malicka (1991).

Plaister (1993) compiled a book of case studies about ESOL teaching and administration, many of which could be useful springboards for discussion of language teacher supervision. Richards (1998) offers an international collection of cases from language classrooms. Johnson (2000) edited a book of case studies written by language teachers and teacher educators.

Jackson (1997) describes the benefits and limitations of case-based learning in preservice training for ESOL teachers. (See also Burton, 2000; Jackson, 1998; and McCabe, 2002.)

Wallace (2000) discusses case studies in language teacher development. Bailey, Curtis, and Nunan (2001) write about teachers using cases for professional development. Reichelt (2000) reports the use of case studies by ESL teachers in training.

Daresh (2001) and Glickman et al. (1998) use cases in their books about teacher supervision in general education. Wise, Darling-Hammond, McLaughlin, and Bernstein (1984) compiled a book of case studies in teacher evaluation. Osunde's (1999) book contains case studies about student teaching. Schwebel, Schwebel, Schwebel, and Schwebel (2002) use case materials (e.g., trainees' journal entries) to convey significant events and concerns. See also the articles by Brobeck (1990); Grimmett and Crehan (1990); Nolan, Hawkes, and Francis (1993); and Weinstein (1989) in general education.

An article by Ackerman et al. (1996) describes a workshop in which teachers write and discuss their own cases.

2 Awareness and attitude

This chapter examines two key issues in supervising language teachers: awareness and attitude. Teachers' awareness and attitudes are central to their professional development. But supervisors' awareness and attitudes are also significant, because they are part of the chemistry – or perhaps the alchemy – in relationships between teachers and supervisors.

Both awareness and attitude play a role in the following case. Please keep this teacher in mind as you read this chapter about awareness and attitude and how they relate to supervision. Of course, you are welcome to change the target language in the case to make the context more relevant to your own situation.

Case for analysis: A question of varieties

You are the new supervisor for a large Spanish as a foreign and second language program for adults in a community college. You have a master's degree in teaching Spanish, as well as seven years of experience teaching at another community college. You are familiar with the program, since all the regional community colleges use the same curriculum.

Needs assessments have shown that most students enroll to improve their speaking and listening skills, to prepare for travel, and to interact with Spanish speakers in the community. There are also some native speakers who wish to improve their Spanish literacy skills. Some students were born in this country, whereas others have emigrated from Latin America as children or young adults.

You observe an intermediate class taught by a teacher who has worked in the program for 15 years. The teacher is a non-native speaker of Spanish with an excellent command of the language, having studied in Spain for many years. He teaches Castilian Spanish, including Castilian pronunciation and vocabulary. The grammar lesson that you observe involves very little communication. The teacher corrects "errors" in Castilian pronunciation made by the students who are native speakers as well as by non-native speakers who have lived in Mexico. Since one of the program goals is to prepare students to interact with Spanish speakers from many countries, you consider this exclusive focus on Castilian Spanish somewhat narrow.

At the post-observation conference, you ask the teacher about his choice of Castilian Spanish as the best model for these students. He enthusiastically tells you about his degree in Spanish literature and his monograph on Cervantes. He also explains how important it is for learners to master "proper" Spanish. In his opinion, it is vital for both native and non-native Spanish speakers to learn Castilian Spanish, including its vocabulary and especially its pronunciation. He feels that knowing this variety of Spanish is important for his students, in case they visit Spain.

Awareness and language teacher supervision

Awareness, as the term is used in applied linguistics and as it relates to the work of language teacher supervisors, is an important concept in psychology. Due to space constraints, I will draw on the work of teacher educators, applied linguists, and supervision researchers, rather than the original research in psychology. With the exception of Freeman (1989a) and Larsen-Freeman (1983), who influenced one another, the frameworks presented here are linked only by their connection of awareness and action and their potential usefulness to our work.

The idea that awareness of one's behavior is the key to changing that behavior underlies the feedback role in teacher supervision. This assumption can be viewed in two ways, which I will refer to as the strong and the weak versions of the awareness hypothesis. The strong version is that people will change their less-than-optimal behavior after becoming aware of it. (This statement implies that a person agrees that the behavior in question is less than optimal.) The weak version is that people must become aware of less-than-optimal behavior before they can purposefully change it. The strong version of the hypothesis asserts that awareness is both necessary and sufficient to bring about change. The weak version asserts that awareness is a necessary condition for change, but makes no claim about its sufficiency.

We will start with the premise that successful teaching entails awareness. To improve as teachers, we must at least be aware of what we hope to accomplish, what we are doing, and what the results are. In general education, Acheson and Gall say that a reflective teacher "is aware of the dilemmas inherent in teaching, is aware of his or her belief systems and feelings and how they affect his or her teaching, considers choices among instructional strategies, and evaluates the effects of those choices" (1997:115). Of course, the people you work with as a language teacher supervisor will be reflective and self-aware in varying degrees.

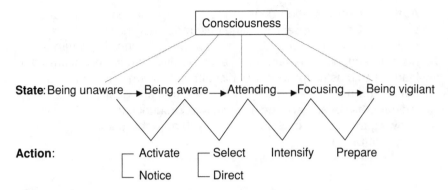

Figure 2.1   Varieties of attention involved in perceiving an object (van Lier, 1996:49)

Definitions of key constructs

Awareness "is the capacity to recognize and monitor the attention one is giving or has given to something. Thus, one acts on or responds to the aspects of a situation of which one is aware" (Freeman, 1989a:33). Initially, awareness consists of becoming cognizant of something. It is a moment of realization. Thereafter, awareness is a way of being – at least with regard to what one has realized (van Lier, 1996; also see Bailey et al., 2001). Awareness varies in intensity according to the attention an individual pays to an issue at any given time.

Two types of awareness have been discussed by van Lier (1995:3). First, in *focal awareness*, an object or event captures our attention, and we focus on it. Second, in *subsidiary*, or *peripheral awareness*, a person is generally aware of something that is not the main focus of his or her attention. For example, a teacher may have focal awareness on one student's question while having subsidiary awareness of other students chatting. Distraction occurs when our focal awareness shifts from the thing on which we are concentrating to something else.

Attention consists of "three separate but interrelated networks: alertness, orientation and detection" (Schmidt, 1995:19). *Alertness* "represents a general readiness to deal with incoming stimuli" (ibid.), *orientation* "refers to a specific aligning of attention" (ibid.:20), and *detection* "is the cognitive registration of sensory stimuli" (ibid.). But "attention (specifically, detection) is not awareness" (ibid.), although focal attention and awareness are basically alike (ibid.).

What Schmidt calls *detection* is what van Lier labels *activating* and *noticing* in Figure 2.1, which identifies different states and actions as components of perceiving something.

An individual moves from being unaware to being aware (the state) by activating and noticing. The state of being aware may, through selection and direction, become attending, and so on. We can see that a supervisor's input may reside with the verbs in the "action" line of Figure 2.1. In other words, it is the teacher's work to move from being unaware to being aware, attending, focusing, and being vigilant, but the supervisor can help the teacher to activate, notice, select, direct, and so on, by raising questions, providing observational data, and discussing the teacher's concerns with him or her. We turn now to a discussion of awareness in language teaching.

Awareness and language teaching

Larsen-Freeman (1983:266) has said that in order to "make informed choices" about their work, teachers need (1) heightened awareness, (2) a positive attitude that allows one to be open to change, (3) various types of knowledge needed to change, and (4) the development of skills. Speaking as a teacher, Larsen-Freeman says,

> I cannot make an informed choice unless I am aware that one exists. Awareness requires that I give attention to some aspect of my behavior or the situation I find myself in. Once I give that aspect my attention, I must also view it with detachment, with objectivity, for only then will I become aware of alternative ways of behaving, or alternative ways of viewing the situation, and only then will I have a choice to make. (ibid.)

Achieving awareness, then, can be the first step for teachers in making a change. Something realized during a moment of awareness either converts to knowledge or skill (Freeman, personal communication) or is ignored or forgotten. Freeman used these concepts in the model of the constituents of teaching (1989a:36) shown in Figure 2.2.

Freeman claims that the traditional knowledge-transmission model of teacher education only addresses skills and knowledge. Yet to bring about long-lasting change and development, teachers' awareness and attitudes must also be involved.

The awareness component of Freeman's model is important because "much of what happens in teaching is unknown to the teacher" (Richards and Lockhart, 1994:3–4). Teaching (perhaps especially language teaching) consists of dynamic, fast-moving, multiperson, multifaceted interactions. It is virtually impossible to be aware of everything that happens while we are teaching, so one important role of language teacher supervisors is to provide information to teachers about what the supervisors notice during observations.

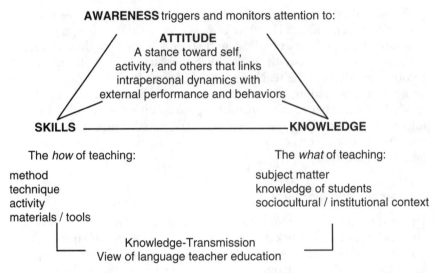

AWARENESS triggers and monitors attention to:

ATTITUDE
A stance toward self,
activity, and others that links
intrapersonal dynamics with
external performance and behaviors

SKILLS ———————————————— **KNOWLEDGE**

The *how* of teaching:

method
technique
activity
materials / tools

The *what* of teaching:

subject matter
knowledge of students
sociocultural / institutional context

Knowledge-Transmission
View of language teacher education

Figure 2.2 Freeman's (1989a) descriptive model of the constituents of teaching

	Known to self	Unknown to self
Known to others	Open self	Blind self
Unknown to others	Secret self	Hidden self

Figure 2.3 The Johari Window (from Luft and Ingram, 1969)

Changes in awareness

The use of another model will help us better understand the concept of awareness and how it changes. Figure 2.3 is known as the Johari Window, named after its creators, Joseph Luft and Harry Ingram (1969).

The Johari Window quadrants show that things about us are either known or not known to us as individuals. These same things are also known or not known to others. For example, a student may know that he is nervous about making errors in class but may not reveal that anxiety. This situation falls in the secret self quadrant, because the anxiety is known to the student himself but not to other people. Or a teacher may not be aware she's calling on male students much more often than on female students, although a supervisor might quickly notice this pattern

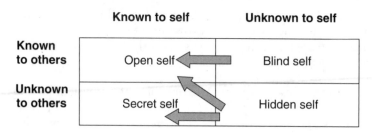

Figure 2.4   The Johari Window and becoming aware

during an observation. This example is an instance of the blind self for the teacher, because the supervisor is aware of the disparity, but the teacher is not. Before the supervisor notices the pattern, if both the teacher and the students were unaware of it, this turn distribution issue would be an example of the hidden self.

When we become aware of something, "in terms of the Johari Window, something previously unknown to oneself becomes known. In this sense, awareness involves both a moment (the act of becoming aware) and a state (being aware)" (Bailey et al., 2001:25). The two quadrants in the Unknown to Self column represent lack of self-awareness. Becoming aware entails moving from the blind self to the open self, or from the hidden self to either the secret self or to the open self, as represented in Figure 2.4.

As language teacher supervisors, we can help teachers discover information about the blind self through awareness building. We can provide a climate for self-reflection and risk taking that allows teachers to uncover features of the hidden self or to share concerns related to the secret self. Finally, we can work with teachers on the open self in two ways: by encouraging teachers to share their successes with colleagues and by addressing areas for improvement with individual teachers, if they agree that some development is needed.

Awareness and competence

Awareness raising for teachers is crucial because "it is a starting point. We cannot develop unless we are aware of who we are and what we do" (Knezedvic, 2001:10). Knezedvic, who teaches in Croatia, says that "developing awareness is a process of reducing discrepancy between what we do and what we think we do" (ibid.). She was influenced by Underhill's (1992) four stages of development:

> (1) *Unconscious incompetence* – I am not aware of something I am not doing well; (2) *Conscious incompetence* – I become aware of doing something in a way that is not what I want;

(3) *Conscious competence* – I find that I can do this thing in a better way as long as I keep my attention on it; and (4) *Unconscious competence* – This becomes natural, leaving my attention free for something else. (ibid.)

In Underhill's terms, *conscious* is not the opposite of a physical lack of consciousness. Instead, it refers to being focally aware, the act of paying attention. In fact, stage three, conscious competence, entails maintaining focal awareness on the task at hand. Thus, stage three, conscious competence, maps onto Figure 2.1 as what van Lier calls focusing (1996:49).

Stage two, conscious incompetence, is both painful and a key developmental point (Underhill, 1992) because of the discrepancy it entails. The teacher is aware of doing something in a less-than-optimal way. This stage "involves reflection, an inner dialogue, and a desire to do something differently" (Knezedvic, 2001:10). To reduce the cognitive dissonance of being aware of doing something in a less-than-optimal way, we must change either the way that we do that thing or our understanding of how it ought to be done. Thus, being in stage two, conscious incompetence, can be a powerful stimulus for growth. Teachers can become aware (by themselves or with input from others, including supervisors) of not doing something well. However, becoming aware may or may not lead to competent performance, as that will require further work on skills and knowledge (Freeman, 1989a).

Attitudes, language teaching, and language teacher supervision

Language learners' attitudes have been studied in second language acquisition research and sociolinguistics for decades. Teachers' attitudes toward linguistic minority groups have also been examined. However, teachers' attitudes toward language teaching have received less attention. Let us now consider how language teachers' attitudes relate to supervision.

Beliefs and attitudes

In language teacher supervision, it is important to understand two related constructs: *beliefs* and *attitudes*. A belief is "any simple proposition, conscious or unconscious, inferred from what a person says or does, capable of being preceded by the phrase 'I believe that...'" (Rokeach, 1971:61). So, for example, one supervisor might say, "Pupils' oral errors should be corrected immediately so they won't learn bad habits." Another might say, "Learners should communicate orally without interruption so they can develop spoken fluency." Such beliefs profoundly influence how we define effective teaching, whether implicitly or explicitly. Beliefs also influence how supervisors respond to and evaluate language lessons. For this reason, supervisors must articulate and examine their own beliefs about language teaching and learning.

In contrast, an attitude is "a relatively enduring organization of beliefs around an object or situation predisposing one to respond in some preferential manner" (Rokeach, 1971:180). In other words, "attitudes are clusters of individual beliefs that survive the immediate moment" (Daresh, 2001:31). Language teachers and supervisors hold certain attitudes, based on beliefs, about, say, the efficacy of treating oral errors. But, Daresh continues, "we can certainly have incorrect attitudes based on false beliefs about language teaching and learning; this does not make the potency of the attitude less real" (ibid.:32).

Attitudes, awareness, and issues of importance

Freeman defined attitude as "a stance toward self, activity, and others that links intrapersonal dynamics with external performance and behaviors" (1989a:36). Sometimes teachers' and supervisors' beliefs and attitudes are in only partial agreement. For example, one day David Nunan and I were discussing what had been helpful for us developmentally, and what hadn't been helpful. I asked him, "What didn't work for you?" His immediate response was "supervision." When I asked him why, he said the supervisor

> was focusing on one issue and I was concerned with other issues or problems. So on one occasion, the supervisor gave me feedback about the way that I introduced a new grammar point, but my concern with that particular class was how to set up and manage group work activities. (Nunan, cited in Bailey et al., 2001:3)

These comments highlight a concern. If the supervisor is focused on issue B and the teacher is focused on issue A, there may be no cognitive or emotional space, in terms of the teacher's attitudes and awareness, to work on issue B.

If you, as a supervisor, focus on an issue that is not important to the teacher, he or she may not be able to process the information you provide. On the other hand, if you focus on an issue that is outside the teacher's awareness entirely, you may or may not be able to introduce the new issue into that person's awareness. More important, if you are unaware of the teacher's focus, you will probably not be much help with regard to that issue. For all these reasons, it is crucial to discover the individual teacher's concerns before conducting an observation.

Sociocultural theory and language teacher supervision

Attitude and awareness are part of the big picture of how teachers learn. In order to promote teacher learning, supervisors can benefit from an understanding of sociocultural theory (Lantolf, 2000a and 2000b; Vygotsky, 1978; Wertsch, 1991). This theory's goal is to "create an account of human mental processes that recognizes the essential relationship between these processes and their cultural, historical, and institutional settings" (Wertsch, 1991:1). Citing work by Wertsch, del Rio, and Alvarez (1995:3), van Lier describes sociocultural theory as an approach to the human sciences that explains the relationships between human mental processes and the cultural, institutional, and historical situations in which those processes occur. Teachers are adult learners, and much of Vygotskian theory relates to learning by children. Still, there is a great deal of useful material in sociocultural theory to inform supervisors' work with teachers.

Definitions of key constructs

A key concept of sociocultural theory is Vygotsky's *zone of proximal development* (ZPD). Lantolf (2000a) describes the ZPD as "the difference between what a person can achieve when acting alone and what the same person can accomplish when acting with support from someone else and / or cultural artifacts" (p. 16). He adds that this process involves "the collaborative construction of opportunities" (ibid.) for individual mental development. In the previously cited case, where Nunan was focused on setting up group work and the supervisor focused on grammar, this collaboration did not occur. We can interpret this situation by saying that the supervisor misjudged the teacher's zone of proximal development, or that the teacher did not enter the ZPD identified by the supervisor.

Who "owns" the ZPD? Are teachers aware of the areas in which they need to develop? Do supervisors have the authority to tell teachers where their next area of focus should be? Or should teachers and supervisors negotiate an understanding of the individual teacher's ZPD, relative to the needs and goals of the particular educational program?

These questions deal with interaction and learning, which are the results of motivation. There are many types of motivation and many discussions of it in the literature. Here I will borrow from van Lier (1996), whose work has been influenced by sociocultural theory. He discusses "externally motivated behavior as following along a continuum from external to internal regulation" (p. 112). In van Lier's view, "externally controlled actions can only be beneficial if they gradually fall in step with intrinsically motivated actions, so that other-regulation can become self-regulation" (ibid.). These issues are related to supervisor-teacher interaction, since teachers may not be intrinsically motivated to adopt supervisors' suggestions.

This connection of action and motivation is a component of activity theory, which is attributed to Leontiev (1978). In this context that *activity* "is not merely doing something, it is doing something that is motivated either by a biological need...or a culturally constructed need" (Lantolf, 2000a:8). Such activities, "whether in the workplace, classrooms, or other settings, do not always unfold smoothly. What begins as one activity can reshape itself into another activity in the course of its unfolding" (ibid.:11) – as every teacher knows from experience.

Internalization is an important element of activity theory and a key component of human development. Lantolf states, "At first the activity of individuals is organized and regulated (i.e., mediated) by others, but eventually, in normal development, we come to organize and regulate our own mental and physical activity" (ibid.:13–14). So, for example, teacher trainees initially will be closely supported and guided by their cooperating teachers, but the trainees will soon take over responsibilities for lesson planning, teaching entire classes, marking papers, and so on.

Principles of scaffolded activity

A helpful sociocultural metaphor is *scaffolding*, through which "assistance is provided from person to person such that an interlocutor is enabled to do something she or he might not have been able to do otherwise" (Ohta, 2000:52). The image is useful because a scaffold is intentionally temporary: When the building has been constructed, painted, or repaired, the scaffold is removed. Six principles of scaffolded activity have been described by van Lier (2004: 151):

1. **continuity**: tasks are repeated with variations, and connected to one another (e.g., as parts of projects).
2. **contextual support**: exploration is encouraged in a safe, supportive environment; access to means and goals is promoted in a variety of ways.
3. **intersubjectivity**: mutual engagement, encouragement, non-threatening participation.
4. **contingency**: task procedures depend on actions of learners; contributions are oriented towards each other.
5. **handover / takeover**: an increasing role for the learner as skills and confidence grow; careful watching of learners' readiness to take over increasing parts of the action.
6. **flow**: skills and challenges are in balance; participants are focused on the task and are in 'tune' with each other.

(See also van Lier, 1996.)

A related concept is *affordance*, which van Lier defines as a "relationship between an organism and a particular feature of its environment" (2000:252). While an affordance allows action, it neither triggers nor causes that action: "What becomes an affordance depends on what the organism does, what it wants, and what is useful for it" (ibid.). For example, van Lier says, a leaf offers different affordances to different organisms: "crawling on for a tree frog, cutting for an ant, food for a caterpillar, shade for a spider, medicine for a shaman, and so on. In all cases the leaf is the same: its properties do not change; it is just that different properties are perceived and acted upon by different organisms" (ibid.).

The concept of affordance is related to supervision in that "an affordance is a property of neither the actor nor of an object: it is a relationship between the two" (ibid.). So a supervisor can represent many affordances: an unwelcome visitor, a spy from the administration, or a source of ideas and possible support. Various teachers will view supervisors differently and those perceptions will not be totally under the supervisors' control. Likewise, teachers will differ in the way they engage with supervisors and make use of supervisors' input and expertise. We will now discuss awareness as it relates to the development of teachers' knowledge and skills.

Working with teachers' knowledge and skills

The interplay of the four constituents of teaching in Figure 2.2 (Freeman, 1989a) suggests that if teachers' attitudes are positive and those teachers are aware, then development in knowledge and skills can follow. Development in skills and knowledge can also lead to changes in attitude and awareness. We can see these four constituents as foci in the zone of proximal development.

Promoting the development of skills and knowledge

If we assume that individual teachers' ZPDs are multifaceted products of the interaction between teachers' competence and local needs, supervisors can promote teachers' knowledge and skills development in various ways. First, supervisors can be resources to help teachers develop their knowledge (e.g., of teaching techniques, syllabus design, language assessment, computer-assisted language learning, classroom management, and the target language itself).

Second, by observing and talking with language teachers, supervisors can determine what skills and knowledge bases need developing, both in individuals and in an entire staff. More important, skillful supervisors can help teachers themselves identify areas for development. Supervisors can aid in skills development through demonstrations, by viewing videotapes with teachers, by team teaching, and by listening to teachers' emerging ideas. Supervisors can promote teachers' knowledge development by sharing resources, setting up peer observation opportunities, encouraging professional discussions, and allocating funds for teachers' professional development (e.g., participation in workshops and conferences).

By observing several language teachers in a program, a supervisor can gauge the overall strengths and weaknesses of the team and decide what topics should be addressed in staff meetings or in-service workshops. Supervisors can also identify teachers with particular strengths to demonstrate teaching ideas or lead discussions at staff meetings.

If we examine the elements identified by Larsen-Freeman (1983) as necessary for teachers to change, we can see that they are not all under the supervisor's control. Table 2.1 lists the supervisor's and the teacher's options in working together, relative to these four elements.

Teachers can certainly attain all four of these components *without* a supervisor's assistance. Sometimes the supervisor's best choice might be to work on awareness and see whether the teacher requests input in the other areas. We will return to these issues in Chapter 3, when we examine the dynamic tension between teachers' autonomy and supervisors' authority.

Five principles for professional development

How can sociocultural theory be applied to professional development contexts? Rueda (1998:1) reviewed research on improving schooling and educational outcomes for learners. He concludes that "effective instructional environments depend on well-trained, effective teachers who are adequately supported in terms of professional development" (p. 1). Based on this work, he summarizes five principles from sociocultural theory to guide supervisors in promoting teacher development.

The first principle is to promote learning through "joint productive activity among leaders and participants" (ibid.). Sociocultural theory views teaching and learning as social rather than individual activities. Learning (including teacher learning) occurs when a common problem is solved by novices and experts working together: "A sociocultural model for professional development therefore involves assisted performance by a more competent other" (ibid.).

The second principle is to "promote learners' expertise in professionally relevant discourse" (ibid.). Sociocultural theory holds that language is an important tool for mediating interaction. Learning the discourse of teaching is part of learning teaching, especially if it helps novices to articulate a problem or reconceptualize the problem somehow (ibid.).

Table 2.1 *Options for working on awareness, attitude, skills, and knowledge*

Component	The supervisor	The teacher
1. Heightened awareness	May be able to create conditions for a teacher to become aware.	Must be receptive to multiple sources of input in order to become aware.
2. Positive attitude	Should avoid creating conditions that lead to teacher defensiveness or rejection of input, and promote conditions that foster positive attitudes.	Should strive to maintain and project positive attitudes and to promote conditions that foster positive attitudes.
3. Knowledge	May be able to provide the teacher with knowledge or guide the teacher to appropriate sources of knowledge.	Can seek out knowledge himself / herself and consider knowledge (or guidance to knowledge) offered by the supervisor.
4. Development of skills	Can assist in the development of teaching skills (e.g., by providing workshops, arranging for or giving demonstrations, engaging in coaching sessions, reviewing videotapes with the teacher, etc.).	Can actively communicate with colleagues and supervisors about desired skill development; can seek out and develop new skills on his / her own and / or accept (or reject) help from the supervisor.

Rueda's third principle is to "contextualize teaching, learning, and joint productive activity in the experiences and skills of participants" (ibid.). Teaching and learning must be based on meaningful everyday activities (ibid.). This principle means that activities and problem-solving tasks should focus on authentic issues relevant to the participants.

The fourth principle is to "challenge participants toward more complex solutions in addressing problems" (ibid.). Rueda says that it is better to view professional development activities as long-term problem-solving opportunities rather than short-term exercises (ibid.). In sum, teachers need "meaningful feedback on efforts that are critical to success" (ibid.).

The fifth principle from sociocultural theory is to "engage participants through dialogue, especially the instructional conversation" (ibid.). These interactions encourage participants to make connections between formal schooled knowledge derived though education and practical knowledge gained by experience.

These five principles all apply to discussions among language teachers and supervisors to promote learning. Note, however, that such influence is not a one-way street: Supervisors can and should learn from the teachers they work with, just as teachers learn from supervisors. Of course, not all learning requires the presence of another person. The next section discusses individual awareness and learning through the vehicle of teachers' journals.

Attitudes, awareness, and teachers' journals

Awareness gained through self-initiated data collection is difficult to deny. Therefore, professional development activities in which teachers collect their own data are very powerful (Bailey, Curtis, and Nunan, 1998).

Keeping a teaching journal is one data-gathering activity through which teachers can gain awareness and express their attitudes (Bailey, 1990; Bailey et al., 2001). The process involves writing about teaching and learning occasions and how we feel about them. It is a record written to ourselves as teachers. Because there is no other audience for developmental journals (unless we choose to share or publish them), we can be totally candid in expressing our opinions, shortcomings, and frustrations.

Acheson and Gall (1997:117) call journal writing "an effective supervisory technique for encouraging the development of reflectivity in teachers." They note that journal keeping must be a regular activity that allows teachers to record their experiences and raise questions about those experiences: "Just as a videotape records the external reality of teaching, so can journals record the internal reality of teaching" (ibid.).

I am not suggesting that supervisors should require teachers to keep journals. That sort of external control would be a corruption of the purpose of making journal entries. I am saying, however, that teachers (and supervisors) who keep journals may be more self-aware than teachers who do not. We will now consider the awareness gained by both an inexperienced teacher and an experienced teacher who each made systematic journal entries over time about their teaching.

An inexperienced teacher's journal

As a relatively inexperienced ESL teacher, Telatnik kept a journal. Later she wrote about how reviewing her journal changed her attitude toward getting feedback:

> After having analyzed myself daily I tended to see other people's analysis of my teaching more objectively. Having learned

> to be honest and objective in my own recording, I found it easier to be more honest and objective about others' comments.... With Observer X, who criticized my authoritarian, teacher-dominated approach, I began to become less defensive. My resentment passed when I accepted the fact that I *did* run a teacher-dominated classroom and that was exactly what I wanted. I no longer secretly raged through our discussions. I even managed to glean from our sessions a few techniques on encouraging student participation (Telatnik, 1978, cited in Bailey, 1990:223).

Teachers who are motivated enough to keep journals of their teaching may differ in their attitudes and awareness from those who do not engage in such a process. However, Telatnik's entry suggests that her awareness increased as a result of keeping a teaching journal. First, Telatnik noted that she no longer "secretly raged through" discussions about her teaching with a particular observer. If her anger was indeed veiled from the observer, then this was an example of the "secret self" (Luft and Ingram, 1969), because Telatnik knew she was angry but the observer did not. Second, becoming more aware by keeping a journal influenced Telatnik's attitude, as she has stated.

Telatnik also recorded the following entry after a visit from the coordinator of the ESL program (her supervisor), who reported that

> during a lesson she observed, she was slightly confused about how an exercise I had the students do was supposed to go. But she said she understood once we got started. This chance remark, in the light of my journal entries expressing my displeasure with sluggish lessons, made me realize that sometimes I gave unclear instructions. (ibid.)

This journal entry documents a moment of becoming aware. When Telatnik connected the supervisor's comment about feeling confused with her own journal entry about "sluggish lessons," she became aware that her instructions were sometimes unclear.

An experienced teacher's journal

Verity (2000) was an experienced language teacher and teacher educator who wrote about the awareness she gained by keeping a teaching journal as a first-semester university EFL teacher in Japan. She used sociocultural theory to frame her insights about herself as an expert teacher who became a novice again when faced with a new teaching context. She writes that "professional identity is a zone of historically situated activity vulnerable to external conditions and influences ... rather than a fixed state of being whose continuity is assured" (p. 180). Verity relates this insight to the sociocultural theory concept "that development is neither uniform nor unidirectional" (ibid.:182).

Keeping a teaching journal allowed Verity's expert self to support her novice self. She says, "private writing, like private speech, allows the self to act as a temporary 'other.'" This duality, in turn, allowed her to "consider possible answers to [her] own internally self-addressed queries" (ibid.:183). Verity says the teaching journal became a zone for thinking in which, "through externalizing and making explicit my thoughts and feelings, I struggled to regain a sense of control in my activity, to sort through the voices, facts, memories, skills, and resources that constituted my shattered sense of expertise" (ibid.:184). By keeping a journal, Verity was able to process these struggles. Her efforts to reconstruct her existing skills and knowledge in her new teaching context are captured in the comment, "My teaching journal reveals someone who is trying not merely to peek into the instruction manual, but to write it all over again" (ibid.).

Verity was uncomfortable about "having regressed to a much earlier stage of what had become a gaping zone of proximal development" (ibid.:186): "In the ZPD, the novice seeks semiotic mediation from external sources, often other people. The dialogue forms that characterize the early entries reflect my need for other regulation, the urge to bounce ideas and questions off a virtual interlocutor" (ibid.). The journal was a record of Verity's frustrations, but "the internally created expert was always at work: each class period became an opportunity for observation and understanding" (ibid.:193). Could she have used a supervisor's help? Perhaps. Or perhaps not. Verity says, "Had I in fact turned outwards for help, I suspect that I would not have been able to follow other people's advice, even had they offered any. I need instead to hear more clearly my own voice, which ... is in sociocultural terms an aggregate of the many voices out of which I had originally constructed my expertise" (ibid.:196).

Verity's analysis reveals that even experienced teacher-educators can return to a state of being a novice if the surrounding conditions change substantially. Keeping a journal is one way to respond to changed states, but supervisors can also support teachers at such times. In the next section, we will discuss some supervisory options using the frameworks already introduced.

Promoting awareness and development

Combining Freeman's (1989a) and Larsen-Freeman's (1983) frameworks with the Johari Window (Luft and Ingram, 1969) can help us think about supervisors' opportunities to promote teacher awareness and development. If we use these frameworks, what is the supervisor's role in helping language teachers make informed choices about teaching?

First, the supervisor may trigger awareness through direct feedback, by asking questions, or by being available if teachers want to talk. In the example on page 48, Telatnik referred to her supervisor's comment (about being confused) as a "chance remark." I find this wording fascinating because it suggests that the supervisor's comment was quite casual, perhaps downplayed in the conversation or given in an offhand way. Yet Telatnik was able to use this statement productively in her thinking about her own teaching.

I am fascinated by Telatnik's perception because *I* was the supervisor to whom she refers. The feedback I gave her was anything but a chance remark: It was intentional and carefully timed. Yet I am delighted that she interpreted it as a casual comment and that she was not put on the defensive. Instead, by making what psychologists call an *I statement* (as opposed to a *you statement*), I simply communicated my own feelings, rather than judging. That is, I said to her, "I was confused about how the exercise was supposed to go" instead of saying, "your instructions were confusing." Her resulting awareness of my confusion, coupled with her own journal entries, allowed her to think about the clarity of her instructions.

Language teacher supervisors can encourage the kinds of awareness that promote teacher development. Supervisors can establish a positive, open tone that allows teachers to examine (and perhaps question) their teaching practice and possibly improve it. Such an atmosphere also encourages teachers to seek help from one another and share information and materials.

Concluding comments

In this chapter we encountered some key concepts from sociocultural theory, including the ZPD, scaffolding, and affordances, which can inform our work as supervisors. We also considered five sociocultural principles for promoting teachers' professional development.

We examined the issues of awareness and attitude and saw that these complex and pervasive constructs underpin the relationship between teachers and supervisors. Throughout this book, we will revisit two frameworks introduced in this chapter: Freeman's model (1989a) of the constituents of teaching and the Johari Window (Luft and Ingram, 1969). We also discussed focal and subsidiary awareness as these terms relate to what teachers and supervisors focus on during and after lessons. Journal keeping was suggested as one means for teachers to create moments of awareness for themselves.

Three key issues for supervisors arise from this chapter: (1) the extent to which supervisors can help language teachers achieve productive awareness; (2) how supervisors can help teachers take appropriate action as a result of new awarenesses; and (3) the need for supervisors to create an environment that will encourage teachers to maintain positive, open attitudes toward professional development.

The following activities are intended to help you develop your supervisorial skills and knowledge. As you consider the case presented earlier in this chapter, I hope you will try to utilize the conceptual frameworks introduced here.

Case discussion

1. In terms of Freeman's model (1989a) and the concepts discussed by Larsen-Freeman (1983), what constituent or constituents of teaching are involved in the case about varieties: awareness, attitude, knowledge, and / or skills? Explain your thinking to a colleague.
2. How would you characterize the Spanish teacher's attitudes in terms of the Johari Window?
3. This teacher may not see himself as needing improvement. How could you describe this teacher's ZPD from his point of view and from the supervisor's perspective?
4. What actions are possible for you in working with this teacher? How might Rueda's (1998) five principles be applicable here?
5. What are your short-term goals, as a supervisor, in working with this situation? What are your long-term goals? Think about goals both for the teacher and for the program.
6. What would be three alternatives that you could suggest to this teacher if you chose to use the alternative model of supervision?
7. If this teacher were to state his belief about the best model of Spanish to teach, he would probably say "I believe that _____."
8. If you, as the language teacher supervisor, stated your belief about the best model of Spanish to teach in this context, you would probably say "I believe that _____."
9. If you were to make *just one suggestion* to this teacher, what would that suggestion be? Compare your idea to those of your colleagues if you are working with a group.

Tasks and discussion

1. Think of a moment when you became aware of something important (about teaching or learning, the target language, the students, and so on). Don't focus on instances where you realized that it was

time to end the lesson or that there weren't enough handouts for all the pupils. Instead, focus on substantive realizations, such as the awareness that a group of students was lost or that an activity was working surprisingly well. What was it that you realized? How did you come to be aware of the issue? Who, if anyone, helped you gain the awareness? What was the effect of this awareness on your attitude, skills, and knowledge?

2. The strong version of the awareness hypothesis states that teachers will change their less-than-optimal behavior after becoming aware of it. The weak version posits that teachers must become aware of less-than-optimal behavior before they can purposefully change it. Which version do you believe is true? Is awareness a necessary *and* sufficient condition to bring about change in teaching? Or is it necessary but not sufficient? Think of an example from your work as a teacher. Share that example with a classmate or colleague orally, or write it down as a journal entry to yourself. Can you think of a counter example?

3. If you believe that awareness is a necessary condition, but *not* sufficient to cause change, what other condition(s) must be present to effect significant, lasting changes?

4. Here, Underhill's (1992) ideas about competence and consciousness are plotted on a grid:

	Not competent	Competent
Not conscious of (unaware)	1	4
Conscious of (aware)	2	3

Think of an example for each quadrant based on your own experience as a teacher.

5. How do Underhill's (1992) four quadrants relate to the cells of the Johari Window (Luft and Ingram, 1969)? How do these two frameworks relate to the zone of proximal development?

6. What does it mean to say that a teacher has a "bad attitude" or a "great attitude"? We make inferences about attitudes based on what people say or do; an attitude itself is not visible. List five behaviors that indicate a positive attitude and five that indicate a negative attitude.

7. Look at your lists of indicators that signal positive or negative attitudes. Are there any behaviors in either list whose meaning might change as you move from one culture to another? Share your list with someone else – preferably someone from another culture. Are there possible different interpretations of the behaviors you listed?

8. How do we know when someone realizes something? List three observable behaviors or direct quotes that would show that a teacher had become aware of something.
9. Think of a language you have learned. Do people hold particular attitudes toward its different varieties? What about your native language – are there notable linguistic attitudes about the value of its varieties?
10. Choose a hot-button topic in language teaching – something such as "frequency of error treatment" or "awarding grades." Complete the following sentence about the topic: "I believe that _____."
Compare your sentence with those of your colleagues or supervisees.

Suggestions for further reading

Larsen-Freeman's (1983) and Freeman's (1989a) articles are both seminal papers about awareness, attitude, knowledge, and skills in teacher development. Winer (1992) describes a practicum for ESL / EFL teachers-in-training using Freeman's (1989a) framework.

Luft and Ingram's (1969) book is not directly related to language teaching or teacher supervision, but it has influenced other authors in our field (Burton, 1987, and Richards, 1990a), as well as supervisors in general education (Glickman et al., 1998).

Teachers' journal keeping has been discussed by Appel (1995), Ho and Richards (1993), Jarvis (1992), McDonough (1994), Numrich (1996), and Oates (1990). Bailey et al. (2001) include a chapter on language teachers' journals. See also Bailey (1990), Gebhard and Oprandy (1999), and Verity (2000).

For more information on sociocultural theory, see Vygotsky (1978), Ohta (2000), Wertsch (1991), van Lier (1996), and Lantolf (2000b).

3 Autonomy and authority

The dynamic tension between language teachers' professional autonomy and supervisors' authority presents challenges for supervisors and teachers alike. This chapter considers *autonomy* and *authority* as the terms are used in supervision and language education. Specifically, we will explore the complex interaction between supervisors' authority and teachers' autonomy in making decisions and taking action. We will also examine the types of power at work in supervision, how and when teachers learn, and whether supervisors' authority is genuine, delegated, or both. We begin with a case in which the supervisor must decide how much authority to exert and how much of a teacher's autonomy to recognize and respect.

Case for analysis: The "teacher's pet" issue

You are the coordinator of an adult basic education program in a large city. Your duties include supervising the teachers who teach literacy, ESL, and citizenship for new immigrants. The program includes students from 40 countries, with the majority coming from Asia and Latin America, though there are also students from Africa, Europe, Eastern Europe, and Russia.

One of the teachers speaks Thai fluently. He has the appropriate credentials for working in this program, including postgraduate training in TESOL and overseas experience. The teacher has worked at the school for eight years and has consistently received good to excellent student evaluations. He has also written materials and placement test items. Occasionally, he has given workshops about teaching Thai learners of ESL.

One evening, three students (from Brazil, Greece, and Morocco) come to your office representing a larger group of students. They complain that this teacher is ignoring them and several other students. They claim the Thai students get all his attention. They say those students bring him Thai food and that he speaks Thai with them during the breaks. These three students also claim the teacher often speaks Thai in class if those students do not understand the instructions or explanations in English. The students who have brought the

---

complaint want the teacher to speak only English in class. Otherwise they want to be switched to another class. You know these three to be hard-working students with good attendance records. You feel that you must take their complaint seriously, so you decide to talk to the teacher.

Autonomy in second language learning and teaching contexts

In the last quarter of the twentieth century, there was an increasing emphasis on student autonomy in language learning (see Little, 1991). Learners were encouraged to pursue their own goals for language acquisition. Needs analyses became routine procedures in syllabus design, and self-assessment was widely used to evaluate learners' skills. The lockstep language laboratory gave way to self-access learning centers. Student-centered teaching was promoted for curriculum development and lesson planning (Nunan, 1988), and the earlier emphasis on monolithic methods gave way to concerns about individuals' learning styles and strategies.

Autonomous learners are self-directed. Knowles (1975:9–11) describes an educational climate conducive to self-directed learning as a warm climate in which the participants care about one another. It would be a climate of mutual respect and "conducive to dialogue" (ibid.:10) in which learners participate actively (ibid.) and are "clear about and secure in [their] respective roles" (ibid.). Finally, it would be "a climate of mutual trust" (ibid.). Although Knowles is discussing language learning, his key points are applicable to teacher development as well.

In autonomous learning, "students take some significant responsibility for their own learning over and above responding to instructions" (Cotterall, 1995:219). Autonomous learning can be coupled with formal instruction but in such a way that learners make important decisions and take steps to further their own progress: "Learners who are autonomous take responsibility by setting their own goals, planning practice opportunities, or assessing their progress" (ibid.).

Autonomy can be related to teacher development as well. In fact, at a time when there is so much discussion about language learners' autonomy, it is surprising that teachers' autonomy is emphasized so little (Blue and Grundy, 1996:245), but recently this topic has gained some attention in our field. For example, Nunan and Lamb's (1996) book is entitled *The Self-Directed Teacher: Managing the Learning Process*. Gebhard and Oprandy (1999) begin their book with the idea that teachers should take responsibility for improving their own teaching. Likewise, *Pursuing Professional Development: The Self as Source*, by Bailey et al. (2001), is based on the idea that teachers can do a great deal to promote their own professional development.

This focus on autonomous individuals, whether they are language learners or language teachers, is consistent with some political and pedagogical changes in the late twentieth century. Following Hargreaves (1994), Corson (1995:7) describes "an almost universal trend away from things such as centralization, mass production, specialization, and mass consumption, including the standardized school systems that used to be the norm almost everywhere." Conversely, he notes "an almost universal trend toward the development of flexible technologies that are developed and used in smaller and more diverse units, including a rapid increase in diversity among schools and greater devolution of educational control" (ibid.).

The idea of self-directed teachers stands in stark contrast to approaches to professional preparation and supervision that try to get teachers to follow a certain method (e.g., the historical case in U.S. government language schools). When we think of the traditional supervisorial role of inspector (Acheson and Gall, 1997) or Wallace's (1991) classic prescriptive approach to teacher supervision, we can see that one characteristic of those approaches is the teachers' lack of autonomy, contrasted with the supervisor's extreme authority. (See also Goldsberry, 1988.) However, nowadays it is not uncommon for supervisors to work with teachers who wish to be quite autonomous. To paraphrase Cotterall's prior comment about students (1995:219), there are teachers who take responsibility by setting their own goals, planning practice (or improvement) opportunities, or assessing their own progress.

Definitions of autonomy

Autonomy lies at the heart of teacher-supervisor relationships. The concept of autonomy relates to "the property of a state to be self-ruling or self-governing" (Boud, 1981:18). In education, autonomy is "the capacity of an individual to be an independent agent, not governed by others" (ibid.). For Benson and Lor (1998:3), autonomy is a process of individuals' "active involvement in the learning process, responsibility for its control over factors such as time, frequency, pace, settings and methods of learning, and critical awareness of purposes and goals." Timing and pace are important in any discussion of teacher-supervisor relationships. Even where teachers and supervisors share purposes and goals, their views of the time needed for learning a skill or acquiring knowledge may differ considerably.

Breen and Mann (1997:134) explain autonomy as "a position from which to engage with the world. . . . [It is] not an ability that has to be learnt . . . but a way of being that has to be discovered or rediscovered."

What an autonomous person thinks and does is determined by the individual and involves "choosing, deciding, deliberating, reflecting, planning and judging" (Dearden, 1972:46). However, complete autonomy, in which "the learner is totally responsible for all the decisions about his or her learning," is rare (Dickinson, 1987:11).

The importance of individual autonomy may vary from one culture to another. According to Pennycook (1997:36), autonomy "has been central to European liberal-democratic and liberal-humanist thought," where it has been defined as

> both mastery over oneself (an internal, psychological mastery) and freedom from mastery exercised over oneself by others (an external, social and political freedom). Thus it is based on a belief in a developed self – a self-conscious, rational being able to make independent decisions – and an emphasis on freedom from external constraints – a sense of liberty bestowed by social and political structures. (ibid.)

Pennycook says this view of the autonomous individual "is a very particular cultural and historical product, emerging from the western model of enlightenment and modernity" (ibid.:38–39). He argues that autonomy is not achieved by handing over power or by rational reflection: "rather it is the struggle to become the author of one's own world, to be able to create one's own meanings, to pursue cultural alternatives amid the cultural politics of everyday life" (ibid.:39). Pennycook worries that promoting learner autonomy globally may be "yet another version of the free, enlightened, liberal West bringing one more form of supposed emancipation to the unenlightened, traditional, backward and authoritarian classrooms of the world" (ibid.). Thus autonomy may be defined or valued differently in various cultures: "To encourage 'learner autonomy' universally, without first becoming acutely aware of the social, cultural and political context in which one is working, may lead at best to inappropriate pedagogies and at worst to cultural impositions" (ibid.:44). We should recall this point about cultural differences in our discussions of supervision as well.

Four "frames" for viewing organizations

The majority of language teachers work within an organizational structure. Organizations, including schools, universities, and other language programs, "host a complex web of individual and group interests," according to Bolman and Deal (1997:163). These authors list the following propositions about organizations:

1. Organizations are *coalitions* of various individuals and interest groups.

2. There are *enduring differences* among coalition members in values, beliefs, information, interests, and perceptions of reality.
3. Most important decisions involve the allocation of *scarce resources* – who gets what.
4. Scarce resources and enduring differences give *conflict* a central role in organizational dynamics and make *power* the most important resource.
5. Goals and decisions emerge from *bargaining, negotiation*, and *jockeying for position* among different stakeholders. (ibid., italics in the original)

By definition, supervisors and language teachers work together in organizations, so it behooves us to be aware of these propositions and how they influence our work and our relationships.

Bolman and Deal (2002) discuss four "frames," or ways in which people view organizations. The first is the *political* frame, which emphasizes the idea that scarce resources cannot meet all the demands placed upon them. With this frame, schools are viewed as "arenas where individuals and groups jockey for power" (p. 3). In this view, the goals of the organization are determined by bargaining and compromise. The political focus sees conflict as a potential source of energy.

The second perspective is the *human resource* frame, which emphasizes the needs and motives of individuals within the organization (ibid.). It assumes that educational programs function best when employees have a supportive work environment. In this frame, "showing concern for others and providing ample opportunities for participation and shared decision making are among the ways to enlist people's commitment and involvement" (ibid). Bolman and Deal say many principals work within this frame and use supervisory styles that involve teachers in daily decision making to give the teachers a sense of ownership over their work.

Third, the *structural* frame stresses the value of productivity and suggests that programs work best "when goals and roles are clear and when efforts of individuals and groups are highly coordinated through authority, policies, and rules as well as through more informal strategies" (ibid.). In this view people are held accountable for their responsibilities. It is a rational approach that values measurable standards (ibid.).

Finally, the *symbolic* frame emphasizes culture, meaning, belief, and faith. Organizations use symbols to promote group loyalty (ibid.). Such symbols "govern behavior through shared values, informal agreements, and implicit understandings" (ibid.). These symbols are preserved and conveyed through stories, metaphors, ceremonies, and so on. In this view, the educational program becomes a meaningful way of life "rather than a sterile or toxic place of work" (ibid.).

Autonomy within organizations

Although language programs are indeed organizations, they differ from industrial organizations that produce consumer goods. Teachers themselves (with a fair amount of variation around the world) are professionals with a particular knowledge base and repertoire of skills. Professions are organizations whose work is "highly uncertain and contingent, requiring professional practitioners to rely heavily on their individual skill and judgement within the norms of accepted practise for their particular professions" (Savage and Robertson, 1999:155).

However, professionals must often use resources that are owned by institutions they themselves do not control, including schools and universities. For example, most teachers do not "own" the buildings in which they teach their classes, or the audiovisual equipment they may use during lessons. These resources are typically owned by the educational organization. Although such organizations are designed to enable professionals to use their skills and their judgment independently, they "nevertheless pose problems because they are most often not owned by these professionals, and their administration is not entirely under professional control" (ibid.). This economic arrangement "creates the potential for conflicts between independent practitioners, who seek to preserve their authority and autonomy, and the administrators...who have responsibilities of their own" (ibid.).

Take as an example the autonomy and authority of physicians in the modern hospital system that has been studied by Savage and Robertson (1999). Complex institutions such as schools and hospitals typically establish standardized procedures, because "one of the main goals of these organisations is...to restrain people from exercising their individual judgement, since deviations from routine patterns may disrupt the entire flow of work" (p. 155). But these authors point out that "hierarchy and centralisation are inappropriate...when there is a substantial amount of uncertainty present in the production process" (ibid.). The difficulty is that in complex, client-centered organizations, some procedures must be standardized, while other actions require interpretation and expert judgment. For instance, in a hospital, medications must be administered as prescribed in order to be safe, but doctors must interpret patients' symptoms and complaints. In schools, teachers must administer testing procedures uniformly to guarantee that different groups of students have equal time to complete the test. But teachers must also use their training, experience, and judgment to determine the content, sequence, and pacing of lessons for the benefit of diverse learners with varied skills and abilities. So the independent decision making of skilled teachers is a key part of their professional abilities (see Chapter 13).

An argument can be made that the standards movement leads to diminished teacher autonomy, since the articulated standards state what teachers should do. We will return to this issue in Chapter 10, when we consider the criteria used to evaluate teachers.

Autonomy, supervision, and power

Given this emphasis on the significance of the individual on the one hand and cultural differences in autonomy on the other, we must ask ourselves if there is still a role for language teacher supervision. Or is supervision an anachronism?

It is likely that the classic prescriptive approach (Wallace, 1991) is no longer optimal in many contexts (assuming it ever was). As we saw in Chapter 1, in that approach the supervisor is an authority figure who judges teachers' work and who may serve as the sole source of expertise about teaching. In preservice training, according to Wallace, such supervisors provide novice teachers with "a 'blueprint' of how the lesson ought to be taught" (ibid.:110). In this approach, during discussions of teaching, the supervisor does the talking, and the trainee is expected to listen. The supervisor may even attempt "to preserve authority as a mystique" (ibid.).

Definitions of other key constructs

Power is an important concept in understanding autonomy. In a sense, power and autonomy are conceptual opposites. *Power* is defined as "the fundamental ability of one person to command some degree of compliance on the part of another person" (Daresh, 2001:187). Power is the "potential ability to influence behavior, to change the course of events, to overcome resistance, and to get people to do things they would not otherwise do" (Pfeffer, 1992:30). In other words, power is taking action that influences other action (Kiesling, 1997; Foucault, 1982).

At some level, supervisors have a certain amount of power over language teachers. On the other hand, language teachers also have a certain amount of power over their supervisors and others in their environment. For instance, teachers can resist or ignore supervisors' recommendations for changes in their teaching. As Canagarajah notes,

> We have to consider power as not necessarily exercised top to bottom; institutions like the school may serve to reconstitute power relations bottom up. At the micro-social level of the classroom, then, teachers and students enjoy some agency to question, negotiate, and resist power. (1999:211)

According to Corson (1995:12), power "can hardly be portrayed in an organizational flowchart . . . because no flowchart or diagram is sophisticated enough to represent the situational effects of language in creating the background to power."

How does power relate to autonomy? Savage and Robertson (1999) say professionals often work in institutions (e.g., courts of law, hospitals, etc.) that they "do not own or manage . . . and that do not, in turn, own or manage them. In such settings, an important issue for professionals is to maintain professional *authority* and *autonomy*" (p. 161). For these authors, "*Autonomy* means that no one except another professional . . . can challenge the day-to-day decisions of a professional" (ibid.). Savage and Robertson contrast the rights and responsibilities of production workers in hierarchical organizations with those of professionals working in institutions. Such individuals are prepared to use independent judgment. "Autonomy represents the formal recognition of their individual responsibility to do so" (ibid.).

The terms *authority* and *power* are sometimes used interchangeably, but in fact their meanings are somewhat different. Authority is "a right granted to a manager to make decisions, within limitations, to assign duties to subordinates, and to require subordinates' conformance to expected behavior" (Reeser, 1973:311). It is a question of position within a hierarchy. Power, in contrast, is the ability "to make others behave in certain ways and is available to most people in society, regardless of whether or not they have formal authority" (Daresh, 2001:188). Both power and authority are important in supervisors' work, but how they operate depends on whether the organization views teachers as workers or as professionals. Authority means that professionals "possess command capabilities" (Savage and Robertson, 1999:161) that are not available to people outside a given profession. A view of language teachers as professionals recognizes that they possess specialized knowledge and skills that the general public doesn't have. But in institutions with hierarchical structures, authority typically is "delegated from the top down, from owners through managers to employees" (ibid.:161–162).

Different types of power

Bolman and Deal (1997) see eight kinds of power functioning in organizations. These kinds of power are all relevant to the work of language teacher supervisors, though a supervisor will probably want to be selective about which type(s) to employ.

The first is position power, which is equated with authority (ibid.:169) and which is also called legitimate power – the control of one person by another based on official status. Position power is the idea that "the person exercising the power has a legitimate right to do so and is supported by a statement of policy, law, or even historical precedent and tradition" (Daresh, 2001:189). According to French and Raven (1960:616), legitimacy involves "some sort of code or standards accepted by the individual, by virtue of which the external agent can assert his power." Supervisors' legitimate power would be defined by their job descriptions, by role statements in faculty handbooks, and so on.

The second type of power is based on information and expertise. Bolman and Deal say that "power flows to those who have information and know how to solve important problems" (1997:169). French and Raven call this expert power. Its strength may vary with the perceived knowledge that one person attributes to another (1960:620–621). This is the "ability to influence others' behavior based on special knowledge" (Daresh, 2001:190). In supervision, expert power depends on the teachers' believing that the supervisor possesses expertise, including the skills and knowledge to be an effective language teacher as well as to be an effective supervisor.

The third type is called reward power (Bolman and Deal, 1997:169). It is based on the ability to reward someone. The person in power controls the likelihood that others will receive tangible or intangible rewards (French and Raven, 1960:613). Tangible rewards include raises, bonuses, promotions, or awards for service or excellence. Intangible rewards involve thanks, positive comments, and the supervisor's demonstrated awareness of the teacher's abilities.

The fourth, coercive power, is "the capacity of one person to provide punishment or negative consequences to another in a deliberate attempt to control the other person's behavior" (Daresh, 2001:189). Coercive power is the logical opposite of reward power, as in the metaphor about the carrot and stick. French and Raven (1960:615) say reward power increases the attraction of one person to another, whereas coercive power decreases that attraction. Coercive power includes providing negative incentives (e.g., a critical report in a personnel file) or withholding positive incentives (e.g., refusing to recommend a promotion or a raise).

The fifth kind of power lies in alliances and networks: "[G]etting things done in organizations involves working through a complex network of individuals and groups" (Bolman and Deal, 1997:170). These authors state that managers who don't spend enough time building staff relations may have trouble getting things done (ibid.).

The sixth type of power is access to and control of agendas. Some groups typically have more "access to decision arenas" (ibid.) than do others. Bolman and Deal add that when important organizational decisions are made, "the interests of those with a 'seat at the table' are well represented, while the concerns of absentees are often distorted or ignored" (ibid.).

The seventh kind of power is framing, or the control of meaning and symbols. Powerful people or groups in organizations can "define and even impose the meanings and myths that define identity, beliefs and values" (Bolman and Deal, 1997:170). Instituting a teaching award or graduation ceremony would be an example of this type of power.

Finally, there is personal power: "Individuals with charisma, energy and stamina, political skills, verbal facility, or the capacity to articulate visions are imbued with power independent of other sources" (ibid.). French and Raven (1960) call this referent power. It is "the tendency of other individuals to be attracted by and to identify closely with the person who exercises the power" (Daresh, 2001:189). In this case, the supervisor's personality is significant. Referent power operates largely on an interpersonal level rather than on a professional level. It often exists in combination with the other types of power.

Other authors categorize power in different ways. For example, in his discussion of industrial workplaces, Welskopp (1999) identifies the power (1) to make decisions, (2) to implement and control, (3) to command hierarchical authority, and (4) to define and determine working conditions. Kiesling adds three other types of power to this inventory. Nurturant power is "the process of helping another, as in teaching or feeding" (1997:68). Demeanor power is "the power of solidarity . . . being liked, being 'a good guy'" (ibid.). A person is using demeanor power "when others feel happy, entertained, involved" (ibid.), and so on. Finally, ideological power "ratifies certain traits as powerful [because it] is the process of power whereby ways of thinking . . . are naturalized into a community's behavior" (ibid.).

Language is used to guide, resist, or mediate power: "For most everyday human purposes, power is exerted through verbal channels: Language is the vehicle for identifying, manipulating, and changing power relations between people" (Corson, 1995:3). This point relates to verbal interaction between teachers and supervisors, especially during pre- and post-observation conferences. (See Chapters 8 and 9.)

However, the power roles of supervisors have changed over time. Research on teacher learning has led us to challenge the view of teachers as blank slates – even very inexperienced preservice teachers – just as we have come to realize that even beginning language learners have a great deal of background knowledge and experience on which to draw.

Autonomy and self-regulated action

This point about supervisors' power can be related to sociocultural theory. In discussing the ZPD, van Lier asks, "How do we, as caretakers

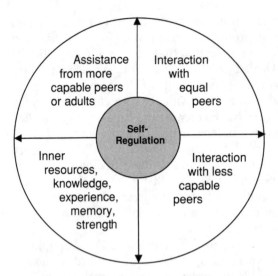

Figure 3.1 Self-regulation and multiple zones of proximal development (van Lier, 1996:194)

or educators, ensure that our teaching actions are located within the ZPD, especially if we do not really have any precise idea of the innate timetable of every learner?" (1996:191). To answer this question, he says, "researchers in the Vygotskian mould propose that social inter-action, by virtue of its orientation toward mutual engagement and intersubjectivity, is likely to home in on the ZPD and stay within it" (ibid.).

In sociocultural theory, what a person can do confidently and indepen-dently comprises an area of self-regulated action. According to van Lier, "beyond that there is a range of knowledge and skills which the person can only access with someone's assistance" (ibid.:190). This material that is within reach, whether it involves skills or knowledge, constitutes the ZPD (ibid.:190–191). However, "anything outside the circle of proximal development is simply beyond reach and not (yet) available for learning" (ibid.). Learners can accomplish productive work in the ZPD by using varied resources, including assistance from and interaction with peers, as well as their own inner resources (ibid.:193). Figure 3.1 depicts these ideas.

In this framework, "a learner's zone of self-regulated action can be expanded in a number of different ways, not only through the assistance of teachers or other experts" (ibid.:193). We can apply the logic of this framework to teacher learning as well. Figure 3.1 suggests that teachers have many resources besides input from supervisors.

Input, intake, and uptake in teacher learning

Supervisors should understand that teachers selectively process the advice they are given. If that information is incorporated at all, it will probably be applied when the teacher is ready to use it. An experience I had as a student teacher illustrates this idea. I remember struggling with classroom management and turn distribution in a university ESL course taught by Marjorie Walsleben, the cooperating teacher. Some students talked a great deal while others hardly spoke. Some of the Asian women were particularly shy about speaking in class, and when called on, they would answer very quietly. So I would move closer, to show my interest and encourage them to speak up. Marjorie did not interfere, but it was clear even to me that when I leaned in to hear the quiet students, many of the others would begin talking among themselves. Then she gave me a simple tip. She said, "You know, I have found that if I can't hear a student well, it probably means the other students can't either. So instead of getting closer, I back *away* from the student who's speaking. It usually makes the student speak louder." I was stunned. What a paradox!

At this point, I will borrow two terms from second language acquisition: *input* and *intake*. (See, e.g., Corder, 1967; Krashen, 1981, 1982.) These terms have important analogies in teacher learning and supervision: "*Input* in the L2 literature refers to the language to which a learner is exposed, either orally or visually (i.e., signed languages or printed matter) and is to be distinguished from *intake*, . . . which is the language that is available to and utilized in some way by the learner" (Gass, 1997:28). Gass points out that the term *ambient speech* is synonymous with *input*. It is the language that surrounds learners living in a second language environment. *Intake*, on the other hand, is that subset of the input that learners process in some way.

Pennington (1996) has also applied the notions of input and intake to language teacher development. She states that in teacher learning and change, input does not equal intake:

> Rather, teachers take in only those aspects of the available input which are accessible to them. *Accessible input* refers to those types of information which the teachers are prepared to attend to because of a high awareness and understanding of the input coupled with favorable attitudes such as preexisting interest in or positive attitudes towards the form of input or the person giving the input, a strong recognition of a need for input or change, or a strong feeling of discomfort at a preexisting clash of values. (p. 340)

Pennington adds that "input for which teachers have low awareness, low understanding, or unfavorable attitudes is *inaccessible input*" (ibid.), and it "will consequently have little or no impact in the way of teacher change" (ibid.).

According to Slimani (1987), a third term, *uptake*, refers to the information or skills language learners claim to have gotten from lessons or other learning events, such as doing homework. Uptake refers to a conscious awareness of having learned something.

These three constructs have parallels in teacher learning. Supervisors should understand these ideas in terms of how we may (or may not) influence teacher development, particularly in relation to time. First, the feedback to which teachers are exposed parallels the input surrounding language learners. However, just because those concepts are available to be learned does not mean that they will all be internalized by teachers and become intake. The ideas that a teacher remembers having learned constitute the uptake. In other words, uptake has occurred if a teacher can recall a particular point at which learning took place. Thus, uptake is a case of meta-awareness – an awareness of becoming aware and learning something.

In the example about my cooperating teacher, I had seen Marjorie move away from students (the strategy was available to me as input), but I hadn't understood her intent. Yet the advice that Marjorie gave me became intake and has shaped my teaching for nearly 30 years. Finally, my rendering of this conversation is an example of uptake. I clearly remember the moment Marjorie taught me how to get students to speak louder and how to build a sense of community in my classes. This anecdote leads to another key concept: the time to learn. Teachers, like language students, convert input to intake on their own schedules.

Time and teacher learning

Most learning occurs on the learner's own schedule, in both language acquisition and teacher development. Supervisors are not fairy godmothers who can, with the wave of a wand, turn a frog into a prince. A better metaphor than the magic wand is the slow process of planting and nurturing a seed. Changes in teaching often need time to grow and flourish.

An illustration comes from Elizabeth Macdonald, who taught EFL in the Central African Republic. She had been trained in the audiolingual method, but the notional / functional approach was also covered in her Peace Corps training. Years later she wrote:

> My Peace Corps technical trainer had told us repeatedly that . . . we did not have to use these approaches once we arrived at our post. In encouraging us to experiment with different techniques and activities, he had presented us with a model lesson using a notional / functional approach. . . . My second year,

however, I realized that the notional / functional approach was applicable at an organizational level. . . . Using a notional / functional syllabus my second year was successful and enjoyable. (Macdonald, personal communication, cited in Bailey, 1992:275)

This comment illustrates the terms defined above. The notional / functional approach was available for some time as input to Elizabeth. She recalls learning about it during her Peace Corps training, and this recollection is an instance of uptake. Finally, when she was ready, she began to implement the concept, thereby converting it to intake.

Training and development

Freeman (1989a) contrasts two important processes: training and development. He defines *training* as a "strategy for direct intervention by the collaborator, to work on specific aspects of the teacher's teaching" (p. 39). *Development*, on the other hand, is a "strategy of influence and indirect intervention that works on complex, integrated aspects of teaching [that] are idiosyncratic and individual" (ibid.:40), as shown in Table 3.1. The *collaborator*, as Freeman uses the term, is someone who helps a teacher learn. That person might be a colleague, a supervisor, a mentor, a peer coach, or the like.

Table 3.1 *Comparison of training and development (adapted from Freeman, 1989a:42)*

	Teacher Training: Process of direct intervention	Teacher Development: Process of influence
Characteristics of aspects of teaching focused on	Generally accessible; can be mastered through specific courses of action	Idiosyncratic and individual; maturation through constant attention, critique, and involvement of the teacher in his or her teaching
Constituent base	Knowledge and skills	Attitude and awareness
Focus	Initiated by the collaborator; work carried out by the teacher	Raised by the collaborator, but work initiated by the teacher
Criteria for assessing change	External; accessible to the collaborator	Internal; personal to the teacher
Closure	Can be within a fixed time period, once criteria are satisfied	Is open-ended; work continues until teacher decides to stop

Freeman's comparison of training and development is related to autonomy and authority. He suggests that some teacher learning, especially at the level of knowledge and skills, can be initiated and promoted by a collaborator and addressed through training activities. However, although attitude and awareness issues may be raised by the collaborator, the teacher must do the actual developmental work in these areas. Therefore, it is important for supervisors to be clear about what constituent base of teaching may be involved in any given context.

Training and development relate to time and teacher learning. As Freeman notes, closure in some work, such as learning a new skill, can occur within a given time period, perhaps even on an externally imposed schedule. Other types of developmental work, however, are ongoing and may not be finished at a certain time.

Training and development are "two complementary components of a fully rounded teacher education" (Head and Taylor, 1997:9). Teacher training "essentially concerns knowledge of the topic to be taught, and of the methodology for teaching it" (ibid.). Teacher development, in contrast, involves "the learning atmosphere which is created through the effect of the teacher on the learners, and their effect on the teacher" (ibid.). Head and Taylor say development is related to people skills and to teachers being aware of their attitudes and behaviors. So, although there will be instances in which supervisors should call on training strategies, at other times development strategies will be more appropriate.

Freeman refers to training as a "process of direct intervention" (1989a:42) and to development as a "process of influence" (ibid.). These ideas are related to our discussion of autonomy, and particularly to the concept of time to learn. In areas where a teacher needs time to develop, the language teacher supervisor may be able to exert influence, but direct intervention may be minimally effective or even counterproductive. The wise supervisor will choose carefully in trying to influence teachers' decisions and actions.

Autonomy in decision making and action taking

Supervision in industrial contexts typically involves overseeing workers on a production line. Factories and other production-oriented firms, say Savage and Robertson (1999),

> are strong at executing known routines in which complex management teams oversee large-scale production and distribution processes of a repeated, consistent and planned character. Such routines tend to be measurable at various stages in production, and so are suited especially well to formal monitoring schemes. (p. 158)

However, "when production involves uncertainty and requires highly flexible adjustment of routines to tasks, then the benefits of knowledge synergy in a hierarchy come at a cost that is large in terms both of agency and of the poor collocation of knowledge" (ibid.). In such contexts, production "is very much a sphere of activity in which uncertainty and task variability are important, and in which rigidly pre-programmed routines work poorly" (ibid.). As a result, schools require professionals rather than assembly-line workers. And, like other professionals, teachers must "wield and apply a wide repertoire of routines to fit widely varying concrete circumstances" (Savage and Robertson, 1999:158).

As professional language teachers, we can practice autonomy in our actions, our decision making, or both. And, as teacher supervisors, we can influence both teachers' decision making and their actions. For example, a preservice teacher may conduct group work alone but at the direction of the cooperating teacher. Although the cooperating teacher makes the decision, the preservice teacher carries out the action independently. In other circumstances the preservice teacher might conduct group work with the cooperating teacher's assistance, no matter whose choice it was to do group work. There are also situations in which the cooperating teacher would turn the class, including the lesson planning, over entirely to the trainee. In that context, both the trainee's actions and decision making would be autonomous.

One developmental process is for preservice teachers to assume greater responsibility for both making decisions about teaching and taking actions during teaching. Many practice teaching opportunities are created with a gradual transition in mind. That is, trainees often begin by observing classes, then help with parts of a lesson, and gradually take responsibility for more teaching, but with guidance from the cooperating teacher.

Both planning lessons and teaching lessons involve risk. Wallace notes that "the risk / cost factor is operational at several levels" (ibid.:89). What if the preservice teacher plans an inappropriate activity, or if an appropriate activity is planned well but poorly executed? One risk is the loss of precious instructional time, another the loss of the students' interest or of the preservice teacher's confidence and credibility. Figure 3.2, adapted from Wallace (1991), depicts "opportunities for varying degrees of safe experimentation" (ibid.) on the increasing cline of risk as teachers in training take on more responsibility for actions and decision making. For example, trainees' observing usually precedes their *microteaching*, "a teaching situation [that] has been reduced in scope and / or simplified in some systematic way" (ibid.: 92).

The ranked activities in Figure 3.2 run from minimum risk or cost to the students and the trainee to fully "individual autonomous professional interaction" (ibid.). However, the reality of teaching is much messier than these neat boxes would suggest. When I have used this figure

69

Degree of risk / cost	Activity	General category
Minimum	Observation / analysis of lessons on film	1. Data collection / analysis activities
	Observation / analysis of live taught lessons	
	Analysis of lesson transcripts	
	Draft exercises Draft lesson plans	2. Planning activities
	Microlessons (nonrecorded)	3. Microteaching activities
	Microteaching (group preparation)	
	Microteaching (individual preparation)	
	Microteaching (peer group)	
	Microteaching (real pupils)	
	Extended microteaching	
	Supervised teaching	4. Supervised professional action
	Auxiliary teaching	5. Shared professional action
	Team teaching	
Maximum	Individual teaching (NB varying degrees of autonomy)	6. Individual autonomous professional action

Figure 3.2   Sample of training and teaching activities categorized according to putative risk / cost (Wallace, 1991:91)

with teacher educators and supervisors, there has often been considerable debate about which activities are riskier than others. For instance, some people have felt that microteaching to one's peers is much riskier, in terms of the potential threat to the teacher's confidence, than microteaching with real pupils. Others have argued that the possible loss of face involved in team teaching is much riskier than is individual teaching. Presumably Wallace's ordering had more to do with the possible risk to the learners, for example, in terms of clarity or instructional time. What is clear is that different teaching activities seem to carry different potentials for risk, depending on who is considering those activities.

Risk-taking is involved in choosing between alternative courses of action, when the result of the choice is not clear. The choice entails an element of possible loss or failure. With teacher learners, as with language learners, the opportunity to take risks must be available if any growth is to occur. In working with novice teachers, cooperating teachers and trainers may wish to start cautiously, limiting the risk. Still, preservice teachers need opportunities to try out new things and then reflect on their success (or lack thereof).

In contexts where in-service teachers (those who are already employed) are recognized as professionals, they typically have a greater range of

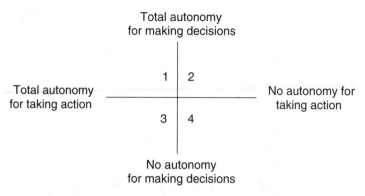

Figure 3.3 Teachers' autonomy in decision making and action taking

autonomy in both their decision making and their actions than do teachers in training. Professional teachers typically plan and carry out their lessons with relatively little input from others, unless the teachers themselves seek such input. Of course, if we enter into a team teaching arrangement, we trade some of our autonomy (in both our decision making and our actions) for the numerous benefits of such a partnership.

The range of language teachers' possible autonomy in both action taking and decision making can be plotted as overlapping continua, as in Figure 3.3.

Any particular teaching context can be plotted on this diagram. For in-service language teachers, most decisions and actions would fall somewhere in the upper left quadrant, because in-service teachers generally have a great deal of autonomy both in making decisions and in taking action. For novice teachers in student teaching assignments, many decisions and actions would fall in or near the lower right quadrant, with the novice teacher's actions and decisions moving further left and upward as the novice gains skill and confidence.

Figure 3.3 reveals possible sources of tension in the relationships of supervisors and language teachers. Consider the following comments of a supervisor to a language teacher:

1. "What would you like to work on next time I visit? I'll be happy to observe whatever you choose to teach."
2. "You decide what areas you want to work on, and write your lesson plan. Then I'll help you conduct the class."
3. "As you plan your lessons, you must think of some ways to increase the opportunities of the students to talk during class."
4. "You need to decrease the teacher talk so the students will have more opportunities to talk. Be sure to incorporate this point in your lesson

planning. Next time I visit, I want to see you using more group work and less lecturing."

Each comment represents a particular quadrant from Figure 3.3. For instance, statement 1 leaves both the decision making and action in the teacher's hands. Statement 4, in contrast, removes both the decision making and the action from the teacher's control.

Typically, a language teacher supervisor observes in order to give feedback on teaching behavior. "Although this approach does focus on teachers' classroom behavior, it does not show how teachers can make their own informed teaching decisions...because the supervisor takes on much of the responsibility for selecting, observing, and offering feedback on teachers' classroom behavior" (Gebhard, 1991:740). Gebhard (1990b:517) also points out the problem of decision making in the classic prescriptive approach. He says a serious problem with this model

> is that it forces compliance with the supervisor's prescriptions, thus keeping the decision-making with the supervisor. In this model, teachers are not provided opportunities to develop decision-making skills.... [D]ecisions about what and how to teach are quite often framed by the supervisor's perceptions about what needs to change in the teacher's teaching.

Here is an example of Gebhard's point from his own work as a teacher (1984:502–503):

> One day a person I had never seen before walked in and sat down as I was in the process of teaching a reading lesson. I was trying out a few new ideas and wanted to see the consequences of not going over vocabulary before having the students read. Instead of presenting vocabulary, I was having the students read a story several times, each time working on a different task such as underlining words which described the person in the story or crossing out words they did not know. The supervisor sat in the back of the room taking notes, and I became nervous. After the class...she smiled and whispered that she would like to meet with me at her office.... At this meeting, she opened by leaning over, touching me on the arm, smiling and saying, "I hope you don't mind. I'm not one to beat around the bush." I sank a little further into my chair. She proceeded to tell me that I should always write difficult vocabulary on the board and go over it before the students read aloud to help them with pronunciation, and that in every class there should be a discussion so that the students have the chance to practice the new vocabulary.

This advice was highly prescriptive. The supervisor preempted the teacher's decision-making autonomy. And had she visited his class again, to evaluate how well he carried out her advice, she would have been exerting control over his actions as well.

Glickman et al. (1998:107) associate high supervisor decision making and low teacher decision making with the directive model of supervision. In contrast, they relate equal teacher and supervisor responsibility for decision making to a collaborative model of supervision. Finally, they relate high teacher decision making coupled with low supervisor decision making to a nondirective supervisorial role.

Authority

There are three major types of authority, according to Daresh (2001). The first type is *traditional* authority. In this situation, "people accept the control of others because it is assumed that those 'others' have some sort of traditionally legitimate absolute right to exercise that authority with no challenge" (Daresh, 2001:191). The second is *charismatic* authority, which is "based on the assumption that the leader has some gift or even supernatural powers" (ibid.). Finally, *legal* authority is "derived from laws, policies, or statutes" (ibid.:192).

What is authority? We can talk about a person of authority or a person who is an authority on a certain subject. As mentioned earlier in this chapter, the terms *power* and *authority* are sometimes used interchangeably, but there are key differences that supervisors need to understand. Of course, a person can have both power and authority or neither or authority without power or power without authority. We will now examine how some of these ideas relate to the work of language teacher supervisors.

Genuine authority and delegated authority

The first point to make is that a language teacher supervisor may have only delegated authority – a matter of appointment. Such a supervisor may lack genuine authority, in the sense that he or she does not possess the knowledge and skills needed to perform the supervisor's role successfully. Or the supervisor may have earned genuine authority in language teaching, through some combination of education and exemplary experience. This part of authority derives from expert power (French and Raven, 1960; Daresh, 2001).

The best-case scenario is that a person is officially appointed to a position of authority and also possesses the required skills and knowledge to be an effective supervisor. This person has expert power, can wield reward, coercive, and legitimate power, and may also possess referent (i.e., personal) power.

The worst-case scenario is a person who is officially appointed as a supervisor, but lacks the needed skills and knowledge to be an effective language teacher supervisor. In other words, this person does not possess expert power, but may wield reward power, coercive power, or both.

Clearly, people working as language teacher supervisors, or aspiring to do so, should have genuine authority, based on training, knowledge, skills, and experience. However, many language teachers are put in supervisory positions without proper preparation to take on that new role. This situation highlights the distinction between two types of knowledge and skills that a language teacher supervisor needs. First, a supervisor needs to be a successful language teacher and possess the knowledge base and skills expertise to talk knowledgeably with teachers. But there is also a knowledge and skills base associated with being an excellent supervisor. Some of these supervisorial skills overlap with those of being an effective language teacher (e.g., communication and organizational skills), but some do not. (For instance, an excellent teacher may be able to explain grammar rules to learners but not be able to provide constructive criticism to a teacher.) For this reason, an excellent language teacher may or may not be an excellent supervisor.

It is important to keep in mind that "the supervisor, simply due to position of authority, does not automatically know what is best for everyone" (ibid., 1998: 142). This point is the distinction to be made between delegated authority (legitimate power, in French and Raven's [1960] terms) and genuine authority (expert power).

A person with only formal or delegated authority may have trouble getting people to cooperate: "A critical concern in assessing a supervisor's potential power rests in the appreciation of how much a supervisor can motivate others to do something" (Daresh, 2001:194). Someone who lacks functional or genuine authority may have to rely on reward power or coercive power to get things done. A person who lacks both genuine authority and coercive or reward power may have no effect whatsoever.

Selectively using directive control behaviors

There are times when a language teacher supervisor must simply exert control. Doing so entails employing directive control behaviors. These are behaviors that supervisors use with teachers when "there is an assumption that the supervisor has greater knowledge and expertise about the issue at hand" (Glickman et al., 1998:144). However, teachers can only be expected to comply with plans imposed by supervisors if they respect the supervisors' judgment. "The supervisor must demonstrate and convince the teachers of this superior expertise" (ibid.). This "superior expertise" entails not only supervisorial skills and knowledge, but also the ability to do the work one supervises – in our case, language teaching.

These authors add that if the supervisor has line authority (also called "position power") over teachers,

> it is more difficult to separate teacher compliance due to respect for the supervisor from that due to a perceived threat to job security. The line supervisor might believe teachers are following orders because of his or her superior knowledge, but the teachers might actually believe the supervisor is an ignoramus. (ibid.)

In other words, if a language teacher supervisor has coercive power, teachers' compliance with directives may not be evidence of the supervisor's presumed expert power.

Glickman et al. note (ibid.:151) that "since directive behaviors raise issues of power, respect, expertise, and line and staff relations," they should be used with caution. These authors state (ibid.) that there are five contexts in which it is appropriate to use directive behaviors:

1. When teachers are functioning at very low development levels.
2. When teachers do not have awareness, knowledge, or inclination to act on an issue that a supervisor, who has organizational authority, thinks to be of critical importance to the students, the teachers, or the community....
3. When teachers will have no involvement and the supervisor will be involved in carrying out the decision. If the supervisor will be held totally accountable and the teachers will not....
4. When the supervisor is committed to resolving the issue and the teachers are not. When decisions do not concern teachers, and they prefer the supervisor to make the decision....
5. In an emergency, when the supervisor does not have time to meet with teachers.

So there are specific circumstances in which directive control behaviors should be used. But employing such behaviors to accomplish a particular goal is not the same as assuming the role of a directive supervisor (in Freeman's [1982] or Gebhard's [1984] terms), or exclusively using the classic prescriptive approach (Wallace, 1991).

Supervisors' roles in teacher empowerment

Murdoch (1998, Establishing Effective Supervisory Relations section, paragraph 2) notes that progressive organizations try to empower trained teachers "to become reflective practitioners, capable, eventually, of independently satisfying the learning needs of their students, developing their own classroom teaching skills, and taking a large degree of responsibility for their own professional development." But what does it mean to say that we wish to *empower* teachers?

75

To empower someone is to provide that person with the knowledge and skills that give him or her a certain amount of power in given circumstances. One can also empower oneself by garnering such knowledge and skills. As an example, teacher research and action research have been promoted as means of teachers' empowerment (see, for example, Edge and Richards, 1993).

Presumably, anything a supervisor does to help language teachers improve their effectiveness and their job satisfaction would be empowering. However, the situation is not that simple. In the supervisorial relationship, empowering teachers is partly a question of control. By this I mean that in the typical interactions between language teachers and supervisors (e.g., scheduling and conducting classroom observations, discussing lessons, conducting evaluations), the balance of power can vary dramatically from teacher control to supervisor control. The issue of variable power is implicit in all the figures presented in this chapter.

We should distinguish between short-term and long-term empowerment. In the short term, supervisors can empower teachers by having them schedule observations instead of imposing a schedule on them. (This seemingly minor point will be explored in Chapter 5.) In conferences, supervisors can empower teachers by listening more than talking. In short, by practicing the classic collaborative approach rather than the classic prescriptive approach of supervision (Wallace, 1991), supervisors can help empower teachers in the short term.

Over time, incorporating more democratic and collaborative processes in supervision can lead to teacher empowerment, but will not *necessarily* do so. Empowerment is both a process and a potential end-state, or product; a journey and a desirable destination. I don't know whether a teacher can reach a certain goal and suddenly say, "Aha! I am empowered!" (as if achieving academic and professional nirvana). It seems more likely that empowerment is ongoing and fluid and that empowerment as an outcome waxes and wanes, depending on the context. There are many situational, systemic variables that influence the extent to which teachers feel empowered. These include (but are not limited to) factors beyond the supervisor's control, such as benefit cuts, shifts in national language policy, changes in administrative personnel, and so on.

With regard to autonomy and authority – the dual themes of this chapter – the empowerment of language teachers depends in part on supervisors recognizing that effective and professionally prepared teachers should have a great deal of autonomy, in both the decisions they make and the actions they take. (It is in working with less effective or marginal teachers that supervisors face challenging questions about teachers' autonomy.) Likewise, teacher supervisors must not abuse the power and authority they have. If the goal of language teacher supervisors is to "refine the process of teaching and improve the effectiveness of the results of schooling" (Alfonso et al., 1984:17), then empowering teachers is consistent with this goal.

Concluding comments

This chapter considered the dynamic tension between teachers' autonomy and supervisors' authority. We considered various kinds of power that individuals might wield, as well as different meanings of authority. And we contrasted delegated authority and genuine authority derived from knowledge and skills. We also borrowed the terms *input, intake,* and *uptake* from second language acquisition research and applied them to teacher learning. We added the concepts of *accessible input* and *inaccessible input* to teachers (Pennington, 1996).

Time and teacher learning are related to autonomy. Teachers, like language students, learn at their own paces and on their own schedules. Supervisors must remember that some learning occurs quickly and some takes a long time.

Autonomy and authority also involve risk, in both the decisions teachers make and the actions they take. Supervisors' intervention in teachers' decisions or actions can range from welcome help to unwelcome intrusion. Although supervisors are sometimes justified in using directive control behaviors, supervisors can also help empower language teachers.

The following Case Discussion section is based on the case that began the chapter. I hope these activities and suggested readings will encourage you to pursue these topics.

Case discussion

1. You make an appointment to talk with the teacher in this case. What is the message you wish to convey? What constituent or constituents of teaching do you need to address – awareness, attitude, knowledge, and / or skill (Freeman, 1989a)?
2. How much authority do you wish to exert here, and how much autonomy should the teacher have in terms of decision making and actions to take? In terms of Figure 3.4, in which quadrant do you want to work in order to deal with this complaint?
3. What are your short-term goals in working with this teacher? What are your long-term goals in regard to his involvement in the program?
4. What is a "teacher's pet"? What should teachers do when a group of students identifies a teacher's pet? What can supervisors do when language students complain about favoritism?

5. If you were to visit this teacher's class, what would be three things you could observe during the lesson in order to have an appropriate database for discussing the students' complaint?

6. Now imagine three possible outcomes of talking with this teacher. He might say,

> (6-A) "Gosh! I didn't realize I was making the other students feel bad! I just like to practice speaking Thai so I won't forget it."

In this case, would you be dealing with awareness, attitude, knowledge, or skills?

Or the teacher might respond with a comment like this:

> (6-B) "Which students said that? I'll bet I know who it was. They are pretty lazy, and they want me to do their work for them. But the Thai students are always very respectful. They ask me for help politely, and they invite me to chat during the breaks. That other gang just goes off together in the breaks to smoke and sulk."

Which constituent(s) are involved here – awareness, attitude, knowledge, or skills?

Perhaps the teacher might say something like this:

> (6-C) "Oh, I didn't know I was hurting their feelings. It's just so much easier to explain vocabulary and sticky grammar points in Thai."

Which constituent(s) are involved here – awareness, attitude, knowledge, or skills?

7. Which kind(s) of authority might be helpful for you to possess in talking with this teacher? Which kind(s) of power might be useful in working with this teacher?

8. How would you characterize this teacher's ZPD? If you could make just one suggestion for change to this teacher, what would it be?

Tasks and discussion

1. As a teacher, what sorts of things do you prefer to learn on your own? When do you prefer guidance? If you are a novice, in the first few years

of employment, your responses may differ from those you would give as a more senior teacher. Write an idea in each box:

	Guided learning preferred	Autonomous learning preferred
Preservice teacher		
Novice teacher		
Experienced teacher		

2. How do the issues you identified in the boxes relate to the concepts of awareness, attitude, knowledge, and skills (Freeman, 1989a; Larsen-Freeman, 1983)?
3. Have you had experience as a teacher with supervisors who clearly possessed or lacked genuine authority? If so, what were you able to learn by working with those people?
4. This chapter suggests that the terms *input, intake,* and *uptake* can be used in talking about teacher learning. Think of an example from your own life as a teacher learning something new. Describe the input, the intake, and the uptake. Was someone else involved as the collaborator (Freeman, 1989a) in this learning? If so, how did that person influence you?
5. Think of an example from your life (as an in-service or a preservice teacher) when you were working on an area open to direct intervention from a collaborator. Think of another example when you were working on a developmental issue that was amenable to more indirect influence. In each case, was there someone who tried to help you? If so, what did that person do or say to you? Were those attempts useful to you as a language teacher?
6. Think of someone who has been your supervisor. What types of power were part of the relationship? Which of these types of power were most important in terms of how that person influenced your work? Why? Thinking of your own work as a supervisor, which of these types of power have you exerted (or would you want to exert)?

Suggestions for further reading

Pennington (1996) reports on the changes undergone by eight secondary school EFL teachers in Hong Kong who were learning about process writing.

For a discussion of power and authority in general education, see Daresh (2001). Blase and Blase (1995) focus specifically on power and authority in supervisory conferences.

Wallace (1991) includes a chapter about language teacher supervision in the context of reflective teaching that relates to autonomy and authority.

For an interesting discussion of empowerment, see the article by Lankshear (1994), who wrote about the impact of literacy and numeracy training in Nicaragua.

Bolman and Deal (1997) present an excellent analysis of how power functions in organizations. In another book (2002), these authors illustrate these frames in a story about a new teacher, a new principal, a veteran teacher, and an experienced principal.

4 Issues in observing language teachers

A fundamental part of language teacher supervision is observing lessons. Supervisors observe language lessons for various reasons, including seeing how well the curriculum is coordinated, monitoring students having difficulty, and so on. But at some point in a supervisor's work, he or she will find it necessary to observe teachers and evaluate their performances. Being in the classroom with the teacher(s) and students is a primary means by which supervisors can gather information to promote teacher development, to help with problem students, or to form judgments. Of course, supervisors can read teachers' portfolios, discuss unobserved lessons, or review teachers' diary entries, but conducting live classroom observations is still a very important part of supervisory work.

This chapter examines the pros and cons of observing teachers and of recording data during classroom observations. A basic concern is that fair and appropriate evaluation procedures are followed. We will see that there are many ways to collect appropriate data, by both manual and electronic means (the topics of Chapters 5 and 6, respectively). A key issue is whether the purpose of the observation is developmental (to benefit the teacher) or evaluative (as a quality control measure). We will return to these points in Chapters 9 and 10, when we consider teacher evaluation. Let us begin with a case to contextualize these issues.

Case for analysis: Getting through the door

You are a newly hired supervisor in a large commercial language program. You have postgraduate training in your language and in language teaching. In addition, you have worked for years as a teacher and a supervisor in another job. You feel confident that you have the skills and knowledge to work well in this new context. Your contract states that you will observe all teachers for at least two one-hour lessons each semester. The teachers' contracts state that they will be observed for evaluation purposes twice each semester. Additional developmental observations may be scheduled at your discretion or jointly negotiated with the teachers.

When the semester begins, you write an informal letter to all the teachers to set a positive tone and convey your enthusiasm for working here. You ask each teacher to choose two hours during the third

---

to sixth weeks of the term when you could observe a class. You also ask each teacher to suggest two hours during the tenth to fourteen weeks for your second observation. Thus, for each teacher, you plan to schedule a one-hour observation between weeks three and six, and another between weeks ten and fourteen. You hope to make the scheduling very convenient for the teachers and to show them how flexible you are.

One teacher writes that it will not be necessary for you to observe her. She has been working in this program for many years and she always received positive evaluations from her previous supervisor. Therefore, she says, you do not need to observe her since there are many other teachers who need your help more than she does. The tone of the note is positive. It is signed "Cordially yours," along with her given and family names. When you see her in the program office, she greets you in a friendly way, but she doesn't stop to talk.

To observe or not to observe: That is the first question

Some may question the wisdom or value of supervisors observing language teachers and learners in classrooms. One concern is that the lessons supervisors observe may differ from lessons when no supervisor is present. Quirke (1996) has gone so far as to say that since both teacher and pupils are usually on their good behavior, observing lessons is a charade.

Should supervisors observe teachers during language lessons? If so, why? If not, why not? The answers to these questions are based on historical, cultural, and political considerations. The main answer for a supervisor, however, rests on logic rather than on research findings. First, let us assume that you, as a language teacher supervisor, are supposed to evaluate the teachers with whom you work and that those evaluations will play a role in decisions about the teachers (e.g., promotions, tenure, and terminations). Let us further assume that the teachers' main responsibility is to teach language classes. It follows that you should have some firsthand knowledge of their teaching. Otherwise, your evaluation will rest entirely on self-reports (by the teacher involved), other sources of data (such as formal student and peer evaluations), hearsay (including complaints and compliments from the students or the teacher's colleagues), or your own assumptions (she's a hard-working employee, so she must be a good teacher). Therefore, to evaluate teachers fairly, it is important that you, the supervisor, see them teach.

Of course, this logic sidesteps the question of whether supervisors should be evaluating teachers at all. But since a key component of the supervisor's role entails evaluation, I will take that responsibility as a given. (We will return to this important issue in Chapters 9 and 10.)

Suffice it to say that if you are a language teacher supervisor, it is likely that some part of your work will be developmental and some will be evaluative in nature. It is difficult to imagine how a supervisor could successfully carry out either of these two broad functions without having firsthand knowledge of teachers' performance. Whether supervisors can influence teachers after having observed their classes is another question altogether.

Conducting "unseen observations"

One alternative to conducting observations in language classrooms is to discuss a lesson you have not observed with the teacher who taught it. An "unseen observation" (Powell, 1999; Quirke, 1996) is based on a structured self-evaluation conducted by the individual teacher and then discussed with the supervisor. It is "unseen" because the supervisor neither attends the class nor views a videotape of the lesson.

There are three advantages of using unseen observations over direct observations, according to Powell (1999). First, this procedure is very time-effective, which is an important issue for supervisors and program administrators. Second, issues such as lesson planning "are actually more susceptible to honest introspection than to observation" (p. 3). Third, the unseen observation procedure "tends to be less judgmental; as a rule, description rather than prescription occurs, and this tends to generate more alternatives" (ibid.).

Unseen observations involve two questionnaires completed by the teachers. The first taps into teachers' belief systems and philosophies of teaching. Teachers fill out this questionnaire before teaching the lessons that are the basis of the unseen observations. The second questionnaire contains categories on error treatment, question types, group and pair work, skills focus, use of authentic materials, and so on. Teachers complete it after teaching their lessons because its purpose is "to reveal what actually happened in the class" (ibid.). Powell says that in post-lesson discussions, these "unseen observation questionnaires ... encourage practitioners to articulate their general principles, then examine them and analyze them for contradictions" (ibid.). In the process, teachers compare what they had planned with what actually happened during their lessons. This last point is particularly important if the purpose of observation is to promote teacher development. Powell adds that "self-observation is a very useful tool for encouraging teachers to increase their awareness of and evaluate their own teaching" (ibid.).

The value of conducting unseen observations rests on two assumptions. The first is that the teacher is aware of what is going on during

83

the lesson. The second is that the teacher candidly reports what occurred during the lesson on the questionnaire.

Both assumptions bear scrutiny. First, it seems unlikely that teachers can be aware of all that transpires during the multifaceted interactions in language lessons. As Richards and Lockhart note, "much of what happens in teaching is unknown to the teacher" (1994:3). Second, it is unlikely that teachers will be able to report on all those factors they are aware of in each lesson. Some issues would be filtered out as insignificant; others might be eliminated because they reveal weaknesses or gaps in the teacher's knowledge and skills.

Conducting surprise observations

The extreme opposite of unseen observations is surprise observations. Some supervisors feel it is important to conduct observations without informing the teacher first. The point in carrying out surprise visits is to see a normal lesson, rather than one the teacher has specially prepared. But, as we saw in Chapter 1, this practice leads to mistrust and defensiveness, as evidenced by the circulating of warnings such as "the ghost walks" and "stand and deliver" (Black, 1993:38). It is difficult to see how a lesson could be "normal" in such a climate of suspicion, especially when simply having a class visitor may be an unusual occurrence.

There are several arguments in favor of telling teachers what class you will visit or negotiating with them about when you could conveniently visit the class. I would go so far as to say it is much better to ask the teacher what class session you can visit. In this way, teachers can have a substantial amount of control over the scheduling process and lesson content.

Gaining entry into the classroom world

In negotiating appointments to observe lessons, you may wish to set some time parameters. For example, if you have one week in which to observe 10 teachers in adult school ESL classes between 6 P.M. and 9 P.M., Monday through Thursday, it is likely that you will get overlapping first choices if you ask all the teachers to tell you their choice of hour when you could observe. It would be preferable to ask for first, second, and third choices. As an alternative, you could distribute a schedule form with blocks of time indicated and ask the teachers as a group to create an observation schedule allowing you to visit each of the 10 classes that week.

You may also want to set some parameters as to the content of the lessons you will observe. Neither you nor the teachers are likely to gain much informative feedback if you observe study periods of silent reading and independent work, when students don't consult the teacher. Nor will

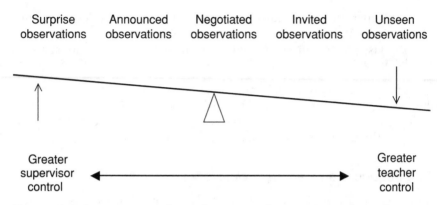

Figure 4.1 Supervisor and teacher control over arranging classroom observations

much be gained if you observe exam periods (unless your focus is on how the students behave during a test or how the teacher gives instructions).

So the first important issue for a language teacher supervisor in conducting observations is to determine how to gain access to the classroom. Will you conduct surprise visits – the emotional equivalent of barging in? Will you tell teachers in advance of your visits? Will you negotiate convenient times and dates with the teachers? Will you ask to be invited or wait to be invited? Or will you be comfortable with unseen observations?

We can think of Figure 4.1 as a scale that can tip in the direction of either supervisor control or teacher control over scheduling classroom observations. The fulcrum, or balance point, is to negotiate with the teacher about when to observe. The opposite situation, of course, is that of supervisor control.

I hope Figure 4.1 makes clear why surprise observations and unseen observations are opposites. In the former, the teacher has no control over the observer's presence in the classroom. In the latter, the teacher doesn't have to deal with an observer at all.

In my opinion, observation appointments should be negotiated for the convenience of both the teacher and supervisor. Or, better yet, language teachers should regularly invite supervisors to visit their classes. Blumberg and Jonas (1987:62) use the metaphor of a teacher-owned swimming pool in discussing how supervisors gain access to classrooms:

> It is not so much a case of manipulating an invitation to go swimming as it is of considering the character of relationships between supervisor and teacher as well as among teachers. . . . If supervision is to be more than ritualistic or cosmetic, the

> supervisor must earn access to a teacher at the level of belief system. It is the teacher who, metaphorically, permits the supervisor to "swim in my pool." It is the supervisor who must attend to things that will result in a much-sought-after invitation.

This perspective may seem strange in contexts where supervisors have a high degree of power (especially reward or coercive power). Nevertheless, gaining physical entry to the classroom parallels the concept of gaining entry to the teacher's psychological and social world.

The frequency and length of classroom observations

Other concerns are the frequency of classroom observations and how long such observations should last. In some contexts, these issues are determined by law or by program policy. For example, in New Jersey, state law and the administrative code specify the evaluation requirements: "The frequency of evaluation is once a year for tenured teachers and three times a year for non-tenured teachers" (Hazi, 1994:198). This distinction between fewer observations of experienced teachers and more of newer teachers is common in both general and second language education contexts. However, it is also common that teachers having problems will be observed frequently regardless of their seniority.

The length of the observation is a parallel issue. Hazi states that in New Jersey "the duration of the class visits is one class period in secondary schools and one complete lesson in elementary schools" (ibid.). In my experience, if teachers and supervisors have the freedom to negotiate the length of the observation, teachers feel they have been more fairly observed if the observer stays for a full lesson, rather than coming in late or leaving early.

To collect data or not to collect data: That is the second question

If the decision is to observe lessons, the next key question about a classroom visit is whether the supervisor should record information in some systematic way or simply gather impressions during the observed lesson without making any written or electronic record.

Systematically recording events (or impressions of events), whether manually or electronically, creates data. According to Bateson (1972: xviii),

> data are not events or objects but always records or descriptions or memories of events or objects. Always there is a transformation or recording of the raw event which intervenes between

the scientist and his object. The weight of an object is measured against the weight of some other object or registered on a
meter.... Moreover, always and inevitably, there is a selection of
data because the total universe, past and present, is not subject
to observation from any given observer's position.

We will use this definition when we consider whether to record data
during observations. There are, of course, arguments in favor of each
choice.

Pros and cons of recording data

When might it be worthwhile *not* to gather data during a classroom
observation? Some teachers feel quite nervous about being observed.
A visitor taking notes, audiotaping, or videotaping can increase that
anxiety. In fact, for teachers, "classroom observation is very often
viewed in traumatic examination-like terms... because of the perceived
linkage between performances during the observation and the offer
of contract renewal" (Murdoch, 1998, Conflicting Discourses section,
paragraph 4).

The image of an observer scribbling furiously or checking off items
on an evaluation form is a familiar stereotype of teacher supervisors. Williams (1989) says, "Classroom observations have traditionally
entailed the familiar scenario of a nervous teacher, trying to perform
correctly, while the trainer sits at the back ticking items on a checklist
and making decisions as to what is 'good teaching' and 'bad teaching.'"
(p. 86). Teachers seem to assume that when a supervisor sets pen to
paper, it is to make a "black mark." This assumption is not delusional;
the image of the inspector looms large in our professional collective
memory.

Administrators, rather than teachers, typically conduct classroom
observations, and peer observations are not common, according to
Sheal (1989). Therefore, "observation tends to be seen as judgmental,
and one more aspect of administrator 'power'" (p. 93). Furthermore,
Sheal claims, observations are often unsystematic and subjective, because
"administrators and teachers generally have not been trained in observation or the use of systematic observation tools. Consequently they tend
to use themselves as a standard, and they observe impressionistically"
(ibid.). In addition, because observation is used for evaluation, "teachers generally regard observation as a threat. This leads to tension in the
classroom, and tension between teacher and observer at any pre- or post-
observation meetings" (ibid.). Finally, conferences focus on "the teacher's
behavior – what he / she did well, what he / she might do better – rather
than on developing the teacher's skills. As feedback from observers is

often subjective, impressionistic, and evaluative, teachers tend to react in defensive ways" (ibid.). Sheal adds that, unfortunately, "given this atmosphere, even useful feedback is often 'not heard'" (ibid.).

In Australia, Burton (1987:164–165) was also concerned with observations and teacher development. She makes five points about observation for developmental purposes:

1. Observation as a means of staff development must be kept separate from administrative supervisory requirements.
2. Observation could beneficially be built into staff development programs as a regular ongoing activity.
3. Observation is effective when it is teacher-initiated.
4. Observation is most usefully conducted by teachers (who might also sometimes be middle managers, because middle managers do often teach).
5. Team teaching incorporating team staff development could be more strongly encouraged.

(This last point will be revisited in Chapter 14, when we discuss supervising native and non-native-speaking teachers.) As for language teacher supervisors, it is important to be clear in our own minds and to communicate honestly with teachers the purpose of any particular classroom visit. Part of the anxiety many teachers feel about being observed relates to not knowing whether an observation is meant to be developmental or evaluative in nature.

The "observer's paradox"

As we have noted, recording information during classroom observations may negatively influence the teacher. The students may also respond to the visitor and the data collection process in unpredictable ways. Indeed, language teachers often tell supervisors in post-observation conferences, "The students were totally different while you were there." Students show a wide range of possible responses to a classroom observation – from being well-behaved to being rowdy, from seeming quite active in the lesson to being passive. Sometimes teachers alter their behavior so much during an observation that the students can be confused by the changes: "The lack of reality about such rituals can be farcical as the students struggle to help out the teacher while trying to cope with unfamiliar tasks, materials, switches of activity and unfamiliar groupings" (Murdoch, 1998, Conflicting Discourses section, paragraph 4).

Whatever the alterations in the participants' regular behavior may be, they are all examples of what Labov (1972) has called the *observer's paradox*. This term refers to the irony that by our presence we influence the very behavior we wish to observe. This result is partly because in most language classes, having visitors in the classroom is not a natural state.

Trust and transparency

Familiarity and trust are the keys to overcoming, or at least lessening, the observer's paradox. If the students and teachers are familiar with the observer and there is a degree of trust among these parties, then the effect of having an official visitor in the classroom diminishes.

The supervisor can overcome the familiarity issue by being a regular, visible, positive fixture in the program life. For example, by sitting in on classes often, talking with students during breaks, and attending school social functions, the supervisor can become a more familiar visitor and thus less threatening.

Achieving a teacher's trust is somewhat more difficult than becoming a familiar figure, however. Part of trust is based on *transparency* – which in this case means congruence between the supervisor's stated purpose and follow-up actions. If you, as the supervisor, tell a teacher you are visiting classes simply to familiarize yourself with the new students, but then proceed to file an official evaluative report of the visit in the teacher's personnel file, it is highly likely that this teacher and others who hear of the incident will not believe you in the future. This issue is related to Burton's point that "observation as a means of staff development must be kept separate from administrative supervisory requirements" (1987:164).

Both interpersonal and contextual factors influence a teacher's perception of a supervisor's visit. Here are four questions to keep in mind: Is the supervisor familiar to the teacher and the students? Is the visit official (e.g., are records kept, does it count as the first of three required observations)? Is the observation evaluative (as opposed to information-gathering)? Does the teacher find the observer to be trustworthy based on past experience, expertise, and reputation?

In my experience, the likelihood of the observer's paradox increases with the number of negative factors. An official evaluative observation, especially one conducted by an unfamiliar person whom the teacher sees as untrustworthy, is a charged event. In contrast, an unofficial observation that is off the record and conducted for information-gathering purposes by a familiar and trustworthy observer is less likely to provoke the observer's paradox. Of course, being observed by a familiar but untrustworthy person is also problematic!

Trustworthiness is a complex social construct. It relates not just to a supervisor and an individual teacher but also to communications in the wider, shared social milieu, including communications with and among other teachers and other members of the administration.

Interactions between the supervisor and any particular teacher may be private, or they can be shared with other teachers and even with many other people, by either party. And those other people can also share information, for example, about the post-observation conference between the teacher and the supervisor, even though they themselves weren't there for the original discussion. Such an unofficial network quickly conveys impressions and influences people's perceptions of a supervisor's trustworthiness – even those of people who were not directly involved in the exchange between a particular teacher and the supervisor.

The problem of selectivity: Means and ends

Another major objection to collecting data during classroom visits is related to the selection of information and how to gather it. If an observer is taking field notes or using an observation form, he or she may be focused on one particular issue while something else of equal or greater importance is occurring outside the observer's awareness. This problem can be partially overcome by conducting a pre-observation conference to learn about the teacher's concerns. It is also partly a matter of choosing appropriate observational means to accomplish our data collecting ends. For instance, a tried-and-true observation instrument designed to record a teacher's error treatment and praise behavior may not provide any information at all about the language learners' use of the target language to accomplish group-work tasks. To take another example, if the teacher is working on getting the students to interact in the target language, an observer who uses a checklist focused entirely on the teacher's question-asking, without recording information about the students' speech, will be able to speak only impressionistically about the learners' target language use.

Likewise, electronic data collection procedures, while quite reliable at capturing the kinds of information they were designed to record, are notoriously poor at gathering other sorts of data (see Chapter 6). Most audiotape recorders, for instance, can miss a great deal in multiparty, overlapped speech (as in group work) and will record those voices loudest or nearest to the microphone, while other voices and sounds become part of the background noise.

Video recordings, in turn, are ideal for studying nonverbal behavior, movement within the physical space, proxemics, and eye gaze, as well as these phenomena coupled with speech. But as comprehensive as video is, the camera cannot record what it is not aimed at, so its "tunnel vision" makes videotaping less than ideal. In addition, videotaping can be highly intrusive, especially if there is a camera person operating the equipment.

Thus, the two main arguments against collecting data during classroom visits are that the process may trigger the observer's paradox and that most data collection processes are inherently selective. It is important to choose the right data collection method(s) to gather information. For these reasons, it is incumbent upon the supervisor to do everything possible to quell reactions – especially negative reactions – to his or her presence. And it is important to select data collection procedures that are appropriate to the issues that the teacher and supervisor are examining.

Data collection and post-observation conferences

Whether supervisors should make records while they are observing is an interesting question. In my experience, it is worthwhile to ask each teacher how he or she feels about my collecting data. If the teacher prefers that I not take notes, I am quite willing to simply visit the class for one or two observations, until the teacher and students are accustomed to my presence.

However, for evaluative purposes, in my opinion it is far preferable to record information than not to record information. Hunter notes that "to be useful, observation must be valid, objective, and recorded" (1983:43). Without recorded data, the teacher and supervisor are left with a discussion based solely on their memories, which probably differ somewhat to begin with and will certainly fade as the time between the lesson and the post-observation conference increases. But with data to form the basis of the discussion (provided that both the teacher and the supervisor think the data are accurate), the post-observation conference can move forward without the participants spending time debating whose recollections are more nearly accurate.

In a review of several key sources about providing feedback to language teachers, Murdoch emphasized the importance of discussing specific events instead of a supervisor's impressions: "If data collected is collaboratively reviewed, it will greatly increase the likelihood of a positive outcome – in terms of a useful dialogue about strategies, and the identification of future foci for lesson preparation / observation" (2000:58–59). Having an agreed-on focus and generating reliable data lead to useful dialogue if two conditions occur. The first is that the teacher and the supervisor will agree on the focus before the observation. (This does not mean the supervisor should dictate what the focus will be.) The second is that the discussion of reliable (i.e., consistent and trustworthy) data forms the basis of the post-observation conference. Through interpreting such data, teachers and supervisors will be able to make sense of

91

teaching. For this reason, the post-observation conference should be a dialogue rather than a monologue (an issue we will revisit in Chapters 7 and 8).

Figure 4.2 shows the role of agreed-on data collection in the observation of language teachers. The left-hand column represents three rough chronological phases in the interaction of language teachers and supervisors about an observed teaching event. These are the pre-observation conference, the observation itself, and the post-observation conference (the essential components of clinical supervision). The flowchart takes into account that the teacher's and the supervisor's perspective on any given teaching event will probably diverge.

Figure 4.2 shows that teaching events are influenced by the teacher's previous experience, thinking, models, feedback, and the like. The observer and the teacher may have somewhat different perspectives on the teaching event. If both the teacher and observer make a record of the event (e.g., the supervisor's field notes and the teacher's journal entry) or if they share a common database (a videotape recording of the lesson), the post-observation conference can be an interpretation of the data, rather than a negotiation or an argument about what really happened. As Murdoch notes, "meaningful discussion of classroom events can only occur when developmental objectives and data collection procedures have been developed" (2000:54).

In the grand scheme of things, supervisors are not always present to observe teaching events. By definition, in a student-teaching situation, for instance, the university-based observer's role ends when the trainee completes the practicum. Supervision of preservice teachers should be predicated on this fact: Responsibility for ongoing professional growth beyond the training program is almost entirely that of the individual teacher. Likewise, very few in-service teachers are constantly observed by their supervisors or their peers. Thus, both preservice and in-service teachers should be prepared to continue the self-evaluation process in the absence of an observer. This context is depicted in Figure 4.3, in which the supervisor's perspective has been removed entirely.

Reflective teachers will continue to improve their work as they continue the cyclic stages of planning, teaching, and evaluating. In this case, the teachers take responsibility for their own ongoing professional development.

Key concepts in data collection

There are three more key concepts to consider before examining specific data collection issues. These are the concepts of observation, feedback, and supervision.

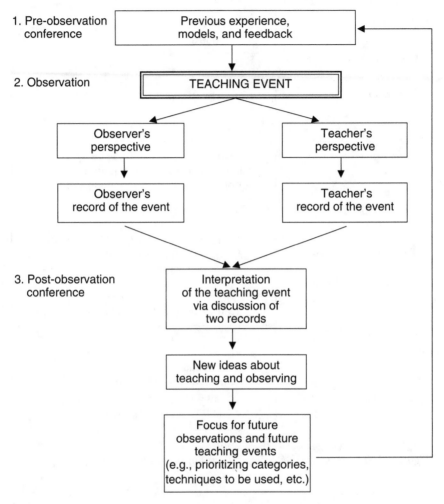

1. Pre-observation conference — Previous experience, models, and feedback

2. Observation — TEACHING EVENT → Observer's perspective / Teacher's perspective → Observer's record of the event / Teacher's record of the event

3. Post-observation conference — Interpretation of the teaching event via discussion of two records → New ideas about teaching and observing → Focus for future observations and future teaching events (e.g., prioritizing categories, techniques to be used, etc.)

Figure 4.2 The processes of observation and feedback in the teaching event cycle

Throughout this book I will use *observation* (in a collective sense) as a technical term to mean the process of systematically watching teaching events. Typically, *observations* (the individual results of the observation process) are recorded or noted in some way (e.g., with a coding system, open-ended field notes, video- or audiotape) to facilitate the feedback process.

Feedback consists of providing a teacher with information about the observed teaching event. Such information ranges along a continuum from low-inference observational data to high-inference evaluative

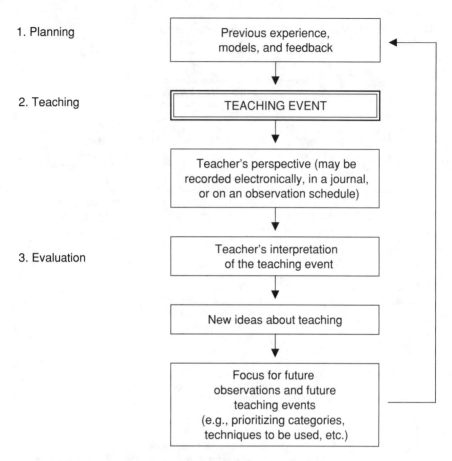

1. Planning

Previous experience, models, and feedback

2. Teaching

TEACHING EVENT

Teacher's perspective (may be recorded electronically, in a journal, or on an observation schedule)

3. Evaluation

Teacher's interpretation of the teaching event

New ideas about teaching

Focus for future observations and future teaching events (e.g., prioritizing categories, techniques to be used, etc.)

Figure 4.3 The processes of self-evaluation in the teaching event cycle

comments. Low-inference data are verifiable and largely objective. The observer does not speculate or conjecture greatly in recording such data. In contrast, high-inference evaluative comments represent opinions in which the observer's data rely heavily on inferences. In other words, feedback can be purely informational in nature; it does not necessarily have to be evaluative.

Many definitions of *supervision* were given in Chapter 1. Here, I will simply restate that supervision entails a host of procedures to ensure the quality of instructional programs, and to promote teachers' professional growth, in part by providing them with information based on observations of their teaching. Observation and feedback are thus key components of supervision. In my experience, the data supervisors discuss with teachers after observations are more reliable and credible if

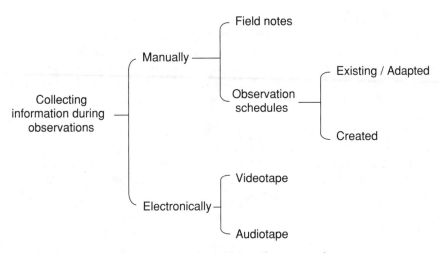

Figure 4.4 Options for collecting data during classroom observations

they have been systematically collected, and this is why I advocate using appropriate data gathering procedures.

To summarize, then, my professional preferences are for supervisors (1) to negotiate observation appointments with teachers, and (2) to collect data systematically during such classroom visits, with the teachers' permission. Given advances in technology, supervisors have many choices for recording data during observations. The basic data collections options, which will be discussed in more detail in Chapters 5 and 6, are depicted in Figure 4.4. Of course, these data collection methods can be used in combination too. We will return to this point at the end of Chapter 6, after examining manual and electronic data collection.

Concluding comments

In this chapter we have considered a rationale for systematically collecting data during classroom observations. We have examined the pros and cons of recording information, including the problem of the observer's paradox (Labov, 1972). We saw that one strategy for dealing with teachers' worries about being observed is to use unseen observations. In addition, we considered the balance between a teacher's power and a supervisor's power in terms of how observations are arranged and whether they are announced or unannounced. We also saw that our observation visits and our supervisory discussions with preservice language teachers will end (in the case of student teachers enrolled in a practicum) or may be infrequent (in the case of in-service teachers). Thus, observations and discussions should ideally contribute to the teachers' ongoing professional development in the absence of the supervisor. Finally, we compared the concepts of observation, feedback, and supervision and noted that feedback is not necessarily evaluative in nature: It can be simply informative.

Data can be collected through a variety of manual and electronic procedures. In the next two chapters, we will consider specific data collection options, examining the advantages and disadvantages of each. Before we continue, however, please answer the following questions, which are based on the case that began this chapter.

Case discussion

1. What constituent(s) of teaching (Freeman, 1989a) are you dealing with, in terms of this teacher's response to your letter: awareness, attitude, skills, or knowledge?
2. What are your short-term and long-term goals for working with this teacher in this program? What strategies will you use as you work toward your goals?
3. This situation is located in a wider context than the interaction between the individual teacher and the supervisor. Think of at least three situational or systemic factors that will influence how you respond to this teacher's note. (For instance, your contract and the teachers' contracts clearly specify that all teachers will be observed twice each term.)
4. One option is to insist on visiting this teacher's class. Role-play with a partner a conversation in which you tell this teacher that you will be happy to visit her class. Afterward, get your partner's feedback on how well you accomplished your goal.
5. You might prefer to write a note to this teacher before (or instead of) speaking with her. Draft the note you would send to this teacher.
6. Figure 4.1 depicts the cline of teacher control and supervisor control over setting up observations. Where would it be most effective for you to position yourself on this continuum in dealing with this particular teacher? Why?
7. Assuming you do eventually visit this teacher's class and observe a lesson, what data collection procedure(s) would you probably want to use, if any? What topics would you want to be sure to discuss during the pre-observation conference?
8. Think about the four variables of transparency and trust. Which factor(s) do you need to deal with in this case? Circle a number after each statement below to indicate the significance of each factor in this

situation. (On this scale, 1 equals "not at all important" and 5 equals "extremely important.")

A. The supervisor is familiar.	1 2 3 4 5
B. The visit is officially on the record.	1 2 3 4 5
C. The observation is evaluative.	1 2 3 4 5
D. The observer is seen as trustworthy.	1 2 3 4 5

9. Think about the various educational cultures with which you are familiar. Would your informal letter be acceptable or unacceptable in those contexts? Why or why not? What about this teacher's written response? Would it be acceptable in those cultural contexts?

Tasks and discussion

1. What is your preference as a language teacher – for a supervisor to observe your class without recording any information or for the supervisor to collect data in some way? Why? Can you think of any other pros and cons of data collection?
2. If a supervisor were to collect data for evaluative purposes while observing your teaching, what would be your first, second, and third choices from Figure 4.4? Why? (Compare your answers with those of your classmates or colleagues.)
3. Do your answers to questions 1 and 2 shift if you think of yourself as a preservice teacher, a novice teacher, a somewhat experienced teacher, or a very experienced teacher? Why or why not?
4. Consider Figure 4.4 from the supervisor's view. If you were to observe a teacher, which options would be your first, second, and third choices for data collection? Do your preferences shift if you imagine yourself observing a preservice teacher, a novice teacher, a somewhat experienced teacher, or a very experienced teacher? Why or why not?
5. Think about times when a supervisor has observed your teaching. What label best characterizes the means by which the observation was arranged? (See Figure 4.1.)
6. We read Gebhard's (1984) account of the person who visited his reading lesson. Taking Gebhard's position as the teacher, circle a number after each statement below indicating how the supervisor probably seemed to Gebhard. (On this scale, 1 equals "not at all" and 5 equals "completely.")

A. The supervisor was familiar.	1 2 3 4 5
B. The visit was officially on the record.	1 2 3 4 5
C. The observation was evaluative.	1 2 3 4 5
D. The observer was trustworthy.	1 2 3 4 5

(We may not know enough to rate that supervisor on some of these categories.)

7. Ask two experienced teachers and two novices about their preferences. Should a supervisor collect data during a classroom observation? Why or why not?

8. Try an unseen observation (Powell, 1999; Quirke, 1996) in which you and a colleague take the roles of the teacher and the supervisor. What are your impressions of this approach?

9. Next, switch roles. Now, what is your impression of unseen observations?

Suggestions for further reading

Allwright's (1988) book, *Observation in the Language Classroom*, provides helpful information for supervisors and teacher educators considering using observation schedules in language classrooms. Burton (1987), Murdoch (1998), and Sheal (1989) have written about the downside of supervisory observation. Each of these articles should be helpful if you wish to implement or improve a program of classroom observation.

Powell (1999) and Quirke (1996) describe the self-evaluation procedure they call "unseen observations." Powell's brief article contains copies of the pre-lesson and post-lesson questionnaires that teachers complete to begin reflecting on their lessons.

Some key references about how visitors should behave during observations are by Master (1983), Murphy (1992), and Zuck (1984).

See Munro (1991) for a feminist interpretation of the imposition involved in supervision.

5 Manual data collection procedures

There is a long history of teacher supervisors recording information manually as they observe lessons, either by using open-ended note taking to generate field notes or by using an observation system. There are advantages and disadvantages to both.

We will begin with a case to contextualize these issues and then examine the use of field notes. We will discuss the pros and cons of note taking as a data collection procedure and learn some strategies for using maps, seating charts, pictorials, and sketches, as well as a shorthand system to record information quickly. In the second part of the chapter we will investigate the use of observation systems. We will see that such systems can increase transparency in the feedback process by making the focus of the observation explicit from the start.

Case for analysis: Wrong place on the audiotape

You observe an experienced language teacher working with six lower-intermediate learners in a 50-minute listening and speaking lesson. Before the lesson, the teacher tells you the lesson will begin with a grammar review, which should last 15 minutes. Then the students will hear a tape-recorded passage from the audio materials that accompany the textbook. They will identify the main idea and note the dates of key events. She tells you they will then talk in pairs, using the target language to compare their answers on a worksheet.

You take field notes during the lesson. After about five minutes of administrative chores, the grammar review begins. It lasts 20 minutes and seems to be very teacher fronted. Although the teacher asks many questions, the students don't appear to be involved in the lesson. In order to document the students' verbal participation in the lesson, you quickly sketch a seating chart. On it you keep track of which students the teacher calls on, who asks questions and makes comments, and which students speak to one another.

When the listening exercise starts, there are some problems with the way the tape recording has been set up. The teacher can't seem to find the segment of the audiotape that she wishes to play. The teacher

---

asks the students to work on a written exercise while she tries to sort out the difficulty with the audiotape. Eventually the teacher does play the listening passage, but the class period ends before the students can complete all the tasks.

The students thrust their belongings into their book bags and hurry out of the classroom, talking eagerly in their first language. No one says good-bye to the teacher.

As the next group of students quietly enters the classroom, you thank the teacher and make an appointment with her to discuss the lesson. You then find a quiet place to flesh out your field notes and check the data you collected using the seating chart.

To avoid overwhelming the teacher in the post-observation conference, you decide to focus first on the seating chart data about the interaction during the grammar lesson. You will then talk with her about the problem with the audiotape, using the data from your field notes as the starting point for the discussion.

Generating field notes as classroom data

In anthropology, field notes are written records of events observed in the field. Depending on the phase of the investigation, these notes may be open-ended or very tightly focused. These days, easy access to electronic recording devices, including easily transported battery-operated units, means that we are no longer restricted to the laborious production of handwritten notes. But there are times when generating field notes can be very useful in collecting data, whether those field notes are recorded with paper and pen or on a laptop.

When might field notes be more useful than other data collection options? Here are several possible situations:

1. When the teacher asks the supervisor to focus on one thing in particular
2. When the supervisor wants to focus on something specific that is not covered in an observation instrument
3. When video or audio recording equipment is not appropriate (e.g., the noisy environment at a workplace language program in a factory)
4. When video or audio recording would be too intrusive or culturally inappropriate
5. When there is no space in the classroom for the equipment
6. When recording equipment is not available

It is also highly desirable to make field notes to accompany audio or video recordings, since both those approaches have limitations too.

100

Some key concepts in the use of field notes

One concern about a supervisor creating field notes is that the human observer is certainly more subjective than video or audio recordings would be. For this reason, if you work with open-ended field notes, it is important to keep in mind the differences among observations, inferences, and opinions. Bailey et al. (2001:165) offer the following definitions:

1. *Observations*: recording facts and events (e.g., in a scientific study); the data resulting from the observational act; comments or remarks based on something observed. (Please note that here the term *observations* is used to encompass the individual products – the data – produced by the process of observation.)
2. *Inferences*: decisions or conclusions based on something known; ideas derived by reasoning; decisions based on facts or evidence; conclusions or deductions.
3. *Opinions*: beliefs not necessarily based on absolute certainty or factual knowledge, but on what seems true, valid, or probable to one's own mind; evaluations, or impressions of the value of a person, practice, idea, and so on.

These three types of records will all occur in your field notes, but it is important to distinguish among them, both in your mind and in your data. For instance, when I record an inference or an opinion in my field notes, I flag it with OC, to indicate an observer's comment.

Systematic field notes can provide a running commentary on the events during lessons. But the field notes must be carefully prepared and sufficiently detailed to be clear and convincing. The supervisor must be disciplined and responsible in recognizing the difference between data-based observations and inferences (or even opinions). This does not mean that the observer should avoid inferences or opinions entirely. Instead, the supervisor must (1) recognize inferences or opinions, (2) support them with verifiable observational data, and (3) check them against the teacher's understanding of the same events. Field notes provide "a human, interpretive dimension to observational data" (Bailey, 2001a:118), which is often missing from videotapes, audiotapes, or structured observation instruments.

One difficulty in generating good-quality field notes is that life in classrooms moves very quickly. To capture detailed data, including direct quotes and nonverbal behavior, note taking must be fast and accurate. Some people like to use laptop computers for generating field notes, but the presence of someone typing in the classroom can be distracting to teacher and students alike (unless the students are also using laptops).

For this reason, I encourage supervisors to develop their own shorthand systems for recording observational data.

Using a shorthand system for note taking

Some supervisors and researchers (see, e.g., Hunter, 1983) use systematic abbreviations to save time while taking observational notes. Here are some common symbols that are very useful in observing language lessons:

@ = at	÷ = divide (divided by)	% = percent
# = number	W/ = with	→ = goes to
& = and	AM = morning	> = greater than
+ = add(ition)	PM = afternoon or evening	< = less than
− = subtract(ion)	e.g. = for example	♀ = female
x = multiply (multiplication)	i.e. = that is	♂ = male

Other abbreviations are not so widely used but can be very helpful for note taking in classrooms. Here are some abbreviations I've found useful for recording nonverbal behavior:

LH = left hand	LA = left arm	T = teacher
RH = right hand	RA = right arm	St = student
BH = both hands	BA = both arms	Ss = students
th = thumb	LL = left leg	CB = chalkboard
if = index finger	RL = right leg	Q = question
mf = middle finger	LKn = left knee	NV = nonverbal
rf = ring finger	RKn = right knee	Rt = right
lf = little finger	LF = left foot	Lt = left
EC = eye contact	RF = right foot	T_1, T_2 = table 1, table 2

Still other shortened forms provide just enough of the word for the note taker to recognize the symbol as unique. Here are some examples that arise often in classroom observations:

wr = write	lgh = laugh	cn = can
dr = draw	(p) = pause	cd = could
er = erase	(sm) = smile	shl = shall
bk = book	pprs = papers	shd = should
rd = read	dsk = desk	wll = will
pt = point	el = elicit	wd = would
y = you	sil = silence	m = may
d = do	info = information	mt = might
ans = answer	diff = difficult	mst = must

The symbols (p) and (sm), representing *pause* and *smile*, are in parentheses because people often smile and typically pause in the middle of an

> T. tells 6 Ss re: tape in TL. Ss lstn for mn idea & dates. All Ss have pprs—T-
> preprd cloze task handout. T strts tape rec. Realizes not at rt spot. Stps—rewinds.
> Ss wait sly. T starts tape agn. Not rt place. T ffwds tape. Starts. Not rt place. Tries
> again 2X. T. tlls Ss wrk prs ex. in bk. (OC: T confused? flstrd?) Some Ss talk q'ly
> to others. Q2 lks in bk bg. ♂1 asks "Why d w have to wrk in prs?" T "Oh." (p)
> "Oh, okay. Uhm, well w cn, hm, lets see. If y dnt want to b inprs, y cn wrk alone."
> T. tries the tape agn. Too sft. Turns up vol. 3 Ss lk up qkly (OC: Annoyed?
> Strtld.) as voice on tape ldly intrudes. 2 Ss pr up, 4 wrk s 'ly alone.

Figure 5.1   Rough field notes

utterance. The parentheses distinguish these symbols from the ongoing quote in which they appear. The point is not that you learn my shorthand system but that you see how one works, so that you can try out a system of your own.

Figure 5.1 gives an example of five minutes' worth of rough notes from a classroom observation. Using the key above, try to interpret these notes.

If you take handwritten field notes, it is a good idea to schedule some quiet private time immediately after the observation to flesh them out. This can be done by entering them as a word-processed computer file, expanding on the original notes and abbreviations as you type the data. An advantage of creating computerized reports is that the database can quickly be searched for key words if you want to look for patterns in several reports or locate all the instances of a certain behavior or event in a particular data set.

As an alternative, you can elaborate your rough notes by writing directly on the original, using a contrasting color of ink, so that you can preserve the distinction between the original rough copy and the subsequent elaboration. Then you can type or word process the elaborated notes as soon as possible, but preferably within 24 hours of the observation. Figure 5.2 shows the elaborated version of the rough notes from Figure 5.1.

This small segment of field notes presents a snapshot of a lesson. It is full of discussable material. In sharing these notes with the teacher, I would ask her first if the record seems accurate and read through it with her, pausing for her to comment on any points of particular interest. I would also ask her to interpret any observer's comments for me, and I would ask about the pair work: Were the students accustomed to working in pairs? What was the activity she wanted them to do in pairs? How did working in pairs relate to the tape-recorded material? The rest of the discussion would emerge largely from the answers to these sorts of questions.

The teacher tells the six students that they will be listening to a tape in the target
language. They are to listen for the main idea and dates the speaker may say. All the
students have papers. The teacher prepared a cloze task as a handout. The teacher starts
the tape recorder but she realizes that the tape is not cued up at the right spot. She stops
and rewinds the tape. Meanwhile, the students wait silently. The teacher starts the tape
again, but it is still not cued up at the right place. The teacher fast forwards the tape and
starts to play it again. Once more it is not in the right place. She tries again twice more.
The teacher then tells the students to work in pairs and do the exercise in the book.
(OC: As the observer, I wonder if she is confused. She seems a bit flustered.) Some
students talk quietly to others. ♀2 looks in her book bag. ♂1 asks "Why do we have to
work in pairs?" The teacher says, "Oh," and then pauses. "Oh, OK. Uhm, . . . well, we
can, hm, let's see. If you don't want to be in pairs, you can work alone." The teacher
tries the tape again. The volume is too soft and she accidentally turns it up too loud.
Three students look up quickly as the voice on the tape loudly intrudes. (OC: Are they
annoyed? Perhaps they are just startled.) Two students pair up, while the four others
work silently alone.

Figure 5.2   Elaborated field notes based on rough field notes in Figure 5.1

Selective verbatim recording

In a technique called *selective verbatim recording*, the supervisor writes
down exactly what the lesson participants say (Acheson and Gall,
1997:73), rather than paraphrasing or summarizing, so no information
is lost. For example, the paraphrase "T. told S. to sit down" could represent statements from "Can you please sit down now so we can get
started?" to "You *sit down* now! Don't get up from your desk again!"
The two statements mean the same (the teacher wants the student to sit
down), but the affective message differs.

This technique is selective in two ways. First, it is almost impossible to
record manually all that everyone says in a classroom, perhaps especially
in interactive, student-centered classrooms. Second, the teacher and the
supervisor choose before the lesson what types of verbal events will be
captured while the lesson is in progress.

The selective verbatim technique is based on the assumption that the
"learning process is heavily influenced by how students and teachers talk
to each other. Therefore, teachers can learn how to improve their instruction by careful analysis of their communication patterns" (ibid.:73).
In our profession, the supervisor who wishes to use the selective
verbatim technique in observing a language lesson will also need to be
proficient in the target language.

There are four advantages of the selective verbatim technique, according to Acheson and Gall. First, it focuses teachers' attention on what
they say to their students (and what those students say to them). Second,
because the data are selective, teachers can focus on specific verbal behaviors without feeling overwhelmed. Third, the protocol produced in a

selective verbatim recording consists of direct quotes, so the data are objective and nonjudgmental. Fourth, this simple, "low-tech" data collection procedure requires only a pen and paper.

This procedure is intentionally selective, so whatever is *not* being focused on can get lost. The data must be interpreted relative to the global context of the lesson (ibid.). And, knowing in advance what will be recorded may cause the teacher to use (or avoid using) certain behaviors. Thus, the data collection procedure can become an instructional intervention (which is not necessarily bad in developmental observations). Another concern is that the focus chosen for selective verbatim data collection could be something trivial, which is easy to record but will not influence learning. Therefore teachers and supervisors using the selective verbatim technique should choose the observational focus carefully.

Data collection using pictorials and sketches

Many times teachers' and learners' nonverbal behavior is important in a learning event. But recording nonverbal behavior without a video camera is especially challenging.

We do have convenient labels for some facial expressions (e.g., *scowl, frown, grimace, grin, squint, smirk*, and *smile*) and some other nonverbal behaviors. For instance, think about the following behaviors: "The teacher stood facing the class with his arms at his sides, bent at the elbow, palms up. He arched his eyebrows while his lower lip protruded slightly, as he briefly raised and lowered his shoulders." This entire description can be summed up in one word: *shrug*.

However, there are many nonverbal behaviors that are not so easily labeled. For example, I once observed a lesson in which the teacher was trying to get a student to produce the phonemic distinction between the soft *L* and the hard *L* in Russian. She listened to the student's pronunciation and shook her head. She repeated the model, but again he produced the form incorrectly. Eventually she placed her left hand above her right, palms turned downward, with her hands touching at the wrists. Holding her left hand slightly cupped but still, she raised and lowered her right hand, while she pronounced the two phonemes in alternation. Meanwhile, I was trying to record this fascinating gestural teaching device, having decided that the teacher's left hand represented the roof of the mouth and the right hand the relative tongue positions used in producing these two sounds. I drew a quick sketch of the teacher's hands, because drawing was a faster and clearer way to collect data than note taking would have been.

I use this anecdote to show that sometimes drawing a picture is quicker and more descriptive than hurried writing might be. For example, the simple image below describes a teacher's orientation toward the chalkboard

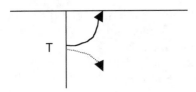

Figure 5.3   Sketch of a teacher's body position and eye contact

and the students. This quick sketch says, "The teacher stood perpendicular to the chalkboard, left shoulder to the board, writing on it and looking at it, but occasionally looking back at the students." The horizontal line represents the board, and the vertical line the teacher's body. The solid arrow indicates where the teacher's gaze was primarily directed, and the dotted arrow where it was occasionally directed. In my notes I make these simple drawings, along with a time notation, to indicate how often teachers change their stance and establish or break eye contact with the class.

Why would it matter how a teacher stands relative to the chalkboard or other communal writing surface? Sometimes students become inattentive when the teacher breaks eye contact with the group. Of course, eye contact differs from one culture to another, and some students remain attentive when the teacher turns away. Yet in my experience, data-based feedback of this sort has often been helpful to teachers concerned about their classroom management.

Data collection using seating charts

There is a tradition in general education research of using classroom seating charts as data collection mechanisms. Acheson and Gall (1997) illustrate several uses of what they call Seating Chart Observation Records, or SCORE techniques.

The advantages of SCORE data are that teachers are very familiar with seating charts and can quickly interpret the records. SCORE data also provide information about individual students, small groups, or the entire class. Acheson and Gall discuss using SCORE procedures for studying students' time on task, verbal flow, and movement patterns within the classroom. Figure 5.4 shows a simplified example based on the data for the teacher and the six students in the case at the beginning of the chapter.

The data in Figure 5.4 say that the teacher asked 30 questions, three of which were directed to individual students (I). The remaining 27 questions were *general solicits* – questions or tasks posed to the group, rather than to individuals. The student data reveal that female student

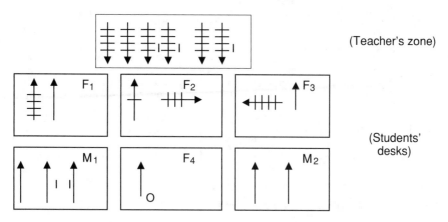

(Teacher's zone)

(Students' desks)

Figure 5.4 Sample SCORE data for a 20-minute grammar review lesson

1 (F1) responded to six of the general solicits, and male student 2 (M2) responded to two general solicits. M1 responded to one general solicit and two individual solicits (also called *personal solicits* or *direct nominations*) that were directed to him. F4, on the other hand, did not respond to any of the general solicits, and she also did not respond to a personal solicit directed to her. The two remaining female students in the front row spoke more to one another than to anyone else. F2 answered two general solicits but also spoke to F3 four times. F3 spoke to F2 five times and responded to one general solicit. The key to interpreting these data is shown in Figure 5.5.

The SCORE data depicted in Figure 5.4 give information about who initiates verbal turns and who responds to them. This simple system provides fast records of who speaks to whom and how often. Of course, these data tell us nothing about the length or content of the turns. Nor do these data convey any information about the participants' target language use, their accuracy, or their fluency. A SCORE chart simply provides a frequency count of turns taken. Nevertheless, for some purposes and contexts, SCORE data are quite helpful and informative.

Once an observer is familiar with the SCORE technique, seating charts can be used to record simple symbols depicting the interaction of larger groups as well. In addition, SCORE data can be collected on just one or two individual students. The narrow focus can yield very helpful information if a teacher is concerned about particular students.

Data collection using classroom maps

Simple maps can also be used to collect classroom data. Maps can help you identify each student, detect interaction patterns, define territories

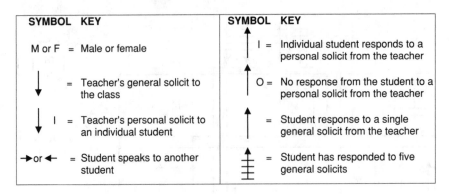

Figure 5.5 Key to SCORE data symbols

within the room, and locate possible distractions (e.g., traffic noise out-side a window). I sketch a map using the following techniques whenever I observe a language lesson, adding the names of the students if they introduce themselves or when I overhear someone call them by name. This strategy allows me to talk more specifically with the teacher after the lesson and ask questions about individual students.

Figure 5.6 presents an actual map from an observation of a math teaching assistant in a university setting. I use these data here, even though the teacher's subject matter is math rather than language, because the particular map reveals a great deal about the environment of the room, and it suggests some simple ways in which the teaching could be improved.

In this map, TR stands for tape recorder; Obs, observer; OHP, over-head projector; □, empty desk; ♂, male student; and ♀, female student. The map is part of a large data set in which I observed 24 teachers work-ing with more than 400 students, so I wasn't able to learn all the students' names. Still, I needed some way to identify each student within each les-son I observed. The strategy I adopted was to identify the student nearest the door at the front of the room as the first person in row one (e.g., ♀ 1,1). The student next to her in the same row was the second person in row one, and so on.

Before you read further, please answer the following questions: What do you know about this lesson, based on the data in the map alone? What questions does the map raise in your mind?

The teaching assistant (TA) for this class was a native speaker of Chi-nese, whom I will call Kwan (a pseudonym). The class was a "discussion section" – a regularly scheduled meeting following a professor's lecture, during which students can ask questions and discuss the material with

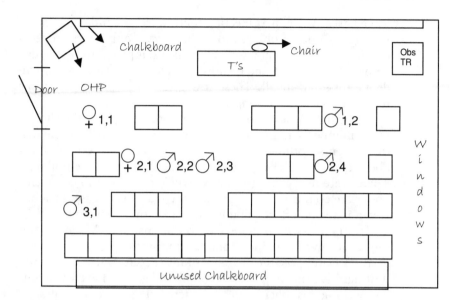

Figure 5.6 Map of a math class taught by a teaching assistant

the TA. There were seven students present, and 35 empty desks. The legs of the desks were clamped together, so that where two or more desks are pictured as adjacent, they are actually aligned in cramped, fixed rows. I was observing the TA for research purposes, rather than as his supervisor, so I am reprinting these data here only to illustrate the use of maps and field notes. We will return to the information contained in this map after learning more about Kwan.

Creating profiles of teachers or learners

One helpful use of field notes is to create a profile of a teacher. To generate a profile or "typical lesson" report, the full-length field notes can be summarized. Three or more sets of summarized notes on one teacher can be combined to generate a profile of the teacher, by looking for the notable similarities across the various summaries.

This profile of Kwan (Bailey, 1984:114–115) is based on three hours of observation over a 10-week term. (This class met for a total of 20 hours that term, so three hours represents 15 percent of the in-class time.) Each set of field notes was condensed into a two-page synopsis. The three summaries were then coalesced to create the following profile:

> Kwan was a native speaker of Chinese who was the TA for a math discussion section. There were seldom many students in his section, and those who did come tended to trickle in late and

109

leave early. At the first meeting there were 18 students present. During two other observations there were only three students one day and seven on another – which happened to be the day before an exam. At one of my scheduled observations, no students appeared at all. These low attendance patterns may be related to Kwan's teaching style.

At the first class meeting, Kwan wrote his name, office hours, office number, and the course number on the board, but he told the students nothing about his background and asked nothing about them (e.g., he apparently did not try to learn their names). There were no "getting-to-know-you" remarks – no comments about the course or himself to put the students at ease. In short, Kwan made no effort to build rapport with the students.

Kwan's classroom style was rather passive. Much of this impression was based on nonlinguistic signals. He seldom used gestures to support the meaning of his speech. When he was not writing, his arms hung limply by his sides – and even when he was writing, his other hand was inactive. His voice was soft, and he sometimes mumbled or talked toward the blackboard. There was little or no difference between the volume or pitch that he used as he spoke to the students and that he used as he did calculations on the blackboard. He did not project his voice when addressing the class; it was as if he were talking to himself. There were also periods of silence as the TA wrote on the board, read his math book, or awaited students' questions.

Kwan didn't call on students during any of the classroom observations. Instead, he would stand silently, waiting for them to ask questions. Then he would usually work problems (rather than explaining them) in response to their requests. Writing seemed to be his main channel for communicating with the students. Indeed, he had what could be called "good blackboard technique" (i.e., clear handwriting, organized layout of solutions on the board, boxes drawn around the answers, vertical lines drawn to separate completed portions of problems from new work, etc.). But as a result of Kwan's involvement with the blackboard, there was relatively little eye contact between him and the students. Instead he would look at the problem and occasionally glance back at the students, with the blackboard holding his attention.

Now that you've read Kwan's profile, please glance back at the map of his classroom in Figure 5.6. Each time I observed Kwan, I drew a map of the room. The three different maps revealed two important bits of information. The first had to do with the number of students present, relative to the number of chairs available. There were eighteen, three, and seven students present in Kwan's class on the three days I observed, so I wondered why his section had been scheduled in such a large room. This issue might not have jumped out at me if I had simply recorded the number of students present at each lesson without drawing a map. However, the number of empty seats was a visual fact that could not be ignored. I became curious about how many students were supposed to be attending Kwan's discussion section. The Math Department secretary told me that there were 35 students enrolled.

Another interesting datum was the overhead projector in the corner. The maps show that it had indeed been present at all three observations, but Kwan never used it when I observed his class. If I had been Kwan's supervisor, we could have discussed the option of using the overhead projector. If the math problems had been written on transparencies before the class, he might have been able to talk through the steps of the solutions, thereby avoiding the long periods of silence in his "discussion" section.

Using field notes, a profile can reveal stable behaviors over time or to generate a typology of teachers or learners. This process is depicted in Figure 5.7. I used this process in the research on the communication

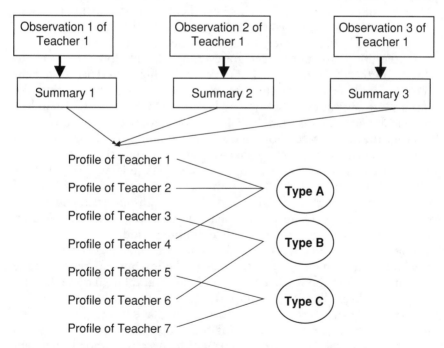

Figure 5.7 Summaries, profiles, and teacher types

problems of non-native-speaking TAs in U.S. universities (Bailey, 1984). Five clear types emerged from the data: (1) the inspiring cheerleaders; (2) the entertaining allies; (3) the knowledgeable helpers and casual friends; (4) the mechanical problem solvers; and (5) the active unintelligible TAs. (Kwan's profile illustrates type 4, the mechanical problem solvers.) These five labels were not predetermined categories taken into the observations. Instead, they emerged as the TAs' profiles were compared.

Using observation instruments

One means of gathering data in classrooms is to use a paper-and-pencil observation instrument (sometimes called an "observation schedule"). Gebhard notes that the use of such observation systems "allows supervisors to describe rather than prescribe teaching" (1984:509).

An observation instrument is essentially a paper form containing predetermined categories that guide the observer's collection of information or the judging process. The categories can be presented as questions to answer or topics to address in writing. Another common format consists of statements with which the observer rates performance (e.g., on a scale of 1 equals "poor," 5 equals "excellent"), or statements followed by evaluative categories (such as "superior," "satisfactory," or "needs improvement") for observers to circle or check.

Observation instrument categories range from "low-inference" to "high-inference" statements (Long, 1980). A high-inference statement requires judgment while the observer is recording (e.g., rating the teacher's organizational skills). Any high-inference category system like this yields data, but note that the data are *not* a record of the lesson events. Instead, they are a record of the observer's opinions of those events. In contrast, low-inference statements are verifiable (i.e., they are observations rather than inferences or opinions), so less judgment is called for on the part of an observer. For example, the statement "positive social climate throughout lesson" is closer to the high-inference end of the continuum than is a category that has the observer tally every time an individual student smiles during a five-minute period.

Observation instruments embody theories of language learning and teaching. The statements or categories in the instruments represent the designers' beliefs about what factors are important. Often these theories are not made explicit. So one important question to ask in selecting an observation instrument is what theory of language learning or teaching the instrument is based on. Knowing that, supervisors and teachers can decide whether the instrument is appropriate. An observation instrument based on the behaviorist principles of the audiolingual method would entail coding or rating behaviors (immediate public treatment of oral errors, for instance), which would not be appropriate in an observation instrument predicated on communicative language teaching and interactionist theories of language learning.

Adapting or designing observation instruments

If an observation system is to be used, one can be chosen from among the available formats, or the supervisor and the teachers could borrow elements of existing systems and adapt them to fit local needs. Such adaptations could include adding or deleting categories, or revising descriptors to make them more appropriate to the context. The team could also add a numerical rating system or spaces for open-ended comments if the existing system lacks these options.

Teachers can also devise their own observation system. This option is very time-consuming, but the process generates important discussions about teaching values. Creating an observation system may also promote "buy in" among the teachers. Murdoch (2000) notes that to empower and motivate teachers, supervisors should involve them in developing evaluative data collection processes. Designing an observation instrument is one way to do so.

If the members of a teaching staff design an observation instrument, it can be based on the goals, philosophy, and content of the specific language program. If, for example, a goal of a particular course is to develop students' fluency and confidence in speaking the target language, it would probably be inappropriate to use categories that rate teachers on their immediate treatment of oral errors. Obviously, designing such an instrument is more straightforward if the program goals are already stated. If they are not, then before teachers can be evaluated on how well they are implementing the program goals, those goals must be articulated and agreed on. In addition, it is important to pilot the instrument in nonbinding practice observations before collecting data that will be used in any official teacher evaluations.

Using existing observation instruments

There is a long tradition of using observation systems to record information about teaching and learning, and many systems are available. In fact, more than two decades ago, Long (1980) contrasted 22 such systems on nine dimensions: type of recording procedure; high, low, or mixed inferences; number of categories used; whether multiple coding is permitted; whether real-time coding is involved; source of the variables; intended purpose (research and / or teacher training); whether the unit of analysis is time or an analytic unit of some kind; and the focus – the "range of behaviors and events sampled" (p. 4). Other systems have been developed since Long published his analysis, but his categories for comparison are still useful. Several observation systems are reprinted in Allwright and Bailey (1991), as well as in Day (1990), so individual formats will not be discussed in detail here.

Many observation instruments were originally designed in the 1960s and 1970s for research purposes, rather than for language teacher supervision. Some, like the Embryonic Category system (Long, Adams, McLean, and Castaños, 1976), were intended for coding data transcribed from audio- or videotapes, rather than for "real-time" coding (live coding during a lesson). Some instruments for observing language lessons are retoolings of systems originally designed for general education classrooms. For example, the well-known Interaction Analysis system (Flanders, 1970, 1976) from general education led to the Foreign Language Interaction system or "FLInt" (Moskowitz, 1966, 1968, 1971).

In a study with student teachers utilizing FLInt, Moskowitz stated that the "main goal in training the teachers in observational systems was to increase their sensitivity to their own classroom behavior and its effects and influence on students" (1968:231). In other words, awareness-raising was a key goal. In reviewing 18 projects in which Interaction Analysis was used to help modify teaching behavior, Flanders wrote, "If there is any common bond which cuts across all of the projects... it is that they all provide some support for the following proposition. *Attention to teaching behavior, practice in analyzing it, and performing it with feedback tends to incorporate such behavior in the teacher's repertoire*" (1970:352; italics in the original). The assumption underlying the use of such observation systems is that feedback is important in changing teaching behavior. Jarvis concluded that "the very use of such instruments may, in fact, be a causal factor in behavior change" (1968:341).

Some instruments have a specific theoretical orientation. One example in our field is COLT: the Communicative Orientation of Language Teaching (Allen, Fröhlich, and Spada, 1984; Frölich, Spada, and Allen, 1985). COLT was designed "to capture differences in the communicative orientation of L2 classroom interaction" (Frölich et al., 1985:27). The two parts of the instrument reflect this orientation. Part A "contains categories derived primarily from pedagogical issues in the communicative language teaching literature" (ibid.:29), including activity, group work, content, topic control, student modality, materials, and the like. Part B of the instrument documents the verbal interactions that occur during class activities. The categories in Part B are derived from first and second language acquisition research findings.

In short, there are many observation instruments available for research or teacher training purposes, though several are quite old and may not

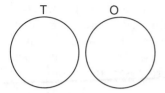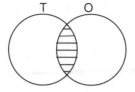

Figure 5.8   Levels of congruity in the teacher's and the observer's focus in an observation

reflect current pedagogy. Language teacher supervisors may use or adapt these instruments to guide their data collection. However, many questions arise in selecting such instruments: Is the focus consistent with the individual teacher's goals for improvement and the supervisor's reasons for observing the class? Are the assumptions underlying the instrument clear to the teachers and supervisors? Are the instrument's theoretical underpinnings appropriate as evaluative guidelines for this program's curriculum and teaching policies? Does the observation instrument provide a mechanism for collecting appropriate data in this particular program? Will the instrument yield useful data for answering questions about language teaching and learning? A supervisor should consider all these questions in selecting or adapting an existing observation system.

Using observation instruments to specify the observational focus

Using an agreed-on observation instrument can serve an important purpose in pre- and post-observation conferences. Observers bring conceptual "lenses" into the classroom, regardless of whether they use observation systems. An observer generating field notes, for example, may focus on issues of interest to him or her, based on his or her beliefs and background knowledge. Using an observation instrument may help externalize and systemize that knowledge and those beliefs. Communication between the teacher and supervisor can be enhanced if the teacher is familiar with the observation instrument used and agrees that it is appropriate. It is even better if the teacher is skilled in its use and thus understands what the supervisor is doing during an observation.

Making both participants' perspectives explicit before the observation can help to focus the feedback on topics of interest to both the teacher (T) and the observer (O). Three possible levels of congruity are depicted in Figure 5.8.

The first pair of circles is reminiscent of both Gebhard's (1984) and Nunan's (in Bailey et al., 2001) personal accounts of supervisors focusing

115

on something quite different from the focus each of these teachers had chosen. In the second pair of circles, the shaded area indicates partial congruity between the teacher's interest and the observer's, while the third diagram indicates a high degree of overlap. The use of an agreed-on observation system, or clear focus setting, in the pre-observation conference can promote such congruity.

In my opinion, teachers should have a major role in devising or choosing any instrument to be used and in directing the supervisor's focus during observations. Consensus about the instrument and familiarity with its categories can help teachers incorporate teaching elements studied in teacher preparation courses or in-service training. Using an accepted observation system seems to lower anxiety (because there are fewer surprises), which in turn allows the teacher to consider the observer's ideas.

Advantages and disadvantages of using observation instruments

Williams explains why many people dislike the use of observational categories. First, for the teachers in Williams's context, observation with a checklist "was threatening, frightening, and regarded as an ordeal" (1989:86). Second, the teacher had no responsibility for the evaluation process. It was trainer-centered, even though the program emphasized child-centered teaching (ibid.). The checklist was prescriptive, and teachers felt it focused on too many things at once (ibid.). There also seemed to be no continuity across three classroom visits. Finally, the established categories didn't accommodate the individual teacher's pace or wishes (ibid.).

The problematic use of decontextualized checklists was summarized by Chamberlin, who wrote that a supervisor typically "observes the teacher's behavior and rates behaviors on a standard scale of measure, which is then placed into the teacher's file. This approach mirrors an attempt to reduce teaching to a technical act that can be measured by a set of prescribed criteria" (2000:654). Chamberlin's concern about a "set of prescribed criteria" can be partially overcome if the teachers themselves either revise or create the categories, but the point that observational categories are often used out of context and can reduce teaching to a "technical act" is still a matter of concern. Furthermore, "almost without exception, such technicist approaches to teacher evaluation fail... because teachers and students do not live their lives in the fragmented and dislocated ways suggested in the observation schedules" (Gitlin and Smyth, 1990:85).

There are both advantages and disadvantages to using observation instruments in language teacher supervision. The advantages are all based on the fact that the predetermined categories don't change from one observation to another. Teachers and supervisors know from the outset on which issues to focus because those features are codified in the particular instrument's categories. Second, ratings on nominal categories or numerical scales can be compared over time, with improvement plotted in subsequent observations. Third, teachers and supervisors can focus on various categories in any given lesson and disregard or downplay the others. For instance, if an instrument highlights promoting student-student interaction, the teacher can plan opportunities for such interaction and attend to this feature during the observed lesson. Finally, observation instruments embody an established, finite number of variables, so teachers may feel they are not facing an unending task or aiming at a moving target.

Ironically, the disadvantages of using observation instruments in language teacher supervision are based on the same facts: The categories on the instruments are predetermined and unchanging. Of course, some of the observation systems (e.g., COLT) include a space for recording open-ended comments, which introduces some flexibility in the data collection process. Nevertheless, supervisors should be aware of the following potentially problematic issues. First, the theoretical position(s) embodied in the instrument may not match the position(s) held by the teachers or espoused by the program. Second, the topics covered in the instrument's categories may not match the issues that arise during a particular lesson. And third, the categories may not match the teacher's professional development issues at the time. In addition, some people argue that if teachers know what criteria (in the form of an observation instrument) will be used, they may teach to the category system instead of teaching as they usually do. This could be either an advantage or a disadvantage, depending on the purpose of the observation.

We saw in Chapter 2 that the teacher's focus and the supervisor's focus in an observation can differ widely. This problem can be exacerbated if the teacher is unfamiliar with or doesn't value the observation instrument used by the supervisor. If the instrument makes the supervisor focus on the teacher's grammar presentation, but the teacher is concentrating on managing group work, then the feedback from the supervisor may fail on two counts. First, it doesn't address the area in which the teacher wanted input (i.e., the desired input is not received). Second, the feedback that is provided may be discounted as irrelevant or unhelpful if it addresses a topic the teacher feels is unimportant at the time (i.e., the input that is received is not desired).

Given these shortcomings, it is important that a supervisor or teaching team carefully analyze any existing instrument to determine whether its underlying philosophy is consistent and appropriate in the program context. Using an observational system that is not appropriate can create serious problems in teacher evaluation and staff morale.

Concluding comments

This chapter examined two manual data collection approaches. The first is the more open-ended, unstructured but systematic use of field notes, maps, sketches, and seating charts. The second involves structured observation instruments, whose categories range from objective to highly inferential.

The following Case Discussion is based on the case that began the chapter. The excerpt from the field notes (Figure 5.2) describes a segment of the lesson that you will discuss with the teacher. The SCORE data in Figure 5.4 are from the grammar review. You have given the teacher your elaborated field notes and the SCORE data prior to the conference.

Case discussion

1. Please reread the field notes in Figure 5.2 and the SCORE data in Figure 5.4. Then decide what areas you can discuss with this teacher as strengths. What issues will you discuss as areas for improvement? Are you dealing with issues of awareness, attitude, skills, and/or knowledge (Freeman, 1989a)?
2. How would you describe this teacher's zone of proximal development? What are your short-term goals for working with this teacher? What are your long-term goals for this teacher in this program?
3. Think about the Johari Window (Luft and Ingram, 1969), reprinted as Figures 2.3 and 2.4 in Chapter 2. What kind of development do you hope this teacher will experience as a result of your feedback? Give some specific examples from the case, using the Johari Window.
4. How would your conference with the teacher be different with and without the field notes?
5. Do the SCORE data (Figure 5.4) support your impression that the grammar review was teacher-centered? What patterns do the data reveal that you could discuss with the teacher?
6. Role-play the conference with this teacher. What are the discourse differences if you use (A) the supervisory or traditional directive option, (B) the alternative option, and (C) the nondirective option (Freeman, 1982; Gebhard, 1984) carefully and consistently in role-playing three post-observation conferences? Are there some issues that could be discussed better using one of these three options?
7. On what areas would you want to focus in a future observation of this teacher? Why?

Tasks and discussion

1. Suppose you are a language teacher whose supervisor observes your class. Afterwards, the supervisor gives you this grid to review before the post-observation conference:

Sample rating grid 1

Categories	Poor	Fair	Average	Good	Excellent	N. A.
Category T			X			
Category U			X			
Category V				X		
Category W						X
Category X		X				
Category Y					X	
Category Z			X			

What questions would you have? What would you want to tell the supervisor?

2. Do your answers depend on the categories? For example, if you were the teacher, would your reactions change if this rating grid included the following categories?

Sample rating grid 2

Categories	Poor	Fair	Average	Good	Excellent	N. A.
Use of authentic language samples			X			
Variety in learning activities			X			
Group work, pair work, and student interaction				X		
Development of the physical environment						X
Appropriate feedback to 2LLs		X				
Positive affect in lesson					X	
Clarity of instructions and explanations			X			

3. You are the supervisor preparing for the post-observation conference with the teacher whose lesson you rated in Sample Grid 2. What would you want to ask this teacher? What would you want to say to him or her? What evidence would you use to explain the ratings of fair, average, good, and excellent?

4. Now consider Sample Grid 3, the ratings made after three visits to one teacher's class. The numbers 1, 2, and 3 represent the supervisor's opinion at the first, second, or third observation. What patterns emerge in these data?

Sample rating grid 3

Categories	Poor	Fair	Average	Good	Excellent	N. A.
Use of authentic language samples			1	2, 3		
Variety in learning activities			1, 2	3		
Group work, pair work, and student interaction				1, 2	3	
Development of the physical environment						1, 2, 3
Appropriate feedback to 2LLs		1, 2			3	
Positive affect in lesson					1, 2, 3	
Clarity of instructions and explanations			1	2	3	

5. If you were the teacher who had taught these lessons, what patterns would you find most interesting? Most troubling? What comments or questions would you have?

6. If you had compiled this grid, what patterns would you find most interesting? What particular information in the grid would you want to discuss with the teacher? With a colleague, role-play the third post-observation conference and discuss these data.

7. In the profile of Kwan, identify all instances of observations, inferences, and opinions.

8. What does each of the following images convey to you? The horizontal line represents the chalkboard, while the shorter horizontal line represents the teacher's orientation. The arrows show the direction

of the teacher's gaze. A dotted arrow represents an occasional glance and a solid arrow shows sustained eye contact.

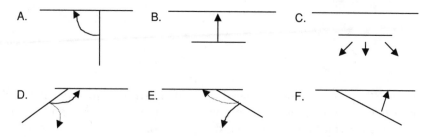

Suggestions for further reading

Allwright (1988) published a history of several observation instruments. The book includes the original authors' ideas as well as Allwright's commentary.

Acheson and Gall (1997) devote four chapters to data collection procedures, each of which is illustrated with clear examples.

Bailey et al. (2001) provide examples of observational field notes and two colleagues' discussion about the information one gathered while watching the other teach.

Abbott and Carter (1985) include a sample checklist for observing trainees' practice teaching lessons. Omaggio (1982) provides an observation instrument and sample data. Rhodes and Heining-Boynton (1993) give an observation form for language lessons in primary schools.

For discussions about the instrument called FOCUS, see Gebhard (1999), Gebhard and Oprandy (1999), and Oprandy (1999). FOCUS stands for "Foci for Observing Communications Under Settings," an influential system designed by Fanselow (1977, 1987, 1988).

Day (1990) discusses ethnography, audio and video recording, seating charts, and other coding techniques. The use of seating charts for data collection in language classes is illustrated in Gebhard, Hashimoto, Joe, and Lee (1999). See also Swan (1993).

6 Electronic data collection procedures

In this chapter we will consider the use of electronic data recording, primarily by audiotaping or videotaping lessons. Videotaping can be intrusive but provides more information than audiotaping does for teachers and supervisors alike. Audiotaping is less invasive and more convenient, but its data yield less information than do video recordings. Both videotapes and audiotapes can be transcribed to create written data for analysis. In addition, electronic recordings can be used along with or instead of in-person visits by the supervisor.

We will consider audiotaping and videotaping and the advantages and disadvantages of each before we review the use of transcripts and some technological developments in supervision. We will also discuss the benefits of using manual and electronic data collection procedures simultaneously.

Let us begin with a case to situate these possibilities. This is a situation where the supervisor could use SCORE data, but due to the specific verbal nature of the teacher's concerns, an audio recording will be useful. The recording will provide detailed data that will enable you and the teacher to examine linguistic and social issues in some depth.

Case for analysis: Working with a transcript

You observe a lower-intermediate ESL adult class that meets Monday through Thursday, from 6:30 to 9:00 P.M. The participants are often tired, since they work during the day. There is a wide range of speaking proficiency, and the class consists of students from many cultures. As a result, some students participate actively, and some seem more reticent or even passive. The teacher, who has had substantial EFL experience, says it is often tricky to get the quieter students to participate, and a few students occasionally dominate the turn-taking.

During the observation, there are several instances that illustrate the teacher's concern. One student in particular gets more than his fair share of the turns and even seems to derail the lesson at times. It seems that Igor (a pseudonym) dominates the turn-taking.

You suggest that the teacher tape-record a lesson and transcribe a brief bit of interaction where she feels she is having trouble managing the turn-taking. She agrees to transcribe a portion of the lesson and bring the transcript to your next meeting.

Using audiotapes to collect observational data

Audiotapes can be very useful in supervision, whether the focus is teacher development or evaluation. Issues of teacher talk, question types, feedback to learners, and giving instructions can all be profitably studied with audio recordings. Student interaction in pair work and small group work can also be recorded, provided the tape recorder is next to the students. Using cassette recorders is not without its problems, however. The following event occurred when Nunan audio-recorded some group work in his Hong Kong university EFL class:

> The lesson, which had begun well enough, ended in confusion, if not chaos. And it was to have been significant, for it was the first day of collecting data for my new research project.... I put the students into small groups, and then placed a portable cassette recorder in the center of each group. However, I had underestimated the time it would take to set up the recorders and make sure they were working correctly. During the lesson, I constantly had to go around the class, checking that the recorders were still working, so I didn't pay sufficient attention to classroom management. My instructions were unclear and some students became confused. Finally, they rebelled. I noticed in several groups that the students were switching off their recorders. Later ... one of them admitted to me that, despite my disclaimer to the contrary, they thought I would be using the data on the tape to evaluate them. (Nunan in Bailey et al., 2001:143)

This problem can often be overcome by familiarizing the students with the recorders and by the teacher's consistent use of recording over time for the purpose of studying the lessons (rather than testing students).

Allwright (1980) used audio recordings in studying turns, topics, and tasks in lower-intermediate ESL classes. He was recording for classroom research purposes rather than teacher supervision, but his data collection strategy may prove useful to you. Allwright suspended two stereo microphones above the students, who were seated in two rows toward the front. Having the microphones suspended eliminates a great deal of noise as people set down books, move chairs, or bump the desks. It also protects the equipment from being knocked to the floor. Using a stereo

123

recording system enabled Allwright to minimize some noise during play-back, which made it easier to transcribe the tapes and identify individual students' voices.

Using Allwright's (1980) data, Allwright and Bailey (1991) discuss an incident when a teacher learned something by listening to the tape of her adult ESL class, in which there was a learner called Chuck (a pseudonym). In the transcripts, "it appeared that Chuck...got a much greater proportion of the speaking turns than did his classmates" (p. 127), but the teacher told us that Chuck seldom spoke. When we showed her the transcript, she thought we had incorrectly identified the student's voice, but when she heard the tape, she was surprised at how much Chuck spoke. What was the source of this surprise? The map of the classroom drawn by an observer revealed that Chuck had been seated directly under one of the stereo microphones:

> The microphone had accurately recorded Chuck's speech, but he had not taken any turns that were loud enough to be notice-able by the teacher. Instead, he took very quiet private turns that went unnoticed except by the microphone. His way of practicing the target language in class was through 'egocentric speech' – talk directed at himself and not shared with anyone else. The teacher was very surprised, since she had viewed Chuck as some-what indifferent and uninterested in participating in the language lessons. In fact, he was working very hard – but not doing so in an easily observable way. (ibid.)

This anecdote shows one benefit of reviewing audiotapes with language teachers. Supervisors may be able to raise teachers' awareness simply by asking questions that encourage teachers to listen to recordings with "fresh ears." In this case, the teacher saw that an apparently unmotivated student was in fact involved and was participating actively, albeit very quietly.

Using videotapes to collect observational data

The added benefit of videotaping is the visual component, which lets language teachers and supervisors analyze students' nonverbal bids for turns and affective responses to activities. It also enables teachers to see themselves teaching. Videotapes have been used in teacher education for many years, and the technology still provides useful data for teachers and supervisors.

Video provides an "objective record of what actually took place," according to Wallace (1981:8), and "individualized training *par excellence*" (ibid.:11). Eighty-seven percent of the in-service and preservice

EFL teachers in his research said that "seeing themselves on videotape had made them aware of habits and mannerisms which they were now trying to change" (Wallace, 1979:13). As an awareness-raising procedure, video provides "a means of objectifying the teaching process and converting what is subjective and ephemeral into something that is experienced in common and capable of analysis" (ibid.:17).

Next, we will review two studies in which video was investigated as a means of language teacher development. The teachers involved were university professors and teaching assistants.

Key components of using videotape with university language teachers

Three University of Minnesota researchers, Stenson, Smith, and Perry, wrote about using video in language teacher development. They noted that "acquiring effective teaching skills is a developmental process" (1979:2), and identified five key components of this process, all of which can be aided though the use of video recordings.

1. *Obtaining Feedback*. In order to determine how effective their teaching is, teachers first need to have information about their performance.... Obtaining feedback is thus the first component of the developmental process.... [A] crucial aspect of feedback is the extent to which the teacher feels able to accept it and work with it....

2. *Becoming Introspective*. Given a source of feedback, the teacher needs to be able to analyze the information.... [T]he most important factor of this component is the ability to be introspective about one's own teaching. The teacher must ... develop the ability for self-evaluation rather than continue to rely on external judgment.

3. *Accepting Responsibility*. The ability to be introspective and to evaluate one's own teaching is a prerequisite to the third component, the teacher's acceptance of responsibility for his / her further growth.... Only from this point of view is it possible to recognize and accept both positive and negative aspects of one's own teaching as a preparation for bringing about appropriate change.

4. *Choosing What to Change*. The fourth developmental component involves the teacher's decision to devote the time and energy necessary to effect change. A major part of this decision will be the teacher's choice of which aspects of teaching s/he is ready to work on. It is ... only when teachers themselves decide when and what to change that any real change occurs.

> 5. *Effecting Change*. The final component...addresses the need
> of teachers who have chosen to change some aspect of their
> teaching and are looking for information on ways of bringing
> about the desired changes. (ibid.:2–5)

Stenson et al. say "introspection, acceptance of responsibility, and internal motivation for change are all aspects of teacher behavior that no trainer / supervisor can control" (ibid.:4), which relates to our discussion of autonomy in Chapter 3. However, judiciously using video recordings of their own lessons can help teachers with these five components.

Videotape and the supervision of teaching assistants

A great deal of language instruction at colleges and universities is done by graduate students working in the role of teaching assistants (TAs), a topic we will explore in more depth in Chapter 12. Videotape has been used productively in this context. For example, Franck and Samaniego (1981) supervised TAs in university language departments. Their method involved "videotaping a TA in his or her regular class and providing prompt replay with feedback" (p. 273). Feedback sessions were conducted by the TA supervisor from the language department and a video analyst from the university's Teaching Resource Center.

The team built in several safeguards. First, the TAs chose whether to be observed or to be videotaped. Second, those who were videotaped could view the recording themselves before it was seen by others. Third, if a TA felt that the lesson was not representative, the tape was erased, and another lesson was recorded. Franck and Samaniego reported that "in the first two years of this program only one out of twenty-one TAs requested a second taping" (ibid.).

Steps were also taken to keep the video recording from intruding on the language lesson: "Tapings are done by an experienced...technician using a small television camera requiring no special lighting. The camera is placed in an unobtrusive location from which both the TA and the students can be observed" (ibid.). The TAs and students reported that they were able to disregard the camera after about 10 minutes (ibid.).

In discussing the videotape, each TA could react first and "pick out aspects of the class hour that made it typical or atypical, successful or unsuccessful" (ibid.: 273). The Teacher Resource Center analyst commented on style and classroom presence, while the departmental TA supervisor focused on language teaching. This process saved time, since it "greatly reduced the need for traditional classroom visits" (ibid.).

The TAs said the process was helpful in making them aware of the amount of Spanish (the target language) they used in the classroom;

the extent to which they monopolized class time; the effectiveness of drilling techniques used; and the effectiveness of their grammar explanations (ibid.:274). They felt that both videotaping and supervisorial visits have advantages and disadvantages, but the videotape procedure promoted "greater learning through self-observation" (ibid.:275). However, the TAs thought the supervisor probably got a clearer impression of the class atmosphere by conducting a live observation (ibid.).

The three-person analysis of the videotapes had four benefits: "(1) it reduced by one-third to one-half the amount of time required for class visitation; (2) it increased substantially the precision and effectiveness of critical commentary; (3) it eliminated, to a large extent, the need to make some of the traditionally most difficult criticisms; and (4) it helped the TAs develop the ability to assess their own teaching and make necessary changes" (ibid.:275). One key advantage for the supervisor was that the videotape provided very credible data: "The problem of convincing [TAs] they said a particular thing or that the students were answering incorrectly ceases to exist" (ibid.:276). Defensiveness diminished, and the TAs became more self-evaluative. Another benefit was that when the TA supervisor and the video analyst differed in their reactions, they openly acknowledged those differences. As a result, the TAs were able to see that there is no single "teaching methodology that is ideal for everyone" (ibid.:277).

Advantages and disadvantages of electronic data collection

There are, of course, advantages and disadvantages to electronic data collection procedures (see Hunter, 1984:186), just as there are in the case of both field notes and observation schedules. Let us consider the disadvantages first.

One disadvantage is the cost of the recording equipment and the tapes. There is also the cost of compact discs if you wish to store the data on CDs, as well as the cost of the software and hardware for doing so. However, many schools and language programs will have purchased this hardware and software for nonsupervisorial purposes, so existing resources for creating electronic databases may be available for supervision.

Second, audiotaping and videotaping can influence participants' behavior in unpredictable ways. However, there is some evidence (see, e.g., Franck and Samaniego, 1981) that teachers and students get accustomed to recording equipment.

There are also limitations to the devices themselves. Audio recordings cannot capture nonverbal behavior in classrooms. Videotaping adds the nonverbal dimension, but the camera can only record what it is aimed at, and sometimes the video sound quality is poor.

One advantage of using videotape for professional development is that it "allows teachers to see themselves from the students' point of view and to obtain an accurate record of what happens in the classroom" (Stenson et al., 1979:6). Videotapes let teachers review the lessons as pure data, rather than through someone's analysis or interpretation. Another advantage is cited by Gebhard: "Teachers can listen (audiotapes) or view (videotapes) segments of a lesson many times, thus filling in more and more details" (1990b: 518).

Yet another advantage, as Wallace notes (1981:8), is that videos provide impartial records. Stenson et al. (1979:6) agree that the value of videotape is its objectivity:

> The tape can show specific aspects of a teacher's performance, such as rate and intensity of speech, nonverbal behavior, techniques of presentation and practice, sequencing of materials, and methods of providing feedback to students. It can show the verbal and nonverbal performance of students, their degree of participation in the class and level of attention, as well as individual student behavior.

Videotape also provides information about the lesson's organization and classroom activities. It can document the use of teaching aids and can be analyzed to compare teacher talk and student talk. Unlike most human observers, "videotape provides the facts without itself making any judgments" (ibid.). Supervision is often both inherently judgmental and assumed by teachers to be judgmental, but the use of videotapes (or audiotapes) as data to inform supervisory discussions can help overcome this problem.

In addition, teaching is very demanding work, so we cannot always observe ourselves during lessons. With videotapes, teachers "can relive the experience from a different point of view [and] become aware of aspects of their own performance, the lesson, or student behavior that they did not notice during the class session because they were too involved in the actual teaching process" (ibid.:6–7). Thus, the recording can help raise awareness. (See Chapter 2.) In terms of the Johari Window, what teachers see on video or hear on audiotapes can help them move from the blind self quadrant to the open self quadrant.

Electronic recordings also provide distance from the teaching event, enabling the teacher and observer to discuss the lesson somewhat dispassionately. Stenson et al. say that videotape gives teachers emotional distance by viewing lessons later: "A teacher may wish that a particular classroom incident had been handled differently. Upon viewing the tape of the class, the teacher can dissociate him / herself from the image on the screen, and with this new perspective, may be able to determine how to handle the situation the next time it arises" (1979:7). This distancing can help diminish teachers' defensiveness and resistance in conferences.

Videotapes can be used collaboratively when teachers watch tapes of their lessons with someone else. Stenson et al. say both experienced and inexperienced teachers benefit from discussing videotapes of their teaching: "The presence of a second person, a facilitator who can focus the attention of the teacher on particular issues, is crucial in motivating teachers to become introspective about their role in the classroom" (ibid.). This facilitator need not be a supervisor. Another advantage of electronic recordings is that they can be replayed at the convenience of the teacher and a facilitator, who may not have been present during the lesson. The collaborator or a facilitator should be open to different viewpoints and take the role of a "concerned colleague rather than expert or authority figure," because such a stance is much less threatening to the teacher engaged in self-evaluation (ibid.:10).

Using transcripts

One benefit of both audio and video recordings is that they can be transcribed to yield a verbatim record of interaction. Although transcription is labor intensive, it can be an excellent awareness-raising activity for both preservice and in-service teachers. Gebhard notes that "teachers quite often discover aspects of an instructional context through concentration on the transcription" (1990b:518). Teachers don't need to spend long periods of time transcribing video or audiotapes because "much can be learned from a few short segments" (ibid.).

The following transcript is based on a few minutes of interaction from a lower-intermediate adult ESL vocabulary lesson. The two vocabulary items that appear in this stretch of discourse are the verb *to claim* and the phrasal verb *to get [someone] to* from a passage about air pollution the students had read. In this transcript *T* stands for "teacher" and *S* for "student." *S2* represents a particular male student, who happened to be from Russia. He was given the pseudonym Igor in Allwright's (1980) research. The *Ss* represents other unidentified students, and *xx* indicates speech that could not be transcribed. There are also parenthetical statements from the teacher's aide, who took notes during the lesson, to provide information about nonverbal behaviors. Ellipses indicate that a speaker's voice trails off, as when Igor says, "He claims..." in line 7. Indented lines indicate that the speaker's turn overlapped another turn in progress. So, in line 11, Igor says "yeah" just as the teacher says "the pollution" (in line 10). Boldface print indicates strong emphasis on a word or syllable (as when Igor says "**Reproduce**" in line 23). These print conventions are meant to convey in writing some of the vocal features of

Transcript 6.1 *"Just a second, Igor" (from Allwright, 1980: 180–181; reprinted in Allwright and Bailey, 1991:125–126)*

1	T:	Yeah. Or to make an accusation. OK. You say he he did, he
2		killed that man, OK. You claim that, but you, if you can't
3		prove it, it's only a claim. Yeah?
4	S2:	It's to say something louder?
5	T:	No. That would be exclaim. To to make shout, say something
6		loud, it's exclaim.
7	S2:	He claims . . .
8	T:	Yeah.
9	S2:	I think they'd better produce electric machine for car to use.
10	T:	For for to to end the pollution problem?
11	S2:	Yeah.
12	S2:	Yeah.
13	T:	Yeah. OK. What does this mean? 'Get to'? Uh.
14	Ss:	xx
15	T:	OK. It says the group has been trying to get the government,
16		the city government, to help uhm draw special lanes, lanes like
17		this (draws on board) on the street. OK. These are for cars.
18		These are for bikes . . . (pointing to the board).
19	S2:	You know, in Moscow they reproduce all all cab.
20	T:	Uhm?
21	S2:	They reproduced all cabs xx
22	T:	They produce?
23	S2:	Reproduce
24	T:	D'you mean uh they they use old cabs, old taxis?
25	S2:	No, no, no, they reproduced all A-L-L cabs.
26	T:	All the cabs?
27	S2:	Yeah, all the cabs for electric electric, you know electric
28		(points)
29	T:	Cab. Oh, you mean they made the cabs in down in downtown
30		areas uh uh use electric uh motors?
31	S2:	Yeah, no downtown, all cabs in Moscow.
32	T:	Where?
33	S2:	In Moscow.
34	T:	Oh. And it's successful?
35	S2:	Yeah.
36	T:	OK. Uhm. Just a second, Igor. Let's what does this mean? If
37		you get someone to do something. Uhm.

the transcribed interaction. As you read this transcript, try to put your-self in the role of the teacher's supervisor. The transcript suggests several interesting discussion topics.

Imagine that this transcript was produced by the teacher in the case that began this chapter. It is reprinted here to illustrate the number and variety of discussable issues that can arise in just a short segment of transcribed interaction. Whether transcripts are used as the basis of a casual discussion or are subjected to coding with an observation schedule or are examined with a fine-grained discourse analysis depends on the teacher's and supervisor's purpose in generating the transcripts.

Transcription can be very time-consuming and tedious. Allwright and Bailey (1991:62) say it can take up to 20 hours to produce an accurate, complete transcript of a one-hour lesson involving full group interaction. For teacher supervision, however, extremely detailed transcripts are probably not needed for most investigations. In fact, teachers may benefit from quickly transcribing just a few minutes of interaction at a point they select in the lesson.

As an alternative, teachers can transcribe several very short segments, based on a particular focus, from different parts of a lesson or even from various lessons. For example, if a teacher wanted to work on giving clear instructions for group work, he or she could transcribe just those instruction instances.

Triangulation in data collection

The concept of triangulation is well known in qualitative research but perhaps not so familiar in language teacher supervision. Triangulation is a geometric concept borrowed from navigation, astronomy, and surveying. Hammersley and Atkinson state that if people wish to locate their position on a map, "a single landmark can only provide the information that they are situated somewhere along a line in a particular direction from that landmark. With two landmarks, however, their exact position can be pinpointed by taking bearings on both landmarks; they are at the point where the two lines cross" (1983:198). Triangulation can also be useful in supervision – especially in evaluation. (See Chapter 10.)

In anthropology, triangulation is used as a process of verification that gives researchers confidence in their observations. Denzin (1978) describes four types of triangulation:

> data triangulation, in which different sources of data (teachers, students, parents, etc.) contribute to an investigation; theory triangulation, when various theories are brought to bear in a study; researcher triangulation, in which more than one researcher contributes to the investigation; and methods triangulation, which entails the use of multiple methods (e.g., interviews, questionnaires, observation schedules, test scores, field notes, etc.) to collect data. (Denzin, 1978, as summarized by Bailey, 2001a:118)

131

There are, as we have seen, advantages and disadvantages to whatever data collection procedures a supervisor chooses. Using data triangulation and methods triangulation can help us overcome the weaknesses inherent in any single data collection source or procedure.

Denzin's (1978) theory triangulation and researcher triangulation appear to have relatively little application for language teacher supervisors. On the other hand, data triangulation and methods triangulation hold great promise for supervisors.

For example, Murdoch (1998, Multiple Data Sources section, paragraph 1) discusses a variety of data collection procedures in teacher evaluation contexts. These include

> student [and] teacher questionnaires; interviews with teachers; samples of student work; teacher diaries; learner diaries; audio tape recordings of lessons; video recordings of lessons; classroom observation reports; interviews with coordinators; interviews with program administrators; careful analysis of teaching materials and curriculum / syllabus documents, reports of testing experts, etc.

This list includes data triangulation (teachers, students, administrators) and methods triangulation (video, audio, diaries, questionnaires, interviews, etc.) in language teacher supervision. Murdoch questions "the wisdom of evaluating teachers solely on the evidence of infrequent observations when the opportunity exists to gather data about the full range of a teacher's program involvement and professional activities" (ibid.). Thus, incorporating triangulation strategies can enhance the validity of teacher evaluations.

Technological developments in supervision

How can recent developments in technology benefit teachers and supervisors? There is little research on this issue in language teaching, but there are some studies in general education. We will briefly review some of that literature before speculating on the roles new technological developments might play in language teacher supervision.

Technological advances and the supervision of preservice teachers

There is some research about the use of technology in supervising preservice teachers, though most of it is from general education. For example, Hsiung and Tan (1999) report on the distance supervision of 36 preservice elementary science teachers in Taiwan. The Distance

Supervision Hot Line (designed by the student teachers using the Internet) consisted of seven components: "overview of research, research group, bulletin, my reflection, teaching resources, teaching difficulties, and meeting in the air." The Internet communications relieved the trainees' task stress and increased the frequency of contact with their supervisors.

Crippen and Brooks (2000) have described the use of e-mail to promote journal keeping by student teachers. They also discuss the use of handheld personal digital assistants (PDAs) for recording in-class notes during observations. By entering preset codes, the observer creates "a time-stamped phrase . . . in the device's memory that elaborates classroom observations" (p. 208). This record is immediately available for discussions with the teacher.

Technology is being used to promote communication between supervisors and teacher trainees, particularly in rural situations. For example, the Electronic Enhancement of Supervision Project at Indiana University Southeast (for training cooperating teachers in special education) was designed to address teacher shortages in rural areas (Shea and Babione, 2001). The project's teachers were to supervise trainees in special education, with the help of webcams, e-mail discussion groups, and Web sites. However, there were difficulties due to mismatches between the university's and individual school's equipment, as well as with the technology bureaucracies of the two systems.

The teacher education program at Valdosta State University in Georgia also uses technology to decrease the time and costs involved in supervisors' travel (Venn, Moore, and Gunter, 2000–2001). The program uses CU-SeeMe videoconferencing software to enable student teachers to communicate with their supervisors frequently. It also allows the supervisors to observe from a distance and promotes interactions among the supervisor, the student teacher, and the local cooperating teacher, as well as among student teachers.

A teacher training program at North Georgia College and State University uses in-class cameras to record student teachers' lessons, which are followed by interactive two-way videoconferencing. Though this system is costly, it allows trainees to return to their own rural communities. It also saves travel time for the university supervisors and increases the visibility of the university in remote areas (Gruenhagen, McCracken, and True, 1999).

In Iowa, a teacher education program uses computer technology "to build community and reduce isolation during student teaching, improve communication and enhance supervision of student teachers, and encourage reflection" (Johanson, Norland, Olson, Huth, and Bodensteiner, 1999:1). The student teachers are given e-mail addresses and participate in at least one of six Listservs: (1) primary school, elementary school, and middle school, (2) music instruction, (3) high school, (4) art instruction,

(5) physical education, and (6) professionalism. The authors report that some student teachers actively engaged in discussing issues and reflecting with their peers via the Listservs. However, the authors felt there was still a need for face-to-face communication among trainees and supervisors.

A study in Australia (Hodder and Carter, 1997) reported on the Remote Area Practicum Supervision Project, which incorporated the Instructional Information Management System, an electronic storage system. The remote practicum site was electronically linked to the university. The technology allowed the university-based supervisors to work with the trainees from a distance, while the local cooperating teachers worked with the trainees in the schools. Results were positive in terms of developing collegial practices and sharing practical expertise.

A similar distance-based system used in North Carolina supported first-year teachers, who worked with local mentor teachers and were linked electronically to a professor from their training program (Thomson and Hawk, 1996). The technology involved videotaped lessons and telecommunications for post-observation conferences. (The videotapes were sent to the university supervisor by snail mail.) The participants deemed the project a limited success, even though they generally felt telecommunication provided "a viable alternative to traditional face-to-face conferencing" (p. 16). The savings in cost and travel time were substantial, however.

A money-saving project in British Columbia used teleconferencing and conference calls for consultations with student teachers (Cross and Murphy, 1990). As in the study by Thomson and Hawk (1996), this project reported only partial success because the student teachers found the telephone conversations impersonal; they preferred face-to-face supervision.

Potential benefits of technology in supervision

Technological advances can facilitate the collection and analysis of classroom data. For example, software programs such as Nud*ist and Ethnograph can be used to find key themes and repeated words or phrases. Concordancing programs (e.g., MonoConc or Wordsmith®) can identify words and phrases that occur together in transcripts and field notes. For training purposes, minidisc or digital video recordings can be edited to produce samples of effective teaching demonstrated by several teachers. Once a lesson has been transcribed, transcript lines can be connected to videotape footage with SMIL (synchronized multimedia integrated language resources). Such a system enables teachers and supervisors (or a teacher alone) to watch lessons while the text of the spoken discourse is scrolling on the screen. Some technological developments will result in savings of time and storage space. For instance, minidisc recorders can create digital audio recordings that are more durable and easier to archive than bulky and fragile audiotapes. In addition, it is possible to place a digital marker at the beginning of key sections on the disc, enabling listeners to move from one section to the next with a single button, a far simpler process than manually forwarding a cassette to particular points in a lesson. Thus, teachers and supervisors can save time by using digital recordings. The added control that digital recorders afford can also accelerate transcription. Turns or segments of lessons can be timed automatically, and it is easy to note points of interest while observing. Digital video recordings offer similar flexibility of handling and durability.

There are also commercial organizations that use Web-based technology to promote teacher development. For example, a group called LessonLab advertises the use of streaming video and digital libraries to promote interactive learning based on case materials. Some organizations (see, for example, www.wested.org) have the technological capacity to support professional development programs for teachers, including language teachers, with videotaping and other technologies in the data collection process.

Concluding comments

This chapter examined the two main electronic means of collecting data – audiotape and videotape. Although both procedures have disadvantages, the main benefits of electronic data collection are its longevity and its impartiality: Although they are selective, unedited videotapes and audiotapes are not judgmental. In addition, teachers, alone or with supervisors, can review tapes repeatedly. The technological advances described above are likely to make electronic recordings faster and easier to use, as well as more economical to store. Electronic recordings also gather the raw data for transcription, providing valuable tools for documenting teachers' strengths and raising their awareness.

Transcript 6.1 is a verbatim record of interaction from a vocabulary lesson. When doing the following case-discussion activities, remember that the teacher in this chapter's case audiotaped her class in order to work on some issues of concern. She transcribed this segment because it typified the difficulty she sometimes had in moving the lesson forward. Use the transcript as the basis of your discussion with the teacher about the concerns she has raised.

Case discussion

1. Have you ever been aware of a student who seemed to dominate turn-taking in classroom interaction? If so, what did you do about it (either

as a teacher or a learner)? On the basis of that experience, what advice would you give this teacher?

2. In dealing with the teacher's concerns, which constituent(s) in Freeman's (1989a) model are you addressing: awareness, attitude, knowledge, and / or skills?

3. What are your goals for the conference, given the data and what the teacher said before the lesson? What strategies will you use and what steps do you plan to take in the conference?

4. Looking at the data, what observations can you offer the teacher? What questions could you ask her to lead her to a new level of awareness? (Think about this teacher's ZPD, based on the issue she has chosen to work on.) If this teacher gained one new insight from talking with you, what would you want it to be?

5. Compare your ability to interpret this transcript under the following conditions:

   A. You conducted the observation as well as taking notes and taping the lesson.

   B. You were in the classroom but did *not* take notes while the tape recording was made.

   C. You were not in the class, but the teacher's aide took notes as the tape recording was made. You read the notes and the transcript as you listen to the tape.

   D. You were not in the classroom during the lesson, nor did anyone take notes. You listen to the tape recording as you read the transcript.

   E. You were not in the classroom, nor did anyone take notes during the lesson. The audiotape has been erased, but the teacher did write in her teaching journal after this lesson, and has given you permission to read the transcript and the journal entry.

   F. You were not in the classroom, and no one took notes. There is no audiotape, so all you have in talking with the teacher is the transcript and her recollections of the class.

   Consider these six situations: How does the decreasing amount of data and contextual information affect the post-observation conference?

6. Role-play the post-observation conference with this teacher under the three different conditions that follow. How does the conference proceed if you choose the role of the supervisory or directive approach, the alternatives approach, or the nondirective approach (Freeman, 1982)?

7. If you were to conduct a live observation of this class at the teacher's request as a follow-up to this conference, what would you watch for during your visit? Why? What data-collection procedures, if any, would you use during your visit? Why?

Tasks for development

1. How can recordings of classroom interaction influence the four constituents that Larsen-Freeman (1983) says are needed to bring about change?

Constituent of teaching	Audiotape	Videotape
Gaining heightened awareness		
Possessing a positive attitude		
Gaining new knowledge		
Developing new skills		

Write a comment in each cell about the potential value of the recording method.

2. Think about the Johari Window, shown in Figures 2.3 and 2.4. How can language teachers and supervisors use audio- or videotapes of classroom interaction to help teachers work on the Blind Self, the Hidden Self, and the Secret Self? Write one comment about how electronic recording relates to each quadrant.

3. You as the supervisor are not present during a language lesson, but have access to an audio- or videotape made by the teacher. In the grid, put plus (+), check (√), or minus (−) in each cell to represent the value of information provided to supervisors and teachers by the electronic data in each category. (Assume high-quality recordings.)

	Audiotape	Videotape
Awareness		
Attitude		
Knowledge		
Skills		

4. Stenson et al. say the five components listed below are needed for teacher development. The horizontal headings are Freeman's constituents of teaching. Put a check (√) in each cell where the ideas from Stenson et al. intersect with Freeman's ideas.

Components of teacher development (Stenson et al., 1979)

Constituents of teaching (Freeman, 1989a)

	Awareness	Attitude	Knowledge	Skills
Obtaining feedback				
Becoming introspective				
Accepting responsibility				
Choosing what to change				
Effecting change				

Where there are no check marks, what explains the lack of overlap?
5. What is the supervisor's responsibility in helping a language teacher achieve each of the five components of teacher development identified in the research by Stenson et al.? For each item on the list, write one statement about what a supervisor can do to help a teacher working on each particular category. Think about van Lier's (1996) six principles of scaffolded activity and Rueda's (1998) five principles for professional development. (See Chapter 2.)
6. Audiotape yourself teaching a language class. Identify some element(s) of your teaching you would like to improve or investigate. Selectively transcribe parts related to the issue(s) you identified. What information does the transcript, or the process of transcription, give you that you did not gain from simply listening to the tape?
7. Videotape yourself teaching. During playback, darken the screen so no picture is available. Note what you learn by listening to the tape and then replay it with the picture. What do you learn by adding the visual component?
8. Transcribe a three- to five-minute segment of a recording of your teaching. What does the transcript reveal about the interaction that the recording alone did not reveal?
9. Next, share your video or audio recording with a trusted colleague. Tell that person what issue(s) you want to focus on before you review the tape together. What insights does that person have to offer that you hadn't thought of yourself?
10. Based on your experience and reading, use this grid to document the strengths and weaknesses of electronic recordings and manual data collection in supervision.

	Strengths	Weaknesses
Electronic recording		
Manual data collection		

Suggestions for further reading

The article by Franck and Samaniego (1981) about using videotape in supervising TAs is a bit dated now, but it contains interesting data and practical suggestions.

Suggested transcription conventions can be found in Allwright and Bailey (1991:222–223), and van Lier (1988) offers a helpful appendix about transcription in classroom research. Edwards and Lampert (1993) provide a more detailed treatment of issues related to transcription and coding. In Nunan and Lamb's (1996) appendices, the teacher's commentary parallels the lines of the lesson transcript. Additional transcripts can be found in Allwright and Bailey (1991).

Bailey et al. (2001) have a chapter on using videotape in which a teacher reports what she learned by watching a video of her teaching by herself. Murphey (2000) discusses a self-videotaping task he uses with EFL teachers in Japan. For more about videotape in teacher development and evaluation, see Batey and Wesgate (1994), Cullen (1991), Curtis and Cheng (1998), Laycock and Bunnag (1991), and Rowley and Hart (1996). Allan (1991) compares the use of videocassette recorders and videodisc players in language education.

For more information about egocentric speech, see Appel and Lantolf (1994), McCafferty (1994), and Vygotsky (1978).

7 The post-observation conference

No matter who you are supervising – preservice or in-service language teachers, native or non-native speakers, full-time or part-time employees – one of the trickiest parts of a job is the post-observation conference. This event can be awkward because supervisors must sometimes give negative feedback to teachers.

This chapter examines feedback in language teacher supervision and factors that affect supervisory discourse. We will begin with a case that demands that some changes be made. As the supervisor, you must decide how to promote the needed changes.

Case for analysis: Classroom control issues

You are an experienced language teacher working as the lead teacher and supervisor in the foreign language department of a large secondary school. You have a postgraduate degree and experience as a teacher educator, as well as experience teaching French and Spanish.

You receive a written complaint from a parent. She claims that her daughter, who studied French for a year at another school, cannot accomplish anything in her French II class because some students are so noisy that others cannot concentrate, and the teacher cannot possibly teach. The parent also claims the teacher does nothing to curb the rowdy behavior.

You arrange with the teacher to visit the French II class. She does not seem thrilled that you are coming, but neither does she seem anxious or defensive. During the pre-observation conference, you ask her what the class is working on and whether she has any particular concerns. She tells you that the students are all 14 or 15 years old and that they will be doing grammar exercises the day you visit. She also comments that she has no major worries about these students. In fact, she says, it is a typical French II class, quite like all the others she has taught during the fifteen years she has worked at this school. Given the teacher's lack of concern, you hope that the parent's complaint was not entirely justified.

> However, when you visit, the teacher has no control over the students' behavior. Most of the 17 students present – eight boys and nine girls – are apparently not learning any French. The girl whose mother complained sits at the front of the class with her book open. She and another girl and a boy are doing grammar exercises. The teacher helps those students and reminds others that they will get detention notices if they don't do their work.
>
> Meanwhile, the other students are engaged in many activities unrelated to studying French. Three girls are applying makeup and laughing loudly. One girl is braiding another's hair while talking excitedly in English about a party. Four boys are reading a motorcycle magazine (in English), and two others are playing a handheld computer game. The teacher ignores these six boys, who are being relatively quiet, and divides her time between the three students who are working on the exercises and those who are making noise. For instance, two girls are calling another student names and tossing his glasses back and forth in a game of "keep-away." The teacher tells them to return his glasses. The girls continue taunting the boy and throwing his glasses around. The teacher's repeated admonishments seem to have no effect on the students.

The role of feedback in language teacher supervision

The post-observation conference is predicated on the concept that teachers can improve by gaining feedback. The assumption is that feedback increases awareness, which enables teachers to change their behavior. The intent of such feedback is to note effective teaching, to identify less effective teaching, and to promote positive change.

Knowledge of results

"Knowledge of results" (Chaudron, 1977:30) can come from our own awareness or through outside agents who give us feedback on the results of our actions. For example, if you are driving a car, you may encounter a roadside radar device that measures oncoming vehicles' speed. If you are traveling at 40 miles per hour in a 35-mile zone, a bold digital sign informs you that you are going five miles per hour over the speed limit. As you decrease your speed, the numerals on the sign change to 39, 38, 37, and so on, until the car is traveling at 35 miles per hour, at which point you stop decelerating and maintain the legal speed. In this situation, the sign flashing how fast you are going provides clear knowledge of results. To deny the accuracy of the machine's feedback

141

or to fail to act on its information puts you at risk of getting a traffic ticket.

Computer-delivered feedback to language learners with a spectrograph is based on the same concept. The language learner says an utterance that the computer records. The intonation contours of the learner's utterance are portrayed on the computer monitor along with a model utterance produced by a native or a proficient speaker of the target language. The learner uses the computerized visual display to "notice the gap" (Schmidt and Frota, 1986:310) between his or her intonation contours and those of the computerized model. The learner then attempts to match the model in his or her own subsequent utterances – as shown by the two intonation contour lines coming together on the screen.

The principle of feedback underlying the speed detector and the spectograph is the same: Knowledge of the results of one's actions is necessary to change those actions. This principle underpins the post-observation conferences between teachers and supervisors. Unfortunately, in language teaching, we seldom know the results as quickly as feedback can appear on the radar detector or the computer monitor. Sometimes we can see that a student has understood or learned a concept, but often learning is not immediate. In some cases, it takes a very long time.

Although driving a car and changing one's intonation are not simple acts, language learning and teaching are even more complicated. Besides striving to develop students' knowledge (of the target language and culture) and skills (in using the linguistic system appropriately), teachers try to promote attitude changes in their students. These attitudinal changes include a heightened level of curiosity and positive stance toward the target language and culture, receptivity to further learning and instruction (Allwright and Bailey, 1991), willingness to take risks while using the target language, respect for people of other cultures, and so on. Because knowledge, skills, and attitudes take time to develop, it is sometimes difficult to know what the results of teaching are. Figure 7.1 contrasts the radar and spectograph feedback with evidence of language learning.

Figure 7.1 reminds language teacher supervisors that evidence of learning as a result of teaching is not always immediately apparent. In observing a lesson, we may or may not see results of teaching because (1) the students are not all learning; (2) the students have only partially mastered the material covered but will learn it eventually; or (3) the students have learned something, but the manifestations of that learning are not directly observable. In addition, if learning is delayed or incremental, even though there may be no obvious evidence during the observation, a teacher may be extremely effective in the long run. Therefore, we need to consider a possible incubation period for teaching's effects to be realized.

142

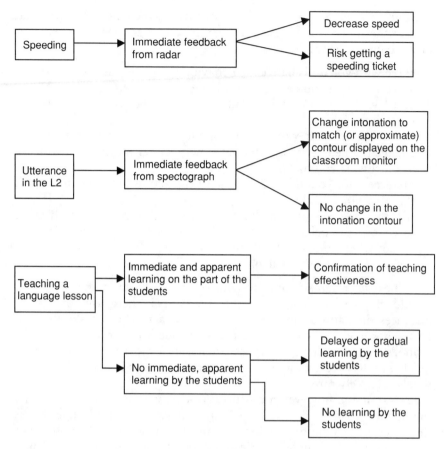

Figure 7.1 Immediate versus delayed knowledge of results

Feedback, awareness, and creating conditions for change

The knowledge of results concept suggests that teachers cannot purposefully change their behaviors without being aware of them. But it does not necessarily follow that teachers' being aware of their less-than-optimal teaching behaviors will automatically lead to change. In general education, Brophy and Good (1974:291) assert that "most inappropriate teaching is due to lack of awareness in the teacher rather than to any deliberate callousness or inability to change" (ibid.). These authors stress that the recipients of feedback must find it to be both relevant and credible. Otherwise, their motivation to change will understandably be low.

143

Many factors can prevent, inhibit, or slow such changes. Imagine that you, as the supervisor, advise a teacher directly that a teaching behavior must change. The teacher may

1. agree with you and change the behavior completely and immediately;
2. agree with you and change the behavior gradually;
3. agree with you somewhat and modify the behavior partially but immediately;
4. openly agree with you, either completely or to some extent, and change the behavior partially but slowly (either incrementally or not as quickly as you had hoped);
5. disagree with you about the value of the action but agree to change the behavior, and do so;
6. silently disagree with you about the value of the action, verbally agree to change the behavior, but fail to do so (or choose not to do so), except when you visit the class; or
7. openly disagree with you and refuse to change the behavior.

A supervisor can seldom say with certainty that a language teacher should change a teaching strategy. Of course, there are some clear instances of inappropriate behavior (e.g., if a teacher breaks the law, harms a student, allows students to hurt one another, or violates the school's written policies). In those situations, a supervisor needs to take quick and decisive action, but in my experience such instances are fortunately relatively rare.

It is common, however, for a supervisor to communicate to a teacher the opinion that an observed teaching activity was not effective. But is the supervisor's opinion any better than the teacher's? In the absence of research evidence, publicly articulated standards, methodological prescriptions, school policy, or legal requirements, we are left to debate the relative merits of particular teaching strategies on the basis of beliefs and attitudes derived from our experience and training alone. But the supervisor's experience and training may differ dramatically from those of the teachers he or she works with, so teachers may not heed a supervisor's opinions.

Supervisors' concerns about conferences

The rise of clinical supervision (Cogan, 1973; Gaies and Bowers, 1990; Goldhammer, 1969; Acheson and Gall, 1997) has all but institutionalized the sequence of the pre-observation conference, the observation itself, and the post-observation conference. It is this third step, the post-observation conference between the supervisor and the teacher, that "carries the potential of being an agonizing experience for both" (Shrigley and Walker, 1981:560) because of the danger of loss of face. In this context, *face* is defined as "the public, socially valued image of self" that people wish to convey to others (Wajnryb 1994a, p. i).

The supervisory discourse of Australian teacher educators was investigated by Wajnryb (1994a, 1994b). She interviewed supervisors and ESL teachers-in-training and analyzed transcripts of post-observation conferences. Teachers also responded to a questionnaire about a post-observation meeting between a supervisor and a teacher (or student teacher), which involved giving the teacher critical feedback. Wajnryb's results (1994a: 370) show that in feedback conferences, supervisors

1. are concerned with the impact of their words on the face and morale of the teachers and accordingly adjust their words, bearing in mind the teacher's unforeseen responses, both immediate and delayed;
2. have to juggle the twin demands of helper (advising, counseling, nurturing, encouraging, guiding, supporting) and critic (judging, assessing, pointing out weaknesses);
3. have to ride a fine line between not hurting the teacher with their words but also getting a clear message across;
4. are aware of staging, managing, and handling the conference in ways that make it productive and facilitate the successful delivery of bad news;
5. work hard at the affective factors of trust and empathy to create a context in which critical feedback might be well received;
6. safeguard their instructive message to counter the mitigating impact that face has on their choice of words;
7. refer to the complexity of their functions, demonstrate an awareness of their own evolution towards more effective practice, and testify to the value that strategic training might offer.

These concerns are reflected in supervisors' linguistic behavior. (See Chapter 8). It is important to understand these variables to avoid communication breakdowns during conferences.

The roles teachers take in post-observation conferences

In general education, Waite analyzed audiotaped conferences between four novice teachers and their three supervisors. He also observed those meetings and wrote detailed descriptions of them (1993:678). In addition, Waite conducted three interviews with each supervisor and shadowed them as they interacted with the trainees.

In these conferences, the novices enacted three different roles, which were labeled "passive, collaborative, and adversarial" (ibid.:681). According to Waite, teachers taking the passive role accept both the supervisor's suggestions and the supervisor's authority to offer them and may try to align their teaching with the supervisor's beliefs.

The second role, that of the collaborative teacher, "correlates with a much weaker supervisory agenda" (ibid.). Teachers taking this role select which suggestions to respond to and how to apply those suggestions. Two possibilities arise, however: (1) Teachers may appear to accept the supervisor's suggestions but not apply them, or (2) teachers may accept the feedback and actually incorporate the supervisor's suggestions.

The third role occurs when both the teacher and the supervisor bring strong agendas to conferences and the teacher does not capitulate to the supervisor's position. Then the teacher may take an adversarial role in the conference. This situation is related to the concept of face-threatening acts (see Chapter 8) because "disagreement is always a face-threatening act" (Beebe and Takahashi, 1989:204).

The implications of Waite's three roles are important. If supervisors wish to promote positive changes, teacher development, and standards of excellence, teachers must be able to take in supervisorial feedback. (In Pennington's [1996] terms, the input must be accessible.) No one benefits (except in the short term) if teachers only *appear* to accept suggestions. Likewise, if teachers become so defensive during conferences that adversarial roles are established, it is unlikely that positive changes in teaching will result.

Successful and unsuccessful conferences

Observations are more effective if they are both preceded and followed by discussions with the teacher, but those communications don't always occur. For example, when supervisors make surprise visits to classrooms, no pre-observation conference takes place. Sometimes a supervisor observes a lesson but does not discuss it with the teacher afterward.

Blase and Blase (1995) analyzed successful and unsuccessful post-observation conferences in general education. Successful conferences were those "that both participants reported as non-threatening and growth-oriented" (p. 68). The dyads consisted of supervisors interacting with teachers with a wide range of experience. Those supervisors also had varied experience, from true novices (in their first supervisory conference) and beginners (in their first year as supervisors) to very experienced supervisors. The conferences followed observations of the teachers during which the supervisors made selective verbatim transcripts and anecdotal records of some events. The supervisors were not responsible for the formal evaluation of these teachers, so no decisions rested on the outcome of the discussions.

These authors found that the teachers and supervisors employed four main strategies: the use of the participants' personal orientations,

Table 7.1 *Strategies and related factors used by conference participants that facilitate or constrain interaction (Blase and Blase, 1995:60)*

	STRATEGY			
	Use of participants' personal orientations	Use of conversational congruence	Use of formal authority	Use of situational variables
R E L A T E D F A C T O R S	*Cognitive framework* • opinions and beliefs • individual philosophy • personal expectations • achievement motivation *Affective framework* • praise • success • shared values • moral commitments • purposes *Interpersonal histories* • shared events • knowledge • experiences *Individual agendas* • congruence on instructional goals and objectives	*Shared meanings* • instructional approaches, concepts, ideas *Shared assumptions* • how to work with children • purpose of conference *Semantic congruence* • jargon, terms, references *Professional credibility* • expertise • experience	*Role expectations* • fulfilling traditional roles *Social proximity or distance* • familiarity • informality *Status* • equality of participants *Rewards* • reinforcement • feedback	*Place and physical arrangement* *Time to confer* *Teaching resources and materials* *Policy requirements* *Topic control*

conversational congruence, formal authority, and situational variables. These strategies, and factors related to each of them, are listed in Table 7.1.

The study by Blase and Blase indicates that successful conferences "differ from less effective conferences in terms of the strategies participants employ" (1995:68). In effective conferences, both supervisors and teachers predominantly used the strategies in the first two columns of Table 7.1. The participants' use of formal authority was limited to "evaluating the status of participants to equalize and balance the conference, to build trust, and to foster openness" (ibid.). Successful conferences also provided opportunities for teachers to talk about their work in a non-threatening context: "In this 'safe haven,' risk is tolerated, suggestions are offered in a positive manner, and mutual goals are emphasized" (ibid.). Such conferences produced discussions that were "more collaborative, nonevaluative, and reflective than did the less successful conferences" (ibid.).

In the less successful conferences, verbal agreements between participants seemed forced and contrived, and they often evolved into brief indications of agreement (such as "uh-huh," "mmm," "oh yeah"), or periods of silence. These conferences were characterized by "a lack of agreement on roles and personal expectations and a lack of shared meaning or assumptions about teaching or learning" (ibid.:69). The supervisors' authority and situational control strategies seemed to inhibit the development of viable conference exchanges (ibid.). In addition, teachers were more resistant in the less successful conferences, although some supervisors were able to change from a formal authority strategy to an emphasis on personal orientation, which seemed to repair the interaction when resistant behaviors occurred.

There were also some notable differences between the experienced and the less experienced supervisors. Blase and Blase (ibid.:66–67) report that experienced supervisors achieved topic control rather subtly, whereas beginning supervisors were more direct. Beginning supervisors seemed to disregard teachers' agendas and their ability to reflect on their teaching, whereas experienced supervisors often requested such information about the former from teachers and reinforced the teachers' reflective talk with comments and questions. Blase and Blase note that "such follow-up comments appeared to be critical to reflective talk; in fact, without these comments, conference participants seemed to wander aimlessly through subsequent talk" (ibid.:67). These authors conclude that "beginning supervisors have difficulty in tolerating high levels of dissonance in conference interaction; consequently, they escalate their attempts to guide or control ensuing conference interactions" (ibid.:68).

Factors affecting supervisory discourse

A number of factors – related to the supervisor, the teacher(s), the context, or any combination thereof – can influence supervisory discourse. It is important to understand supervisory discourse because "discourses themselves exercise their own control" (Foucault, 1981:56). The post-observation conference (especially if it remains unexamined) can be one of those "ritualized sets of discourses which are recited in well-defined circumstances" (ibid.). Both teachers and supervisors wield power and are influenced by the power struggle inherent in many forms of supervisory discourse.

Situational factors and unequal power discourse

The critical discussion of one person's teaching by another person is potentially difficult, even if the teacher's interlocutor is a peer or a good friend. If the interlocutor is a more powerful person, the discussion is a type of unequal power discourse and can be face-threatening. Examples of unequal power discourse include doctor-patient conversations, employment interviews, and classroom interaction. Chamberlin (2000:653–654) states that the power imbalance of typical supervisory approaches "does not promote a collegial interpersonal setting that is conducive to self-disclosure and exploration of beliefs and practice." This power imbalance can have profound effects on the behavior of the conference participants.

Many factors contribute to the inherently threatening nature of the post-observation conference. For instance, the supervisor usually has a higher rank than the teacher in the structure of the program. Typically the supervisor is older and has more experience teaching, teaching language(s), teaching in the program, teaching the particular age group or type of student, and / or teaching the subject matter. The supervisor often has more or better training and may hold an advanced degree or diploma in the field.

Occasionally the supervisor even has some other (potentially veiled) form of power. This point may sound unnecessarily mysterious, but it should not be ignored. In some instances the supervisor may be the outright owner / operator of the program. In other cases, that person may be the significant other, sibling, child, protegé, or best friend of the person who runs the program. All of these scenarios suggest the possible existence of a power base that is not derived entirely from the supervisor's qualifications.

Typically, the supervisor has some actual administrative power over the teachers being supervised. That power may be limited to making suggestions about changing one's teaching, which can even be off the record, or it could include putting such suggestions on record in the teacher's file, with or without scheduled follow-up visitations. Supervision often entails writing developmental evaluation reports about the teacher. These reports document the supervisor's suggestions. In other contexts, supervisors may write recommendations for or against raises, promotions, contract renewals, or tenure. In extreme cases, supervisors may even make summative evaluations leading to dismissal. So, for any given post-observation conference, the supervisor should be aware that a differential power base may influence the discourse. Furthermore, the teacher's *perception* of the supervisor's power should not be ignored.

Teachers' respect for supervisors

Another important variable is the respect teachers have for the supervisor. If the teachers you supervise don't respect you, as a person and as an educator, why should they incorporate your ideas in their teaching? If you respect someone, you normally value his or her judgment and give credence to his or her opinions. Thus it is important for supervisors to create the conditions in which the teachers they supervise can respect them.

Gaining someone's respect can be difficult and time-consuming. Losing it, on the other hand, can be easy and instantaneous. Some of the ways supervisors can lose teachers' respect include lying, gossiping, going back on a promise (e.g., not writing a letter of recommendation after having promised to do so), and being duplicitous (e.g., saying one thing to the teacher and another to the administration). Supervisors can also lose (or fail to gain) teachers' respect by lacking expert power: If you do not possess the skills and knowledge to carry out your responsibilities, the teachers will see little reason to respect you.

Macroanalyses of the post-observation conference

This section reviews some research and practical advice from both general education and language teaching about conducting conferences. Much of the published literature contains suggestions (whether they are based on practice, research, or opinion) about how supervisors should conduct post-observation conferences to get teachers to heed the input.

Wallace's three models of teacher education

Wallace (1991) has proposed three models of teacher education: the craft model, the applied science model, and the reflective model. Each model has had an impact on our field, and each has implications for how supervisors interact with teachers.

In the craft model, a novice serves an apprenticeship with a master teacher. By observing the master, imitating his or her behavior, and getting

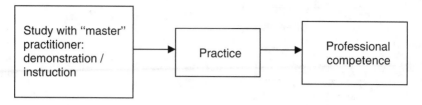

Figure 7.2 The craft model of professional education (Wallace, 1991:6)

feedback, the novice learns the trade. An example in teacher training is placing practicum students with experienced cooperating teachers. The novice teachers observe and assist the experienced teachers and learn by doing whatever they do. Sometimes the novices work on one increment of the task at a time, before moving on to the next step. Wallace's craft model is shown in Figure 7.2.

The craft model has been very important in terms of learning the technical skills of teaching. But over the years, language teaching has moved beyond being a collection of techniques. These days the profession is influenced by theories and research findings too.

These developments have led to the use of the applied science model, in which teachers receive knowledge, based on research and theory, from experts. The implications of this model are that experts conduct research and generate theory. The teachers are then taught that research and theory, which they must somehow apply as classroom practices. Thus, the responsibility of teacher educators and supervisors in the applied science model is to convey theory and the findings of research to teachers, as depicted in Figure 7.3.

The applied science model is predicated on research findings and theory that can inform language teaching. That knowledge is conveyed to trainees, who somehow utilize it in their teaching. Professional competence results from applying scientific knowledge and practicing procedures based on that application. Since the body of knowledge is constantly changing, teachers need regular updating (e.g., through in-service workshops).

Wallace's third framework, the reflective model, acknowledges the importance of research and theory, referred to as the "received knowledge" of the field, but it also gives equal emphasis to teachers' experiential knowledge, as shown in Figure 7.4.

The reflective practice model also explicitly recognizes the influence of the trainees' background knowledge and experience on their practice and reflection. It is important for supervisors to understand teachers' experiential knowledge, because it serves not only as a motivating force, but

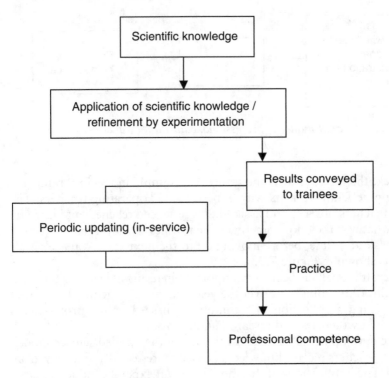

Figure 7.3 The applied science model of professional education (Wallace, 1991:9)

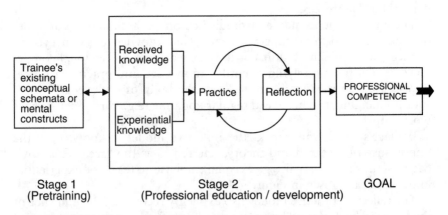

Figure 7.4 The reflective practice model of professional education / development (Wallace, 1991:49)

also as a screen through which incoming information (including feedback) is filtered.

Wallace's models and language teacher supervision

Wallace's three models have implications for teacher supervision. The craft model exerts a powerful influence in the practicum system of placing novice teachers with cooperating teachers. Wallace and Woolger (writing about a supervisor training program in Sri Lanka) note that in the applied science model of teacher education, "the expertise is seen as basically residing *outside* the trainee: the trainee's job is to imbibe the expertise in the best way that he or she can. In this model, the trainee's role is essentially passive or reactive; the supervisor is the 'expert'" (1991:320–321). These authors point out that novice teachers are often happy to comply with the applied science model because it places the responsibility for their development on the supervisor. Of course, "supervisors also find this model congenial, albeit for different reasons (often related to status and self-image)" (ibid.:321).

Wallace and Woolger relate the applied science model to the discourse that occurs during a post-observation conference: "It becomes essentially (and sometimes literally) a monologue, in which the supervisor 'sorts out' the trainee's problems, the latter dutifully taking notes" (ibid.). They conclude that "neither party finds much professional satisfaction" (ibid.) in this model even though it initially seems attractive. The authors say the problem

> is that the two participants are much more evenly balanced than they seem. Although the supervisor usually has superior knowledge and expertise *in general terms,* the trainee usually has greater knowledge of *this particular class* and also, of course, a different perspective on *this particular lesson* – from the *inside* as it were. (ibid.)

Wallace and Woolger prefer the reflective model, because "the responsibility for the development of professional expertise is seen as essentially residing with the trainee, by a process of reflecting on his or her own practice" (1991:321). In this model, the supervisor's role is to help the novice develop his or her powers of reflection. Wallace and Woolger believe the reflective model is more demanding than the applied science model, and "will fully extend the supervisor's knowledge and expertise, but will also probably be found more rewarding" (ibid.). They contend that, in the reflective model, "a true supervisory dialogue is essential, because the supervisor must *start with the trainee's experience.* Common ground must be established. There must be agreement on what happened, and what was intended to happen" (ibid.:320–321).

Stages in the post-observation conference

Wallace and Woolger (1991:322) recommend using four stages in the post-observation feedback conference. The first they call "establishing the facts," which relates to what happened during the lesson. These authors recommend that supervisors ask two questions in this stage: "What did the teacher do?" and "What did the pupils do?" (ibid.) during the lesson.

The second stage also has two key questions: "What was achieved?" and "What did the pupils learn?" (ibid.) in the lesson. Wallace and Woolger say an important corollary to the last two questions is, "How do you know?" In other words, what evidence is there that the students actually learned something?

The third stage entails generating alternatives and asking, "What else could have been done?" Wallace and Woolger note that "there are almost always alternatives worth considering, even when both participants agree that the lesson has been very successful" (ibid.:322), which clearly relates to the alternatives option (Freeman, 1982; Gebhard, 1984, 1990b).

In the fourth stage, self-evaluation, teachers are asked, "What have you learned?" Wallace and Woolger (1991:322) note that the supervisor must listen carefully in this crucial phase for evidence of the trainee's self-evaluation skills and ability to improve (ibid.:322). They add that the question "What have you learned?" should apply to the supervisor too.

The delivery of criticism

Criticism of teaching is often taken as criticism of the person. The phrase "Don't take it personally" refers to this issue: Don't apply the criticism of your action to yourself as a person. Of course, such advice is easy to give and hard to follow. In fact, the social strictures against giving criticism are so strong that most people avoid it, including supervisors. Wajnryb (1994a:82) borrows Olson's (1982) metaphor of a theatrical performance. She says supervisors

> avoided a rational analysis of the teaching they observed and instead assumed an uncritical, supportive role.... The specific role assumed was that of "a friend in the audience." Teaching was deemed a stage performance, and while a "drama critic" role was in fact required of them, the supervisors opted for a support role.

Olson (1982:77) provides an apt summary statement about cooperating teachers' lack of critical feedback to student teachers: "[W]hen the performance was over, [they] applauded warmly or lukewarmly, but did not write a critical review of its elements."

154

Wajnryb (1994a:84) also cites a study by O'Neal (1983), which found that although cooperating teachers were able to make judgments, they were not willing to share those ideas with the novice teachers they supervised. Instead, the cooperating teachers chose primarily to provide support and encouragement. The responsibility of delivering criticism was left to the university-based supervisors who occasionally observed the lessons.

In spite of the value of feedback, "research evidence suggests that various processes operate within informal face-to-face interactions between supervisors and subordinates that militate against supervisors' ability to give negative feedback" (Wajnryb, 1994a:87). For supervisors, "there is a natural reluctance to deliver bad news" (ibid.). Likewise, "on the subordinate's side, there is a set of feedback-seeking strategies that produce, as intended, mitigated negative feedback" (ibid.). Thus there is a delicate balance managed, almost out of awareness, by both parties in the conference.

The concept of account behavior is relevant here. According to Wajnryb (ibid.:88), *account behavior* is "language behaviour intended to extricate one from a tight spot – wherein the mitigation of messages is documented as strategic management of failure events." So in a case where one person (e.g., a supervisor or peer) finds another person's actions (e.g., teaching during a language lesson) to be less than fully successful, the first person may use account behavior to temper the discussion of the problem. Wajnryb also points out that although the role expectations of the post-observation conference demand the "transmission of bad news" (ibid.), the supervisor "may be unable to keep silent, but may choose other ways to muffle the message" (ibid.). We will examine specific ways supervisors "muffle the message" in Chapter 8.

The supervisor's account behavior was a factor in an Australian study of a teacher called Lucy (a pseudonym), whose teaching was supervised in a 12-week ESL training program (Wajnryb: 1995b). Lucy was 25 years old and had already taught ESL / EFL for two years in Australia and Europe. She had enrolled in the program for professional development purposes. Lucy kept a journal about receiving feedback during the training program. In addition, Wajnryb interviewed Lucy at the halfway point and at the end of the training program.

Wajnryb concluded that the trainers "found it quite difficult, especially early in the course, to point out weaknesses and shortcomings without resorting to redressive verbal strategies to protect the trainee's face" (1995b:56). The author posits that as the trainers got to know the trainees, they learned how direct they could be with each individual, and they subsequently altered their language in the post-observation conferences. Although the helping role predominated at the beginning of the course, "the evaluative side of the trainer's role-set" (ibid.) gained prominence as time went on and the supervisor's account behavior decreased.

Supervisors' nonverbal behavior during post-observation conferences

In any spoken communication involving visual contact with one's interlocutor, the nonverbal behavior of the participants conveys meaning. Supervisory discourse in post-observation conferences is no exception.

Chamberlin investigated teachers' reactions to supervisors' nonverbal behavior. In the study, 266 participants from 22 TESL programs rated the behavior of four actors portraying supervisors in "simulated teacher-supervisor conferences viewed on videotape" (2000:659). The teachers who rated the videotapes were all seeking advanced degrees at U.S. universities. They had a range of teaching experience: 28 percent had less than one year, 45 percent had one to five years, 12 percent had six to ten years, and 15 percent had more than ten years. Sixty percent of the respondents said that they had been supervised before.

In the videotapes, each actor was filmed from the teacher's viewpoint (i.e., the video camera faced the supervisor) in an office setting. The verbal script was the same for all four actors, but two of them delivered the script using nonverbal behaviors associated with a dominant role. These included "limited eye contact and facial expressions, indirect body orientation, and placement of a large desk between a teacher and supervisor" (ibid.:660–661). The other two actors used nonverbal behaviors associated with affiliation. These included "smiling, head nods, eye contact, direct body orientation, and close proximity of the participants" (ibid.:661).

Chamberlin wanted to know whether supervisors who used affiliation-related nonverbal behaviors were perceived as more trustworthy than those who displayed nonverbal behavior related to dominance. Her reason for studying supervisors' perceived trustworthiness in supervision was that if we do not trust our interlocutor, we will probably not be self-disclosive. Under circumstances of mistrust, teachers are unlikely to divulge concerns about their teaching, and discussions that could lead to development are not likely to occur.

To investigate this issue, Chamberlin used the Individualized Trust Scale (ITS; Wheeless and Grotz, 1977). She operationally defined *trust* as "a teacher's overall perceptions of honesty, safety, sincerity, and respect in a supervisor as measured by the ITS" (Chamberlin, 2000:657). The analysis showed that those supervisors displaying "nonverbal behaviors of affiliation received statistically significantly higher scores . . . than those displaying nonverbal behavior of dominance" (p. 662). Those who used affiliation-related nonverbal behaviors were seen as more trustworthy than those using dominance-related nonverbal behaviors.

The teachers also rated the supervisors' appropriateness and effectiveness. Chamberlin found strong, statistically significant correlations between the trustworthiness ratings and both the appropriateness and the effectiveness ratings. That is, the more trustworthy a supervisor seemed, the higher his or her ratings were on the appropriateness and effectiveness scales. Chamberlin's findings suggest that supervisors' nonverbal behavior influences the extent to which teachers find supervisors trustworthy.

Concluding comments

This chapter focused on post-observation conferences and on some strategies for coping with them. We saw that such meetings are usually examples of unequal power discourse (Hatch and Long, 1980), since supervisors have more power than teachers in most contexts. We reviewed some literature from general education and second language contexts about how supervisors should structure the discourse in the post-observation conference. We also noted, however, that the supervisor's role in these discussions is seldom easy.

The case at the beginning of this chapter portrayed a situation in which the supervisor must either deliver some critical feedback or lead the teacher to serious self-evaluation. The following activities are meant to help you apply the concepts covered in this chapter to that case and to situations you may face.

Case discussion

1. Is it appropriate for you as the supervisor to take any action *during* the French II lesson you are observing? If so, what action would you take?
2. What would you say to this teacher immediately after the lesson, assuming that you have already set an appointment for a conference? As you leave the room and confirm the date and time of the conference, would you ask her to think about any issues? Would you give her any feedback? Or would you refrain from commenting at that time?
3. Which of Freeman's (1989a) constituents of teaching are you dealing with here – awareness, attitude, knowledge, or skills? What are the implications for how you will proceed with the post-observation conference?
4. How would you begin the post-observation conference with the teacher? (Assume that you have both scheduled 30 minutes for the discussion.)

5. What specific issues will you address in the conference with the teacher? If you could get her to change (or begin changing) just one or two things, what would they be?
6. How do the concepts of autonomy and authority apply to observing the French II class and to the post-observation conferences with the teacher?
7. If this teacher does choose to change, what are three specific things you could do to help her?
8. You decide to observe this teacher's class at least once again this term (and possibly more often). On what will you focus, and how will you collect data?
9. What is appropriate for you to do in terms of responding to the parent who complained? If you feel you should not communicate with the parent, explain why. If you feel you should, how would you do so (by phone, face-to-face, by letter), and what would you say?
10. What is the students' role in this situation? Do you have a responsibility to interact with the students in some way? If so, what is the best course of action for you to take?

Tasks and discussion

1. Think of times when you received supervisorial or peer feedback on your teaching. What sorts of knowledge of results did you gain that you would not have had otherwise?
2. With a colleague, role-play a post-observation conference in which the supervisor and the language teacher hold radically different views on the value of a teaching or learning activity (e.g., the treatment of oral errors, reading aloud, pair work, etc.). Tape-record the role play.
3. Review Wajnryb's (1994a) list of seven concerns of language teacher supervisors in feedback conferences. Think of an example of each from your own experience, either as a supervisor or as a teacher in a feedback conference. Which of these seven concerns were you aware of at the time?
4. Think of a time when you have been teaching a language lesson or tutoring someone. What observable indications have you had that learning was actually occurring? List three to five ways a teacher (and a supervisor) can know that language learning is happening.
5. Think of a conference in which you participated as a teacher or supervisor. Could that discussion be characterized as unequal power discourse? List the variables (e.g., training, seniority, experience, etc.) that influenced the equality or inequality of that discourse event.

6. As a language teacher supervisor, how can you know for sure, during or after a post-observation conference, that a teacher will indeed change a less-than-effective behavior that the two of you discussed? List three types of information you would find convincing.

7. How do supervisors show respect for teachers, and vice versa? What are the signs of disrespect? Think of an example for each of these four situations: teachers showing respect for a supervisor, a supervisor showing respect for teachers, teachers showing disrespect for a supervisor, and a supervisor showing disrespect for teachers. Share your list with your colleagues and compile a list of do's and don'ts for supervisors.

8. Look back at Wallace and Woolger's (1991) suggestions for the sequence of a post-observation conference. If you have a recording of an actual conference, see how closely the phases of that conference paralleled their recommendations. As an alternative, you could analyze the role play of the post-observation conference from Task 2 or enact a real conference in which you try to use their suggestions.

9. View a videotape of a post-observation conference with Chamberlin's categories and findings in mind. Or try to observe a real conference or even a role play. Identify the supervisor's nonverbal behaviors that might indicate dominance or affiliation to the teacher.

Suggestions for further reading

For work on the post-observation conference in general education, see Holland (1989a), Shrigley and Walker (1981), Waite (1992a, 1992b, 1993, and 1995), Zahorik (1988), and Zeichner and Liston (1985).

Wallace and Woolger describe a workshop for language teacher supervisors designed to improve "the ELT supervisory dialogue" (1991:320). It has several quotes from the participants. Wallace's (1991) book has a chapter on supervision.

8 Mitigation and the microanalysis of supervisory discourse

In microanalyses of post-observation conferences, the researcher analyzes detailed transcripts of conference exchanges between teachers and supervisors. Research in which data are examined closely (Wajnryb, 1994a:86) reveals patterns in supervisory discourse. This approach has been taken in both general education and second language contexts and has yielded several important findings for language teacher supervisors.

One consistent pattern, noted in Chapter 7, is the use of mitigation devices to soften criticism. The current chapter summarizes some research about how supervisors use mitigation devices in post-observation conferences. We will begin with a case that involves trying to raise an issue in a post-observation conference.

Case for analysis: A tricky post-observation conference

You are taking a seminar to help supervisors improve their conferencing skills. Each participant observes language lessons and holds post-observation conferences with the teachers. The conferences are videotaped so the seminar participants may analyze their performances.

A classmate named Lee asks you to view a videotaped conference that was difficult to conduct. The teacher and Lee are seated on opposite sides of a desk. Lee has several pages of notes. The teacher sits with a relaxed posture, legs crossed, hands resting quietly. (Lee tells you the teacher is experienced, but the program's two-week orientation session is the only formal training this teacher has had.) In the following transcript, S stands for the supervisor (Lee) and T represents the teacher. Nonverbal behaviors are given in brackets.

S: Thank you for coming. I really enjoyed watching your lesson. It seemed, uhm, is this—uhm, how long have you been teaching adult students?

T: Oh, several years now.

S: Several years. OK. Uhm, what were the goals of this particular lesson? I mean, uh, what specifically did you want to accomplish? Or maybe it would be better to say, what did you want the students to, ah, accomplish during the lesson?

T: [2-second pause] The students?

S: Well, yes, I mean, uh, what did you want them to know or be able to do at the end of the lesson, that, uhm, that they didn't know or maybe they couldn't do before?

T: Well, I just wanted to cover Chapter 6.

S: Yes, well, what I mean is, what did you want them to, ah, get from this chapter? I mean what exactly was the point of covering Chapter 6? Uhm, or perhaps I should say the purpose. What were your goals for the students?

T: Do you mind if I close that curtain? The sun is shining right in my eyes. [Walks behind desk and closes curtain. Returns to seat and sits down.]

S: Oh, sure, of course, no problem [as the teacher is walking].

T: ⌈What did you ask—   ⌉ [Their turns overlap. They both

S: ⌊What I was wondering was— ⌋ stop speaking.]

T: You go ahead.

S: Well, what I was wondering, I mean, Chapter 6 was on the syl– was scheduled as the lesson, but wh–what did you hope they would learn from it?

T: Well, Chapter 6 is the past tense.

S: Yes, right. I understand, but, I mean, what did you want them to learn?

T: The past tense.

S: [3-second pause] Yes, but what about it? How it's formed? Regular verbs? Irregular verbs? How it's pronounced? Or maybe how it contrasts with other verb forms?

T: Yes.

S: Yes—what? [Leans forward in chair, hands clasped on desk.]

T: All of those things. The past tense. My goal was to cover Chapter 6.

S: Oh, OK. Uhm—OK. [Exhales audibly.] So you didn't have specific, ah, learning objectives that you wanted the students to, to master?

T: Well, yes, the past tense. [Shifts in chair, uncrosses and recrosses legs.]

S: [Leans back in chair.] OK, let's go over my notes about your class, OK?

T: OK.

S: OK. I've written here—[straightens papers, begins to read from notes] uh, the class begins at ten o'clock. Twelve students are seated near the front of the room. The desks are arranged in six neat rows of six chairs. The teacher stands, turning the pages of the book. Three students enter the room and sit down quietly. Several students have their workbooks open and three are comparing what they have written.

At 10:08, the teacher says, "All right. Are you ready? Open your workbooks to Chapter 6. Today your homework was, uh, Chapter 6. We'll start with Exercise 1. Turn to page 128 please." (The teacher writes p. 128 on the blackboard.) "OK, everyone? Please start." (The teacher nods at the first student in the first row.) The student says, "Me?" The teacher says, "Yes. Number 1, please."

The students read their answers aloud. Each student along the row takes a turn in sequence. The task is to underline the one verb out of four verbs that appears in the past tense. Each student reads a single word aloud. The teacher says "yes" or "right" or "good" if the choice is correct, and "no" or "not quite" or "try again" if the choice is incorrect. At the end of Exercise 1 the teacher looks at the book, turns some pages, looks up at the students and asks, "Any questions?" No students speak.

The teacher glances around and then says, "OK, turn to page 135. Lets do Exercise 2. Who's next, please?" One student nudges another, who says, "Me?" The teacher says, "Yes, please," and the student reads his answer aloud. The turns proceed sequentially along the rows. The exercise involves changing present tense verbs to the past tense. Again the teacher indicates whether answers are right or wrong. [Lee stops reading from the field notes.]

S: What do you think of this record?

T: What do you mean?

S: Well, let's start with whether it's, I mean, do you think the, the record is accurate?

T: Yes.

S: Yes. You do. OK, uhm, well what do you think about the lesson, uhm, the record of the lesson up to this point? [Voices are heard in the hallway. Somewhere a door slams.]

T: Can I close the door? [The teacher stands and closes the door.] The noise is distracting.

S: No problem. [The teacher sits down, leans back, legs crossed, hands relaxed.]

T: [Silence.]

S: So what do you think about the record of the lesson up to this point?

T: Oh, it's fine.

S: OK. Well, what I'm try—really trying to get at here is your evaluation of the lesson. How do you think the lesson was going up to this point?

T: Fine.

162

S: Right. Let's see. [3-second pause, as Lee glances at the notes] Well, what exactly did you think, uhm, what were, say, three things you thought were good about the lesson?

T: [2-second pause] Well, all the students got turns to speak.

S: Yes.

T: [3-second pause] And the students were quiet. I mean, they weren't unruly.

S: Yes.

T: And it was organized. That's three things.

S: Yes. Uhm, what do you mean exactly when you say it was organized?

T: Well, I worked through Chapter 6 systematically, one exercise at a time. And I gave every student feedback. And after each exercise I let the students ask questions.

S: Yes, these are all good points. Uhm, I, uh, I notice that you stick to the book. Uhm, as I look at my notes here, I don't see any references to any other materials. [3-second pause] Uhm, do you ever bring in any photographs, or songs, or any kind of authentic materials?

T: What do you mean by "authentic materials"?

S: Oh, well, I mean nonpedagogic materials. Language that was, uh, generated for purposes other than language teaching. Things like newspaper or magazine articles, movies, radio programs, video-tapes of television programs, or even, uh, tape-recorded conversations.

T: Oh.

S: So have you tried using any authentic materials?

T: No.

S: OK, well, uhm, why do you only use the book—the, the workbook?

T: Well, it's the required book for this level.

S: Yes, but why do you use *only* the workbook? Why don't you supplement it at all?

T: Oh, I don't know. [Glances down and then up.] The students like the book, and it's well laid out. It's clear. They're not very high-level students so they need the book. They kind of, you know, rely on it. They know what's expected of them.

S: Uh-huh. [Nodding and maintaining eye contact.]

T: And, uh, we're supposed to do this whole workbook. And, uhm, I'm supposed to finish all the lessons this term. So we do one chapter every week and that will leave a little time for review, before the students take their exams, so they will be prepared.

S: Yes, I see. I just don't know, I mean, of course you do have to help them prepare for the exams and all, but, well, I'm just—uh—and, I can sympathize with you, be—because I've been in your shoes before, but I just, I couldn't help but but feel that perhaps the lesson, I mean the exercises in the book, maybe they were a bit dry.

T: Dry?

S: Yes, you know, uhm, just working the exercises in the book the whole time.

T: [3-second pause] Well, the students like it. They can get the exercises right, at least sometimes. Without the structure of the exercises they can barely say a word!

S: Well, I suppose you can't make a silk purse out of a sow's ear. I just was wondering if, uhm, if the students ever got a chance to, well, to ah use the past tense, maybe to express their own ideas—or even to talk to each other about their own lives.

T: Oh, they're not advanced enough for that. They have to learn the grammar first.

S: Ah. [Leans back in chair, lips pursed, looking at the remaining pages of notes.]

At this point, Lee stops the videotape and asks you, "Well, what do you think?"

Face-threatening acts in the feedback conference

Criticism involves delivering a face-threatening act (FTA). *Face* is defined as "the public, socially-valued image of self which participants in an encounter claim for themselves and each other" (Wajnryb, 1994a, glossary, p. i). A face-threatening act is "a communicative act which runs contrary to the face needs of speaker or hearer" (ibid.). Beebe and Takahashi (1989:200) say expressions of disapproval are one face-threatening act: "In performing face-threatening acts ... speakers must integrate personal and societal values with linguistic competence and, most importantly, gain some knowledge of 'face-work' (Goffman, 1976)." Brown and Levinson (1987) examined FTAs in their work on politeness strategies. Figure 8.1 provides their categories of strategies for carrying out FTAs. The numbers in Figure 8.1 indicate a hierarchy of politeness. Refraining from doing the FTA (5) is the most polite course of action, whereas doing the FTA on-record, baldly and without redressive action, is the least polite (1).

If a supervisor wants to tell a teacher about a problem, the first issue is whether to engage in an FTA. Having decided to proceed, the next choice is whether to be "on-record" (very direct and explicit) or "off-record" (hinting, indirectly suggesting, or implying). An on-record statement is unambiguous: It has only one acceptable

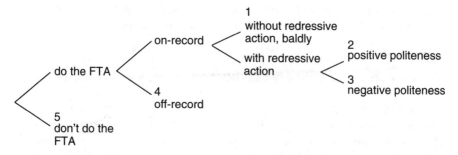

Figure 8.1 Possible strategies for doing face-threatening acts (Brown and Levinson, 1987:69)

interpretation. Off-record strategies "are generally more polite than on-record" (ibid.:20), and "off-record strategies are a solution halfway between doing the FTA on-record and not doing it at all" (ibid.).

Having decided to go on-record, the supervisor's next decision is whether to offer the criticism "without redressive action, baldly," or "with redressive action" (ibid.). On-record FTAs are more efficient than potentially ambiguous off-record FTAs, but on-record FTAs are problematic because they can be offensive to the hearer (the teacher). In fact, an on-record FTA that is delivered without redressive action means doing the FTA "in the most direct, clear, concise way possible" (ibid.:69). The social circumstances in which one can be so direct are limited, however. The alternative is to go on-record but "with redressive action" (see Figure 8.1). This option "attempts to counteract the potential face damage of the FTA by doing it in such a way, or with such modifications or additions, that indicate clearly that no such face threat is intended or desired" (ibid.:69–70). Many supervisors use on-record FTAs with redressive action to support teachers in conferences and sustain positive working relationships.

After choosing an on-record FTA with redressive action, the supervisor is faced with issues of positive and negative politeness. *Positive politeness* is aimed at the "positive self-image that the [hearer] claims for himself" (ibid.:70). The speaker (the supervisor) indicates to the hearer (the teacher) that they have some wants in common (by treating the hearer as someone who is liked). In this situation the supervisor seems to convey to the teacher that the FTA doesn't suggest a general negative evaluation of the teacher's face (ibid.). *Negative politeness* is aimed at partially satisfying or redressing the hearer's "basic want to maintain claims of territory and self-determination" (ibid.). It is "characterized by self-effacement, formality and restraint" (ibid.) on the part of the speaker, who uses apologies, deference, and "other softening mechanisms that give the addressee an 'out,' a face-saving line of escape" (ibid.).

Mitigation in supervisory discourse

Mitigation refers to the "linguistic means by which a speaker deliberately hedges what he / she is saying by taking into account the reactions of the hearer" (Wajnryb, 1995a:71). Wajnryb describes three major types of mitigation in supervisory discourse: (1) *hypermitigation*, meaning there is so much mitigation the message is overly softened, often at the expense of clarity; (2) *hypomitigation*, meaning there is too little mitigation and the message is so direct as to be blunt; and (3) *above-the-utterance-level mitigation*, meaning the softened criticism is accomplished at the discourse level.

Wajnryb video-recorded actors delivering three versions (hypermitigated, hypomitigated, and mitigated above-the-utterance-level) of the same supervisory message, based on an actual post-observation conference. Questionnaire responses about the videotaped conference were elicited from 231 preservice and in-service teachers in Australia, Israel, and the United States.

Hypermitigation in supervisory feedback

The following text is Script A from Wajnryb's research (1994a, Appendix 33; see also 1995a:76). Script A represents a supervisor's comments in a post-observation conference:

> I think that, um, I think that, I've mentioned here in my notes that um, it's just a little thing really. It seems to me you were sort of tending to explain things, rather than concept check things. Now you do explain very well. You're very good at explaining and I think people ah get it, so they get the idea which is fine, so this is only a little point. The thing is um that for those who don't get it, if they miss the explanation for whatever reason, and there hasn't been a concept check, then they can get left behind, can't they? And I think that can be a little bit of a problem, because, I think, and I'm pretty sure you'd agree, that it's important at a low level, which this class is at, ah, I think it's important that learning is always, well, it's two things really, ah, it's important that learning is presented through concept questions, so it sort of narrows down the possibilities, and so they can't help but understand. And also that the learning is then checked, with a comprehension a concept checking question ah to make sure that they've

sort of got it, um, and you do, you you do that but I don't think it's early enough um I feel perhaps you could do it maybe just a little earlier in the piece.

Here the supervisor is "attending to the face of the supervisee / teacher" (1995a:74). The supervisor "undercuts his own authority, seeks to reduce the impositive nature of what he is saying, dilutes the gravity of the message, redresses his criticism with hedges and undercuts the rhetorical force of his assertion" (ibid.). This pattern is common in supervisors' speech.

Hypomitigation in supervisory feedback

In this version, the propositional content is the same, but the supervisor's delivery of Script B is different (Wajnryb, 1994a, Appendix 33; 1995a:76):

> You tend to explain, rather than concept check things. Now I must admit that you do explain quite well, and so most of the students do grasp the idea. The difficulty is for those who miss the explanation. If you don't follow up with a comprehension check, or use concept questions through the explanations, then students can get left behind. So, with a low-level class like this one, you should do two things. Firstly, you should present learning, through concept questions to narrow down the possibilities, so they will definitely understand. And secondly, you should use a concept-checking question to check that learning has happened, to make sure that they have understood it. Now you do use concept checks, but you use them too late in the lesson.

This message is shorter and more direct than Script A. In Script B, "the supervisor is up-front, blunt and totally frank. He uses bald unredressed language, . . . avoids gift-packaging his language and delivers his message with attention to the transaction (the transmission of information) rather than to the interaction (the 'face' of the interlocutor)" (ibid.: 74). The danger is that while the message is clear, it may not be received by teachers at all. If feedback is so direct that it puts teachers on the defensive, they may not absorb the information. If threatened, teachers may take the passive or adversarial roles described by Waite (1993).

The challenge for the supervisor is to deliver negative feedback (or to elicit self-assessment from the teacher) in such a way that the message is neither so obscure as to be uninterpretable, nor so pointed as to be harmful. Achieving that balance is difficult but not impossible. However, it does require supervisors to be very aware of how they communicate with teachers, especially in the post-observation conference.

Above-the-utterance-level mitigation

The third alternative, between the extremes of hypermitigation and hypomitigation, is what Wajnryb (1994a) calls "above-the-utterance-level mitigation." This option, illustrated in Script C, occurs at the discourse level:

> I think that I think that um I've mentioned in my notes here that um you tend to explain rather than concept check things [mm] now I also said you tend to explain in brackets which you do quite well you're very good at explaining and so I think people get it they get the idea which is fine but um for those who don't get it if they've missed the explanation [mm] and there hasn't been the comprehension check [mm] or during the explanation if there hasn't been the concept check then they can get left behind [mm] and I think that if I think it's important at a low level at which this class is I think it's important that learning is always well it's two things really it's learning is presented through concept questions so that it sort of narrows down the possibilities so they can't help but understand [mm] and also that the learning is then checked with a concept checking questions um to make sure that they've got it um and you do you do that but perhaps I feel you could do it a little bit earlier in the piece. (ibid.)

Here mitigation is accomplished through more direct means than in the hypermitigated speech of Script A. In this case the softening occurs at the discourse level – hence the label "above-the-utterance-level mitigation." The language is almost the same as in Script B, but prior to delivering the criticism, the supervisor "seeks to prepare the teacher for the forthcoming criticism by ... building on her strengths, affirming the positive side of her teaching, engaging in interaction, and setting a tone of trust and professionalism" (Wajnryb, 1995a:74).

An analogy will help clarify the concept of above-the-utterance-level mitigation. Many years ago, Vigil and Oller (1976) noted that language learners get two kinds of feedback while interacting with target language speakers. *Cognitive feedback* provides information about their target language use. *Affective feedback* consists of the interlocutors' emotional responses to the learners' speech. Affective feedback indicates the interlocutors' interest and willingness to continue conversation, while cognitive feedback indicates whether the learners' output is unintelligible, slightly flawed, and so on. The concepts of affective and cognitive feedback are useful in analyzing the messages supervisors send to teachers. Once again, we can picture two overlapping continua, representing these two types of feedback, as shown in Figure 8.2.

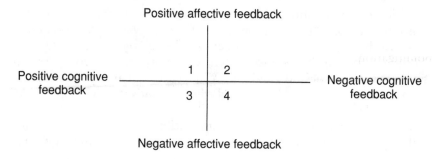

Figure 8.2 *Possible combinations of cognitive and affective feedback*

Cognitive supervisory feedback is information about the teacher's teaching. Positive affective feedback conveys the idea that the supervisor is interested in and values the teacher. Negative affective feedback sends a dismissive or belittling message. The concept of above-the-utterance-level mitigation is related to Quadrant 2 in Figure 8.2. The supervisor's affective message is positive (conveying an attitude of interest and support), even if the cognitive message is critical (negative). This dual message is delivered through speech and nonverbal behavior.

Types of utterance-level mitigation

Wajnryb notes that the actual linguistic markers of mitigation take many forms in the discourse of post-observation conferences. These linguistic signals include

> distancing effects, such as using the past tense ('I *thought* the lesson was quite good'), or through minimisers ('*one little* thing I thought I might *just mention*'). A supervisor can mitigate his / her appearance of certainty through a first-person preambling statement (for example, '*I feel* that') and can take the sting out of a criticism by a pre-emptive warning ('I *hope this isn't going to upset you, but...*'). Another mitigating mechanism is to opt for the third person rather than the confrontational second person ('*the lesson* began', instead of '*you* started the lesson'). Also, questions used in place of statements ('*have you considered...?*') tend to take the harsh edge off criticisms. (1995a:71)

There are "many degrees of indirectness by which a supervisor can render communication imprecise and hence mitigated" (ibid.). The prevalence of mitigating devices stems from supervisors' natural reluctance to criticize: "[M]itigation is a natural, pervasive, functional and largely subconscious feature of supervisors' language, which yields itself to certain configurations and clusters, especially at the pivotal point of giving negative criticism" (ibid.:73). Wajnryb adds that "while mitigation is natural and indeed 'authentic' and while its motivation is 'respectable,' it nonetheless could be problematic" (ibid.).

Both hypermitigation and hypomitigation can lead to problems, although the results of these two forms of mitigation differ. Evidence suggests

> that supervisors who mitigate their language too greatly (by 'beating about the bush') are likely to confuse the hearers through an unclear, ambiguous message. On the other hand, supervisors who under-mitigate . . . could alienate the teacher and create unnecessary and counter-productive enmity. (ibid.)

Thus the balancing act for teacher supervisors becomes one of delivering criticism gently enough that teachers can listen to it but clearly enough that they can hear it.

Wajnryb's research shows that supervisors achieve mitigation in post-observation conferences through a variety of verbal and vocal mechanisms. The main types of mitigating strategies are syntactic, semantic, and indirect, as shown in Figure 8.3.

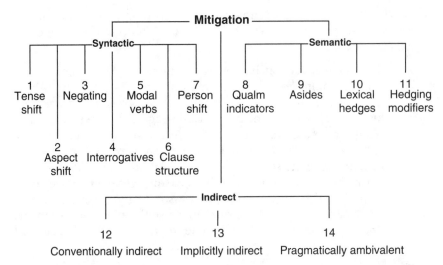

Figure 8.3 A typology of utterance-level mitigation in supervisory discourse (adapted from Wajnryb, 1994a:230)

In conferences, these mitigating devices appear in multiple, fluid combinations. We will examine each in turn, starting with syntactic mitigation.

Syntactic mitigation devices

Wajnryb breaks down the syntactic means of mitigation (see Figure 8.3) into subcategories. These are summarized in Figure 8.4.

Shifts in tense and aspect

Shifts in tense and aspect often occur in supervisory discourse. For example, instead of saying "I'm worried about your classroom management," a supervisor might say, "I was worried about your classroom management." The use of past tense seems to separate the participants temporally from the teaching event. Supervisors also sometimes shift to present tense when discussing an event that occurred in the past. Shifts from the past to the present suggest "collegiality, symmetry, and a seeking of harmony" (Wajnryb, 1994a:236).

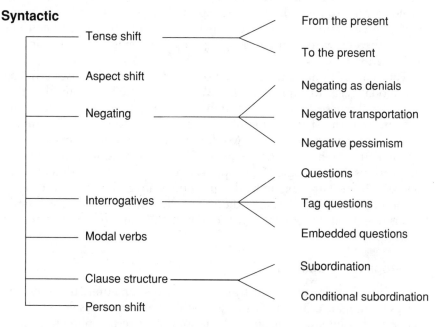

Figure 8.4 Types of syntactic mitigation (adapted from Wajnryb, 1994a:234)

Shifts in aspect "make the action more vague, less precise, less able to be pin-pointed and located in time" (ibid.:237) – so the durative [continuative] seems to soften the criticism by making it less absolute. For example, instead of saying, "The instructions confused your students," the supervisor might say, "The instructions were confusing your students."

Negating devices

Negating, another syntactic mitigation strategy, takes three forms (see Figure 8.4): (1) as denials, (2) as transportation, and (3) as pessimism. In discussing negating as *denial*, Wajnryb suggests that the utterance "It wasn't always consistent" has the underlying expectation that something should be consistent (ibid.:241). Leech says the quality of understatement in such an utterance permits a positive interpretation by disguising the negative message (1983:148).

Negative transportation (also called *neg-raising* and *negative left-shifting*) often appears in supervisory discourse. This is the tendency "to attract to the main verb a negative which should logically belong to the dependent nexus" (Jesperson, 1917:53, as cited in Wajnryb, 1994a:242). Instead of saying, "I think you weren't sure of yourself during the grammar explanation," a supervisor might say, "I don't think you were sure of yourself during the grammar explanation." The threatening power of direct criticism is reduced in transported negatives (ibid.). The pragmatic force of the transported negative is "to implicate rather than assert, thereby weakening or hedging the claim being made" (Wajnryb, 1994a:243).

The syntactic mitigation strategy of *negative pessimism* uses adverbs and modal verbs to express doubt. Wajnryb (1994a:244) notes that this type of politeness "has a deliberately awkward, convoluted nature" to indicate that the speaker doesn't wish to impose too much. Examples include utterances such as "I wouldn't use that sequence myself" (as opposed to "Don't use that sequence") and "Why don't you put the instructions on the board?" (as opposed to "Put the instructions on the board"). In the latter example, the question is not really asking for information (the reason the teacher didn't put the instructions on the board) but is a suggestion, couched in the indirect *Wh*-question ("Why don't you...?").

Interrogative structures

As the preceding example illustrates, supervisors sometimes use interrogatives to mitigate criticism. Using question forms introduces doubt about the speaker's intended meaning. A question "converts a potential statement of criticism into an apparent inquiry" (ibid.:246). So as an alternative to a direct comment about a lesson's organization, a supervisor might ask a teacher, "How did you feel about the organization of your lesson?"

Tag questions are powerful mitigating devices. In English, tag questions take two primary forms. The first is the syntactic tag, which uses the copula verb and the subject of the sentence, as in "You were a bit rushed at the end of the lesson, weren't you?" This tag softens the actual content of the comment "by seeking cooperation rather than obedience" (ibid.:247). The second form, invariant tags, uses a lexical tag, such as "OK?" or "huh?" or "right?" appended to a statement with rising intonation. Instead of saying, "You were a bit rushed at the end of the lesson," a supervisor might say, "You were a bit rushed at the end of the lesson, huh?" The lexical tag softens the directive by inviting agreement: "It'd be good to cue up the audiotape, right?" This structure softens a clear directive: "Next time, cue up the audiotape before class."

In Wajnryb's final type of interrogative mitigation, embedded questions, interrogative structures are embedded in another statement, such as "I was wondering why you used that particular exercise." Such utterances put the core message of the question ("Why did you use that particular exercise?") in the larger sentence. This process implies the speaker's doubt or curiosity, since the already-mitigated question form is further distanced through embedding.

Modal verbs and clause structure

Modal verbs such as *might* and *may* can soften directives. Contrast the following statements: "Try giving the instructions in writing as well as orally" versus "You might try giving the instructions in writing as well as orally."

Clause structures can also soften a directive through subordination or conditional subordination. Subordination often involves embedding the core proposition into an utterance that begins with "I think / thought" or "I feel / felt," or "I notice(d)" as in "I noticed that you seemed a bit rushed at the end." The first-person subject and the verb of perception (such as *think*, *feel*, or *notice*) introduce subjectivity into the speaker's assertion, giving the hearer room to express an opinion or disagree. This strategy provides an "offer of negotiability to the hearer" (Wajnryb, 1994a:256). The face-threatening act (e.g., "you seemed rushed") is placed in the embedded clause and thus is distanced.

Conditional subordinate clauses are introduced by *if*. Consider the following:

1-A. "Cue up the audiotape before you come to class."
1-B. "If you cue up the audiotape before you come to class, it will go more smoothly."

2-A. "Write the instructions on the board instead of just saying them."
2-B. "If you write the instructions on the board instead of just saying them, the students will do better on the task."

The use of *if*-clauses and the presence of the subsequent rationale (in 1-B and 2-B above) turn blunt directives into more indirect suggestions.

Person shift

Finally, syntactic mitigation is accomplished by "person shift" (Wajnryb, 1994a:259), which is realized by substituting an impersonalized form for *you* (representing the listener), as in "There was quite a bit of confusion among the students." (The use of *there was* depersonalizes the event.) And the utterance "It's important to finish one task before moving on to the next" is a mitigated version of "You should finish one task before moving on to the next." Using *it's* depersonalizes and softens the criticism.

Supervisors tend to use first-person instead of second-person subjects, frequently in the middle of a sentence. Wajnryb found utterances such as "Were you perhaps hoping in the middle of it, I wish this were a bit shorter?" (ibid.). This sentence contrasts with the alternative, "Were you perhaps hoping in the middle of it that it was a bit shorter?" The insertion of *I wish* suggests that the supervisor can relate to what the teacher was thinking during the lesson.

Semantic mitigation devices

Semantic devices are also used to mitigate direct utterances. Wajnryb found four main semantic mitigation strategies in her data: (1) qualm indicators, (2) asides, or shifts in footing, (3) lexical hedges, and (4) hedging modifiers, as depicted in Figure 8.5.

Qualm indicators

Qualm indicators are "a mixed bag of acoustic and linguistic signals" (Wajnryb, 1994a:266) that include such insertions as *uh*, *er*, *uhm*, *well*, and *you know*. They have sometimes been called *dysfluency markers* (Hatch, 1992). Other qualm indicators are hesitation markers (both silent and filled pauses), reformulations, and false starts. All of these qualm indicators tell the listener that the speaker is somewhat hesitant – even uneasy (Wajnryb, 1994a:267). Because they make the speaker sound somewhat diffident, these qualm indicators "make the forthcoming assertion more tentative and equivocal" (ibid.).

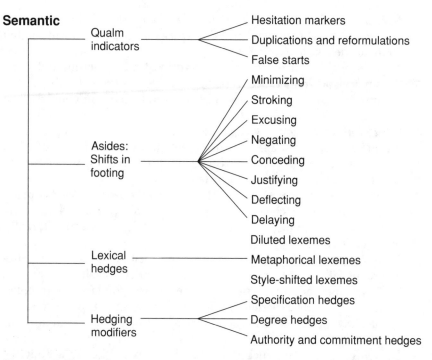

Figure 8.5 Types of semantic mitigation (adapted from Wajnryb, 1994a:267)

Asides: "Shifts in footing"

The second main category, *asides*, is a metaphor from drama, where it refers to an onstage action by an actor who turns aside briefly to share information with the audience but not with his fellow characters. In linguistics, an aside allows the speaker to shift footing and momentarily depart from his or her core message to add another concept. The aside often embodies a different point of view from the very point the speaker is making.

Wajnryb discusses the eight types of asides presented in Figure 8.5 in detail, but here I will just give brief definitions and illustrations:

1. *Minimizing asides* "minimize the harshness" of the criticism (Wajnryb, 1994a:277). Examples: "The only problem I saw was..." or "You might disagree, but I think..."
2. *Stroking asides* provide praise that counteracts "the sting of the face-threatening act and shore[s] up the positive feelings" (ibid.:278) of the teacher. Example: "During the dialogue, and it was a great dialogue, I felt that..."

3. *Excusing asides* make allowances for whatever is being criticized. Example: "Maybe the activity didn't work because the students hadn't all done their homework."
4. *Negating asides* "deny the critical nature of the criticism, and show the supervisor's reluctance to being perceived as critical" (ibid.:280). Examples: "Don't get me wrong, I just think that you could..." or "It's no big deal really, but I think..."
5. *Conceding asides* acknowledge the teacher's efforts, even if the results weren't entirely satisfactory. Examples: "I know you put a lot of effort into your quiz, but..." or "Your drilling techniques, which you've clearly practiced, need to be a little more fluid."
6. *Justifying asides* make excuses for the supervisor's own behavior, rather than the teacher's. Examples: "I think you could go more quickly, as you yourself said" or "You shouldn't worry about it, really, but I want you to try..."
7. *Deflecting asides* momentarily shift "the focus from hearer to elsewhere, usually to the speaker" (ibid.). This effect is achieved through self-disclosure or other attempts to establish solidarity. Examples: "You know, in my experience, this is a tough grammar point to teach, so I usually..." or "Once when I was teaching modals, I ran into this problem..."
8. *Delaying asides* announce that a criticism is forthcoming, but the supervisor "is loath to get to the point" (ibid.:283). This function is served by compliments, hesitations, and vocalized fillers. Examples: "I thought it was really great that you got all the students involved, but I just wondered..." or "I see that, uhm, you've been improving your error treatment techniques, and, uhm, I noticed that..."

Some asides appear in combination with one another and with other types of mitigation. Although they are used by supervisors to soften criticism, they can also obscure the message.

Lexical hedges

Lexical hedges include three subdivisions: diluted lexemes, metaphorical lexemes, and style-shifted lexemes. In these cases, word choice is used to mitigate the directness of criticism.

A *diluted lexeme* is a word "chosen over its less marked equivalent for its softened or attenuated meaning" (ibid.:284). In the following sentence, the more direct lexeme that was not selected is given in brackets: "It's very important to let [make] people realize that one thing is finished and the next one is starting" (ibid.).

Metaphorical lexemes signal "an appeal to intimacy, establishing solidarity through the presumption of shared ground" (ibid.). So for example, when a supervisor says that "people can't sort of slip through the net" (ibid.), both the supervisor and the teacher understand that the metaphor of slipping through a net represents going unnoticed or being ignored by the teacher.

Finally, *style-shifted lexemes* use colloquial language to "reduce distance, increase solidarity and level out the asymmetry" (ibid.:288) in post-observation conferences. Examples include utterances such as "the timing was a bit out" (instead of "the timing was a bit wrong"). Such register shifts indicate that the discussion is informal and therefore perhaps not serious.

Hedging modifiers

Hedging modifiers consist of words or phrases that minimize the message's impact. Examples are *just, sort of, maybe, a bit, somehow*, and *really*, as in "You don't really want to do that" or "I sort of thought the pace was just a bit fast." These devices commonly occur with one another as well as in combination with other mitigating devices.

In my experience training supervisors, these hedging modifiers are frequently accompanied by paralinguistic and nonverbal behaviors that further minimize the negative message. For example, the word *just* is often uttered at a relatively high pitch. Likewise *really* and *maybe* are often attenuated (the sounds are prolonged) and are accompanied by slight head-tilts, small shrugs, and raised eyebrows. Phrases such as *a little* and *a bit* seem to trigger hand gestures indicating small amounts or that a point is being downplayed. The message of these verbal, nonverbal, and paralinguistic features is that the issue is not particularly grave.

Indirect mitigation devices

The third component of Wajnryb's typology is indirect mitigation. These forms are either conventionally indirect, implicitly indirect, or pragmatically ambivalent. Indirect mitigation is a key concept, because, as Wajnryb explains (1994a:299):

> One of the main motivations for indirectness is politeness, which serves an important social role in lubricating interactions that might otherwise be abrasive.... In the context of supervision and specifically in the delivery of FTAs, indirectness furnishes supervisors with an important means of resolving the competing demands of their role – the need to save face vis-à-vis the transmission of bad news messages.

Thus the role of the language teacher supervisor necessarily entails "a tension that exists between the competing demands of clarity and politeness" (ibid.).

Conventionally indirect mitigation

The first indirect mitigation category is *conventionally indirect mitigation*, in which "the criticism is built into the surface level meaning of the utterance" (ibid.:304). This is the most direct of the indirect mitigation types. An example is the use of questions as requests. If the hearer correctly interprets the question "Can you please close the door?" the proper response will be closing the door, instead of saying, "Yes, I can." Wajnryb cites examples from her data such as "Can you think of a way you might have been able to address that?" and "Can you see how that led to a problem?" (ibid.:310).

Implicitly indirect mitigation

Implicitly indirect mitigation is less direct than the conventionally indirect type. Wajnryb says, "Here the inferential path that the hearer must traverse is utterance-specific" (ibid.:311). The teacher must infer the supervisor's meaning by "forcing an interaction between what is said and the context in which it is said" (ibid.:312). Occasionally proverbs (e.g., "This too shall pass" or "The proof is in the pudding") are used for this purpose.

Sometimes implicitly indirect mitigation involves a great deal of verbiage when a simpler comment would suffice. Wajnryb cites this example: "Do you think perhaps it might have been good if they had known a little bit about the context of the dialogue?" (ibid.:315). Here the supervisor uses a lengthy, convoluted utterance to convey and simultaneously soften the message, "Tell the students about the content of the dialogue." In using implicitly indirect mitigation, the message can get lost or softened out of existence.

Pragmatic ambivalence

The third form, *pragmatic ambivalence*, is the most indirect. Wajnryb states that "an utterance is ambivalent when the hearer cannot be certain of its intended force, as this force is not derivable from the sense and context" (1994a:317). In this category, the illocutionary force of the utterance is veiled, or perhaps even masked. For example, consider these data from Wajnryb's corpus: "Do you think the kids like the book?" or "You tend to use capitals a lot when you write." The teacher may interpret these comments as if their apparent meaning had been intended:

"Yes, the kids like the book." Or the teacher may wonder, "Is my supervisor suggesting that the children don't like the book, or that it's not appropriate for them, or that I should have chosen another?" Pragmatically ambivalent utterances can be interpreted as neutral observations, praise, criticism, or a combination of praise and criticism (ibid.:318).

Supervisory discourse contains many indirect mitigation strategies. Sometimes the speaker's meaning is conveyed through nonverbal behavior and / or suprasegmental phonemes. For instance, the question "Do you think the kids like the book?" can be a simple request for information, if said in one tone of voice and with a neutral or pleasant facial expression. In contrast, a supervisor may ask, "Do you think the kids like the book?" while stressing *you* and *kids* and giving strong primary stress to the word *like*, with a furrowed brow. Here the paraphrase of this version is closer to "Do you actually think those kids really like that ridiculous book?" This interpretation becomes more or less likely depending on the stress, pitch, and intonation contours, as well as the incredulity or disgust in the supervisor's facial expressions.

Concluding comments

This chapter has considered supervisors' mitigation devices, as well as their suprasegmental phonemes, voice quality, and nonverbal behavior. We examined face-threatening acts in the post-observation conference and saw that many "processes of supervision can happen subliminally" (Wajnryb, 1995a:73). We also studied hypermitigation, hypomitigation, and above-the-utterance-level mitigation (Wajnryb, 1994a) and reviewed the syntactic, semantic, and indirect mitigating devices in the speech of supervisors.

As usual, the chapter ends with activities to help you internalize these concepts. We will begin with the Case Discussion. Please reread the case at the beginning of the chapter and think about how you would respond to your friend Lee.

Case discussion

1. What is your impression of this conference up to the point where Lee stops the videotape? Would you characterize the session as successful? Why or why not?
2. What were Lee's main goals in this feedback session? What did Lee want the teacher to realize? Was Lee using a particular supervisorial role, or set of supervisorial skills?
3. Based on Waite's (1993) research reviewed in Chapter 7, was this teacher taking a collaborative, a passive, or an adversarial stance in

the discussion? Or did this teacher take a different stance from the three Waite identified? What evidence supports your conclusion?
4. Based on the videotape, does Lee use hypomitigation, hypermitigation, or above-the-utterance-level mitigation? Explain your answer.
5. Using Figure 8.1, trace Lee's apparent decision making regarding how to deliver the face-threatening action. How is the FTA eventually conveyed?
6. Which categories of syntactic mitigation in Figure 8.4 occur in these data? Tally the occurrences of each type of syntactic mitigation.
7. Identify the subcategories of semantic mitigation that occur in this excerpt.
8. Finally, tally the occurrences of the three types of indirect mitigation devices – the conventionally indirect, the implicitly indirect, and the pragmatically ambivalent utterances.
9. What advice can you give Lee, based on your analysis of the transcript? What sort of feedback might help Lee become a more effective language teacher supervisor? Rewrite the transcript so that it represents a more successful discussion.

Tasks and discussion

1. In a post-observation conference when you were being supervised, was your role passive, collaborative, or adversarial, in Waite's (1993) terms? Have you taken different stances in different conferences? What conditions cause teachers to be passive, collaborative, or adversarial during a post-observation conference? List three factors that might lead teachers to take each of these stances.
2. How could you, as the supervisor in a post-observation conference, tell if a teacher was being passive, collaborative, or adversarial? List three observable indications of each stance.
3. Does the teacher's stance depend in part on the supervisor's role? If we consider the directive, nondirective, and alternative approaches (Freeman, 1982), what teacher stance is each supervisorial approach likely to trigger?
4. Audio-record a post-observation conference and locate the mitigating devices that occur.
5. In this chapter look back at Scripts A, B, and C regarding hypermitigation, hypomitigation, and above-the-utterance-level mitigation. How do they compare? Which feedback style would you prefer as a teacher? Does your answer vary depending on the situation and your interlocutor?
6. Using each quadrant in Figure 8.2, role-play the delivery of the same feedback to a teacher in four different ways. How do these four approaches access the teacher's ZPD?

7. Listen to an interaction that involves a face-threatening act but that is not from a post-observation conference with a teacher. What mitigating devices occur in that context?

Suggestions for further reading

Wajnryb's dissertation (1994a) contains a glossary and a clear literature review. Her articles (see, e.g., Wajnryb, 1994b, 1995a, 1995b, and 1998) report on her doctoral research.

Hayashi and Hayashi (2002) analyzed the discourse of conferences with preservice secondary school teachers. Chamberlin's (2000) research on trust and supervisors' nonverbal behavior is also relevant to the issues discussed here.

9 Purposes, participants, and principles in language teacher evaluation

Evaluating teachers' work is in some regards the most fundamental and most difficult part of a teacher supervisor's responsibilities. Brazer (1991:82) has called teacher evaluation "a theater of the absurd." Popham (1988) says that it is "with few exceptions, an anemic and impotent enterprise – promising much but producing little" (p. 269). Nunan and Lamb (1996) say that for many teachers, supervision and evaluation

> are mandatory aspects of their terms of employment. Others are never evaluated (not in a formal sense at least). External evaluation, particularly when it is for purposes of certification or continued employment, can be extremely threatening [and may be] the most anxiety-creating situation the teacher is ever likely to face. (pp. 238–239)

Because of this extreme (but completely natural) sensitivity to evaluations, it is important that evaluations be conducted professionally and sensitively.

This chapter examines teacher evaluation and discusses the various sources of such evaluations. We begin with a case about two teachers and then examine the basic purposes of evaluation, in hopes of understanding the problems in the language teacher supervisor's role.

Case for analysis: Summative evaluation of two teachers

You are the assistant coordinator for a small intensive language program. For several years it has been staffed by one full-time administrator (the director), ten full-time teachers, and a part-time staff of eight to twelve teachers (depending on enrollment). Last year you were hired as a half-time teacher and half-time assistant coordinator. In the latter role, you observe classes, give teachers feedback, monitor the curriculum, and deal with students' complaints.

Because of declining enrollment (and revenues), some teachers' contracts will not be renewed next term. The administration has assured the faculty that this is purely a financial consideration, and that any teachers whose employment must be terminated will be given positive recommendations as they look for new work.

You have observed two part-time teachers whose contracts are about to expire – Maria and Anna. You have given them formative feedback after each of four observations (two observations per semester). The program director (who must eventually let one of the teachers go) has asked you to recommend which of these teachers should be retained and which should be let go. (The other teachers are in the middle of their ongoing contracts.) Here is a summary of your notes based on four observations of each teacher.

Teacher 1: Maria

Maria started working part-time in the program four years ago. She has an MA in the field plus a variety of part-time experience in the local area. She works especially well with lower-level classes and prefers not to teach at advanced levels. She devotes a considerable amount of time to the program's extracurricular activities.

Strengths: Maria is strong in communicative language teaching, materials development, and curriculum design. She served on the needs assessment team and developed the new language curriculum for tourists and short-term travelers. She has also taught the drama course and has directed the end-of-term skits performed by the students. She was the faculty adviser to the International Fair last term. (There were some organizational problems, but by and large the event was successful.) Last spring she attended the state teachers' conference, and she has implemented some ideas that she had gathered there in her own classes. Maria is well liked by the students. She has consistently received good to excellent ratings in student evaluations.

Areas of concern: Maria has not pushed herself professionally. She is known as a solid teacher rather than an inspirational leader. Her teaching materials are creative, but she prefers to work with levels and topics with which she is familiar, rather than branching out into new areas. She has declined to take on student teachers from the nearby university, although her teaching skills and subject matter expertise are certainly strong enough for her to be a good role model.

Teacher 2: Anna

Anna has taught part-time for two years. She has an MA plus three years of teaching experience. She works well with advanced academic classes. She helped revise the curriculum for and then teach the test preparation courses (with very good student evaluations).

Strengths: Anna's strengths include teaching public speaking in the target language, her work in the computer lab (e.g., the Web page design class she taught in the target language), and her leadership among the teachers. (She and two colleagues gave a presentation at the state conference about their team teaching. Anna got the project going.) She works well with new faculty members (having helped in the new teacher orientation program for two semesters), as well as novice teachers. She has supervised two student teachers.

Areas of concern: Anna may not be totally committed to working in this program. She has sometimes not participated in faculty meetings. Of course, she has had to teach in the evenings to make ends meet, but she also has talked about returning to graduate school for a PhD. Based on four observations, she needs to work on her classroom management skills (in her work with younger students). However, Anna was open to working on this problem.

Purposes of teacher evaluation

Two basic types of evaluation are discussed in the program evaluation literature. As the term suggests, *formative evaluation* is conducted to provide feedback to an ongoing project, to improve the program. *Summative evaluation*, on the other hand, is a final assessment, a make-or-break decision at the end of a project or funding period. Summative evaluation results often determine whether funding will be continued or whether a program will be maintained or canceled. According to Daresh (2001:283), summative evaluation "is the 'last chance,' the final point where an ultimate disposition regarding a person or thing is made."

Teacher evaluation is not straightforward. Popham (1988) has referred to the "dysfunctional marriage of formative and summative teacher evaluation" (p. 269). If a teacher's contract renewal depends on a supervisor's judgment, summative evaluation is involved. However, much of the evaluative work supervisors do is formative in nature. Formative evaluation is used "to gain intermittent feedback concerning the nature of some activity or practice while it is in progress" (Daresh, 2001:282). While formative evaluation is associated with helping, summative evaluation is associated with "terminating" (Hazi, 1994:200).

Formative and summative evaluation serve different functions. Darling-Hammond, Wise, and Pease (1983:302) say that staff development is the individual goal of formative evaluation and that school improvement is its organizational goal. In contrast, summative evaluation's individual and organizational goals are to make job status decisions and school status decisions (e.g., the program's suitability for accreditation), respectively.

A gray area in language teacher observation makes the apparently clear-cut distinction between formative and summative evaluations somewhat messy. If a supervisor visits a teacher three times during a term, at what point does formative evaluation end and summative evaluation begin? Are the first two visits completely developmental and formative, with the formal, summative evaluation resting on the last observation? Or do events from all three observations inform a summative report at the end of the term? Or are all observations formative in nature, except in times of contract renewals? No matter what the observational purpose may be, it is important that teachers know what sort of evaluation is being conducted.

Daresh describes a third purpose, *diagnostic evaluation*, which is used "to determine the beginning status or condition of something... prior to the application or intervention or treatment" (2001:281). Diagnostic evaluation provides baseline data about the normal state of affairs prior to any attempt at change, so it is sensible to conduct diagnostic evaluations first, followed by formative evaluations. Only after an extended period of systematic formative evaluations would a supervisor engage in summative evaluation. Hazi has described a context in which formative evaluations were informal (i.e., the results were not formally filed in the teachers' records) or formal (i.e., written records were kept and officially filed). Unfortunately, in our field these processes are sometimes collapsed, or their distinctions get muddied. Hazi asks, "Should we ask supervisors to wear a white hat on the day of informal-formative-supervision and a black hat on all other days? And if they did, would teachers believe it?" (1994:215).

Sources of input: Participants in the language teacher evaluation process

Language teachers are evaluated by many people: principals, headmasters, department chairs, lead teachers, program directors – in short, by any number of individuals in positions of authority in the program hierarchy. Language teachers are also evaluated by students and by parents (of their students) or by employers (of adult students). Where the evaluative responsibility lies varies greatly in different educational systems around the world. In this section we will consider several possible participants in the evaluation process.

Evaluation by regional inspectors

Sometimes language teachers are evaluated by outsiders who have authority in the educational system. In countries with a strong central ministry of education, traveling supervisors may observe teachers throughout large regions of the country. The teachers being observed may not know or even have a chance to talk with the person conducting the evaluation.

The regional inspector system of Cyprus was discussed by Mansour (1993). He says "the outcome of the supervisory process is mainly determined by the situational and contextual influences on the performance and effectiveness of the individual supervisor" (pp. 48–49). He says even a competent supervisor must at times compromise his or her values and goals (p. 49):

> Let us consider as an example a newly appointed supervisor in a Ministry of Education in a country with limited resources: Our new supervisor has gone through a brief training programme – something like two days – where he has been lectured about the golden rules of supervision; he now wants to expunge his disbelief in supervision, a reminiscence of his days as a teacher. He has envisaged that he will get to know each of his teachers individually and allocate several hours a week for each teacher. When he starts working, our supervisor is disheartened to find that he has 80–110 teachers to supervise in 100–110 days of actual teaching in a semester. He realises that the best he can do is to visit each teacher twice in a semester – just as it is stated in the regulations.

Mansour adds that the supervisor should "organise in-service training courses, plenaries, and workshops for his teachers, and counsel them, both individually and in groups, about the curriculum and the implementation of the textbook(s) for all levels" (ibid.).

The regional inspector system in Slovenia has been described by Gaies and Bowers (1990). They cite that one inspector supervises "50 English teachers and 15 German teachers in 28 primary schools, and a total of 48 language teachers (30 English, 10 German, 5 French, and 3 Russian) in 14 secondary schools" (p. 172). A supervisor with this workload will have little time to devote to developmental pre- and post-observation conferences. The inspector's role typically remains that of an outsider to, and perhaps an unwelcome visitor in, the teachers' professional lives.

Is there any value to the external inspector approach to supervision? Perhaps it is helpful to have someone who is not a regular colleague be the person who delivers feedback, in terms of maintaining collegial relations at any particular school. Maybe an external inspector can provide useful cross-fertilization, by telling teachers in one area what solutions were reached in another area. In countries where educational resources are scarce, regional inspectors may have been selected because they are better educated than the teachers. And perhaps when the inspector validates a teacher's practice, the inspector's status as an outsider may lend credibility to the praise. The difficulties with the regional inspector system remain, however: (1) The supervisors may not be familiar with the students and the local conditions, and (2) time constraints and geography work against inspectors' having any real positive impact on the teachers.

Evaluation by school-based supervisors

The evaluation system at the University of the United Arab Emirates (UAE) was described by Murdoch (2000). EFL teachers in 12-person teams have one supervisor responsible for each team. The evaluation involves "a series of instruments and processes which are implemented sequentially during each 16-week teaching semester" (ibid.:57). The data are the teacher's action plan, a teacher-generated questionnaire, the observation(s) and follow-up conference(s), the students' evaluation, and finally, the supervisor's report (ibid.).

There are several advantages to having supervisors working in the same program as the teachers they supervise. These supervisors are in a position to understand the students, the curriculum, and the conditions under which teachers work. Second, their physical proximity is an advantage over regional inspectors, who often travel great distances to visit classes. This proximity makes school-based supervisors more accessible and more familiar to teachers and students. As a result, their opinions may be more credible to teachers than those of an outsider.

Evaluation by students

In both language and general education, there is a process known as Student Evaluation of Teaching (SET), but in language courses there are often students from many first languages and cultures. The students may hold disparate views about appropriate teaching behavior, and at least some of those views will differ from the teacher's ideas. And, as Nunan and Lamb point out, "being evaluated by students can be a frightening prospect for some teachers. It can also be considered culturally inappropriate in many contexts and situations" (1996:244). They add that "most learners feel that it is somehow improper for a student to pass judgment on the teacher" but that "data from students can be extremely illuminating" (ibid.).

SET typically involves a questionnaire with statements followed by numerals for rating the teacher. The numbers (usually 1 to 5 or 1 to 7) indicate the extent to which the respondent agrees with each statement. For example, the statement "This teacher is consistently well organized for class" is followed by the numerals 1, 2, 3, 4, and 5, where 1 equals "strongly disagree," 2 equals "disagree," 3 equals "no opinion," 4 equals "agree," and 5 equals "strongly agree." Individual students then circle the number that best represents their opinion. Or the respondents may indicate their opinion of the teacher in particular categories. (For instance, the topic "organization" is followed by the numerals 1, 2, 3, 4, and 5, where 1 equals "poor," 2 equals "fair," 3 equals "average," 4 equals "good," and 5 equals "excellent.")

Numeric ratings can be averaged, and the standard deviation can be calculated to show how much variation there is in each category. Some systems only provide a space for students to write comments about the teachers' performances in various categories. Others combine the open-ended, qualitative format with quantitative ratings.

> In the student evaluation of teaching process used at the University of the UAE, [a] questionnaire is administered to at least one of a teacher's classes. The purpose of this questionnaire is to get feedback directly from students on aspects of the teacher's performance which they can usefully comment on. The questionnaire covers such basic areas as a teacher's speed of speech; the clarity of his / her explanations; the effective use of groups; the ability to establish a rapport with students; the teacher's ability to give attention to all the students, and to make learning interesting. (Murdoch, 2000:59–60)

The students mark a scale where 5 represents "agree strongly" and 1 represents "disagree strongly." They may also write open-ended comments. The supervisor then averages the ratings and analyzes the students' comments in case there are any issues to discuss with the teacher. Murdoch adds, "If a negative response pattern emerges related to a particular topic item . . . then this could become a mutually agreed area for future professional development" (ibid.:59–60).

A viable alternative to paper-and-pencil rating scales is to hold action meetings, conducted by the students without the teacher, according to Nunan and Lamb (1996): "The purpose of the meeting is for the students to review the progress of their course, to record what they liked as well as what they were not happy with, and to make recommendations about what they would like more of in the future" (pp. 244–245). The discussion at action meetings should include both course content and teaching methodology. If action meetings are properly conducted, they may be able to provide "invaluable information to teachers about their performance in a way that is less threatening than more direct feedback" (ibid.:245).

Whether the data come from action meetings or written questionnaires, learners' input is useful in teacher evaluation, especially if it is collected from different classes over time. The diverse input often reveals patterns of strength and areas for potential improvement.

Peer evaluation

Sometimes language teachers are evaluated by their peers. For instance, a teacher's colleagues may write letters of support to inform a tenure or promotion decision. Such letters may or may not be based on casual or formal peer observations. There is little published research on this topic in language education, though there are articles available about peer evaluation in first and second language education contexts. (See Bailey et al. [2001] and Nunan and Lamb [1996] for examples of peer observation reports.)

In general education, Walen and DeRose (1993) reported on nine elementary school teachers who undertook a peer appraisal program, with their principal's support. These authors described four prerequisites to a successful peer observation process: "support from district and building administrators is crucial...(p. 48); trust—the foundation for productive communication—opens the door for self-evaluation (ibid.);...as with anything else that we hope to learn and grow from, this process also takes time, sometimes above and beyond the school day (ibid.); [and]...the alternative appraisal process should be voluntary" (ibid.).

Peer observation can be used either for developmental or evaluation functions. In some professions, peer evaluation is "part of the professional's ethical responsibility to clients and to the profession itself, because it furthers the continual development, transmittal, and enforcement of standards of practice" (Darling-Hammond, 1986:558).

Alfonso (1977) took a less charitable view of peer supervision. He noted that demands for accountability based on attaining objectives can create "a competitive environment that will detract from honest attempts at peer evaluation" (p. 597). But he also acknowledged that peer supervision could "breed a new sense of responsibility not only for teachers to support their colleagues but also to improve their own instructional practice" (ibid.:599).

Self-evaluation

Language teachers themselves can also provide information for evaluation. As Wajnryb notes, "Few would dispute the place of self-evaluation in the process of learning teaching" (1986:69). She counsels, however, that it is not easy to learn the skills of self-criticism (ibid.).

Glickman et al. (1998:315–316) have suggested six different ways that teachers can promote their own professional development through self-evaluation:

1. Visits to the classrooms of several expert teachers for the purpose of comparing expert teaching to one's own teaching

      and identifying self-improvement goals based on such comparisons.

2. Videotaping one's own teaching, then analyzing teaching performance while reviewing the videotape.
3. Designing and selecting or analyzing results of surveys or questionnaires administered to students or parents.
4. Interviewing supervisors, peers, students, or parents about effective teaching and learning or about one's own instructional performance.
5. Keeping a journal of teaching experiences, problems, and successes, accompanied by critical reflection for the purpose of . . . improvement.
6. The development of a teaching portfolio for . . . self-reflection and analysis.

These suggestions were made for experienced teachers, but they could also be used with novice teachers – especially those who are working with a supervisor or mentor teacher.

I am not aware of research on language teachers' self-evaluation. Presumably self-evaluation occurs as part of teachers' professionalism, and some teachers write formal self-evaluations as part of their dossiers. With the increased use of portfolios for evaluation (see Portfolios in Evaluation, this chapter), self-evaluation by teachers may receive more attention in the future.

There are many common-sense reasons to invite input from teachers and their peers in both formative and summative evaluation, particularly in situations where the supervisors are not teaching in the program along with the teachers. In that case, it is important that someone be involved – whether it be the teacher or one of his or her colleagues – who is actually in the trenches and regularly experiences the same working conditions as the teacher being evaluated.

Evaluation by people outside the program

Outsiders who evaluate language teachers include parents in elementary and secondary schools. Parents' input is usually not solicited (e.g., with a rating form). Instead, parents may or may not show an interest in their children's language classes.

In some programs, parents are welcome to observe lessons at any time. In other cases, parents may actively complain about students' poor marks or other concerns. The extent to which parents give feedback on their children's education varies from one place to another. If you are working somewhere other than your home culture, the norms for parental interaction with school officials may be different from what you expect.

Likewise, if you are teaching in your home culture and the parents are immigrants, they may not know what is acceptable or expected in this context. Or they may lack the language skills to interact with school officials.

As a language teacher supervisor, you may be responsible for fielding parental complaints. What you and the teachers choose to do about any given complaint depends in part on the contents of the charge, but it is important that you systematically implement a uniform and fair set of procedures, such as the following:

1. Listen carefully to the parent's complaint if it is delivered orally (e.g., over the telephone). Write down the key points and read the statement back to the parent.
2. Deliver the written message (a parent's letter or your summary) to the teacher immediately. Keep a copy and a written record of the date of delivery.
3. Talk with and listen carefully to the teacher as soon as possible. Sometimes parents complain only on the basis of what their children have told them, so it's very important that you understand the teacher's perspective as well.
4. Make a note about what you and the teacher decide to do about the complaint.
5. Follow up later with the teacher to make sure you can provide an informed response if the parent calls again.

It is extremely important that you behave consistently toward all the teachers on the staff in handling parental input. Charges of favoritism can be very damaging to your credibility as a fair supervisor and terribly harmful to the teaching team's morale.

In tertiary, professional, or workplace contexts, teachers may be evaluated (either directly or indirectly) by "user agencies" – organizations that employ the language students taught by the teachers being evaluated. Such evaluations can be quite distant, anecdotal, and indirect, or more formally structured and regularly solicited from the graduates' employers. They sometimes focus on assessing the entire program rather than individual teachers.

Using multiple sources of information

Pennington (1989) says data collection tools for language teacher evaluation are either *fluid-response instruments* or *fixed-response instruments*. In the former category she lists "conversations, letters, and open-ended questionnaires" (p. 168), whereas the latter consists of "limited response questionnaires, rating scales, tests, and different kinds of summative descriptive data" (ibid.). Fluid-response instruments encourage

191

individualized comments about a teacher's work, but they are "difficult to interpret, to tally, and to score in any reliable manner" (ibid.:169). In contrast, fixed-response instruments permit easy tallying and scoring, but they "discourage reflective, thoughtful responses and do not allow respondents to convey detailed, specific information" (ibid.). Pennington concludes that both types of instruments should be used in teacher evaluation because they provide complementary information.

It is often possible to include input from multiple sources in the evaluation of language teachers. Murdoch (1998, Multiple Data Sources section, paragraph 1) notes that there is a "trend towards gathering data from different users' perspectives: teachers, students, testing experts, course coordinators, teacher trainers, outside experts, etc."

In Chapter 6 we considered triangulation. Two of Denzin's (1978) four kinds of triangulation can be helpful in language teacher evaluation. *Data triangulation* refers to the sources of data: which participants supply the information. In teacher evaluation, the potential data sources include students, regional inspectors, local supervisors, the teacher's colleague(s), the teacher being evaluated, and the parents (or employers) of the students. *Methods triangulation* refers to how the data are collected— via rating forms, classroom observation reports, teachers' journal entries, letters (e.g., from students, parents, or students' employers), video- and audiotapes, and so on.

There are at least three good reasons to triangulate data from multiple sources in teacher evaluation. First, more information from knowledgeable sources will provide a more valid and reliable basis for evaluating the teacher's work. Second, the evaluation will be ethically and legally sounder, if more than one person has influenced the decision. Third, all parties, including teachers and supervisors, will have more confidence in the outcome if data triangulation and methods triangulation are employed in the evaluation process.

Principles for language teacher evaluation

Murdoch (2000:55–56) states that "a progressive teacher-performance review system needs to be founded on five key principles or aims": (1) to encourage reflective practice; (2) to empower and motivate teachers; (3) to assess all aspects of a teacher's professional activity; (4) to take account of students' views; and (5) to promote collaboration. These principles bear further scrutiny, because they inform both the selection of teacher-evaluation procedures and the ways in which they are implemented (ibid.).

The first principle, *to encourage reflective practice*, is directly related to reflective teaching. This model of teacher development emphasizes reflecting on one's own practice as a means of improving that practice (Bailey, 1997; Richards and Lockhart, 1994). Reflective teaching entails gathering data about our own teaching, interpreting those data, and using our reflections to implement change. Supervisors do not follow novices into the real world when they complete their practice teaching and get actual positions. Nor do supervisors constantly monitor the work of in-service teachers. Ideally, language teachers will keep improving without close supervision. For this reason, teacher evaluation should encourage reflective teaching.

The second principle is *to empower and motivate teachers*. Murdoch (2000:55) says effective performance reviews give teachers active roles in developing the instruments and procedures used to evaluate their work. He says empowerment can be promoted by having teachers set their own objectives based on the program activities they work on most intensively (e.g., tutoring, materials development, etc.). Teachers can also review "their own achievements, and provide feedback on outcomes during performance appraisal interviews" (ibid.).

Murdoch's third principle is that an effective evaluation system will *assess all aspects of a teacher's professional activity*. He argues that "a common failing of many teacher-performance reviews is that they make judgements about teachers based on unrepresentative samples – usually isolated observations – of a teacher's work" (ibid.:56). This unfortunate fact is partly a result of time pressure, on both teachers and supervisors.

An evaluation system should *take account of students' views*, the fourth principle. Evaluation should

> reflect a student-centered philosophy. One obvious manifestation of a focus on students will be the importance attached to collecting students' views about their teacher and the classroom environment. This also makes practical sense, since they are the ones who spend the most time interacting with a teacher. (ibid.)

Using the students' ideas provides a viable source of data for triangulating evaluations.

Murdoch's final principle, *to promote collaboration*, is directly related to some of the supervisorial roles discussed in Chapter 1, but diametrically opposed to others. Murdoch says "the relations between a supervisor, senior teacher, or director of studies with the teachers whom he / she evaluates must be built on dialogue. . . . In order to tune in on the teacher's perspective, a non-dogmatic approach to teaching issues is essential" (ibid.). It is difficult to see how someone who chooses the "inspector" role or who practices only the classic prescriptive approach (Wallace, 1991) could enter into collaborative relationships with teachers.

This last point reminds us that the different ways to enact the supervisory role carry certain assumptions. (See Chapter 1.) For instance, it is

193

more likely that you would embrace Murdoch's five principles if you saw yourself in the role of a counselor or coach (Acheson and Gall, 1997) than if you were enacting clerical supervision (Clark, 1990) or traditional directive supervision (Gebhard, 1984). Indeed, the implementation of Murdoch's five principles presumes a democratic and collegial environment with open, reciprocal communication.

Portfolio assessment

Recently, language teacher education programs, influenced by the use of portfolios for evaluating language students' work, have begun to use teaching portfolios in teacher evaluation. This development is related to teacher autonomy discussed in Chapter 3. Someday, supervisors' evaluative work may regularly include the use of teaching portfolios.

Definitions of teaching portfolios

The concept of portfolios is familiar in art, architecture, photography, and modeling. Wenzlaff and Cummings (1996:109) explain:

> A portfolio was originally defined (Olson, 1991) as a portable case for carrying loose papers (*port* meaning to carry and *folio* pertaining to pages or sheets of paper). In current usage, a portfolio is a collection that relates to one or more dimensions of a person's professional life: methods used, artifacts of the work itself, feelings about the work, and indicators of professional growth.

Wenzlaff and Cummings point out that choosing portfolio contents shifts from being "merely an 'assignment' toward a process of making selections that represent the student [teacher] as a person and as an educator" (1996:109).

Porter and Cleland define a portfolio as "a collection of artifacts accompanied by a reflective narrative that not only helps the learner to understand and extend learning, but invites the reader of the portfolio to gain insight about learning and the learner" (1995:154). In preservice education, the "learner" is a novice teacher, but even experienced teachers can learn about language teaching and benefit from compiling portfolios. When the portfolio compiler is a teacher, the supervisor can gain insights by reading the portfolio.

According to Stronge (1997), portfolios should contain "commentaries and explanations of . . . carefully selected examples of both student and teacher work" (p. 195). Enclosing samples of students' work allows teachers to demonstrate the learners' progress, to reveal the curriculum in action, and to display the accomplishments of individual students or groups. Students' work is particularly powerful when it is directly related to the objectives of the program, because it provides tangible evidence that those goals are being accomplished.

Brown and Wolfe-Quintero (1997:28) define a portfolio as "a purposeful collection of any aspect of a teacher's work that tells the story of a teacher's efforts, skills, abilities, achievements, and contributions to his / her colleagues, institution, academic discipline or community." They say that "because of the reflective nature of portfolios, developing one inevitably enlarges one's view of what teaching is" (ibid.). In this sense, creating a teaching portfolio is a professional development activity.

Portfolios for professional development

Teaching portfolios "give teaching a context, accommodate diversity, encourage teachers to capitalize on strengths, allow teachers to self-identify areas for improvement, empower teachers by making them reflective, encourage professional dialogue, and integrate all aspects of teaching" (Green and Smyser, 1996:4–8). Teacher development and evaluation are connected to the use of teaching portfolios because "the best assessment is self-assessment. Teachers are more likely to act on what they find out about themselves" (ibid.:x). This assertion may contradict traditional supervisory roles, but it is consistent with both the alternatives approach and the nondirective approach to supervision (Freeman, 1982; Gebhardt, 1984).

Portfolios have also been used to evaluate preservice language teachers in the practicum context. Liu (2000) says it is helpful for each practicum student's portfolio to include

> the student's lesson plans, journals, observation reports, and the instructor's written feedback on the student's work, including teaching. . . . The various forms of information that come from the practicum students' experiences at different sites and in different contexts also make it easier for the university course instructor to conduct multiple-index evaluations of the practicum students. Using multiple indexes to assess practicum students' performance enhances the validity of the student evaluation. (p. 21)

Thus, preparing teaching portfolios gives the compilers opportunities to present their own professional personae by selecting specific materials.

The contents of teacher portfolios

What can a teacher's portfolio include? McLaughlin and Vogt (1996) describe five sorts of content: educational philosophy, professional

195

development, curriculum and instruction, student growth, and contributions to school and community. Stronge (1997:195) says portfolios "should be structured around sound professional content standards and individual schools' goals." The connection to the goals of the program provides shared, external criteria the teacher and the supervisor can use to evaluate the teacher's work.

Johnson (1996a:12) has identified four types of documentation for preservice teachers' portfolios. *Artifacts* are produced during the normal coursework of the teacher education program. These include lesson plans, teaching materials, tests, and the like. *Reproductions* represent typical events in the teachers' work that are not captured in the artifacts. For example, if a teacher videotapes students' presentations, including the videotape in the portfolio is an example of a reproduction. *Attestations* are documents about the work of the teacher prepared by someone else, such as peer observation reports. *Productions* are items prepared especially for the portfolio (e.g., cover notes explaining the sections). Johnson's list was based on her work with preservice teachers, but these categories can be used for in-service teachers' portfolios. For example, productions might include a teacher's review of his or her own professional growth over the past year.

Portfolios in evaluation

Writing in Italy, Calzoni says it takes time to gather the materials to include in a teaching portfolio. To do so "is a way of showing who you are, your teaching beliefs, theories, [and] achievements in the light of a continuous process of self-evaluation" (2001:13). She adds that "a teacher who decides to start his / her personal portfolio needs to believe that what he / she is doing is worthwhile and subject to evaluation" (ibid.).

Calzoni lists three key ways that teaching portfolios might be used as assessment tools: "to find out the teacher's level of performance; to find out what level of performance the teacher is capable of at a certain time; and to find out whether, after a given period, the educational goals identified at the beginning of the assessment process have been reached" (ibid.:15). She adds that teachers whose portfolios are assessed must be told the objectives and the criteria with which they will be evaluated. That knowledge will enable them to tailor their portfolios to meet the requirements. However, she notes, there should also be room for "structured discussion, assessed against the teacher's own aims and not against a set of established general criteria, aimed at focusing mainly on individual development" (ibid.:16).

Calzoni acknowledges that using teacher portfolios for evaluation might not be widely accepted (ibid.:16). But she mentions that teacher portfolios are useful for global evaluations and also to gain a holistic view of the teacher's development. Some people will argue that portfolios lack standardization. Calzoni counters that the structure and components of the portfolio could be based on uniform requirements, while the material selected to meet those requirements could be personal and individualized.

How can teachers' portfolios be useful in evaluations? One objection teachers have to supervisorial evaluation is that it is "done to them." They typically have little say or power in determining how they will be evaluated. Using portfolios in teaching evaluations combats that top-down imbalance, because the teachers themselves have some control over what goes into the dossier. Even in cases where set criteria determine the *types* of items included (e.g., lesson plans, course syllabi, etc.), the teachers select the examples in each category.

Why should supervisors consider the use of language teacher portfolios? Wolfe-Quintero and Brown (1998:24) note that administrators regularly hire teachers, evaluate their performance, and make decisions about retaining, cutting, or promoting faculty members:

> Such decisions are most often based on the administrator's opinions (formed from classroom observations), and a cursory summary of the teacher's background (as found in a resume or curriculum vitae). Such information can prove valuable, but may not be sufficient for making responsible decisions about a teacher's real strengths and weaknesses.

These authors add that teachers seldom have the chance to present a coherent picture of their overall, multifaceted professionalism, and compiling a portfolio can provide that opportunity.

According to Wolfe-Quintero and Brown, teacher portfolios are directly connected to two important goals of teacher evaluation: "(1) The act of creating and maintaining a portfolio may motivate teachers to improve their performance and develop themselves professionally ... [and] (2) the information included in a portfolio can assist administrators, as current or prospective employers, in evaluating the teachers' qualifications" (ibid.). These authors give an example of portfolio evaluation in the Hawaii English Language Program, in which a committee annually evaluates the full-time teachers: "The evaluation committee found that the portfolios added an important dimension to the annual review because they intersected with student evaluations and administrators' observations to reveal a deeper picture of instructors' strengths as well as areas of recommended growth" (ibid.:26). Wolfe-Quintero and Brown acknowledge that some teachers felt that preparing portfolios for evaluation was "intrusive, time-consuming – perhaps even frightening" (ibid.:26). But they note that advertisements for employment now include a statement about "documented evidence of teaching ability and curriculum development" (ibid.), the intent being to see evidence of what the teacher has actually accomplished rather than just a list of years of experience and letters of recommendation.

Problems in language teacher evaluation

As you can see, the problems in language teacher evaluation are legion, in part because language teaching is almost always influenced by complex social factors that differ widely from one context to another (e.g., class size, student motivation, availability of well-prepared teachers, access to appropriate materials). Consequently, it is virtually impossible to identify universal criteria for language teacher evaluation. (We will return to this issue in Chapter 10.)

In spite of its significance to the program and the individuals involved, language teacher evaluation is often not given enough time, attention, or resources. Murdoch notes that professionally oriented programs commit resources to "revising curricula and teaching material, ensuring that the evaluation of students' progress keeps pace with course developments, providing opportunities for professional development, and introducing new technology" (2000:54). But, he laments, "teacher evaluation matters are often perceived to be of secondary importance, and as a result, tend to be poorly developed in many institutions" (ibid.).

In many teaching contexts, performance reviews are based on infrequent observations by a supervisor who has little time for observations and conferences. As a result, Murdoch says, these ad-hoc evaluation procedures "can only produce universal teacher anxiety, a lack of belief in the validity of observation, and a subtle undermining of other institutional initiatives to support teachers' efforts to deliver courses effectively" (ibid.). It is important to remember these comments even if evaluation is taken seriously and is well supported by the available resources. In the best of circumstances, however, evaluation can take much longer than expected, simply because it often entails differences of opinion. Thus, much time is consumed in communicating appropriately and carefully documenting both the processes and the products of teacher evaluation.

The worst-case scenario is that supervisors are sometimes responsible for making (or contributing to) decisions to dismiss teachers. Decisions about whether to renew a teacher's contract can be difficult and are often traumatic for those involved. Very little has been written about supervisors dealing with unsatisfactory performance in language education, but some information is available from general education.

Summative evaluation procedures in general education contexts

Acheson and Gall (1997) list the steps involved in K–12 teacher evaluation in general education. First, distinct standards are set defining the criteria for effective teaching (a topic we will consider in Chapter 10). Second, job descriptions are written detailing the expected performance in particular teaching situations. Third, goals are set, based on the standards and the job descriptions. These steps provide the context for both formative and summative evaluation.

Formative evaluation, in Acheson and Gall's terms, involves planning classroom observations, collecting data during observations, and discussing the feedback based on the data. Where improvement is called for, a plan for assistance can be negotiated between the teacher and the supervisor. If follow-up observations and feedback discussions indicate that the intervention was successful, the employment continues. If not, the teacher may choose to resign or may eventually face a negative summative evaluation.

In cases of summative evaluation, according to Acheson and Gall, a formal evaluation report is filed, and a post-evaluation interview is conducted with the teacher. If the teacher's work does not improve, a dismissal procedure is initiated. If the teacher chooses to contest the dismissal (depending on local laws), grievance procedures, hearings, arbitration, and legal proceedings may ensue. We should note that Acheson and Gall were writing about the U.S. context and almost entirely about elementary and secondary public school situations. These procedures may not apply in other circumstances or cultures.

Personnel issues in language program administration

Geddes and Marks recommend 16 procedures for feedback and problem solving in managing intensive English programs. They say that administrators (including supervisors) should "objectively observe and monitor all employees regularly" (1997:212). They stress the value of positive recognition and feel administrators should "identify and recognize significant contributions and commitment to the program, regularly acknowledge and, if possible, reward exemplary performance, and support and encourage competent employees" (ibid.).

It is also important for administrators and other supervisors to "identify problematic behaviors when substandard performance is observed, ascertain the severity of the problem, determine the source of the problem, [and] determine the course of action to be taken" (ibid.). Geddes and Marks also note that if action is needed, the administrator should "initiate corrective intervention or move to dismiss as soon as possible, establish a timeline for meeting expectations, [and] complete

199

all required documentation" (ibid.). It is also important to "support the employee and all other members of the program when corrective measures are being pursued, [and] maintain open communication with all employees" (ibid.).

Geddes and Marks list several procedures for making personnel changes. They say that dismissing a teacher can be less painful if the administrator has "objective criteria for promotion, reassignment, non-renewal, layoff, and dismissal" (ibid.:213). They also recommend following both "institutional and legal guidelines" (ibid.:212–213). In addition, supervisors should assist departing employees with stress management, morale building, and reorganization. These authors stress that supervisors should not neglect the rest of the staff but rather "maintain open lines of communication to dispel rumors and negativism" (ibid.) and "facilitate the redistribution of duties and support ongoing program services" (ibid.). Dismissing even one faculty member can lead to disillusion and mistrust among those who remain.

Ethical documentation of procedures

Following institutional and legal guidelines is essential, even though they can seem quite bureaucratic and / or idiosyncratic, depending on the culture where you work. The practices of dismissing teachers vary greatly from one country to another. Even within a particular country, the laws may differ across states or provinces. And where regional or local governing bodies are the policy-making entities, the policies may vary from one district or program to another.

White, Martin, Stimpson, and Hodge emphasize that labor laws must be reviewed before a dismissal is undertaken. They also state that in the United Kingdom there are two broad categories for dismissing a teacher: inefficiency, which includes incompetence and continued absences without certification (e.g., a legitimate illness); and misconduct, which includes "breaking the regulations of the organization, unreasonable refusal to carry out legitimate instructions, neglect of duty, violence, [and] criminal activity" (1991:88). The last two categories are usually labeled "gross misconduct" (ibid.) and can lead to immediate dismissal.

Lawrence, Vachon, Leake, and Leake (2001) have written *The Marginal Teacher*, which is targeted for school principals in the U.S. K–12 context who must document attempts to deal with unsatisfactory teaching performance leading to dismissal. The authors' guidelines for fair procedures are based on four assumptions about evaluating teachers: (1) the evaluator has "established administrative and instructional credibility with the staff" (p. xii); (2) the evaluator has "effectively monitored the instructional climate in all classrooms, and...provided assistance to those teachers who are having difficulties" (ibid.); (3) the evaluator realizes "the physical and psychological demands inherent in the dismissal process" (ibid.); and (4) the evaluator has "discussed the process with individuals in central administration as well as the attorney for the school district to obtain their support and to ensure that legal and contractual obligations are met" (ibid.). The authors list monthly steps to be taken and provide sample letters and protocols for legal procedures.

Careful recordkeeping should not be confused with "clerical supervision" (Clark, 1990) or degenerate into "nominal supervision" (Goldsberry, 1988). Keeping careful records documents what supervisors have done to advise teachers of problems, and should also guarantee that teachers are not dismissed without due process.

In dismissing a teacher, an administrator in the U.S. K–12 context must demonstrate that the employee's "just-cause requirements" have been met. Lawrence et al. list the following key questions for administrators to answer:

1. Was the evaluation process for the school district made known to all teachers working at the school(s)?
2. Was the evaluation process consistently applied to all teachers?
3. Was the teacher treated consistently with other teachers and not singled out?
4. Did the observations include all phases of the teacher's assignment, morning and afternoon?
5. Was there a continuous and accurately dated file of all conferences with and observations of the teacher?
6. Did the teacher receive written memoranda of concerns specifying exact deficiencies?
7. In each memorandum of concerns given to the teacher, did the teacher receive a list of specific suggestions for correcting deficiencies and ways to achieve a satisfactory level of performance?
8. Was an intensive assistance plan established and implemented for the teacher, using school and district resources?
9. Was the teacher given a reasonable period of time to improve teaching performance?
10. Was the teacher informed in writing that failure to achieve an acceptable level of performance by a specified date would result in the issuance of an unsatisfactory evaluation? (2001:xiii–xiv)

According to Lawrence et al., an administrator or supervisor who can answer "yes" to these questions has a greater chance of winning a dismissal case than someone who cannot do so.

Dismissal and all the trauma it creates (for the teacher, for the rest of the staff, for the students, and certainly for the supervisor) are the last resort. If new teachers are carefully screened during the hiring process, and if formative evaluation is properly done, supervisors should seldom have to resort to dismissal during summative evaluation.

Concluding comments

In this chapter we considered three primary purposes for language teacher evaluation: formative, summative, and diagnostic. We saw that the evaluative function characterizes the supervisor's role and that there are many sources of information for language teacher evaluation. We examined Murdoch's (2000) principles for a performance review system, considered portfolio assessment, and discussed some of the problems in language teacher evaluation.

Teacher evaluation may be done for program-internal purposes (e.g., promotion, retention, or dismissal) or for external audiences, if a teacher is seeking an award or a new job. Reasons for evaluation include the need to decrease the teaching staff, "to provide supporting documentation for granting / denying a promotion, to do what has always been done (i.e., performance of a ritual act), or to see what is going on in the program" (Oprandy, 1999:120).

The case presented at the beginning of the chapter was based on the need for staff reductions. Please reread it before answering the following questions.

Case discussion

1. What questions would you ask the director before you undertake this prioritizing task? Think about what you don't know and what you need to know.
2. What issues will influence the decision of whom to retain and whom to let go? List five programmatic factors to be considered in recommending which teacher's contract to renew.
3. What role should student evaluations play in determining which teacher to retain? How should the supervisor compare the two teachers' student evaluations?
4. The director asks you for your input at the beginning of the final three-month term in Anna's and Maria's current contracts. Also

imagine the director assigns you the task of mentoring both teachers as they compile their first teaching portfolios. What could you suggest that Anna and Maria include? Using Johnson's (1996a) categories, write one idea in each box below:

	Maria	Anna
Artifacts		
Reproductions		
Attestations		
Productions		

5. Suppose that Maria says she appreciates your guidance, but she wants to be more proactive. She asks you to tell her three things she should do differently (or refrain from doing) in the immediate future to increase her chances of being retained. What advice would you give her? If Anna asked you the same question, what advice would you give her?

6. How useful is advice? What could you say that would actually help Anna or Maria?

7. Choose which teacher you would retain and which you would let go. Write a memo to the director in which you articulate your reasoning. (Your summary notes about Anna and Maria, printed in the case at the beginning of the chapter, would be attached to your memo.)

8. Imagine a conversation in which you explain to Maria that you have recommended her contract not be renewed. What would you want to say? What would you avoid saying?

9. Imagine explaining to Anna that you have recommended her contract not be renewed. What would you want to say to her? What would you avoid saying?

10. Suppose the director asks you to write a letter of recommendation in support of the teacher whose contract is not being renewed. Draft an all-purpose letter for one of these teachers in which you talk realistically about her work in your program, explain briefly why her contract was not renewed, and encourage potential employers to look favorably upon her application.

Tasks and discussion

1. If you were a teacher about to undergo a formative evaluation procedure during the first year of a three-year contract, what types of data would you like to have used? Consider the manual and electronic data collection procedures discussed in Chapters 5 and 6, respectively.

2. Under the conditions described in Task 1, whose input would you want to be considered? Put a plus sign (+), a check (√), or a minus sign (−) in front of each source below:

____ regional / district inspector's report

____ school-based supervisor's report

____ students' evaluations

____ your teaching peers' input

____ parents' (or employers') opinions

____ your own self-assessment

____ other: _____

Compare your list with those of a classmate or colleague.

3. If you are currently teaching, is compiling a portfolio part of the evaluation process? If so, what guidelines are available about materials to include in your portfolio?

4. If you have compiled a teaching portfolio, list three things you learned in the process. If you have not, ask a teacher who has created a portfolio. List three things he or she learned.

5. As a teacher, do you have a job description? If so, how could your job description be used in a formative or summative evaluation process? (If you don't have one, use someone else's job description to do this task.)

6. If you are currently teaching, who are the participants in the teacher evaluation process in your context? Do the different participants' ideas have equal weight in the process? How well does the current system work?

7. If you are a preservice teacher, try to find out about the various participants in the evaluation process where you hope to teach. Also try to learn from people who already teach there how well that system works.

8. If you were a language teacher whose contract might not be renewed, what input would be useful from your supervisor? List three sorts of guidance that you would find helpful, and three that would be unhelpful.

Suggestions for further reading

Brown and Wolfe-Quintero's (1997) paper contains practical suggestions for developing portfolios. (See also Bastidas, 1996; Tanner, Longayroux, Beijaard, and Verloop, 2000; and Wolfe-Quintero and Brown, 1998.) Johnson's (1996a) ideas about portfolios in preservice teacher education are applicable to experienced teachers.

Yu (2000) has written an interesting case study about the use of reflective teaching portfolios in a teacher education context.

Green and Smyser (1996) is geared for elementary and secondary schools teachers, but many of the ideas are applicable in other teaching contexts. Other useful references from general education are Lyons (1998), Van Wagenen and Hibbard (1998), Wolf (1996), Campbell, Cignetti, Melenyzer, Hood Nettles, and Wyman (1997), and Martin-Kniep (1999).

Geddes and Marks (1997) have written a very practical chapter about personnel matters. Only a few parts of this article have been cited here.

Omaggio's (1982) article about personalization in language classrooms (discussed in Chapter 10) includes an example of a form for student evaluation of teaching.

Acheson and Gall's (1997) work on evaluation in general education in the United States is well worth reading. Davis (1964) discusses the history of teacher evaluation up to the middle of the twentieth century. Wise et al. (1984) studied teacher evaluation in four states in the United States. Also in general education, Stodolsky (1984) presents an interesting review of research. Rooney (1993) wrote about her work as an elementary school principal, when she and her staff decided to change their evaluation system. Gitlin and Smyth (1990) provide a provocative challenge to top-down teacher evaluation systems.

Blue and Grundy's (1996) article about team evaluation includes a self-evaluation checklist which could be used by a group evaluating its language program. For more information about peer observation, see Head and Taylor (1997).

White et al. (1991) offer procedures for conducting performance reviews. Pennington's (1989) article on language faculty evaluation concludes with recommendations related to supervision. See also Pennington and Young (1989).

10 Criteria for language teacher evaluation

This chapter examines the thorny issue of the criteria against which language teachers are evaluated. It draws on some early research on the concept of teacher effectiveness – a construct that has been questioned in recent years. We will see that – far from the supervisor's opinion being paramount – many critieria are now involved in language teacher education.

Evaluation entails "the necessary existence and use of a *criterion* or standard to which the 'something' being evaluated may be compared to determine *relative worth*" (Daresh, 2001:281). But evaluating language teachers is not as straightforward as appraising a used car or an antique chest. The main difficulty lies in determining the standards against which teachers' work will be compared. In fact the criteria "by which quality teaching is assessed may not be made fully clear to the teacher via an observation schedule or specific criteria for judging competent teaching" (Murdoch 1998, Conflicting Discourses section, paragraph 3). Supervisors must answer the fundamental question of what specific criteria will be used in language teacher evaluation. As McGreal (1988) notes, "an essential element of any effective evaluation system is a clear, visible, and appropriate set of evaluation criteria" (p. 13). This chapter discusses the various criteria that can be used in evaluating language teachers' performance.

The following procedures have been recommended by Geddes and Marks (1997:211) for evaluating programs and teachers. First, supervisors should examine evaluation research and reassess the program's existing evaluation model. Second, the purpose of the review and the intended outcomes should be stated accurately and objectively. Third, supervisors should determine whether the evaluation will be formative or summative. Fourth, one should design, adopt, or adapt the appropriate evaluation model, including the methods and instruments. Fifth, the standards to be used during evaluation must be identified.

Geddes and Marks identify several steps to take, including establishing workable timelines, adhering to the set standards, and following legal and program guidelines. They say supervisors should make "recommendations based on information gathered during the evaluation process" (ibid.) rather than on other sources of data. The supervisor must also write an accurate report and assure that the employee has an opportunity to respond to it.

Case for analysis: Letter of recommendation

You are the supervisor for the part-time teachers in a university language program, a position you have held for a year. You previously taught in the program yourself.

A woman who was once your classmate is now finishing her degree. She has taught language classes for six hours per week for the past year under your supervision. (She also taught last year under the former director.) You held post-observation conferences with and provided written feedback to this teacher each time you observed her class, and a copy of each report was kept in her personnel file. This person is a brilliant graduate student, whose work in discourse analysis, syntax, and materials development is lauded as exemplary. Recently she mentioned she would need a letter of recommendation, since she is applying for several teaching positions. For various reasons, you have not yet drafted this letter. In fact, you'd rather not do so.

One day this teacher writes you a note saying she wants a letter of recommendation from you, since you have seen her teach. However, based on your three observations of her lessons, you have serious reservations about writing such a letter. If she lists you as a reference, potential employers will ask you if you would hire this teacher. Your honest answer, based on watching her teach and having worked with her, would be that you would not hire her. As a result, you'd prefer *not* to write a letter of recommendation for her.

The three observations revealed some clear patterns. This teacher is very well versed in grammar and is consistently able to answer students' questions by drawing on her linguistic knowledge. However, her lessons tend to become extemporaneous minilectures as she answers questions about grammar rules and their exceptions. There were no student-centered activities in the classes you observed, nor was there any interactive language practice. And while the teacher relates well to four of the more advanced language learners (in a class of 20), she does not call on students who don't ask questions, and at each observation she told some students that their questions had already been covered. When you raised these issues with her, she said that most of the students are lazy or their proficiency is too low for them to be in her class.

The teacher's behavior and attitude outside of class have also been problematic. She has not shared materials or exam scoring

---

responsibilities with the other teachers, she does not reliably keep her office hours, and she refuses to use the materials selected by the teaching team for the course she has been teaching. She is also easily upset and has had public arguments with other teachers and with some of her students. You have discussed these issues with her during the post-observation conferences and after faculty meetings where she had become quite agitated. However, there has been no apparent change in her subsequent work or out-of-class behavior. When you think of her, the label "prima donna" comes to mind unbidden.

The teacher has assumed that you would be willing to write a recommendation for her. She says three potential employers need your letter in two weeks. She has also given you two forms, supplied by two other potential employers; both forms ask if you would hire this teacher yourself. All these jobs involve teaching in university language programs similar to yours.

Evaluative criteria

We will now examine the sorts of criteria used in conducting teacher evaluations. Not all of these will be appropriate in all circumstances. It is important to decide, in collaboration with the teachers involved and other stakeholders, which criteria are appropriate in your context.

Individual opinions and group consensus

Historically, the most common criterion for evaluating language teachers has been the evaluator's judgment or opinion, which derives from attitudes and beliefs. Such judgments or opinions are often based on supervisors' implicit ideas and values rather than on explicitly codified criteria. The evaluator's experience and status presumably lend credibility to his or her opinions, and hence to the evaluation.

Difficulties emerge when the supervisor and the teacher hold different values or have different beliefs about how languages are learned or should be taught. The concept of values is related to that of beliefs and attitudes (see Chapter 2): "In many ways, values represent our permanent view of reality, formed and fashioned out of our more temporary beliefs and attitudes as well as the beliefs and attitudes of others in our family, neighborhood, or larger societal environment" (Daresh, 2001:32). In our context, the "larger societal environment" includes the programs in which we work and those in which we received our professional preparation. One thing to keep in mind is that "values are not typically articulated directly by their bearers; more often than not, behavior is the strongest demonstration of our values" (ibid.).

Sometimes an evaluation is done by a group of people (supervisors, peers, etc.) acting by consensus, rather than by one person. In this context, the various viewpoints may balance negative and positive impressions of a teacher. Sometimes, however, a dominant person can sway an evaluation team to his or her position, so that the value of multiperson input is lost.

Teaching method as a criterion

One difficulty in evaluation is that a teacher may have been trained in the natural approach or communicative language teaching, for example, whereas a supervisor – often someone older and more experienced – may have been trained in another method, such as grammar translation or the audiolingual method. If one method rather than another serves as a criterion for evaluation, then teachers' and supervisors' differing beliefs about appropriate methods can be a serious source of disagreement.

Consider the issue of error treatment in language lessons. A supervisor or teacher trained in the audiolingual method (or any method that emphasizes accuracy) may believe that all oral errors should be treated immediately and publicly. A supervisor or teacher trained in communicative language teaching may believe that oral errors should be treated only if they interfere with meaning and that students' attempts to communicate should not be interrupted. A supervisor holding one set of values might give low evaluations to a teacher who espouses the other, on the grounds that the teacher was "ineffective" in treating students' errors. As a further example, consider the different possible meanings of the phrase *student-student interaction*. What one person might see as a lively, intentional communicative activity, another might see as pointless, noisy behavior – perhaps even evidence that the teacher had lost control of the class.

If the program espouses a particular method, the issue is a bit simpler, because teachers can be evaluated on how well they enact that method. For instance, if courses are based on a certain method, the teachers' contracts can specify that they will use that method. And if the method's behavioral manifestations are clear, then a supervisor can watch for its implementation.

In my experience, however, this sort of methodological monism is rare. I once worked as an observer in a study designed to assess the effectiveness of Suggestopedia for teaching beginning Russian as a foreign language. One teacher was thoroughly trained in the method, but was also quite sympathetic to the students' wishes. One day another visitor observed the same lesson I was watching. That visitor was a representative of the Suggestopedia training program in which the teacher had studied. After the lesson the visitor said to the teacher in an exasperated tone of voice, "What are you doing? This isn't Suggestopedia!" The teacher replied, "I know, but what can I do? The students beg me for error treatment and grammar explanations." This comment reveals that teachers must sometimes make decisions to depart from a prescribed method. Professionally prepared teachers who work directly with learners are the people who really know those students' needs, abilities, and learning styles. The very depth and breadth of their exposure to the learners gives the teachers knowledge that is probably not available to supervisors. An important reason to hire well-educated teachers is that they will be intellectually and experientially equipped to make good judgments about alternatives. Therefore, judging teachers on how well they adhere to a prescribed method is a shaky proposition.

In addition, "the achievement of excellence is not a question of selecting this or that method. Methodology is sometimes an important factor, but it is virtually never the overriding reason for the achievement of excellence" (Strevens, 1989:81). Likewise, Smith, Stenson, and Winkler (1980:9) state that supervisors who require "adherence to a particular teaching method may find that some teachers are unwilling to adopt the method in question because they do not believe in it, while others, though willing, may be unable to comply." Furthermore, we do not have convincing evidence that any one method is superior to another. The large-scale methods comparisons of the 1960s and 1970s were, for the most part, inconclusive. (See, e.g., Politzer and Weiss, 1970.) In the absence of clear data supporting any given method, it is risky to use methodological criteria for judging teachers' performance. And given the frequent swing of the methodological pendulum in our field, different generations of teachers and supervisors may have been prepared to work with widely divergent teaching methods. In fact, with the plethora of teaching methods and the lack of evidence as to the superiority of one method over another, method is seldom a viable criterion for language teacher evaluation.

Competencies and performance standards

Teacher competencies are statements about what novice teachers are supposed to know and be able to do. Rhodes and Heining-Boynton published a list of competencies for elementary school foreign language teachers in North Carolina. These competencies include the following:

> 1. An understanding of second language acquisition in childhood and its relation to first language development

2. Knowledge of instructional methods appropriate to foreign language instruction in the elementary school
3. Knowledge of instructional resources appropriate to foreign language instruction in the elementary school
4. Knowledge of appropriate assessment and evaluation for foreign language instruction in the elementary school
5. Ability to develop reading and writing skills in learners who are simultaneously acquiring literacy skills in their first language
6. Ability to teach aspects of the target culture appropriate to the development needs and interests of students, including children's literature appropriate to the target culture
7. Knowledge of K–12 foreign language curriculum and the elementary curriculum, the relationship among the content areas, and ability to teach, integrate, or reinforce the elementary school curriculum through or in a foreign language
8. Knowledge of elementary school principles and practices, effective classroom management techniques, and the ability to apply such knowledge to create an affective and physical environment conducive to foreign language learning
9. Proficiency in the foreign language
10. Knowledge of child development
11. Knowledge of the history of foreign language education in the United States and the rationale for various program models in the elementary school
12. Awareness of the need for personal and professional growth
13. An understanding of the need for cooperation among foreign language teachers, other classroom teachers, counselors, school administrators, university personnel, and community members
14. Awareness of skills for program (1993:167)

If you evaluate novice teachers, competency statements may be helpful, but some competencies (e.g., proficiency in the foreign language) are more directly observable and assessable than others (e.g., awareness of the need for professional growth).

Evaluators may judge teachers' work against specified standards, which can be stated as performance goals or embedded in an observation instrument. (See Chapter 5.) When the desired behavior is described in objective terms, teachers are able to see what is expected, because the descriptive language provides a common frame of reference for teachers and supervisors. An explicit statement of objectives works to the supervisors' advantage as well, because it provides criteria for evaluating teachers' performance. Teachers are more likely to teach to performance

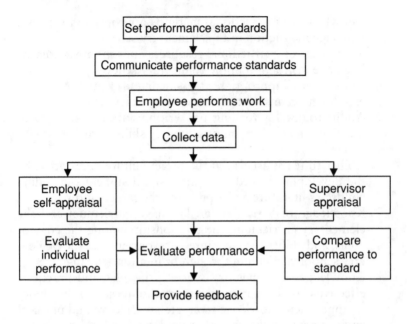

Figure 10.1   Appraising and rewarding performance (Daughtrey and Ricks, 1989:251)

standards and give them credence as evaluative criteria if they have helped develop those criteria. Figure 10.1 depicts Daughtrey and Ricks's process of evaluating teachers (employees) on the basis of performance standards.

Of course, setting performance standards is one key to the success of this approach to teacher evaluation. Whether the standards have been developed by a professional association, a ministry of education, or the local teaching staff, it is important that the teachers acknowledge them as being helpful and appropriate before those standards are used for evaluation.

Performance reviews

Why should a supervisor conduct performance reviews? From the teacher's perspective, "a performance review enables him or her to get to know clearly what the job consists of and what standards are expected" (White, Martin, Stimson, and Hodge, 1991:68). For the manager, administrator, or supervisor, a performance review can be "a way of encouraging staff and giving feedback on the work undertaken" (ibid.).

Performance reviews typically take one of three forms, according to White et al. The first, *comparative reviews*, involves comparing teachers to one another and rank ordering the members of the staff in terms of their value to the program. The main problem is that comparative reviews are highly subjective. If the criteria for ranking are not clearly and publicly articulated, the person(s) doing the ranking have tremendous power and responsibility. In addition, team-building and professional development are often undermined in comparative reviews because "it is very difficult to give individual feedback and encourage development with such a system" (ibid.:69). Comparative reviews parallel norm-referenced tests: The value of one person's performance is interpreted relative to that of another person. A second approach is *absolute methods* (ibid.:65), in which supervisors evaluate "the performance of an individual by reference to objectively defined standards of performance and not by comparison of others" (ibid.:69). This approach is analogous to criterion-referenced assessment. A third common approach to performance reviews is referred to as *results oriented methods*. In this context, "performance is viewed as a series of expected results which can be compared to actual performance results" (ibid.:72). Here, there is an assumption that "shared goal setting will gain individual commitment and that managers will also support and provide resources to jointly agreed plans" (ibid.:74).

Problems in defining effective teaching

Teacher evaluation depends on some understanding of effective teaching, but over the years there has been much debate about teacher effectiveness – what it is, as well as how it can be measured and promoted. Much of the research on effective teaching was conducted from the 1960s to the 1980s, using the *process-product approach* to educational research (i.e., documenting classroom processes in order to connect them empirically to learning outcomes).

Teaching effectiveness is not a simple construct. It is influenced by many factors, including the content being taught, the learners' ages, and the cultural values of the educational system. Nevertheless, it is important for language teacher supervisors to understand teacher effectiveness, because it is directly related to evaluation. As Stodolsky (1984) noted, "Evaluation of teachers rests on the assumption that the characteristics of good or effective teachers are known and recognizable" (p. 11). In addition, helping language teachers become more effective is an important part of supervisors' developmental work.

Some definitions of effective teaching are generic. For example, in the mid-1900s Rosencranz and Biddle defined teacher competence as "the ability of a teacher to behave in specified ways within a social situation in order to produce empirically demonstrated effects approved by those in the environment in which he functions" (1964:241). This definition is both global and safe, and emphasizes a particular social situation, but it does little to help either classroom teachers or evaluators to identify effective teaching. In addition, there are very few language teaching contexts where clear-cut "empirically demonstrated effects" of teaching are readily available to inform judgments about teacher competence.

Biddle defined teacher effectiveness as "the ability of a teacher to produce agreed-upon educational effects in a given situation or context" (1964:20). This definition hinges on articulated objectives or goals – the "agreed-upon educational effects" that the teaching is supposed to produce – but it does not specify *how* teachers achieve those effects. As Biddle's definition suggests, one approach to measuring teacher effectiveness compares the teacher's behavior with an established standard of performance. In this model, the agreed-upon standards are presented as clear behavioral statements, rather than in vague, theoretical terms.

As noted above, teachers have often been evaluated in terms of "how they matched profiles of good teachers derived from the opinions of experts, despite the fact that there was no evidence that teachers having these characteristics were actually successful in bringing about higher levels of learning in their pupils" (Richards, 1990b:4–5). This point brings us to another possible criterion: students' achievement.

Acheson and Gall also connected teacher effectiveness to context: "a teacher is more or less effective depending on how much of the academic curriculum is mastered by his or her students" (1997:25). This definition doesn't address differences in students' ability, study habits, or motivation, or the impact of situational variables on the school or program. Such definitions are useful, since they can be applied in any context, but they often sidestep the very situational factors that influence the teacher's impact on the students' learning.

In summary, definitions of teacher effectiveness are directly connected to the teachers' success in helping students to master the curriculum. For many years, researchers in general education felt that effective teaching must be measured by student achievement (see e.g., Medley and Mitzel, 1963; Rosenshine, 1971). This stance implies that program curricula must be clearly specified if teacher effectiveness is to be judged.

Student achievement as a criterion

Language teachers can be evaluated, in part, based on their students' achievement. Strevens views teaching excellence as "the repeated association of a particular sort of teaching with high rates of success on the part of the learners. . . . Indeed, excellence in teaching has no meaning unless it is in relation to superior achievement in learning" (1989:74). If we believe that effective teaching must be determined by students' learning, then we are faced with the need to document that learning to establish the criterion against which teachers are judged.

However, measuring student achievement is fraught with problems. In order to determine what students have learned in a particular course, it is essential to assess what they knew or could do at the beginning of the course and again at the end, and then determine the difference. This approach to evaluation is only credible if both the before and after measures are appropriate, valid, and reliable. In addition, the procedures and instruments used at these two points in time must measure the same thing and be of equal length and difficulty. In other words, they must be equivalent but not identical measures. If the same test is used at the beginning and the end of the course, the results may be susceptible to the *practice effect* – the "potential influence of the measures on each other" (Brown, 1988:35). Sometimes students remember items from the pretest or learn something by doing the pretest, which can influence their performance on the posttest.

We must consider student achievement data in light of other factors. Language learners, even in homogeneous classes, may differ on several variables: aptitude, motivation, learning styles, study habits, test-taking skills, and so on. Pennington (1989) calls student achievement "an unstable measure" (p. 171) and says "there is a great deal of unpredictable individual variation in test scores produced in a specific course or courses as taught by a particular teacher" (ibid.). For these reasons, teachers should not be evaluated solely on the basis of student achievement. However, measures of students' learning and interest in the subject can provide useful information as part of a broader evaluation process.

Serviceable definitions of effective teaching

In spite of the difficulties in defining effective teaching, we do know enough about the construct to discuss it sensibly and use it cautiously. In a review of teacher effectiveness research in general education, Acheson and Gall (1997:23) acknowledge that "teaching cannot be researched and analyzed because the criteria of effective teaching differ for every instructional situation and every teacher." They add, "We are sympathetic to this argument, but our experience suggests that most teachers and supervisors can develop serviceable definitions of effective teaching to guide the supervision process" (ibid.).

To illustrate this point, Acheson and Gall ask readers to list five characteristics of a good teacher in a particular context: elementary school, secondary school, tertiary education, and so on. They also suggest listing the "characteristics of an *ineffective* teacher" (ibid.). They say most educators find this task easy and that their lists usually agree with one

215

another: "Rarely do we find a controversial characteristic – one that some educators think represents good teaching and other educators think represents bad teaching" (ibid.). Instead, they say, the disagreement is usually over the relative importance of the characteristics listed.

In fact, one of the problems in identifying effective teaching is that everyone feels he or she is knowledgeable about teaching. Everyone at some point has been taught something, and most people have had experience teaching someone something. As a result, "most people, including teachers, supervisors, school administrators, the owner of the neighborhood hangout, the person on the street . . . believe that they can identify good teaching when they see it" (Gebhard, 1984:503). For this reason, it is important for supervisors to go beyond the folk wisdom about effective language teaching and understand the research on this topic.

Some research on effective teaching in general education

Over the years, research in general education has found that teachers whose students learn more than other teachers' students display certain behaviors, attitudes, and skills in common. Citing an early synthesis by Rosenshine and Furst (1973), Acheson and Gall list the following characteristics of successful teachers: (1) clarity; (2) use of varied materials and methods; (3) enthusiasm; (4) a task-oriented, businesslike approach to teaching; (5) avoidance of harsh criticism; (6) indirect teaching style; (7) emphasizing content covered on achievement tests; (8) using structuring statements to provide an overview for what is about to happen or has happened; and (9) use of questions at many cognitive levels (see Acheson and Gall, 1997:25–26). These authors note that studies after 1970 "have continued to demonstrate the effectiveness of these teacher characteristics in promoting student learning" (ibid.:26).

More recently, Glickman et al. (1998:91) found four key patterns in research on effective teaching in general education:

1. Effective teachers have a sense of being in charge, a "can do" attitude. Although effective teachers face the same kinds of problems as ineffective teachers, they see them as challenges to be met, not suffering to be endured.
2. Effective teachers spend whatever time and effort is necessary to assure that all students learn. They give special attention . . . to slower students.
3. Effective teachers have realistic professional attitudes toward students. They possess neither romantic nor cynical views of their students. They see themselves as "diagnosticians and problem solvers," rather than as "mother substitutes" or "disciplinarians" (Brophy and Evertson, 1976:45).

216

4. Effective teachers expect their students to achieve. They believe that all students can learn essential knowledge and skills.

Each statement above is also applicable to language teaching.

Factors influencing teacher effectiveness

Identifying teacher effectiveness is not straightforward, particularly in cross-cultural contexts. Medgyes states that "outstanding teachers cannot be squeezed into any pigeonhole: all outstanding teachers are ideal in their own ways, and as such, are different from each other. The concept of the ideal teacher resists clear-cut definitions, because there are too many variables to consider" (2001:440). Zahorik notes that defining good teaching on the basis of students' learning "would require that that teacher's classroom acts caused the learning" (1992:394). He says that in attributing student learning to the teacher's teaching we would have to "discount students' prior knowledge, aptitude for the particular task, interest, and many other possible causes, such as conditions of the learning environment, the mix of students in the classroom, instructional materials, administrative policies, and involvement of parents" (ibid.). He concludes that "using student learning to measure teaching quality is fraught with conceptual problems" (ibid.).

We also cannot ignore the importance of contextual factors. A teacher who is excellent at one school or with a particular age group might be average in another context. As Strevens notes, "informed teaching in the primary school calls for many differences in practice as compared with, for example, teaching English for specific purposes to mature adults" (1989:84). Language teacher supervisors must be aware of the situational factors – particularly the constraints – that influence teachers.

Strevens (1989) has identified three constraints on excellent language teaching: (1) institutional conditions, (2) students' intention to learn, and (3) the teachers themselves. First, institutional conditions must at least be adequate. These conditions include the materials and equipment available, class size, hours of instruction, and the caliber of teacher preparation. Second, the "learners' 'intention to learn' needs to be raised and maintenanced" (1989:81). Strevens defines *intention to learn* as "the commitment, usually unconscious, on the part of a learner to give his or her attention and effort to learning" (ibid.:81–82). Thus, effective teaching is not just teaching that promotes language learning, but also teaching that improves and sustains students' motivation to go on learning. The third condition is that "teachers need to be capable of 'informed teaching,' that is, to display professionalism in their work" (ibid.:82). Informed teaching requires time and professional

217

commitment, as well as high quality preservice and in-service training programs.

Features of "informed teaching"

Strevens further asserts that "a set of regularly co-occurring features can be identified, so that one may refer to 'informed teaching' as the type of instruction and learning / teaching conditions that commonly produce effective learning" (1989:73). He identifies six features of informed teaching: (1) the teacher has specialized training and experience; (2) the methodology and materials employed are varied, interesting, and perceived by the learners as relevant; (3) the teacher maintains a high "intention to learn" on the part of the learners; (4) the teacher promotes good relations with the learners and makes special efforts specifically for them; (5) there are ample opportunities for practicing the target language, in learner-centered and communicative ways; and whenever possible, (6) teaching and learning are conducted at a high rate of intensity (20 to 25 hours per week).

Strevens concludes, "the informed teacher is an active, reactive, and interactive participant in a two-part learning / teaching process, the other part of which is actively supplied by the learner" (ibid.:82). Therefore supervisors must remember that students are essential parts of the equation. No teacher's effectiveness can be assessed in a vacuum.

Personalization and effective teaching

Increasing students' interest in language learning may be related to personalizing the lessons. Omaggio (1982) reported two parallel studies in the teaching of French as a foreign language in which measures of university French teachers' effectiveness were correlated with the personalization in their language lessons. Strong, positive, statistically significant correlations were found between the teaching effectiveness measures and the following personalization variables: percentage of personalized teacher talk; percentage of personalized student talk; percentage of personalized student talk within the whole-class hour; and percentage of time the teacher prompted or facilitated student response.

These positive correlations were found in two contexts. In the first, two French program supervisors at Ohio State University ranked the instructors on their overall effectiveness as teachers. At the University of New Mexico, students' evaluations of teachers were the criterion variable. Omaggio summarized the findings as follows: "When teacher effectiveness, as measured by subjective supervisory ratings and by end-of-semester student evaluation, was compared to in-class variables relating to degree of personalization, ... there was a high positive correlation between those measures" (1982:265). Personalized communication was defined as "any verbal exchange that involves (1) requesting or sharing facts about oneself or one's acquaintances; (2) requesting or expressing personal concerns; (3) sharing or eliciting private knowledge; [and] (4) remembering or restating the personalized content contributed by others" (ibid.:257). Omaggio concluded that "the more effective teacher...is one who tries to incorporate such personalized language practice into daily lesson plans" (ibid.:266).

These findings about personalization don't suggest that weak teachers can immediately become effective simply by personalizing their lessons. They do suggest, however, that effective language teachers are able to connect language lessons to their students' lives.

Allocated time and engaged time

Following from these points, let us temporarily describe effective language teaching as those sorts of teaching that promote both students' learning and students' intention to learn (Strevens, 1989). Measuring student learning is more difficult than one might assume at first. Measuring their intention to learn is also tricky, but we will focus on student learning here.

Some research in language teaching has used student achievement as the criterion variable. In an early landmark study, Politzer (1970) examined videotaped lessons taught by seventeen secondary school French teachers. He correlated the students' achievement on several different French tests with various teaching behaviors. Theoretically, a strong positive correlation between a given teaching behavior and student achievement would indicate that the particular teaching behavior was "good" or "effective."

Some correlations were found, but Politzer's interpretation of the results is more interesting than the statistical findings. His main point is that there is no simple linear relationship between teaching behavior and student achievement: "With most teaching behaviors measured it is quite obvious that the correlations cannot possibly indicate 'the more the better,' 'the more the worse'" (ibid.:38). Instead, Politzer suggests that there is an optimum range for the use of various teaching behaviors, so what different teachers do in classrooms cannot be easily characterized as "good" or "bad" teaching (ibid.:41). He says there are

> probably very few teaching behaviors or devices which can be classified as intrinsically "bad" or "good." Ultimately, most teaching activities...have probably some value, but each activity is subject to what might be called a principle of economics.

219

> Each activity consumes a limited resource – namely time. Thus the value of each activity depends on the value of other activities which might be substituted for it at a given moment.

Politzer is also careful to point out that good teaching is determined in part by individual student differences and the specific teaching setting. Given this interpretation, "the 'good' teacher is the one who can make the right judgement as to what teaching device is the most valuable at any given moment" (ibid.:43).

Politzer's "principle of economics" leads to an interesting problem: Teaching behaviors are observable, but teachers' decision making typically is not (see Chapter 13). Supervisors do not have direct access to the mental processes teachers use in taking one course of action over another. Thus the principle of economics reminds us that supervisors should ask teachers why they make particular choices and listen carefully to their responses.

Nerenz and Knop reviewed the literature on the use of classroom time in general education, as well as the few studies that had been done on second and foreign language learning. They concluded that teachers influence achievement "only inasmuch as they have an effect on the student's *active involvement* with the material to be learned. Simply put, the things teachers do determine the activities available to students; students' involvement in these activities determines, in large part, the learning outcomes" (1982:244). Nerenz and Knop define two key variables in their own research: The first was *allocated time*, "the amount of time which teachers set aside for particular aspects of the curriculum program" (ibid.:245). Allocated time is directly related to student achievement. Another key construct, *engaged time*, is "the amount of time in which a student was actively working on appropriate curriculum content" (ibid.:244). (This variable is also called *time on task* in some studies.)

Nerenz and Knop hypothesized that engaged time would predict success in foreign language learning as well: "The effective teacher is one who provides students with opportunities to learn the requisite curriculum content *and* who structures instruction so that students are actually involved – not merely 'busy' – with that content" (ibid.: 245). It follows that good teaching "provides students with a maximal amount of exposure to the material within the construct of the school-wide program" (ibid.:246). In other words, an effective teacher addresses the curriculum to be covered, allocates sufficient time in lesson planning, and then executes those lessons so that students' engaged time is maximized.

This relation is depicted in Figure 10.2. Teachers must cover a particular curriculum in a given term, and a certain amount of time is designated

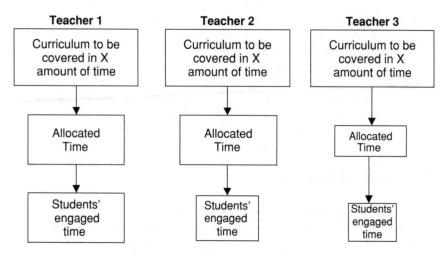

Figure 10.2   Three different teachers' uses of time

during lesson planning for teaching and learning activities (allocated time). The time that is actually spent on such activities during lessons (the students' engaged time) may be the same as or different from the amount of time the teacher chose to allocate, as shown by the size of the boxes in Figure 10.2.

Teacher 1 allocates a certain amount of time for covering a portion of the curriculum. (Some time is dedicated to administrative matters and assessment.) If the teacher successfully involves the students in the subject matter, the engaged time will be nearly equal to the allocated time. Teacher 2 allocates the same amount of time as Teacher 1 for covering some portion of the curriculum, but is less successful in involving the students, so their engaged time is less than that of the students of Teacher 1. Perhaps Teacher 2 is less skillful in those areas of classroom management that get students actively engaged in the material. Teacher 3, in contrast, allocates less time for conveying the same curriculum and also apparently lacks the skills to engage the students' interest and attention. As a result, the students of Teacher 3 spend very little engaged time actually dealing with the curriculum.

This relationship of allocated time and engaged time is pertinent to supervisors' observations. It may be important to ascertain how much time the students are really working on the course objectives. In postobservation conferences, supervisors should provide teachers with clear, credible data about when the learners were and were not engaged with the concepts, and should help teachers develop strategies for increasing the amount of allocated and engaged time.

There is at least one danger in using time on task as an indicator of effective teaching: "The demand that teachers strive for increasing levels of time on task with their students means that fragmentary relationships are elevated in importance above ones that are more communicative, discursive, and democratic" (Gitlin and Smyth, 1990:90). Supervisors must keep this caveat in mind: Focusing on purely observable behaviors in assessing time on task may obscure the importance of time spent on less easily observed cognitive processes.

Concluding comments

This chapter has considered the criteria for evaluating language teachers, including individual opinions, group consensus, teaching methods, competencies, and performance standards. We also reviewed some early research on effective teaching. As Gebhard notes, "The search for effective teaching goes on. For these reasons, since we do not know much about the effects of our teaching behaviors on learning it is difficult to justify what teachers should do in the classroom" (1984:503). Nevertheless, some teacher effectiveness studies provide concepts, such as personalization, upon which language teacher supervisors can draw. We have also seen that allocated time and engaged time are useful constructs in classroom observations.

The following discussion questions are based on the case that began the chapter. Please reread it in the light of all the information you have gained on evaluative criteria.

Case discussion

1. Given only the details in the case, do you consider this teacher effective? What information (from the case, the literature review, or your own experience) influences your opinion?
2. What are your options, as the supervisor, in terms of how to respond to this request for a recommendation? List several possible responses before you decide what course of action you would take. Do your options (or your preference for which option to take) change if you imagine yourself as an experienced teacher supervisor and not as a former peer of this teacher? If so, why? What factors would make your response change?
3. In this case, what constraints influence this teacher's ability to practice "informed teaching" (Strevens, 1989:81–82)? Consider factors related to institutional conditions, the students' intention to learn, and the teacher herself.

4. In the section Some Research on Effective Teaching in General Education, four key points about effective teaching were listed in the research synthesis by Glickman et al. (1998). Which, if any, of these four statements apply to this teacher?
5. If you do decide to write a letter of recommendation for this teacher, what points would you make? Draft your letter and compare it to one written by a colleague.
6. Which constituent(s) of teaching are you dealing with here: awareness, attitude, skills, or knowledge (Freeman, 1989a)? Explain your answer.
7. With a colleague, role-play a conversation with this teacher a day after she asked you for a letter, after you have thought about your reply. (Or you could write a dialogue in which you tell the teacher your decision.)
8. Role-play a conversation with a respected professional who is considering hiring this teacher for a position in an academic language program. What would you say to that person if you decide to write the recommendation, or if you decline to write the letter?

Tasks and discussion

1. Try this activity from Acheson and Gall (1997). First, specify a particular language teaching role and context (e.g., a postsecondary English teacher in an EFL context). Second, list five characteristics of an effective teacher in that role. Next, list at least five characteristics of an ineffective teacher in that same role. Compare your two lists with those of your classmates or colleagues, and discuss any discrepancies.
2. One important goal for us as language teacher supervisors is to be aware of our own beliefs, attitudes, and values. Make a list of five beliefs you have about language learning. How do they translate into your own "serviceable definition" of effective language teaching?
3. What are the behaviors that you think language teachers should use in lessons? What should teachers avoid doing during lessons? List five behaviors that should be incorporated and five behaviors that should be avoided in any language lesson, regardless of the language, the students' age or proficiency level, the curriculum, or the method(s) being used.
4. Rosenshine and Furst's (1973) list of the characteristics of effective teachers is more than 30 years old. (See the section Some Research on Effective Teaching in General Education.) Are there any items here that you think do *not* characterize effective teaching? Are any of the items on this list particularly important in effective *language* teaching? Are there any that are *not* important in language teaching?

5. There may be characteristics of effective *language* teaching that are not part of Rosenshine and Furst's list. If you were to add to the list, what factors would characterize effective *language* teachers?
6. Think of yourself as a supervisor using Rosenshine and Furst's nine characteristics of effective teaching. Which factors would be easily and directly observable? Which are not directly observable and would require inferences on your part? Locate each factor on a continuum ranging from directly observable to highly inferential.
7. What are the parallels and contrasts between Rosenshine and Furst's list and the six features of "informed teaching" identified by Strevens (1989)? How do these ideas relate to the ZPD?
8. Think about allocated time and engaged time as these constructs are manifested in your work as a teacher. Tape-record three of your own language lessons and determine what percent of the time that you allocated is actually realized as engaged time.
9. Politzer's (1970) principle of economics says the value of any teaching activity is determined in part by whatever other activities might have been selected but weren't, because all classroom activities consume time. Think of an outstanding language teacher and decide how well that teacher understood and enacted Politzer's principle of economics. Give an example.
10. Figure 10.1 depicts one system of performance appraisal in the United States. If you work in some other context, either as a language teacher or as a supervisor, how well does this model represent your situation? What parts of the figure fit your context? What parts don't fit? What elements of your work are not represented here?

Suggestions for further reading

For research on teaching effectiveness in general education, see Acheson and Gall (1997) and Glickman et al. (1998).

Omaggio's (1982) research about personalization in language lessons raises interesting issues and questions for further research. Her article and the one by Nerenz and Knop (1982) are a bit dated now, but they present useful constructs for language teacher supervisors.

11 Supervising preservice language teachers

Working with preservice language teachers is a typical work context, especially for new supervisors. People who supervise preservice teachers usually serve one of two key roles. In the first the supervisor is connected with a training program in which those novices are enrolled. (This person is often referred to as the university-based supervisor.) In the second, supervisory responsibilities may be shared with (or held by) the classroom teacher who oversees a novice's field experience (the cooperating teacher).

Some preservice training programs run by colleges, universities, or commercial language schools conduct all their practice teaching within their own classes. But if novices are preparing to work in K–12 contexts or with nonacademic adults, their practice teaching should prepare them for work at those levels. In these cases, university-based supervisors will often visit preservice teachers placed in nearby elementary, secondary, or adult school programs.

This chapter compares the work of cooperating teachers and university supervisors, and examines a model called "situational leadership." It reviews two studies on the relationship between student teachers and cooperating teachers, as well as the findings of a supervisor about her own feedback to trainees. We will also learn about an innovative program in Hungary that trains in-service teachers to supervise preservice teachers.

Case for analysis: The practicum student

You are a teacher educator at a postsecondary institution. Your responsibilities include teaching the practicum, visiting the novices as they complete their student teaching in local schools, and giving them feedback. You must write a final report on each trainee's progress, which is a key part of the summative evaluation for teacher candidates in your program.

Dee, a student in your practicum class, is a native speaker of the language she will teach. She is currently in her final semester, having completed all the coursework for her diploma. Your colleagues who have been her teachers say Dee has done good to excellent work.

In the practicum, Dee is quiet and seems a bit anxious, though she contributes ideas to the discussion if you call on her. She is one

---

of the less experienced teachers in the class. You place her with a well-respected teacher for her student teaching. He has been the cooperating teacher for other trainees and is known to be helpful and reasonable. After three weeks, he tells you Dee is a very weak teacher. He says she lacks confidence, can't make up her mind, doesn't carry out her lesson plans, and seems very tentative in class. The teacher asks you to observe her as soon as possible.

You observe Dee teaching a few days later. Indeed, the cooperating teacher has not exaggerated. Dee's teaching is so hesitant that she appears incompetent. In preparing for the post-observation conference, you decide to focus on one five-minute segment of data from the lesson. (Your elaborated field notes appear in Chapter 5 as Figure 5.2.)

The prevalence of research on preservice teacher supervision

Much of the research about language teacher supervision deals with preservice teacher training. Why is this so?

First, in some countries, much of the preservice training in the language teaching profession occurs at colleges and universities, where faculty members are typically required to "publish or perish." So it is logical that university teachers faced with publication requirements would conduct research on their teacher preparation work.

Second, supervising trainees fits well in the research on language teacher education. How novices join the profession has become an important research focus over the past two decades. (See, for instance, Casanave and Schecter, 1997; Flowerdew, Brock, and Hsia, 1992; Freeman, 1989a, 1989b; Freeman and Richards, 1996; Johnson, 1996b, 2000; Li, Mahoney, and Richards, 1994; Pennington and Richards, 1997; Richards and Nunan, 1990; Sachs, Brock, and Lo, 1996.) Many of these resources deal with supervision directly, in chapters on this topic (see, e.g., Wallace, 1991) or indirectly, through discussions of supervision embedded in other topics.

Third, supervising preservice teachers is less laden with problems than supervising in-service teachers, and therefore it is easier to write about. Why? Normally preservice teachers put themselves into contexts where supervision is expected, if not welcomed. The trainees acknowledge that they have something to learn about teaching. They typically enroll in a practicum course, which is the "major opportunity for the student teacher to acquire the practical skills and knowledge needed to function as an effective language teacher" (Richards and Crookes, 1988:9). Therefore, as the supervisor, you are working with people who expect you to talk with them about their teaching. And the regular practicum meetings provide both a venue for talking openly about teaching and a critical mass of people interested in doing so.

In the in-service context, in contrast, teachers are supposed to be competent. That's why they were hired. Unless you hold regular staff meetings or workshops to examine teaching, most of your discussions with the in-service teachers will be conducted on an individual basis. Ironically, having private meetings to discuss teaching can increase the likelihood of sensitivity and the teacher's loss of face. (In large groups, an individual can think, "Surely that statement doesn't apply to me!" In one-on-one discussions, it is difficult for teachers to deny that particular statements are directed at them.) Likewise, in the absence of a practicum course or staff meetings for discussing teaching, you'll need a particular time and place to discuss an observation or other concerns. Such a discussion is thus marked as an other-than-ordinary form of interaction.

In addition, busy supervisors who are not required to publish research findings may not be motivated to do so. As a result, the supervision of in-service teachers in primary, secondary, or adult schools, commercial programs, or community colleges is not as well represented in publications as is the supervision of preservice teachers.

One of the challenges in supervising preservice teachers is that these teachers are so varied! Some will be true novices. Others will have teaching experience, but not in *language* teaching. And sometimes (e.g., in master's degree programs), the trainees will have a wide range of experiences. Therefore, the supervisor must ask, "What is the most effective form of supervision to use in any given circumstance with the individual concerned?" (Clark, 1990:39). Clark says that "the answer should be determined by the two people in consultation. Individualized supervision will lead to individualized development" (ibid.).

Situational leadership and language teacher supervision

The situational leadership model provides a framework for approximating Clark's idea that individualized supervision leads to individualized development. This model originated in management but has been used in education and can be helpful for language teacher supervisors. It suggests that effective leaders tailor their behavior to meet the needs of their followers.

Based on her experience as an EFL teacher trainer in China, Osburne (1989) discusses two components of leadership behavior: *task behavior*

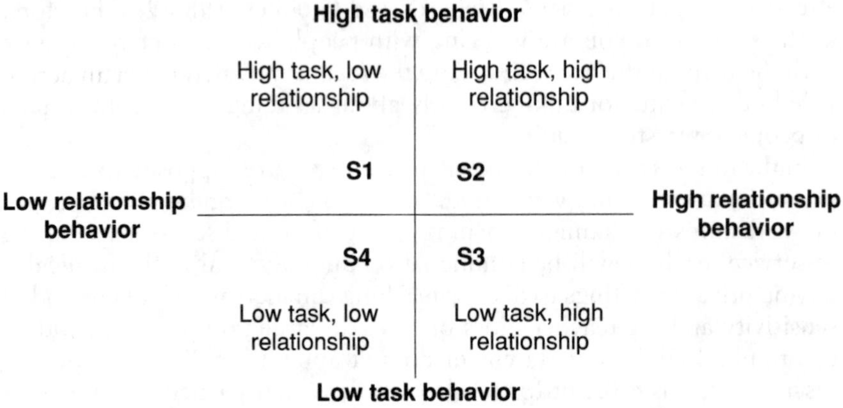

High task behavior

High task, low relationship	High task, high relationship
S1	**S2**

Low relationship behavior ————————————————————— **High relationship behavior**

S4	**S3**
Low task, low relationship	Low task, high relationship

Low task behavior

Figure 11.1 Continua of relationship and task behaviors in situational leadership

and *relationship behavior*. These terms are defined as follows (Hersey and Blanchard, 1982:96):

> *Task behavior* is "the extent to which leaders are likely to organize and define the roles of the members of their group (followers); to explain what activities each is to do, and when, where and how tasks are to be accomplished"; [and] *relationship behavior* is "the extent to which leaders are likely to maintain personal relationships between themselves and members of their group (followers) by opening up channels of communication [and] providing socioemotional support."

We can apply these concepts to language teacher supervision, where the supervisor must attend to both task behaviors and relationship behaviors while interacting with teachers.

The supervisor's leadership style

Leadership style is "the behavior . . . [a] person exhibits when attempting to influence the activities of others as perceived by those others" (ibid.:95–96). Effective leaders are flexible in emphasizing or de-emphasizing relationship and task behaviors. They can use either high or low task behaviors, as well as high or low relationship behavior orientations. These two constructs are plotted as overlapping continua in Figure 11.1. The *S* in each quadrant stands for "style."

The S1 quadrant represents high task, low relationship strategies. In this combination, the supervisor would not attend to maintaining relationships or providing socioemotional support but would provide clear guidance about the tasks to be accomplished. Consider the example of the field notes in Chapter 5 (where the teacher couldn't find the right place in the audiotape). In using S1 that supervisor might say, "I'll be back to visit again next Wednesday, and I want to see you lead an activity where you start with the tape properly cued."

Quadrant S2 represents high task and high relationship behavior. In this style the supervisor might say, "It was great that you used audiotape to provide varied input to your students. I'll be back next Wednesday, and I want to see another audiotape activity. If you start with it properly cued, you'll feel more confident." In this style, the clarity about the task is maintained, but the supervisor also provides emotional support and builds a positive relationship.

In quadrant S3 (low task, high relationship behavior), the supervisor would not be specific about a task, but would maintain or build a positive relationship. The supervisor might say something like, "That was a very nice lesson. I'll be back Wednesday. I'll look forward to observing any activity you choose. I know you felt badly about the tape recording, but these things happen. You'll do fine – you're a natural language teacher."

Quadrant S4 represents a nonjudgmental, nondirective style that is neutral as to affect and also minimalist as to specific guidance. In this case, the supervisor would exhibit low task, low relationship behavior, and might just say, "I'll be back to visit again on Wednesday."

What guides the selection of these various combinations of task and relationship behavior? To answer that question, we must examine the concept of readiness.

The trainees' readiness levels

One factor that determines what leadership style to use is the person being supervised. Is the teacher a novice who lacks confidence and experience, or an experienced, confident teacher? One can also be confident but inexperienced, or experienced but lacking in confidence. In situational leadership, these combinations are referred to as readiness.

Readiness is people's "ability and willingness . . . to take responsibility for their own behavior" (Hersey and Blanchard, 1982:151). There are two components of readiness: *job readiness*, the "knowledge, ability and experience to perform certain tasks without direction from others" (ibid.), and *psychological readiness*, the "confidence and commitment or . . . willingness to do something" (ibid.) These constructs can also be depicted as overlapping continua, as shown in Figure 11.2.

This model posits that certain leadership styles are most appropriate for working with people at given readiness levels. That is, leaders will be more successful if they select the combinations that will work best with particular followers, as portrayed in Table 11.1.

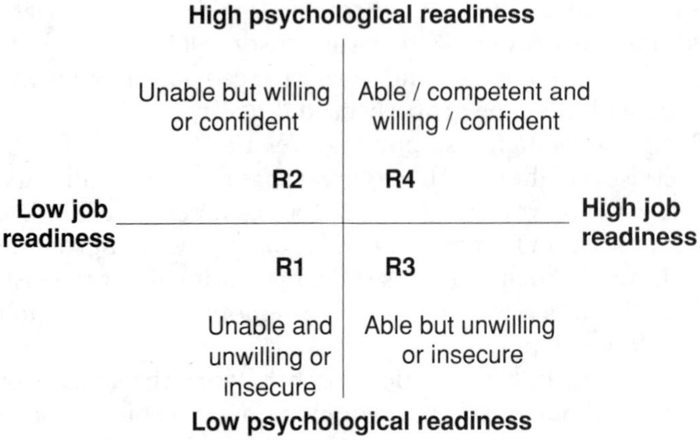

High psychological readiness

Unable but willing or confident	Able / competent and willing / confident
R2	**R4**

Low job readiness ———————————————— **High job readiness**

R1	**R3**
Unable and unwilling or insecure	Able but unwilling or insecure

Low psychological readiness

Figure 11.2 Continua of job and psychological readiness in situational leadership

Table 11.1 *Connecting readiness and style using the situational leadership model (Hersey, 1984:71, adapted from Daughtrey and Ricks, 1989:333)*

	Readiness	Style	Descriptor
R1	Unable and unwilling or insecure	*S1* HT / LR	Provide specific instructions and closely supervise performance
R2	Unable but willing or confident	*S2* HT / HR	Explain decisions and provide opportunity for clarification
R3	Able but unwilling or insecure	*S3* LT / HR	Share ideas and facilitate followers in decision making
R4	Able and willing or confident	*S4* LT / LR	Turn over responsibility for decisions and implementation

Of course, confidence and willingness are two different things, even though they are treated similarly in these quadrants. This distinction is not so significant in quadrant R1 (where the trainee is unable, unwilling, and experiencing self-doubt), or in quadrant R4 (where the trainee is willing and / or confident). However, the contrast is important in quadrants R2 and R3. In quadrant R2, the unable trainee is characterized as being willing or confident, while in quadrant R3 the able trainee is characterized as being unwilling or insecure. The combination that is not depicted is the possibility (e.g., in quadrant R3) that the trainee is able and willing but insecure, or secure but unwilling. Likewise in quadrant R2, the trainee could be unable and unwilling but confident, or willing but unconfident. The intervention strategies a supervisor might select would vary under these contrasting situations.

Situational leadership and the zone of proximal development

Job readiness is related to Vygotsky's zone of proximal development (ZPD), which, as discussed in Chapter 2, refers to the distance between a person's "actual developmental level as determined by independent problem solving and the level of potential development as determined through problem solving under adult guidance or in collaboration with more capable peers" (1978:86). Vygotsky was discussing children's learning, but the ZPD construct is applicable to learning by preservice teachers too.

People approach learning tasks or problems with their own perspectives – their own subjective ways of making sense of those tasks or problems. Through discussion, two or more individuals may develop shared understandings that are mutually agreed on, or intersubjective (Nyikos and Hashimoto, 1997). These authors add, "through collaboration within each person's zone of potential understanding, the knower and the learner may reach intersubjectivity or a shared understanding" (p. 508). A further connection to teacher learning is that *intersubjectivity* means "participants are jointly focused on the activity and its goals, and they draw each other's attention into a common direction" (van Lier, 1996:161).

In the context of supervision, determining teachers' levels of job and psychological readiness is partly a process of coming to understand those teachers' ZPDs. As supervisors talk with teachers in pre- and post-observation conferences, intersubjectivity can be built.

Two processes promote intersubjectivity, according to Nyikos and Hashimoto. The first is the *cognitive apprenticeship*, during which learners "are encouraged to monitor their performance in the context of the task, to compare their performance to the experts' ways, and to move between the roles of knower and learner" (1997:508). A cognitive apprenticeship is similar to scaffolding, but in the former, "responsibility for learning is primarily on the learner / apprentice, whereas in scaffolding the more knowledgeable person assumes the responsibility of offering the learner support to facilitate learning" (ibid.). So while the preservice teacher is engaged in a cognitive apprenticeship, the supervisor can provide scaffolding. But these authors caution that it is "critical to acknowledge the inherent power relationships between the knower and the learner" (ibid.). They add that "power-sharing and mutual understanding (i.e., intersubjectivity) are required for the ZPD to function" (ibid.).

231

This point suggests that some supervisory roles may be more appropriate than others: "If social interaction takes place between an individual who continually dominates learning and a student who always follows, co-construction of knowledge may not occur" (ibid.). For this reason, they add, "more knowledgeable persons must continually be aware of the learners' ranges of potential growth and must calibrate the power balance for mutual understanding" (ibid.).

The second process that promotes intersubjectivity is *critical thinking*, which the authors define as thinking "from different points of view, acknowledging bias when solving given problems" (ibid.:509). Cognitive development occurs through the accommodation of new ideas into one's existing cognitive framework through social interaction. Nyikos and Hashimoto suggest that critical thinking consists of two key components: "(1) a frame of mind that allows examination of multiple viewpoints, and (2) a number of specific mental operations, such as determining reliability of a source, distinguishing relevance, detecting bias, identifying assumptions, and recognizing inconsistencies or fallacies" (ibid.). A related concept, *dialogic thinking*, is "the ability to see any issue from many points of view and realize people can address an issue constructively without necessarily agreeing with each other" (Pugh, 1996:2, as cited in Nyikos and Hashimoto, 1997:509). Supervisors can clearly promote teachers' dialogic thinking (e.g., in discussing different viewpoints about the success of an activity), but supervisors too must be able to view the issue from many perspectives.

Matching leadership styles and readiness levels

These situational leadership frameworks and sociocultural theory provide useful concepts for language teacher supervisors. We can choose from among these styles to accomplish our goals with particular language teachers. And the decision is not a one-time-only choice: Effective supervisors can determine teachers' readiness and choose an appropriate style. The situation might demand focusing on the task at hand or attending to a teacher's confidence level, or both. At times one style will be more appropriate, and in other cases another style may be preferable.

One difficulty for language teacher supervisors is having responsibility to the administration, the language students, the cooperating teachers, and the preservice teachers themselves. In addition, the supervisor's role entails both helping and evaluating. There may be occasions when you are working with a trainee who is unable but willing, when support and guidance are needed to help the teacher develop as an effective professional. However, if that teacher does not make sufficient gains in knowledge and skills in a given time period, it may be your responsibility to file a critical observation report or summative evaluation, which might negatively influence the trainee's ability to graduate and find desirable work. Other trainees may be confident and experienced, but nevertheless have serious weaknesses in their work. In this situation, different strategies for guidance are called for, so it is important to determine whether a teacher is unable but willing, able but unwilling, or both unable and unwilling.

The choice of high or low task orientations is determined largely by the person(s) you are supervising: Some teachers work well with minimal explicit guidance; others benefit from clear discussions, demonstrations, or even written contracts for change. And while some supervision involves individuals, some entails working with groups in a practicum (or an entire staff in an in-service context). In those cases it may not always be possible to tailor your behavior to suit the needs of all the individuals present.

The choice of high or low relationship behaviors is related to your preferred style and how you believe people change. Is change generated by giving direct instructions, by making suggestions, by modeling and patient forbearance, or by having people experiment on their own? The answer may vary depending on the teachers' training and experience.

Participants in the supervision of student teachers

Practice teaching (also called student teaching) is a component of many professional preparation programs for teachers. (In 1979 Clifton said it was a part of virtually every teacher education program in Canada.) It is predicated on the assumption that novice teachers need guided practice in learning how to teach. The teacher-in-training is placed with an experienced teacher but is also observed by a representative of the program providing the training. Placing the novice in the classroom of an experienced teacher is a clear illustration of the craft model of teacher education (Wallace, 1991), which was depicted in Figure 7.2. The typical participants in this context are the trainee, or student teacher, the classroom-based cooperating teacher, and the university-based supervisor, as shown in Figure 11.3.

Practice teaching is widely used, but it is not a universal requirement in language teacher preparation around the world. In many contexts, subject matter knowledge (e.g., a degree in Spanish, or postgraduate studies in Russian linguistics) is considered a sufficient qualification for teacher candidates. However, as teaching has come to be recognized as a profession, an emphasis on pedagogy has emerged. For this reason, many preservice programs require practice teaching. While practice teaching

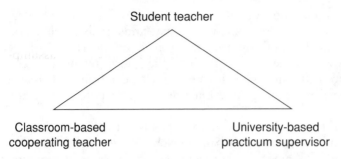

Figure 11.3 Participants in the traditional practicum context

may be seen as optional where there are teacher shortages, elsewhere it is an important component of teacher education. The practicum is also the context in which many new teacher educators first work as supervisors.

Cooperating teachers in language classrooms

In the practice teaching context, teacher learners are frequently paired with experienced teachers who are recognized as knowledgeable and skilled. The cooperating teachers serve as models, pedagogical tutors, sounding boards, and allies to the student teachers. Their very presence can make the university-based supervisor's role much easier.

Unfortunately, cooperating teachers are seldom specifically prepared to supervise novice teachers: "The assumption, apparently, is that anyone who can teach can also supervise" (Goldsberry, 1988:4–5). And coordinating the supervision by two people (the cooperating teacher and the university supervisor) is "more of a challenge than it may seem" (ibid.:5). Goldsberry observes that "the overwhelmed college supervisor often jettisons the baggage of supervising to her school-based counterpart, intervening only when someone complains" (ibid.). In my experience, this abdication of responsibility by the university supervisor is not common, but neither is it rare. We should at least acknowledge that good communication between the two supervisors is important for the trainee as well as the language learners.

Sometimes this triangular relationship can make the practicum supervisor's job more difficult. Some cooperating teachers try to buffer the student teachers from criticism by the supervisor. Others may refuse to turn over teaching or planning to the student teacher. Still others may see the concepts the novices have been learning in their training program as irrelevant to their language students' needs. Conservative cooperating teachers may insist that the trainees not experiment with new methods or ideas but stick to "tried and true" procedures.

234

A student teacher in a general education context

Lemma (1993) published a case study of a cooperating first-grade teacher trained to work with novices. In the training sessions, three key assumptions emerged. First, cooperating teachers who were themselves competent and effective educators should be chosen. Second, they should be reflective and articulate about their teaching in order to promote reflective thinking in student teachers through modeling and discussion. Third, cooperating teachers providing systematic observation and feedback "should supervise the student teacher experience for improved and enhanced classroom instruction" (ibid.:331).

Some studies show that "cooperating teachers do not provide critical feedback to their student teachers, and that when [cooperating teachers] do critique lessons, they are careful not to mention negatively evaluated areas, instead couching their criticism in the form of 'pep talks'" (ibid.). But other studies suggest that cooperating teachers can be effective, "especially when provided with some type of preparation for their supervisory role" (ibid.).

Lemma reports on a survey of 201 cooperating teachers and 209 student teachers in Connecticut. Data were also collected from focus groups (20 cooperating teachers and 20 trainees) to determine the training program's success in preparing cooperating teachers for supervision. The overall results were positive, but many questions arose. Lemma's case study addressed those remaining issues. She found the following (ibid.:332):

> A large majority (88 percent) of cooperating teachers reported meeting daily or more often with their student teacher until the fourth week of the placement. Thereafter, a downward trend occurred; after the third week, only 54 percent of the cooperating teachers reported daily contact. Also during the first three weeks of the field experience, a large majority of the cooperating teachers (80 percent) said they observed their student teacher's teaching 75 percent or more of the time. But again, by the fourth week of the student teacher independently teaching lessons, a decline occurred with 43 percent of the cooperating teachers claiming such frequency of observation.

So after the fourth week of the semester, the majority of the student teachers did not receive much systematic feedback from their cooperating teachers.

Because of the cooperating teachers' flexibility, many student teachers regarded the relationship with their cooperating teachers positively. The cooperating teachers were often willing to suspend their normal routines to let trainees experiment, and they helped the student teachers feel like part of the team by involving them in all aspects of teaching: "Direct statements mention working on discipline, working on methods, creating a positive environment, and providing materials" (ibid.:333). Unfortunately, however, the cooperating teachers' discussions did not guide the student teacher to consider "teaching itself or the impact of teacher behaviors on learners and learning" (ibid.). Lemma speculates, "One wonders if student teachers are led to self-evaluate, thus developing skills of assessment for later use, or if they are dependent upon the evaluations of the cooperating teacher" (ibid.).

Lemma used three data sources: "(1) interviews with both the cooperating teacher and the student teacher, (2) the cooperating teacher's journal writing, and (3) audiotaped conferences between the cooperating teacher and student teacher" (ibid.). Thus she could triangulate her findings and investigate both parties' perspectives.

In the case study, the cooperating teacher focused on helping the trainee raise her own awareness. The teacher's pseudonym is Ms. Anderson, and the novice teacher is called Amy. In discussing what it means to supervise a student teacher,

> Ms. Anderson saw both a direct and indirect involvement with Amy. She stated, "In the beginning, supervising would be a situation of exposing [her to] what's being talked about. To talk about what she's doing, to bring up things that she may not see as a problem, but I may. Heightening her awareness would be one of my jobs." Ms. Anderson . . . compared her [observational] skills with those of the school principal and thought they still needed developing. (ibid.:335)

Support of the novice by the cooperating teacher was a key theme. Prior to working with the student teacher, the cooperating teacher saw herself in a support role:

> She predicted she would use classroom observations followed by conferences with the student teacher. She also saw herself as a model for the student teacher, sharing ideas and expertise, serving as a resource. Ms. Anderson acknowledged that reflection and self-analysis should be part of the student teacher's experience. (ibid.)

Ms. Anderson did indeed fulfill her intention of providing support to Amy, but she was less rigorous in conducting observations and holding post-observation conferences. She did not discuss any observational data, though she had been present while Amy was teaching:

> Instead of relying on data collected during the observed lesson, the conferences seemed to concentrate on perceptions of "how

things went." The conferences conveyed a sense of two teachers talking about teaching in general, rather than a cooperating and student teacher analyzing a specific lesson. (ibid.:336)

This stance could be appropriate, if the student teacher were showing sufficient professionalism and progress. Here, the cooperating teacher adopted the low task, high relationship style mentioned previously. One possible interpretation is that the cooperating teacher would have adopted the same strategy regardless of the student teacher placed with her. However,

> Ms. Anderson's statement that she "faded into the background" *once* she was confident of Amy's abilities suggests that the behavior of the cooperating teacher was based on her perceptions of Amy's competence. She may have behaved quite differently with a less able student teacher. (ibid.:339)

Lemma concludes that training programs must build effective partnerships with cooperating teachers, especially "if they continue to employ the triad made up of student teacher, cooperating teacher, and university supervisor" (ibid.:342). These partnerships could link "research-based and principle-based views of knowledge represented by the university supervisor, and experience-based knowledge generated daily in schools by teaching practitioners" (ibid.).

A student teacher in a second language context

What do teacher trainees think about the relationship among themselves, the university-based supervisors, and the school-based cooperating teachers? Little research has been done on the trainees' perspectives, but Johnson investigated the tensions inherent in a TESOL practicum. She focused on a preservice ESL teacher called Maja, who was completing the practicum. Johnson (1996c) made field notes during weekly observations and interviewed Maja before and after each observation. Three lessons were also videotaped. Finally, Maja used a teaching journal to record her daily reflections on her practicum experience.

Based on her observations and the student teacher's input, Johnson (ibid.:31) describes Maja's 15-week ESL practicum in an urban secondary school:

> Her cooperating teacher, Joan, was responsible for two different groups of ESL students. The first group were refugees, mostly Vietnamese and Amer-Asians, who lacked literacy skills and formal schooling in their native language. These students were placed in ESL literacy classes... where they received basic reading and writing instruction in English.... The second group

were first-generation immigrants...who arrived in the United States after having attended school in their own countries, and who were literate in their native languages. [They] were enrolled in ESL content-based science and social studies classes...[and] also took more advanced-level composition and literature classes, designed to upgrade their academic reading and writing skills in English.

Johnson adds that Maja "was excited about her practicum placement. These were the type of students with whom she wanted to work. This was the type of school where she wanted to teach" (ibid.), so the conditions allowed Maja to prepare for her future career.

Maja made some comments about her relationship with the cooperating teacher, Joan, in her diary entries. About halfway through the practicum experience, Maja wrote:

> I don't feel like I'm really "teaching" this semester...[Joan] decides what needs to be done, and so there doesn't seem to be much room for changes. This sort of upsets me...I have to fit into what she wants me to do, even though I don't really feel comfortable with it. I'm not really uncomfortable, but I know if I had my own class, I'd do it my way. I guess it's just part of this practicum thing. It's not real teaching. (ibid.:40)

This entry illustrates a central tension in the practicum. The cooperating teacher has a vision of the course and what the trainee's role can be. The student teacher also has a vision, which may differ from the cooperating teacher's view. Maja felt Joan's teaching was

> "winging it" and "picking and choosing." She explained, "All they do is...mountains of dittos. She just picks out activities...and there is no well thought-out plan for why these activities are done." She said, "All of the assignments are disconnected and unrelated to each other. The stuff they do in class has no purpose, is never corrected, and the students know this, so they really don't care about any of their assignments." (ibid.)

Maja made allowances for their differences, however: "It is not that Joan is a bad teacher, but that she has a different vision of what she believes is good teaching" (ibid.).

Maja's remarks illustrate another dilemma in the practicum: Sometimes the student teachers are more organized and better prepared than are the cooperating teachers with whom they are placed. If you work as a supervisor in a context where you have access to a variety of well-qualified, open-minded, and flexible cooperating teacher candidates, it is important to be very selective as you place student teachers in their classes.

One function of the practicum is to help novice teachers enter the real world of the classroom. Sometimes this is an uneasy transition. Halfway through the practicum,

> Maja's initial enthusiasm had dissolved into complaints about "realities" that seemed beyond her control. The realities of teaching had begun to overwhelm her to the point that she appeared to be separating herself from the practicum experience. Her sense of having no control over what happened during the practicum seemed to trouble her the most. She seemed ready to give up, and might have done so if Joan had not suggested that she take over the advanced-level ESL literature class for the remainder of the practicum. (ibid.)

This suggestion gave Maja the freedom she needed to spread her wings. In fact, she was granted almost an absence of structure: "Joan told Maja that she could teach whatever she wanted in the advanced-level ESL literature class as long as the students read some literature and wrote about it. This opportunity seemed to excite as well as frighten Maja" (ibid.).

Maja set up lesson plans, created materials, and designed a 17-page unit plan for her literature students. She said, "I told my supervisor that I wanted my lessons to be organized, that I couldn't stand up in front of them without things all laid out. So she helped me plan out each week, all organized, all related to each other, all leading up to a final project" (ibid.:41). Maja and Joan had established a balance between freedom and guidance that allowed Maja to exercise her ideas and try new activities, while still being supported by her cooperating teacher.

The practicum should give trainees "a reasonable amount of control over what and how they will teach . . . so that they can test their emerging conceptions of teaching" (ibid.:47–48). Finding the right amount of freedom and support for preservice teachers is a delicate balancing act for both the cooperating teacher and the university-based supervisor.

A team teaching practicum arrangement

Alternatives to the traditional practicum have sometimes been used with considerable success. For example, two novices can be placed together in a team teaching arrangement. Since there is no cooperating teacher, the two novices coach each other and receive feedback from the university-based supervisor, as depicted in Figure 11.4.

In this situation, the two novices have freedom to experiment with and collaborate on lesson planning, teaching, and follow-up actions. This

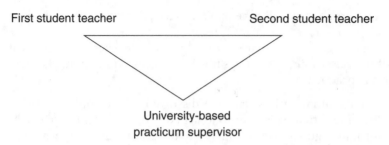

Figure 11.4 Participants in the team-taught practicum context

experience was described by Knezevic and Scholl (1996), two student teachers who team-taught a Spanish class. They say that

> the need to synchronize teaching acts requires team teachers to negotiate and discuss their thoughts, values, and actions in ways that solo teachers do not encounter. The process of having to explain oneself and one's ideas, so that another teacher can understand them and interact with them, forces team teachers to find words for thoughts which, had one been teaching alone, might have been realized solely through action. (p. 79)

Collaborating on lesson plans was important to Knezevic and Scholl, for whom collaboration was "a conscious way of approaching teaching, based on respect for and appreciation of the other's presence" (ibid.). Collaboration created opportunities to recognize, articulate, and understand their own tacit knowledge about teaching by sharing responsibility (ibid.). If we contrast the previous comment with Maja's initial practicum, we see that these two teachers apparently had a much richer experience in terms of what they were able to do.

Perhaps placing two novice teachers together without the guidance and support of a cooperating teacher would be considered risky by some university-based supervisors. Nevertheless, these authors conclude that team teaching is a viable alternative for preservice candidates: "Collaboration can serve as a catalyst and a mirror for exposing, expressing, and examining ideas. It can lead to enriched learning and improved instruction" (ibid.:95).

Responsibilities of university-based supervisors

The university-based supervisor of preservice teachers represents the training program and serves as an ambassador of that program to the schools where the candidates do their student teaching. Part of the supervisor's role is to help novice language teachers make connections

240

between the material in their training courses and the classroom contexts they face. If the trainees are enrolled in a program that emphasizes the applied science model of teacher education (Wallace, 1991; see Figure 7.3), the supervisor may need to guide them as they build bridges between the research and theories they have studied and the realities of classroom teaching.

Unfortunately, the university-based supervisor may have little time to devote to individual trainees. Freiburg and Waxman (1990) point out that each practicum supervisor may work with 10 or 12 student teachers and may only observe each one three or four times during the practicum semester. In addition, "much of the supervisor's time is consumed in travelling to and from the various sites, with little time remaining for quality feedback" (p. 8).

In other cases, the university-based supervisor who is responsible for observing the trainees may or may not be the instructor for the practicum in which the trainees meet to share teaching ideas, raise questions, and support one another. Nevertheless, the existence of the practicum as a forum for discussion is one key distinction between supervising preservice and in-service teachers.

Supervising preservice teachers is different from working with in-service teachers in other ways too. First, university-based supervisors must answer to the novices whom they supervise, because the supervisors' input is part of the trainees' education. But in the practice teaching context, the supervisor is also responsible to the cooperating teacher and the language students in the classroom where the trainees are placed, the program in which the preservice teachers are enrolled, and the profession at large. The cooperating teacher and the language students are going about their regular teaching and learning. The preservice teacher should contribute positively to that context. At the least, the trainee should do no harm in the cooperating teacher's classroom. A trainee who is inept, wastes the learners' time, does not have a good command of the language, or does not incorporate feedback from the cooperating teacher will probably not accomplish much in terms of the learners' progress. In the worst-case scenario, a novice teacher can do so much damage that the cooperating teacher will no longer accept student teachers from the teacher training program.

A supervisor working for the preservice training program (rather than as a cooperating teacher) has a twofold evaluative responsibility to that program. First, the supervisor must determine whether the trainee meets the program's exit requirements (a summative evaluation). Making that judgment is more straightforward if those requirements are stated as clear goals (e.g., the candidate can plan a syllabus based on a needs assessment), rather than on "seat-time" (e.g., the candidate completes a three-unit seminar on syllabus design and needs assessment). But it is also the supervisor's responsibility to promote the trainee's professional development, because the training program markets, and has a contractual obligation to provide, that person's education. In this sense, the primary focus must often be on formative evaluation.

The responsibility to the profession is somewhat nebulous but just as important. University-based supervisors and cooperating teachers occasionally supervise some trainees who are not ready to assume professional responsibilities. They may even work with some trainees whom they feel are not "cut out" to be teachers. While a supervisor may be convinced of the latter position, asserting that someone should not be a teacher is quite different from saying that person is not yet ready to be a teacher. We will now explore the concept of readiness.

Readiness, declarative knowledge, and procedural knowledge

In situational leadership, the trainees' *job readiness* is one key to how supervisors carry out their responsibilities. The focus on job readiness entails both *declarative knowledge* (articulated knowledge about the subject matter and teaching) and *procedural knowledge* (the ability to do certain things). In language teaching, procedural knowledge encompasses the ability to teach and the ability to use the language proficiently. Declarative knowledge is sometimes characterized as "knowing what," while procedural knowledge refers to "knowing how."

Novice teachers may have credible declarative knowledge (e.g., of linguistic rules). In Freeman's (1989a) terms, these novices will be strong in the knowledge constituent of teaching. However, they may lack the skills for working with real language students.

In other cases, novice teachers may have strong procedural knowledge (in teaching or in the use of the target language). These teachers exhibit strengths in the skills of teaching (Freeman, 1989a). They may or may not have the declarative knowledge to explain the rationale for their teaching decisions or to make informed decisions in the first place.

Given the myriad factors present in practice teaching, there can be no one-size-fits-all advice for supervisors. Likewise, the preservice teachers themselves bring a variety of experiences, strengths, and needs to this situation. For all these reasons, it behooves supervisors of preservice teachers to be professional, creative, supportive, honest, and flexible.

Problems in giving feedback to preservice teachers

As we saw in Chapter 8, the provision of feedback potentially involves face-threatening acts and supervisors are particularly sensitive about giving critical feedback to novice teachers. For instance, Freiburg and Waxman summarized the research on the feedback to preservice teachers in general education in the United States. They found that "most supervisors of student teachers receive very little preparation or training, and many do not have the expertise to supervise beginning teachers effectively" (1990:8). These authors contend that cooperating teachers are often aware of problems but don't feel comfortable giving student teachers critical feedback. In addition, "training the cooperating teacher receives affects the quality of the early field experience" (ibid.). These results confirm Lemma's (1993) finding that Ms. Anderson was more concerned with supporting Amy than with giving her input about her teaching.

Freiburg and Waxman (1990:8–9) make the following key point about time in a typical practicum:

> An eight or fifteen-week student teaching experience ... will consist of at least two weeks where the student teacher observes the cooperating teacher. A gradual transfer of teaching responsibility occurs over the following few weeks. Many teachers who are concerned about accountability on test scores will require that the student teachers return to the classes several weeks prior to the end of the semester.

They conclude that "the end result is a highly contracted experience with reduced contact hours with students and subsequent reduction in opportunities for feedback" (ibid.:9).

Research on feedback to preservice teachers

Some research has investigated teachers' perceptions of whether feedback is helpful. A study of preservice teachers in Finland (Jyrhama, 2001) found that about 60 percent of the trainees felt their supervisors' advice was useful, but a small percentage thought their advice was not at all useful. Jyrhama concluded that *why* questions from supervisors helped student teachers consider the elements of successful teaching.

Lewis examined the feedback she herself provided to teachers in New Zealand. She states that in a training program, a supervisor's feedback serves at least five purposes (1998:69):

1. Feedback can establish a bridge between theory and practice, but this link needs to be made explicit in the observer's written comments (Freeman, 1994).
2. The lecturer's comments can reinforce the teacher's developing professional language which will establish their membership of the TESOL community (Freeman, 1996).

3. Feedback can provide formative evaluation in that it offers advice which can make a difference at the time it is given, rather than simply establishing a final grade.

4. The follow-up session in which the teacher and the observer discuss the evaluative comments establishes a process of collaborative reflection which is important during a practicum (Dufficy, 1993; Wajnryb, 1992).

5. The evaluation of teaching practice can make a difference to teaching by turning input into uptake or intake (Pennington, 1996).

So in addition to providing practical tips, supervisors' feedback can promote reflective practice and socialize novices into the professional discourse community. These points pertain to feedback from both cooperating teachers and university-based supervisors, although the latter may be more comfortable bridging theory and practice.

Lewis analyzed her own feedback to the ESOL practice teachers in New Zealand at the University of Auckland's postgraduate Diploma in English Language Teaching. The author's comments to the teachers (the database for this study) were originally written during 28 classroom visits. Lewis selected nine typical data sets to analyze: three sets of data written for teachers working at each of three levels (primary schools, secondary schools, and adult teaching). She also selected data sets from four trainees with high grades, three with low grades, and two with average grades. These teachers had between four and twenty years of teaching experience, so none were true novices.

In her original notes, Lewis focused on the topics the trainees had asked her to watch for. Lewis gave the teachers the evaluative comments immediately after each lesson without rewriting the notes, and a copy was also retained for discussion. Lewis says that "the teachers were told that the comments were their own property and would not be shown to school principals or supervisors" (ibid.). Thus the data in this study were authentic, naturally occurring examples of feedback written with only the student teachers as the intended audience.

There were four categories in Lewis' content analysis of 99 feedback comments: (1) commendations, (2) questions and suggestions, (3) other, and (4) beyond the lesson. Lewis was surprised to find that "there were almost twice as many questions or suggestions as commendations" (ibid.:75). She also found that teachers who weren't doing so well in their teacher-training courses got more commendations than the others. She speculated that this was "an attempt to boost the morale of good classroom teachers whose C grades in course assignment work suggested they found formal study difficult" (ibid.:78). (These are the teachers whose procedural knowledge was stronger than their declarative knowledge.)

Lewis also analyzed the data using four topical categories, with accompanying subcategories given in parentheses (ibid.:73):

1. Other roles of the teacher (providing language input, types of activities, materials, the structure of the lesson).
2. Teacher talk (amount, type, and modifications; questions; feedback on oral language; formal instruction, explanation, differential interaction).
3. Learner behavior (learner production; input generation / receptivity; learner interaction, grouping; learner strategies).
4. Other (general climate; links with mainstream; evaluating progress).

The most frequently occurring topic was "*activities and materials,* having almost twice as many comments as the next category, *formal instruction and explanation*" (ibid.). Lewis observed that "whether the teacher-readers understood the comments in the same way as they were intended could only be answered by asking them at the time or by recording the post-lesson discussion" (ibid.:79). She raises four questions for further investigation (ibid.): "(1) How do suggestions posed in the form of questions appear to the teacher-reader? Are they seen as patronizing? (2) Would a direct suggestion be more acceptable? (3) Are question forms seen as a more polite way of suggesting something which might otherwise be seen as a criticism? (4) Would different teachers give different answers?" These are important questions for supervisors working with preservice or in-service language teachers.

A practice teaching program in Hungary

A preservice program in Hungary, in which novice EFL teachers gain experience during their university studies, has been described by Bodóczky and Malderez (1994). Like Knezevic and Scholl (1996), these novice teachers work in pairs, but an innovation in the Hungarian program is that the novice team teachers are given full responsibility for a primary or secondary class for the entire school year (about five or six contact hours with the language learners each week). In this new plan, the practice teaching lasts much longer than it had previously.

The school-based supervisors are considered "co-trainers," a title that conveys equal status with the university-based supervisors. Bodóczky and Malderez explain that extensive training was necessary, because "previously in Hungary the universities had particular schools designated as training schools. The better teachers got jobs there and, as they became more experienced, they took on trainees for the supervisory work. However, they were not actually trained themselves in supervisory responsibilities" (1994:67). In addition, training was necessary because the cooperating teachers no longer worked as in-class models. This program has intentionally "moved away from the craft model of teacher training" (ibid.).

The authors explain that such preparation for the school-based co-trainers was necessary because the program was trying to make a fundamental change in what had been a traditional supervisory role. The training the novices received was quite different from the

> training the [co-trainers] had undergone. They had probably experienced the authoritarian supervisor, the one who tells you: That was right, that was wrong, and so on. With our teacher trainees we were trying to develop something different and we felt that our model of a supervisor and the traditional model would clash. (ibid.)

Thus this program addressed the problem of having trainees and supervisors from different generations working together by overtly departing from directive supervision.

The university requires that the teachers-in-training be assessed, but in this new system, the evalution is "divided among the university-based classroom studies tutor, the [co-trainer], and the trainee" (ibid.). Since the trainees now teach for a year, the university-based tutors provide them with feedback over that entire time. This lengthy period led the team to revise the traditional assessment role of the university-based tutor: "We didn't want 'exam lessons' when the tutor comes in as God and sits in judgement. So we devised the idea of having a series of lessons over the year to assess and we worked out an assessment sheet, so the whole process becomes more gradual" (ibid.:68).

The role of the school-based co-trainers is generally one of support. They "introduce the trainees to the school and the staff, help with lesson planning, choice of materials and so on, observe lessons and give feedback, troubleshoot when necessary, organize remedial work, and write progress reports for the university" (ibid.:69). Such support is crucial because the first year of teaching often results in young teachers leaving the profession: "We don't want our teachers to drop out. So one of our aims is that they develop a sense of professionalism and the knowledge, the skills, and the confidence to be able to teach and stand on their own feet at the end of the year. We want them to be able to continue their own development" (ibid.:71). To achieve this goal, the program designers built in opportunities for extended research and reflection. In addition, the co-trainers' preparation provided quality teacher education, as did the role restructuring for both the school-based and the university-based supervisors.

Concluding comments

In this chapter we have considered issues related to supervising preservice language teachers. Quite a bit of research has been done on this topic, partly because many people who supervise teachers in training are college professors who must "publish or perish." In addition, since preservice teachers often constitute a captive audience, it may be easier to study their experiences than those of in-service teachers.

We also looked at the situational leadership model's applicability to supervising preservice language teachers. We considered the trainees' psychological readiness and job readiness and saw that skilled supervisors can use task behavior and relationship behavior, the key components of leadership style, to provide appropriate input for preservice teachers. These issues were connected to intersubjectivity and the zone of proximal development.

We also examined the constructs of declarative knowledge and procedural knowledge and reviewed two case studies based on the practicum context. We saw that team teaching and training for supervisors are both recent developments in this area. To conclude, we will analyze the case of the preservice language teacher presented at the beginning of this chapter.

Case discussion

1. What is your single most important goal for the upcoming one-hour conference with Dee? If she could leave that discussion with one new insight, skill, or strategy for action, what would it be? (The short-term and long-term goals for Dee may differ.)
2. What would you say to the cooperating teacher after the classroom observation?
3. Given what you know about Dee so far, what constituent(s) of Freeman's (1989a) model are you dealing with here: awareness, attitude, knowledge, or skill?
4. What can you infer from Dee's behavior about her declarative and her procedural knowledge of teaching? What can you infer about her ZPD?
5. How would you characterize Dee's level of psychological readiness and job readiness based on reading the case and reviewing the field notes in Figure 5.2? Identify the quadrant in Figure 11.2 that represents Dee's current state of readiness.
6. Look back at the Johari Window in Figure 2.3. In which quadrant(s) is Dee working now? What can you do to help her move to another quadrant?

7. Given your informed interpretation of the situation, what issues will you discuss with Dee? Prioritize your list in terms of the sequence you would use in the discussion.
8. Given what you know about Dee (from the case and the field notes), what would be an appropriate supervisorial role (or roles) for you to take in the post-observation conference? Which leadership style would be the most effective to use with Dee? (See Figure 11.1.)
9. If Dee decides to collect data to address her concerns, on what issues should she focus? What data collection procedure(s) should she utilize? List three areas Dee could work on over the next three months, and suggest an appropriate data collection method for each.
10. Before observing Dee's class again, you hold a pre-observation conference to determine her specific concerns. However, there are also issues you are interested in, based on your first observation and conference. List three concerns on which to focus during the second observation, along with the appropriate data collection procedure(s) to use in addressing each issue.

Tasks and discussion

1. If you are a preservice language teacher, what are your three biggest worries about teaching? If you are an experienced language teacher, what were your three biggest worries when you were beginning your teaching career? If you are a novice teacher, share your three main concerns with an experienced teacher, and vice versa.
2. Think about your first official visit(s) from a supervisor. If you are a novice, what are the three main concerns you have about being observed by a supervisor? If you are an experienced teacher, what were three of your concerns about being supervised?
3. If you are an experienced teacher, think of a person who was your supervisor in the past. How would you characterize that person's task and relationship behaviors in dealing with you? How well did that person's leadership style work for you?
4. What are your own preferences for task behavior and relationship behavior when you are the supervisor? On Figure 11.1, put an *X* where you think you would work best.
5. How would you describe your readiness level for your work at a particular time when you were supervised? What was the task behavior and relationship behavior of your supervisor? What did your supervisor do to determine your ZPD?
6. Place an X on Figure 11.2 to show your own readiness for taking on supervisory responsibilities. Explain your thinking to a classmate or colleague.

7. The situational leadership model is not limited to work with novices. Use the concept of readiness to describe the experienced French teacher with unruly students (see Chapter 7).

8. Given what you know from the case in Chapter 7 and your assessment of the French teacher's readiness level, what leadership style would you use to help her improve the situation in the French class? Use Figure 11.1 to explain your rationale.

9. Imagine you are supervising four trainees who have the following characteristics: (A) One teacher has both procedural and declarative knowledge. (B) One teacher has procedural knowledge but lacks declarative knowledge. (C) One teacher lacks procedural knowledge but has declarative knowledge. (D) The last teacher lacks both procedural and declarative knowledge. You are about to observe each teacher teaching a grammar lesson with a communicative activity. What problems might appear and what strengths might emerge? Write your prediction in each cell of this grid:

	Teacher characteristics	Likely problems	Likely strengths
A.	[+ procedural knowledge] [+ declarative knowledge]		
B.	[+ procedural knowledge] [− declarative knowledge]		
C.	[− procedural knowledge] [+ declarative knowledge]		
D.	[− procedural knowledge] [− declarative knowledge]		

10. If you are an experienced teacher, look back to your first teaching experiences. What would have been the single most important thing your supervisor could have done for you or said to you in your practicum or first job? If you are a novice teacher, project yourself years into the future. What might be the most important thing a supervisor could do or say to you now to support your commitment to language teaching as a career?

Suggested readings

Articles about practicum courses for language teachers in training include papers by Brinton and Holten (1989), Flaitz (1993), Freeman (1990), Gebhard (1990c), Kamhi-Stein (1999), Pennington (1990), Richards and Crookes (1988), and Winer (1992). Johnson (1996c) discusses the relationship between novices and cooperating teachers.

Yu (2000) wrote a case study about ESL teacher learners that includes a discussion of post-observation conferencing and reflective portfolios. For references in general education, see Cooper and Seidman (1969), Cohn (1981), Cohn and Gellman (1988), Copeland (1980, 1982), Kremer-Hayon (1986, 1987), Shapiro and Sheehan (1986), Stones (1987), and Zahorik (1988).

Osburne's (1989) article about situational leadership was influenced by Hersey (1984) and Hersey and Blanchard (1982). Glickman et al. (1998) discuss situational leadership in their supervisor-training book.

Lemma's (1993) research was conducted in general education, but the findings concern language teacher educators as well. (See also Bunting, 1988.) Korinek (1989) surveyed cooperating teachers about their preferred compensation for supervising student teachers.

Abbott and Carter (1985) discuss the clinical supervision model in foreign language education. There are many reports of student teaching arrangements in various countries: Yeung and Watkins (1998) in Hong Kong; Deal (2000) in Kenya; Dayan (1999) in Israel; Van den Berg, Sleegers, and Geijsel (2001) and Lunenberg (1999) in the Netherlands; Martinez (1998) in Australia; and Celep (2000) in Turkey. The EURYDICE European Unit (1999) has published an overview of preservice teacher training (including supervision and evaluation) in Estonia, Latvia, Lithuania, Cyprus, and Slovenia.

12 Supervising teaching assistants

This chapter examines the challenges and rewards of supervising teaching assistants (TAs) in university language programs. We will begin with a case and then discuss the central dilemma of supervising TAs. Next, we will consider the advantages and disadvantages of the TA system and the particular challenges it presents to TA supervisors. In addition, we will look at issues related to the coordination of teaching assistants' work within and across levels of language courses in a multilevel program. Finally, we will consider several strategies that supervisors can use to support TAs.

Case for analysis: Rater reliability

You are supervising 12 teaching assistants in a university language department. The five-level program employs 30 people, but in this case we are focusing on the 12 TAs teaching at the upper-intermediate level. Their responsibilities include rating the final examination essays of all the upper-intermediate students. There are 12 sections of the course, each taught by a different TA. Each section has 24 language students.

For the past year a team of four TAs has been working with you to devise a scoring rubric for the upper-intermediate students' exit exam compositions. The other eight TAs have had opportunities to comment on the drafts and to participate in the revision process by using the scoring rubric on five composition assignments written by their own students during the term. All 12 TAs were involved in pilot-testing the scoring rubric throughout the semester. Several staff meeting discussions were devoted to this process, including training and regular scoring practice. For these reasons, you feel confident that all the TAs at this level have understood and bought into the new scoring rubric.

The program policy is that the TAs score the exam compositions of students they themselves have not taught. (So, for instance, the teacher of section 1 will read the compositions of the students in sections 2 and 3, and so on.) Each exit exam essay will be rated independently by two TAs, so each TA must score 48 essays. The

---

student who wrote the composition will be awarded the average of the two raters' scores. In the event of a wide discrepancy between the raters, a third rater will evaluate the composition. These policies and procedures were all discussed with the teaching assistants during the rater training program.

As the semester draws to a close, you set up a rater norming session. Using final exams from previous terms, the TAs score the practice essays independently. They then compare ratings and discuss any discrepancies. When you calculate the inter-rater agreement indices, you are pleased to see that the figures are quite high – in fact, over 95 percent for all the rater pairs. As a result you feel confident that your team is ready to score the final exam essays, so you set up the rater pairs and a system for exchanging the students' essays. Individual TAs pick up a batch of essays from you but may read them elsewhere, as long as those essays are returned for timely distribution to the second reader. The smooth exchange of papers is essential to the success of the system, because you are working against a very tight, important deadline for submitting the students' final grades to the university administration. The TAs work on scoring the compositions for two full days.

When the scoring is done, as the results are being recorded, you notice that one TA has consistently given lower marks than the others, even though he participated in the rater training and norming sessions and achieved high inter-rater reliability indices prior to marking the exams. Some of his marks are drastically low – in fact, the thought occurs to you that they are almost punitive. During the training program, he had not raised any objections to the scoring rubric or asked any questions about the categories, although his scores had typically been somewhat lower than those of the other teachers. Now, however, it appears that virtually all 48 of the papers he marked will need to be scored by another rater – quite possibly you – before tomorrow morning's deadline for submitting the grades.

You call this TA to arrange a meeting in your office in order to discuss the scores he has submitted. You have scheduled a full hour for this meeting early this afternoon.

The work of teaching assistants

In North America and elsewhere, postsecondary institutions try to attract and support outstanding graduate students by offering them stipends for teaching part-time. These positions are referred to as graduate assistantships (GA-ships) or teaching assistantships (TA-ships). They often involve teaching in undergraduate courses, and the application process is typically highly competitive.

The TA label can be something of a misnomer, however, because the teaching assistants in many disciplines do much more than assist someone else. In linguistics, mathematics, and the sciences, a TA may indeed assist a faculty member by grading examinations or running homework review and discussion sections following a professor's lecture. In engineering and the physical sciences, TAs regularly guide students' laboratory experiments and grade their lab reports. But in language departments, TAs often teach their own courses and may have major responsibilities for planning, instruction, and evaluation of students' work.

The use of language TAs has been widespread in the United States for many years. In fact, in 1981 Franck and Samaniego asserted that "most beginning and intermediate foreign language courses at larger American universities are instructed by graduate teaching assistants" (p. 273). In 1987, Rogers stated that it was becoming "increasingly common for foreign language departments that have both graduate and undergraduate programs to look to a cadre of graduate teaching assistants . . . to provide instruction in their beginning-level courses" (p. 403). In several contexts TAs carry out this work "under the guidance of a master teacher or a TA supervisor" (ibid.).

It is an economic fact of life that many universities use TA-ships as a way of providing instruction for undergraduates, and financial support for graduate students. Many people who accept TA-ships have little or no teaching experience, and some have only limited interest in teaching. So although employing graduate students as teachers is economical, it can also be risky in terms of instructional quality. Here is the issue in a nutshell: "Entrusting basic language instruction to new, young teachers carries with it a responsibility to provide them with in-service training. Such training has taken various forms, including orientation programs, methods courses, micro-teaching, and class observation by supervisors" (Franck and Samaniego, 1981:273).

The central dilemma in supervising teaching assistants

The key dilemma in supervising teaching assistants is that first and foremost TAs are graduate students rather than teachers. Their primary attention is supposed to be on their own studies. Barnett and Cook (1992:88) see fundamental dichotomies in "a staff whose members are simultaneously students and teachers." They note that graduate programs need graduate students "in mutually supportive and dissimilar ways, both to keep alive graduate programs and to teach basic language courses" (ibid.). Professors may view the TAs primarily as young scholars, while some administrators think of TAs as "functionaries who teach required or large undergraduate courses at a bargain price" (ibid.).

Unfortunately, but not unexpectedly, TAs themselves sometimes feel ambivalent: "Concurrently pursuing both solitary research and active communication with students, [TAs] face the standard academic dilemma, but rarely realize how normal it is. They consider this conflict difficult (as indeed it is), abnormal (which it is not in an academic setting), and temporary" (ibid.). Thus, TAs in language departments may be pulled in two directions: When time is short will they attend to their teaching or to their own graduate studies?

Because of legal and administrative constraints, a faculty supervisor is often put in charge of the language TAs. This coordination can be as loosely structured as giving the TAs the required textbooks when the term begins. Or it can be a highly coordinated process of negotiating course syllabi, holding weekly staff meetings, conducting regular class observations, writing standardized examinations, and doing periodic formative and summative evaluations of the TAs. Sometimes the TA supervisor is the instructor of record for the courses taught by all TAs, which means that the supervisor is responsible for submitting grades and defending the assessments, a context that creates a number of interesting challenges.

Unfortunately, however, the TA supervisor position is not a very popular one. The work is typically seen as time-consuming and even unpleasant. Some professors feel it detracts from their time for research and publishing. As a result, this responsibility often falls to the junior professors. In other words, those people with the least experience of university teaching are regularly put in charge of TA supervision.

Five challenges in supervising teaching assistants

Supervising language TAs presents at least five challenges. First, the TAs' primary focus may be on their own studies rather than on their teaching. This problem is especially serious in language programs without coherent curricula, where the TAs are responsible for curriculum design and materials development.

Second, TA appointments are part-time. TAs typically teach five to ten hours per week, and they may or may not be required to keep regular office hours. Their salaries reflect these duties and restricted working hours. Consequently, they may not be enthusiastic about attending committee meetings, developing test items, meeting students during office hours, or carrying out other responsibilities expected of full-time employees.

Third, as mentioned above, although TAs earn their stipends by teaching, they may have little or no interest in language teaching as a career. They may be preparing for careers as researchers, language testers, literature professors, curriculum developers, materials writers, or program administrators instead. As a result, they may be less than enthusiastic about doing high-quality teaching, about having their lessons observed, or about discussing teaching with you.

Fourth, TA-ships last only as long as the person is working on the graduate degree. Therefore, if you supervise TAs, you must be prepared for frequent, regular turnover in your teaching staff. Each year, and sometimes each term, you will need to orient new TAs to the curriculum, to departmental expectations, and to your system of observation and evaluation.

Finally, the range of experience in any group of TAs may vary widely. Some students enroll in graduate programs and receive TA-ships immediately after finishing their undergraduate studies and have little teaching experience. As Rogers explains, "many of these TAs, who are themselves students, have no basis either in preparation or experience to carry out the tasks to which they are assigned" (1987:403). She also says that in such contexts TA supervisors should provide guidance and coordination of instruction by all the TAs, and developmental guidance to the less experienced TAs.

However, other TAs working on the same staff may have substantial teaching experience. They may feel that supervision is unnecessary or unhelpful in their cases – at best benign intrusion, at worst troublesome meddling. Either way, the variety of experience among the members of your staff can present interesting challenges for you as a TA supervisor.

These factors can create contexts in which the TA supervisor will sometimes be working with people who don't want to spend much time being observed or engaging in follow-up discussions about their teaching. As Barnett and Cook note, "serious graduate students are conditioned to pay the greatest attention to subject matter and much less to teaching techniques or style – except when they find the latter annoying" (1992:97). This situation can lead to numerous tensions and competing pressures, so supervisors of teaching assistants must be sensitive to the TAs' dual roles as teachers and graduate students.

Disadvantages of the TA system

In a scathing review of the TA system, Lnenicka (1972:97) claimed that using TAs as anything other than assistants is detrimental to the education process:

> The undergraduate student and his parents, who suffer financial strain in order to provide for their children's college education, have a right to feel cheated and resentful when they find even one of the important courses in the undergraduate curriculum

being taught by a graduate student, one who, in all probability, is inexperienced, unrehearsed, untrained for teaching, and whose primary interest lies not in his teaching, but rather in satisfying requirements for his own degree.

This comment was written over three decades ago, but the sentiment is still common today. Barnett and Cook (1992:87) cite several critical remarks that reveal various peoples' discomfort with the TA system:

- In a conversation with parents: "I certainly don't want my son to attend *that* university, where he'll be taught by TAs."
- In a student council meeting: "We're paying a lot to attend this university, and we shouldn't be taught by TAs."
- In the graduate student lounge: "The supervisor expects too much; she doesn't realize all the other work we have to do."
- In a conference between a faculty member and a group of TAs: "Don't let those 202 exam committee meetings get in the way of your own work."
- In a graduate admissions committee meeting: "We can't be *too* selective in our admissions policy; after all, we do have to staff our required language courses."

As the TA supervisor, you will hear many of these comments in your work. (In my experience, these remarks are very realistic.) These attitudes may be "givens" that you must work with, rather than variables you can control.

Advantages of the TA system

Barnett and Cook (ibid.:87–88) also report positive comments about the use of TAs:

- From deans of students: "The TAs in the Language Department do a fine job of keeping us posted about students who are having problems."
- From undergraduate students: "I didn't plan to take any more French / German / Italian / Spanish, but my TA was really great . . . "
- From TAs: "It's the teaching that keeps me going in graduate school."

These comments are also realistic. Sometimes TAs are the most enthusiastic teachers students encounter during their college careers. In addition, many TAs find language teaching rewarding. Some devote a great deal of time to preparing and following up on their lessons. So there are advantages to the TA system for the administration, the students, and the TAs themselves.

Among other advantages, staffing courses with TAs is much more economical than paying professors. In addition, for those graduate students who do pursue teaching careers, working as TAs provides valuable teaching experience. And, as Rogers notes, "teaching assistants can be used quite effectively in the beginning [foreign] language classroom, provided that the person who supervises them is willing and able to carry out the necessary organizational tasks" (1987:406).

Thus, there are pros and cons to using TAs to provide undergraduate instruction. "For the sake of the undergraduates whom TAs teach and for the health of our TAs, graduate students, and programs, we must deal with the contradictions inherent in these disparate views" of the teaching assistants (Barnett and Cook, 1992:88). Much of that responsibility falls to the supervisor.

International teaching assistants

In Chapter 5 we read field notes about a math class taught by Kwan, a non-native-speaking TA at a U.S. university. Kwan was teaching in English, his second language, to undergraduate students who were both native and non-native speakers. There are thousands of international teaching assistants, or ITAs, like Kwan, whose graduate education is funded in part by TA-ships. The term *ITA* normally refers to TAs who are teaching some subject matter other than their native language. Many of them teach in the sciences and mathematics.

The supervision of ITAs is usually the responsibility of the departments that employ them. It is rare for language teachers or applied linguists to be involved in their supervision, but quite typical for the university's ESL program faculty to train ITAs and test their English proficiency. Sometimes such programs involve follow-up classroom visits by the ESL trainers.

Of course, there are many similarities between supervising language TAs and supervising ITAs in other subject areas. Both contexts involve observing and giving feedback to part-time employees who may be more focused on their own graduate education than on their teaching. There are also many linguistic, cross-disciplinary, and cross-cultural challenges involved in the ITA context. If ESL trainers are involved in ITA supervision, it is important to coordinate with the departmental supervisors, who can help the ITAs in terms of their subject matter competence. The topic of ITAs will not be treated further here, but research data can be found in Bailey (1984), Plakans (1997), and Rounds (1987).

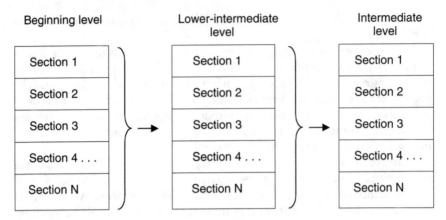

Figure 12.1   Multiple sections in a multilevel language program

Coordination and quality control

Even in the most positive contexts, language departments that employ TAs typically rely on the supervisor for coordination and quality control. This practice is partly because language students typically move through a multilayered curriculum, which must be coherent across and systematic within levels of instruction.

Coordination within and across levels of language courses

Figure 12.1 illustrates that there can be many sections of any given language course.

This situation demands cohesion across levels, as well as comparability across sections of the same level, since a different TA will teach each section. Students from different beginning sections, for example, will end up in the same intermediate classes, as shown in Figure 12.2. For this reason, supervisors must provide TAs with guidance about the curriculum at each level, as well as the interface between levels. This interface is related to articulating the goals and the course content, but also to the assessment procedures used in the program.

Inter-rater reliability in assessment

Coordination within levels and across levels is very important when we consider testing issues in multilevel and multisection programs. Terry says, "whether the tests from all sections are combined and graded by all instructors or individual instructors grade their own tests, the

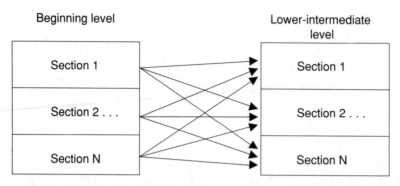

Figure 12.2   Transition of students from various sections of one level into the next level

fundamental problem that arises is ensuring consistency" (1992:229). This consistency is called *inter-rater reliability*. Henning (1987:193) defines it as the "correlation between different raters' ratings of the same ... performance." Thus inter-rater reliability represents the correspondence of scores awarded by two or more raters to the same samples of speaking or writing. Ratings scales requiring evaluators' judgment are often used to test these productive skills.

As Terry points out, "high inter-rater reliability is important in order to ensure that course goals are being met and that student knowledge and performance are measured with a common yardstick" (1992:230). If one TA is consistently a very lenient grader, another is very strict, and a third falls somewhere between the two, language students enrolled in their three different sections of the same course may receive very different marks even though their skills are approximately the same. Likewise, if the TAs' grading standards are very different, students with very different skill levels may receive similar grades. These same problems of grading inconsistently occur with other teachers too – not just with TAs.

Terry suggests ways to improve the consistency of raters' scoring across multiple sections of the same course. The first is that TAs should go through intensive training to "familiarize them[selves] with the techniques for scoring student work, allow for discussion of these techniques, provide sample texts for evaluation, and examine why selected samples were given certain scores" (ibid.:259). He adds that in multisection language courses, clearly defined scoring criteria promote "equal expectations and equivalent results on common tests that are scored by a number of different TAs" (ibid.). This equitable evaluation of the language learners' work may particularly be an issue in courses taught by less experienced TAs (ibid.).

These suggestions about improving inter-rater reliability are very important. TAs' evaluation responsibilities are only part of their duties, however. The next section discusses some ways for supporting TAs in other areas of their work.

Strategies for supervising teaching assistants

TA supervisors are often in middle-management positions. They are responsible both to the program's administration and to the teaching assistants who work in the program. Their responsibilities to the program are normative and evaluative, whereas their responsibilities to the TAs may demand a more developmental, formative approach. Let's first consider the administrative need for coordination and conformity.

Promoting coordination

Given the challenges above, how can a supervisor ensure coordination within and across levels of language courses that TAs teach? Of course, the context in which you work will greatly influence possible solutions. In departments where the curriculum is well developed, where course objectives are clearly articulated and widely understood, and where valid and reliable assessment mechanisms are in place, your role as supervisor will be more straightforward.

Rogers has described an intervention she used with TAs who had little or no teaching experience but were responsible for beginning level Spanish courses at a large university. Many of the TAs exhibited several "patterned weaknesses" (1987:404), including (1) a lack of distinction between communicative activities and oral drills; (2) an inability to conduct classes in the target language; (3) an overreliance on the textbook and a resulting lack of "authentic cultural elements" (ibid.); (4) a lack of variety in teaching techniques and pacing; (5) no facility in switching between teacher-centered, full-group activities to more student-centered group work; and (6) limited preparation for assessing students' writing and speaking skills.

The intervention Rogers devised was to write a series of detailed lesson plans, supported by accompanying materials, for the TAs' use. The plans all covered the initial presentation of new content as well as communicative activities based primarily on the new material. Given her classroom observations and data collected from the TAs themselves, Rogers concluded that the instruction was improved through the use of these shared lesson plans. She suggests that this sort of interaction between the TAs and the supervisor "seems to hold strong promise for addressing a very real problem facing many large postsecondary institutions" (ibid.:407).

Here are some additional strategies promoting coordination in multi-level programs:

1. Make sure the objectives for each level of the curriculum are clearly articulated and open to scrutiny, discussion, and possible revision.
2. Discuss the specific course objectives with the TAs, both as a full teaching staff and in smaller groups defined by the levels of the courses taught.
3. Visit classes regularly, perhaps focusing on a particular level each week, so you gain a sense of the content being covered in the various sections of the same level of instruction, as well as across the different levels of the program.
4. Set up a schedule for peer observation and cross-training. TAs can observe others at the same level, the next highest level, and the previous level of instruction. Supervisors can facilitate peer observations by substituting in the TAs' classes occasionally.
5. Make sure the exit mechanisms for the various levels reflect the course objectives.
6. Hold regular meetings with the TAs at each level. On a less frequent basis, have the TAs meet as an entire group or as subgroups from adjacent levels.
7. Solicit the TAs' input about successes and difficulties in implementing the curriculum. Listen to their concerns and implement agreed-on changes.
8. Share with the group of TAs the successful teaching techniques you observe by publishing a brief electronic or paper news bulletin. Or designate portions of staff meeting time for TAs to demonstrate teaching ideas or creative uses of materials.
9. Have the TAs at each level prioritize the challenges to achieving the course objectives. Then have a brainstorming session to generate ideas for dealing with those challenges.
10. Help the TAs develop their own strategies for time management. It can also be helpful to implement a buddy system. For example, if one TA is collecting dissertation data or preparing for oral exams, you or another TA could teach his or her class for a few days.

In addition, if you can produce a booklet or a Web site of information for new TAs and establish an obligatory training program as part of their employment conditions, you can set the tone and direction of the program before the term starts. In my experience, it is beneficial to involve the continuing TAs in both the planning and the execution of the TA training. The experienced TAs can serve as role models and provide new TAs with strategies for juggling their dual roles.

Promoting creativity

As a language TA supervisor, your primary legal and administrative responsibilities involve ensuring that the university provides viable educational opportunities to the students. For this reason, a great deal of your time and energy will involve communicating course objectives to the TAs; helping them utilize appropriate teaching strategies, activities, and materials to meet those goals; and making sure they apply uniform evaluation procedures with their students.

There is also an important developmental side to the TA supervisor's work. As the supervisor of language TAs, you may have numerous opportunities to promote their careers. If you see TAs using creative teaching techniques or producing innovative materials, you can encourage them to share their ideas in conference presentations or journal articles. Their work can be publicized in faculty meetings or on departmental bulletin boards or Web sites. Encouraging TAs to share their teaching techniques and materials helps create the contexts for their first experiences in teacher training. It also generates an atmosphere of collegial interaction and support. Some materials TAs produce will be appropriate for academic or commercial publications. As a more senior person in the field, you will be in a better position to recognize such options than TAs who are relatively new to the profession.

You may also be in a position to directly help TAs locate employment as they finish their graduate work. You will certainly be asked to write letters of recommendation, to review drafts of TAs' resumes, or to provide feedback on TAs' teaching portfolios. Some TAs may incorporate your written observation reports about their lessons in their portfolios.

As a TA supervisor, you will face many challenges, but you will also experience many rewards. If you can balance the dual roles of ensuring coordination and promoting creativity, you will help to launch the careers of many young professionals. Any TA you supervise may have the potential to be a leader in the next generation of language educators.

Concluding comments

This chapter has discussed the challenges faced by supervisors working with language TAs in university or college settings. We have seen that there are advantages and disadvantages to the TA system and that junior faculty members are often given the responsibility for supervising the TAs. ESL faculty members in English-speaking universities often train ITAs and may sometimes observe their classes along with their departmental supervisors.

The case at the beginning of this chapter and the following activities were designed to help you think about the context of TA supervision. Although this can be a challenging situation, it can also be one of the most rewarding for a language teacher supervisor.

Case discussion

1. What are your short-term goals in this situation? What specific outcomes do you want?
2. What are your long-term goals for this TA? (He has a full year left on his TA-ship.)
3. Role-play the conversation with this TA, laying out your concerns and eliciting a response from him. What role(s) from Chapter 1 will you adopt in talking with this TA? Why?
4. When you tell the TA his essay ratings are unacceptably low, he may respond to your concerns in various ways. Please consider the two following possibilities:
   A. The TA says, "Look, I'm really sorry, but the final paper for my dissertation adviser's seminar was due today. I just didn't have time to read the students' essays very carefully, so maybe I rushed and didn't give the students the benefit of the doubt."
   B. The TA says, "Look, this rating system is ridiculous! It's too cumbersome. In your efforts to be fair, you created way too much work for the TAs. Why should I have to read essays by 48 students who weren't in my class? It'd be more efficient if I just read my own students' essays. I already know what grades most of them would get anyway!"

   What are your options if the TA replies with comment A or comment B?
5. You have responsibilities beyond the professional development of this particular TA. List your immediate responsibilities to the following persons: the 48 students whose papers this TA scored, the two TAs who taught those 48 students, the two TAs who were this TA's reading partners, and the university administration. What steps must you take in the next 24 hours to meet these responsibilities?
6. As this TA's supervisor, it is likely that you will be asked to write a letter of recommendation for him when he finishes his degree. Draft a letter for this person under these circumstances:
   A. This TA voices the sentiment stated in comment 4A and agrees to spend the afternoon rereading the 48 student essays.
   B. This TA voices the sentiment in comment 4B and refuses to reread these 48 student essays. You must take over his scoring responsibilities.

7. Which constituents of Freeman's (1989a) model are you dealing with in this case: awareness, attitude, knowledge, and / or skills? How does your answer to this question change if the TA's response is closer to statement 4A or statement 4B?
8. Suppose this TA refuses to rescore the compositions. Is it preferable for you to score them yourself or to ask another TA to score them? What are the factors that influence your choice?
9. Imagine you decided to ask another TA to score these compositions. Role-play the conversation with that person. What would you say about your reason for asking a TA – who has already successfully scored the 48 original compositions he or she was assigned – to do additional work? What would you refrain from saying?
10. List three clear steps that you could take to prevent this problem from arising again.

Tasks and discussion

1. There is wide variability in the training provided to language TAs. As Barnett and Cook (1992) have said,

> Too often the learning about teaching that supposedly happens by osmosis when one takes a master teacher's course is vague, if not imaginary. Serious graduate students are conditioned to pay the greatest attention to subject matter and much less to teaching techniques or style – except when they find the latter annoying. Unreflective imitation, even of the best teachers, is not an adequate way to equip students to establish and maintain effective teaching practice. (p. 97)

Do you agree or disagree with these authors? What are the implications of this quote for people who supervise language teaching assistants?
2. Did you yourself work as a TA during your graduate studies? If so, were you supervised in some way? What did you learn about language teaching in the process?
3. If you didn't work as a TA, talk to someone who did. Find out whether that person was ever supervised in the TA role. If so, what effect did the supervisory experience have on his or her professional development?
4. If you have access to a university language department, ask the department administrator or TA supervisor if there is a job description for the teaching assistants. It may be useful to compare several job descriptions and see what they encompass.

5. Talk to some college students who have been (or are now) enrolled in language courses taught by teaching assistants. Get the students' views about the advantages and disadvantages of the TA system.

6. Think about your own time-management skills. Are you ever in a situation where equally important responsibilities compete for your limited time? When this situation arises, what criteria do you use for determining what to do first?

7. What challenges will you face if you have 20 new teaching assistants to supervise who have a wide range of teaching experience? Imagine simultaneously supervising a TA staff made up of the following people: (A) five new PhD candidates who have all taught at universities or community colleges for at least five years; (B) five master's candidates in their second year of graduate school who did not have TA-ships last year; (C) five new teaching assistants just starting the MA program, who all have one to three years of language teaching experience elsewhere; and (D) five new TAs who are just beginning the master's program and have no teaching experience. What strategies can you employ to meet the diverse needs of these various TAs? List three to five specific actions you could take.

8. Imagine that you are the supervisor of the teacher described at the beginning of Chapter 10 (the case about the request for a letter of recommendation) and that the teacher involved was actually a TA. You will recall that although this person does excellent work in discourse analysis, syntax, and materials development, she was problematic as a member of the teaching team. Based on three observations and her work on your staff, you personally would not hire her. The lessons you observed tended to be minilectures about grammar rules and their exceptions. While the teacher worked well with the most advanced language learners, she ignored the students who didn't ask questions.

   One day, two students complain that this teacher never calls on them and gives them low marks they don't deserve. They want to move to another section so they can have a different teacher. Unfortunately, the only other sections that will fit in these students' schedules are already too crowded. What do you say to these students while they are in your office? What do you refrain from saying?

9. Role-play the conversation with the TA from Chapter 10 in which you tell her about the students' complaint. Based on your observations, you feel the complaint is justified. Decide what actions you want the TA to take (or to desist from taking). Explain your points to her or lead her to suggest her own solution to the problem.

10. Two or three weeks after the conversation described above, what evidence would suggest that this TA has indeed successfully addressed

the problem raised by the students? List three types of information you would find convincing.

Suggestions for further reading

The chapters by Barnett and Cook (1992) and Terry (1992) are both part of Walz's (1992) collection on training and supervising TAs in language programs. The chapters by Herschensohn (1992) and Kulick (1992) contain sample observation and evaluation forms for supervisors working with TAs.

Franck and Samaniego (1981) wrote about the use of videotape in supervising TAs. Rogers (1987) includes a sample lesson plan and a questionnaire for eliciting TA data.

Effective time management can be a serious issue for teachers and supervisors in any context. Two good sources on this topic are the article about program administrators' time management skills by Christison and Stoller (1997) and Chapter 5 in White et al. (1991).

For more information about international teaching assistants, consult the annotated bibliography compiled by Briggs, Clark, Madden, Beal, Hyon, Aldridge, and Swales (1997). TESOL's Web site (www.tesol.org) features information about the ITA Interest Section.

13 Supervising in-service language teachers

One of the most challenging and rewarding supervision contexts is working with in-service language teachers. The term *in-service* refers to teachers who are already employed, as opposed to those who are completing their professional preparation. A further distinction is that the first two years of in-service employment are often referred to as the induction years, whereas teachers who have been working longer are thought of as "experienced."

This chapter explores issues related to supervising in-service language teachers, whether they are in the early years of their careers or have had substantial experience. Topics include teacher decision making, reluctance and resistance, professional fulfillment, and burnout. We will also consider in-service teachers' ideas on effective supervision.

There are three categories of in-service teachers (Beerens, 2000:56). *Experienced teachers* have three or more years of successful teaching experience. *Beginning teachers* have two years of experience or fewer. This term is potentially confusing, however, since *beginning teachers* also refers to preservice teachers who are not yet employed. In-service teachers who need to make improvements are called *marginal teachers*, whether they are new in the profession or highly experienced.

The tricky thing about working with in-service teachers is that by definition, as employees, such teachers are already supposed to be competent. The idea that they could improve their performance (or might be having difficulty) is a problem for a static view of teacher professionalism. As a result, there is the potential for serious loss of face if in-service teachers receive negative evaluations or even get suggestions for improving their teaching.

Case for analysis: The curriculum issue

You are a supervisor in an elementary school district with a large population of linguistic minority students. There are curricula in place for the early grades (ages 5 through 7), the next grades (ages 8 to 10), and the middle school (ages 11 through 12). These curricula must be uniformly implemented since your program's federal funding requires

---

set curricular and assessment guidelines. Fortunately, the curricula were designed by well-educated materials writers who are familiar with your district's students. The materials and supporting activities are based on appropriate research and current language learning theory.

At the beginning of the year you start to observe the teachers. There are 60 teachers, some of whom have had training to work with linguistic minority students. District policy states that teachers in their induction years are observed twice each semester. The more senior teachers are observed once each semester.

You see many teachers using the curricula in creative and age-appropriate ways. In other classes, you witness activities ranging from audiolingual techniques to grammar-translation exercises, which seem inappropriate for the cognitive development of the young language learners. In your judgment, about half the faculty members are teaching appropriately while the others are using less than optimal procedures for teaching linguistic minority children.

There is no pattern related to the teachers' ages, in terms of how they implement the curriculum. Some more senior teachers have adopted the new curriculum and are using teaching techniques that work well for the children. In other cases, you witness both more experienced and less experienced teachers using decontextualized exercises in which students work individually to fill out worksheets that are not based on the curriculum the school district adopted.

In nine months, by the end of the academic year, you need to have all the teachers working consistently with the approved curriculum. At that time there will be an evaluation by educators representing the federal funding agency, as well as the regional Department of Education and the local school board. Their visits will include classroom observations.

You have four months in the first term, followed by four months in the second term. One day per month is set aside for in-service development. (The children are taken on field trips by other school personnel on those days.) You are responsible for planning and conducting the training sessions, the first of which is scheduled in two weeks. Each in-service program lasts from 8 A.M. to 5 P.M. and includes lunch for the teachers. All 60 teachers are expected to attend each session. You have videotape filming capabilities and large-screen playback equipment, as well as a budget for photocopying and honoraria for guest speakers.

Teacher decision making and language teacher supervision

In Chapter 3 we considered autonomy in language teacher supervision. Part of in-service teachers' autonomy is related to their actions, but teachers' autonomy also relates to their decision making. (See Figure 3.3.) In fact, teaching is essentially a series of actions based on decision making. Shavelson (1973) says decision making is the basic teaching skill. Freeman (1989a) describes teaching as a dynamic decision-making process. He notes that while teachers face both macro decisions (such as goal setting) and micro decisions (e.g., whether to treat an error), "the decision as a unit of teaching remains constant" (p. 31).

Teachers' in-class decision making

Language teachers make hundreds of decisions related to every lesson. Some, called *preactive decisions*, are made prior to teaching, as teachers plan their lessons. Others are made after lessons, as teachers reflect on their work or mark students' papers. Still others, called *online*, or *interactive decisions*, are made during real time, as teachers work with learners.

Some of the decisions teachers make are observable, or at least noticeable, because teachers articulate their decision making aloud. Malcolm (1991) has written a paper entitled, "All right then, if you don't want to do that..." The title is based on a teacher's quote when the students resisted the planned activities. Similar comments include, "We're not done, but we'll pick this up again Monday." Such remarks are often related to the reallocation of time: "Well, I was planning a review here, but you're all doing so well that I think we'll just move ahead." These verbal flags indicate the teacher is deciding to alter the planned lesson. They reveal teachers' understanding of Politzer's (1970) principle of economics: "The value of any... technique depends, in part, on the relative value of other techniques that could have been used in the place of the one actually selected by the teacher" (p. 41).

However, many decisions are not readily observable. They happen privately and in seconds as teachers conduct lessons. Supervisors seldom directly witness the decisions that inform teachers' actions. We can only witness the actions themselves, and only those that occur when we visit classes. Observers may be aware of teachers' decision making if it is verbalized. For example, a teacher might say, "We're running late, so finish this exercise for homework." Without such comments, however, observers may not know what decisions are influencing teachers' actions. Figure 13.1 shows that teachers' articulated decision making during lessons observed by supervisors is a very small subset of all the decisions teachers make.

269

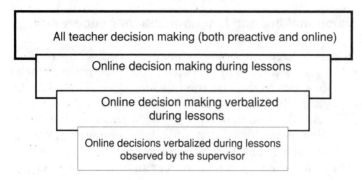

Figure 13.1 Subsets of teacher decision making

For supervisors to make sense of teachers' actions, they need to know why teachers choose to do what they do. Except in the relatively infrequent cases where teachers comment on the decisions they make during observations, supervisors will have no way of understanding what those decisions are unless we ask. This fact is underscored by Larsen-Freeman's comment: "There is only scant research looking at what teachers believe – and yet this is what teachers act upon" (1990:266).

The stimulated recall procedure

One way to learn about online decision making is *stimulated recall*. In this procedure, "it is assumed that the use of some tangible (perhaps visual or aural) reminder of an event will stimulate recall of the mental processes in operation during the event itself" (Gass and Mackey, 2000:17). For example, in the case study of Maja's practicum (see Chapter 11), three lessons were videotaped so Johnson (1996c) could discuss them with Maja using the stimulated recall procedure.

Videotapes, audiotapes, transcripts, field notes, selective verbatim quotes, and observation schedules can all be used for stimulating a teacher's recall during a post-observation conference. The data types are listed here in order of specificity: Videotapes provide more information than audiotapes, which render spoken discourse more accurately than do transcripts. However, transcripts, detailed field notes, and selective verbatim quotes can provide more information than observation schedules, particularly if the teacher and the observer negotiate the focus of the observation beforehand so that data are based on issues of interest to the teacher.

Stimulated recall can be used in watching videotaped lessons regardless of whether the supervisor was present originally. With a television monitor and a remote control, the supervisor or the teacher can stop the tape to discuss events in the lesson. Having the teacher operate the remote control allows the teacher to take ownership of the process (Freeman, personal communication). By controlling the pauses, the teacher can note decision making that is not visible and thus may not be known to the supervisor without the teacher's guidance.

Research on teachers' decision making in general education

Much of the research on teachers' decision making has been conducted in general education contexts. One important early study was done by Peterson and Clark (1978), who used the stimulated recall procedure with junior high school teachers as they discussed the videos of their lessons. These authors identified four possible trajectories, or "paths," through a lesson that emerged in the data. Path 1 was "business as usual." In this case, since everything is proceeding well, there is no apparent need for teachers to change their plans or behavior. In the second path, the teachers see problems occurring but have no viable alternatives readily available. Without workable options at hand, the teachers continue with their plans in spite of evidence that those plans are not working. This situation indicates powerlessness or surprise on the part of the teachers. In the third path (the least frequent in these data), teachers perceived problems and had viable alternatives available, but stayed with their original plans or previous behavior. The last pattern, path 4, was the second most-frequent, and seemed to increase with experience. In this case, teachers perceived problems, had alternatives available, and changed their lessons. The choice of path 3 had a negative correlation with student achievement and attitudes, while path 1 was associated with the learning of facts. In contrast, path 4 was associated with students learning higher order ideas. So Peterson and Clark's analysis suggests that when teachers choose viable options for altering lessons, students' learning increases.

Leinhardt and Greeno (1986) also studied teachers' decision making in general education. They describe teaching as "a complex cognitive skill" that "requires the construction of plans and the making of rapid on-line decisions" (p. 75), and note that "skilled teachers have a large repertoire of activities that they perform fluently" (ibid.:76). They were concerned with the dynamic tension between preactive decisions and interactive decisions: "The conscious planning activity of teachers reflects only a small fraction of the planfulness that actually characterizes skilled teaching" (ibid.). Part of the tension is that having planned an action, it can be difficult to make a real-time decision to abandon that action.

Westerman (1991) contrasted expert teachers' decision making with that of novice teachers (again, in general education). The expert teachers were consistently more aware of the students in the preactive phases (before lessons) and monitored more often for student cues during the lesson. Such awareness and monitoring are largely invisible to supervisors

271

observing lessons, however, unless we ask teachers about their decision making.

Research on language teachers' decision making

Woods (1989) describes two types of teachers' decisions. A *sequential decision* occurs when one decision follows another but is independent of (rather than part of) the previous decision. While planning a lesson, an ESL teacher may say, "After the spelling test, the students will do group work on their written summaries about environmental issues in their countries." A *hierarchical decision* occurs when decisions are made to achieve a previous decision. So, for example, the same teacher might say, "The students have been reading about ecological problems in order to write about environmental issues in their home countries. Today we will review the vocabulary on the environment. Then the students will do the in-class reading and then they will brainstorm about ecological problems in this area before writing their compositions." These are all *planning*, or *preactive*, decisions. Teachers' decisions made online in "real time" are also sequentially or hierarchically related.

Language teacher supervisors should understand the distinction between sequential and hierarchical decision making. When we are observing lessons, we may witness only one very small part of a larger, well-organized plan of instruction. If we don't know how the teacher's goals and decisions inform the lesson plan, we will not understand how the teacher's online decision making is intended to further the plan.

Johnson (1992a, 1992b) used stimulated recall to investigate the interactive decision making of six preservice ESL teachers. She examined the frequency of student performance cues, teachers' interactive decisions, and their use of prior knowledge during instruction. These teachers relied on "a limited number of instructional routines and [were] overwhelmingly concerned with inappropriate student responses and maintaining the flow of instructional activity" (1992a:129). She concluded that preservice teachers must recognize the "routines and patterns which experienced ESL teachers rely on to lessen the number of conscious decisions necessary during instruction" (ibid.). In fact, this is one characteristic of skilled teachers – using teaching routines that move lessons forward coherently and fluidly.

Nunan (1992a, 1996) studied the decision-making strategies of nine ESL teachers in Australia. Three had taught for less than a year, whereas the other six had from one to fifteen years of experience. Nunan obtained the teachers' lesson plans, audio-recorded the lessons, and made field notes. After each lesson, he asked the teacher to identify departures from the lesson plan. Then the tape recordings were transcribed, and the teachers annotated the transcripts.

Nunan noted that an inexperienced teacher "felt that she could not abandon her predetermined course of action, even though the students were evidently experiencing difficulty with it and the flow of classroom events was obviously affected" (1996:48). This case is an example of Peterson and Clark's (1978) path 2, where teachers see problems but don't have viable alternatives readily available. Nunan said the data also suggested that "the more experienced teachers were much more comfortable with monitoring the class and modifying their lesson in the light of ongoing feedback" (1996:48) from the students. This finding is interesting since many observation checklists include categories about the teacher's skill in covering the lesson plan within a given time period. It may be that the more highly skilled teacher knows when to abandon the plan and take an alternate course of action instead.

The teachers Nunan studied were clearly capable of drawing insights from their lesson transcripts. Nunan quotes the following comments from six teachers about their own lessons:

- Quite a wordy explanation, now that I see it in black and white.
- I ask a lot of questions without waiting for the students to answer them.
- Quite a complicated explanation. Maybe a demonstration would have been simpler.
- Maybe I should have got on to the vocabulary activity earlier instead of spending so much time talking in rather vague terms about the article first.
- I find difficulty in controlling the level of my language when talking *about* the target structure or function at this level.
- Maybe it would have been better to have them do something oral here and delay the writing.
- I realize it would have been more useful to get the students to summarize by feeding back to the class, rather than concluding the lesson with a lengthy monologue. (ibid.:53–54)

Nunan concludes that with collaborative data interpretation "teachers can reflect upon their work and grow professionally as a result of that reflection" (ibid.:54).

These findings suggest that one way to incorporate the alternatives model of supervision is for supervisors to review with teachers the data collected in their classrooms. In the process, the supervisor can keep quiet and allow the teachers to interpret the data and generate their own alternatives. Second, in the nondirective approach, supervisors' responses to teachers' ideas should not be to agree or disagree immediately but to encourage teachers' reflection and draw out further ideas based on that reflection.

Consider these same comments from the teachers in Nunan's research as if these utterances had been made by a supervisor to the teacher involved:

- Quite a wordy explanation, now that we see it in black and white.
- You ask a lot of questions without waiting for the students to answer them.
- Quite a complicated explanation. Maybe a demonstration would have been simpler.
- Maybe you should have got on to the vocabulary activity earlier instead of spending so much time talking in rather vague terms about the article first.
- You seem to find difficulty in controlling the level of your language when talking *about* the target structure or function at this level.
- It would have been better to have them do something oral here and delay the writing.
- It would have been more useful for you to get the students to summarize by feeding back to the class, rather than concluding the lesson with a lengthy monologue.

These small syntactic adjustments to Nunan's data illustrate the huge difference between a teacher's self-criticisms and the same propositions made *to* that teacher by a supervisor.

Principles underlying language teachers' decision making

A study I conducted of decision making (Bailey, 1996) involved ESL teachers ranging from those in their induction years to those who had taught for several years. Based on students' evaluations, all the teachers were skillful and successful. I obtained copies of their lesson plans and audio-recorded the lessons while making field notes. The tapes were then transcribed. In follow-up interviews, the teachers commented on the transcripts, focusing on where they had departed from their lesson plans. I then asked each teacher to articulate her reasons for departing from the lesson plan as if she were explaining the principle behind the decision to a novice teacher. The teachers said they would change course during a lesson under the following circumstances:

1. If an opportunity arose to "serve the common good" (Bailey, 1996:26), teachers would leave the lesson plan. This decision entailed responding to one learner's question or problem that was perceived as an issue for the other students as well.

274

2. Teachers chose to "teach to the moment" (ibid.:27–28) when an unexpected opportunity arose to teach something timely and significant.
3. The teachers would depart from the plan in order to "further the lesson" (ibid.:28–29) if an alternative arose that would apparently accomplish the same goals better than the teacher's preactive decisions would have done.
4. These teachers also deviated from their lesson plans when doing so would better "accommodate the students' learning styles" (ibid.: 29–31).
5. Teachers departed from their plans to "promote students' involvement" (ibid.:31–34). Such decisions entailed eliminating or condensing some activities so others could continue longer.
6. Finally, teachers chose to "distribute the wealth" (ibid.:34–36) in order to "keep the more verbal learners from dominating activities and encourage the less outgoing students to participate more" (ibid.:36).

In using these principles, the teachers departed from their lesson plans because they believed the alternative was more efficacious than what they had planned. In each case, they were able to articulate convincing reasons for the choices they made. Yet, as supervisors visiting language classes, we are not usually privy to the teachers' thought processes unless we ask them.

Decision making and three models of supervision

Goldsberry (1988:7) posed three key questions related to supervision and the kinds of decisions in-service teachers must constantly make:

> How does one prepare a teacher to make decisions that take into account the unique mix of setting, learners, and circumstances he may face? How can supervision help a teacher adapt strategies and techniques even when her supervisor isn't there to supervise? How can the expertise we assume supervisors to have be systematically established among classroom teachers?

Goldsberry rejects both nominal supervision and prescriptive supervision because the former offers no substantive input and in the latter, the supervisor controls many key decisions. In short, nominal supervision leaves decision making unexamined, and the prescriptive model presumes that the supervisor is better prepared to make decisions than the teachers. Therefore, Goldsberry says the reflective model is best suited for promoting responsible decision making by teachers. In this approach, "the supervisor uses her superior organizational status to mandate and to guide critical consideration of teaching purposes, procedures, and consequences" (ibid.:9).

The induction years

The induction years, the first few years of in-service work, can be trying times. Battersby wrote a two-part paper (1984a, 1984b) based on his general education research on New Zealand teachers during their first year of professional service. In that context, a senior teacher is often responsible for supporting and evaluating new teachers. Battersby was concerned about the "high drop-out rate of young, beginning teachers from the profession" (Battersby, 1984a:11). He identified two themes in the beginning teacher research: "[N]ot only do they seem to have high, and sometimes unrealistic, expectations about their pupils... but teacher training tends to foster in student teachers the development of ideal images of pupils" (ibid.:16). He found that "first-year teachers are influenced by pupils in a number of different ways as evidenced, for instance, in beginners' dreams and nightmares about pupils" (ibid.:17).

Battersby collected data from 38 first-year teachers in primary schools, using interviews, telephone conversations, questionnaires, and other documents. He also gathered information from senior teachers, principals, inspectors, and the teachers' colleagues to understand the socialization processes by which teachers enter the culture of the schools.

When he analyzed these data sets, Battersby found that many novice teachers are "unaware that one of their senior colleagues will probably be entrusted with responsibility for them during the first year of teaching" (ibid.:22). He cites research that stresses the value of the supervising teacher's guidance and support. Unfortunately, he notes that "lukewarm and negative attitudes about supervising teachers generally prevail amongst beginners" (ibid.).

Based on his review of the literature, Battersby states that beginning teachers often receive what he calls a *remote style of supervision* (1984a:24–25):

> The inference is sometimes made that remote supervision, referred to by Cooper and Sidman (1969) as the "shotgun approach," is inappropriate for beginning teachers and often frustrates them. However, the evidence from the present study suggests that some beginners are, in fact, satisfied with remote supervision... while others, probably the minority, may be dissatisfied with it.

Battersby says official visits by inspectors were rare: "In the present study, most of the Year One teachers were certificated after having received two formal inspections" (1984b:81).

For supervisors working with induction year teachers, Battersby's research suggests three things. First, who will supervise and support new teachers should be made abundantly clear. Second, remote supervision may be accepted, but may not be effective. Third, in order to influence new teachers, supervision should go beyond expectations and meeting requirements.

Attitudinal factors in the supervision of language teachers

Freeman (1989a) defined *attitude* as "a stance toward self, activity and others that links intrapersonal dynamics with external performance and behavior" (p. 36). Two of the interesting challenges for supervisors working with in-service language teachers are (1) understanding the teachers' various attitudes, and (2) working with those attitudes to ensure program quality and promote teachers' continued professional development. An additional complication is that in any faculty, you will encounter a wide range of attitudes, from totally discouraged to wholeheartedly enthusiastic. Some important attitudinal issues are reluctance and resistance and the juxtaposition of burnout and fulfillment.

Reluctance and resistance

Faced with the need to change, teachers sometimes embrace the change and carry it out. However, as teachers we are often reluctant or even resistant to change. And resistance to change can be magnified by resistance to supervision. In fact, Anderson (1982) says "prevailing definitions and modes of teaching nurture resistance to supervision" (p. 181).

In the United Kingdom, Kelly (1980) reported on a study in which 142 teachers were trained to implement a new secondary school science curriculum. At the end of the training, the teachers were asked if they would do one of the following: adopt the curriculum early, try out and then adopt the new curriculum, try out the new curriculum, or consider trying the new curriculum. Four follow-up questions were posed a year later, when the same teachers were asked what they had actually done. The tallies are reported in Table 13.1.

As someone who performs in-service training, I find Kelly's data both incredibly sobering and wonderfully uplifting. These data reveal the following patterns:

1. Only 5 of the 42 teachers who said they would adopt the new curriculum early actually did so. At first glance, this datum appears discouraging.

Table 13.1   *Teachers' intentions and subsequent actions following a curriculum workshop (Kelly, 1980:71)*

Actions one year later	Intentions				
	Adopt early	*Try out and then adopt*	*Try out*	*Considering trial*	*Total*
Adopted early	5	4	12	6	27
Adopted late	7	13	6	9	35
Partial adoption	19	19	5	8	51
Not adopted	11	2	7	9	29
Total	42	38	30	32	142

2. Of the remaining 37 teachers who originally thought they would adopt the new curriculum early, 7 adopted it somewhat later, and 19 adopted it partially. Eleven people who had originally thought they'd adopt the new curriculum never did so. For an in-service trainer, these data are reasons for serious reflection.
3. Reading down the columns "Try out and then adopt" and "Try out," we find cause for cautious optimism. People who were initially moderate in their commitment to enact the new curriculum did so with varying degrees of alacrity.
4. Six of the 32 teachers who only considered trying out the new curriculum initially actually adopted it relatively early. More than 25 percent of them adopted it later, and another 25 percent partially adopted the new curriculum.

Kelly's data suggest trainers and supervisors should not be discouraged by initial reluctance or skepticism, but neither should they be too encouraged by initial enthusiasm.

Sometimes experienced EFL teachers "develop a sense of complacency and confidence" (Saraswathi, 1991:76). Confidence is not a bad thing, but teachers who become complacent can be resistant to change. Writing specifically about India, Saraswathi states that some teachers feel they have mastered teaching and there is nothing more to learn:

> They resist change as it shatters their sense of security. Often they fail to understand the rationale of suggested changes. They therefore reject innovations without making any effort to understand them. Their irrefutable argument is: "The method through which my teacher taught me English is good enough for my learners. If it has worked for me, why won't it work for my learners?" (ibid.)

This point about teachers' own learning is important. Lortie (1975) has written about the *13,000 hour apprenticeship of observation* – the idea that before teachers begin their professional preparation, many have already observed approximately 13,000 hours of teaching during their own education. This period of observing teachers creates lasting images about what teachers do. If such conceptions go unchallenged, these implicit models become the "default position" for teachers. How we ourselves were taught can easily form the invisible blueprint for how we teach.

Of course, not all teachers get stuck. Kawachi's (2000) research with university EFL professors in Japan suggests that there is a peak in professional development activities when teachers are in their early 40s. However, these teachers disagreed as to whether older or younger teachers were better. Some felt younger teachers were more popular with pupils, able to innovate, and willing to improve. Others thought older teachers were more relaxed, had acquired teaching skills, and could understand students' thinking well.

Rinvolucri wrote about teachers' resistance in in-service workshops, but many of his ideas pertain to supervision as well. As an experienced teacher educator, he gained awareness based on his own resistance in another trainer's workshop. He wrote (1981:47–48),

> As a learner of teaching techniques I have come to recognize inner resistance to a new set of ideas as a sign that these ideas are important and worthy of consideration. They cause resistance because they demand that previous knowledge be re-appraised, seen through new eyes, partly superceded or even completely discarded. If there has been heavy personal investment in some of the previous ideas, these fight back, both at a conscious and sub-conscious, dream level. This causes something in my mind akin to the turbulence one sometimes gets while flying: I am buffeted and thrown around without being able to see clearly the reason why – at the time, that is. The clarity of hindsight is all too easy.

Rinvolucri offers a useful definition: *Resistance* is "the refusal to face or deal with something we know is valuable" (ibid.:49). This notion is quite different from the dismissal of a new idea that is "simply a stupid non-starter" (ibid.). He continues,

> When I started teacher training I viewed trainee resistance as a purely negative force, something I had to break down and brush away. I now regard it much as a transplant doctor views the patient's immune system: something that must be worked on but

at the same time something vital to the learner's integrity and shape as a person. (ibid.:49)

Rinvolucri discussed five strategies to overcome resistance (ibid.: 49–51): Minimize trainee resistance to the trainer's personality; give the trainees time to come to terms with their resistance to new ideas; protect the "resistant" from the "acceptant" in feedback sessions; valorise the trainees' own knowledge; and help trainees to become conscious of their resistance.

The causes of reluctance or resistance to change, as Rinvolucri notes, are not just stubbornness or laziness. In fact, Blumberg and Jonas point out that

> Teachers who are concerned about high-quality performance tend to have a deep intellectual and emotional stake in what they do – a deeply ingrained belief system about the process of teaching. It is not so much that veteran teachers, for example, do not want to alter the way they do things. Rather, any changes need to fit their established belief system about good teaching (1987:59).

This comment implies that if supervisors suggest that in-service teachers change their teaching, the changes need to mesh with what those teachers believe to be right.

Freeman has also commented on teachers' resistance: "The experienced teacher may react to the observer in a variety of ways, ranging from passive tolerance to outright hostility" (1982:28). It is important for the observer to "understand the source of these reactions and not merely abandon in-service work with experienced faculty, as is so often the case" (ibid.). Teachers' resistant reactions "seem to stem from the observer's failure, either intentionally or not, to recognize and to affirm the teacher's experience" (ibid.). This view is connected to Rinvolucri's suggestion that supervisors and trainers should "valorise the trainees' own knowledge" (1981:51). Here we find an interesting contrast of perspectives: What Freeman views as the observer's failure to recognize the teacher's experience, supervisors may attribute to teachers' defensiveness or stubbornness. It may be helpful to adopt Rinvolucri's metaphor of the human immune system as a way to understand teachers' resistance.

It is important for supervisors to listen carefully to teachers' ideas and to try to understand the causes of resistance. Since there is so little hard evidence about effective teaching, we must acknowledge that there is often more than one good way to reach an instructional goal. Listening to teachers' ideas is one step toward overcoming resistance.

Burnout

Experienced teachers and others working in the helping professions sometimes experience burnout, but what exactly does this mean? *Burnout* is "a syndrome of emotional exhaustion, depersonalization, and reduced personal accomplishment that can occur among individuals who do 'people work' of some kind" (Maslach, 1982:3). Maslach studied burnout in police officers, prison guards, social and health-care workers, and teachers. She describes burnout as a type of job stress, that is, "a response to the chronic emotional strain of dealing extensively with other human beings, particularly when they are troubled or having problems" (ibid.).

There are three constructs involved in the burnout syndrome: *emotional exhaustion, depersonalization,* and *reduced personal accomplishment.* A language teacher supervisor should understand each of these concepts, because each can influence teachers' work, as well as the interaction between language teachers and supervisors.

Emotional exhaustion occurs when a worker is overextended or overinvolved emotionally. As Maslach describes this response, "people feel drained and used up. They lack enough energy to face another day. Their emotional resources are depleted and there's no source of replenishment" (ibid.). Symptoms of emotional exhaustion are increased absences from work and a lack of energy for carrying out regular duties.

Depersonalization, the second component, is a negative reaction to people. It is a psychological defense mechanism by which the clients (in our case students) are depersonalized in the view of the service provider. Depersonalization involves seeing individuals as cases or types, rather than as individual human beings. Maslach describes this negative stance as "viewing other people through rust-colored glasses" (ibid.:4).

The third element is reduced personal accomplishment, in which teachers "have a growing sense of inadequacy about their ability to relate to recipients [students], and this may result in a self-imposed verdict of 'failure'" (ibid.:5). When teachers experience a reduced sense of personal accomplishment, they feel unfulfilled in and dissatisfied with their work.

Using Maslach's research and definitions, Pennington and Ho (1995) investigated possible burnout among ESL / EFL educators. They surveyed 95 teachers, predominantly from the United States and Canada. Compared to Maslach's norming group, the ESL / EFL teachers experienced less emotional exhaustion, less depersonalization, and a greater sense of personal accomplishment. These authors concluded that, at least among the language teachers they investigated, burnout was not as prevalent as it is in some other people-oriented professions.

Burnout "culminates in a build-up of negative feelings about students, colleagues, and administration" (Barduhn, 1989:2–3). If unchecked, it becomes a downward spiral: "As motivation decreases and frustration increases, we lose the desire and energy to be creative, developing teachers" (ibid.). Eventually this pattern takes its toll, and "physical and emotional stress play on our self-esteem as we lose the sense of being in charge of our lives" (ibid.).

Supervisors can influence all three factors related to burnout. First we can be aware of teachers' emotional exhaustion: low energy level, absenteeism, or symptoms of depression. Second, if the same problems arise term after term, if students have become types rather than individual learners, then depersonalization may be occurring. Finally, teachers' sense of personal accomplishment can be influenced by interactions with supervisors.

Fulfillment in the workplace

If you ask a longtime language teacher why he or she has stayed with the profession, that person may tell you that the work is enjoyable and satisfying – that teaching people languages is highly fulfilling. Verity (2000) wrote about job satisfaction in our field. Intentionally setting aside factors such as compensation and status, she says that satisfaction means "leaving most classes, on most days, in most semesters, feeling good about a job well done" (p. 181). She continues, "From this perspective, a major reward of teaching well is the pleasure inherent in the activity itself; it serves as a creative enterprise" (ibid.).

Some research has suggested that supervision is a factor in teacher job satisfaction. For example, a survey of 208 university teachers in Nigeria (Mallam, 1994) identified supervision as one of seven key factors contributing to faculty turnover. (The other six were pay, promotion, coworkers, commitment, work, and the job in general.)

Blumberg says an individual feels fulfilled in his or her relationships with the organization when seven conditions are present (1980:86–87; italics in the original):

- He feels a *communicative openness*, when it is all right for him to share his concerns about himself with his supervisor, to disagree, to feed back to his supervisor any reactions he may have about their relationship, and so forth.
- He feels a sense of his own *professional competence* by way of helpful feedback from his supervisor and colleagues. This feedback, though it may be critical, is given in a supportive manner, inducing growth and confidence.

- He feels that his relationships with his supervisor and co-workers give him a *sense of colleagueship*, a collaborating share in the enterprise.
- He senses that his supervisor and his colleagues value his *worth as a person*; when he is not merely a cog, no matter how skillful or important, in a larger machine.
- He senses that the organization, primarily through the behavior of his supervisor, is concerned with his *personal and professional growth*, with providing the climate and opportunities for the individual to mature, to reach whatever potential his skills and pre-dispositions permit.
- He feels a sense of *personal independence and freedom*, when he can make decisions affecting his work on his own or with the help of his supervisor or colleagues. The decision to seek help is not seen as a confession of inadequacy.
- He feels a sense of *support for risk-taking* and a concomitant sense that the failure of a new venture is not taken as a sign of immaturity and incompetence.

Your first reaction to this list might be that such affective variables are the employee's business and not the responsibility of the supervisor. But all emotions take place in a social context and are influenced, to some extent, by factors in that situation. A supervisor could have an effect on all seven items listed here. Supervisors can foster conditions for fulfillment so that language teachers are motivated to seek out developmental opportunities instead of avoiding them.

Fostering faculty development

One way to combat burnout and promote fulfillment is to provide regular opportunities for faculty development. As a supervisor, you may be able to influence administrators about investing in teacher development.

Richards (2002) uses the acronym T-R-U-S-T in discussing a program manager's perspective on teachers' professional development. The letters represent *Trust, Respect, Understanding, Support*, and *Time*. Richards argues that consistently using this approach with in-service teachers builds "a culture of support within an organization" (p. 77).

Geddes and Marks recommend several procedures for program administrators (including supervisors) to promote faculty development. Based on their experience as a college ESL program director and as an elementary school principal, respectively, they say it is important to be committed "to an ongoing professional enrichment program" (1997:215). In planning such a program, one should solicit input from the program staff to prioritize training activities "based on recent needs assessments, evaluations, and long-term individual, program, and institutional goals" (ibid.). To carry out coherent faculty development, the program manager must "commit internal resources to professional enrichment" (ibid.). Finally, Geddes and Marks say, managers should provide teachers with appropriate incentives and rewards for development. All of these steps could be taken by supervisors in language programs: "When people share a sense of purpose, work cooperatively, and have a supportive management system, performance and productivity are enhanced" (Alfonso et al., 1984:18).

The next section examines some research on teachers' opinions of supervisory practices, which is related to teachers' resistance, burnout, and fulfillment. Where supervisors are effective, teachers' fulfillment will be enhanced, and resistance and burnout will decrease.

Research on supervision in in-service contexts

The research on the effective supervision of in-service teachers has been conducted mostly in general education rather than in language education contexts. In this research, effectiveness has not been defined in terms of teacher change or learning, but rather by teachers' opinions about effective supervision. This section summarizes three studies of supervisor effectiveness and returns to Freeman's (1982) ideas about training and development to connect them to research on effective supervision with in-service language teachers.

Productive relationships

Blumberg and Jonas asked experienced teachers to describe situations in which a supervisory relation had been highly productive for them. A productive relationship was defined as "one from which [the teachers] had derived both a sense of professional effectiveness and of deeper insight into self" (1987:60). They found 12 teachers who recalled such experiences. After eliciting descriptions, the interviewers asked, "Did the supervisor do anything that said to you, in effect, 'it's okay to open the door'?" (ibid.:60). In other words, they wanted to know how trusting relationships between teachers and supervisors were established.

The teachers then described their supervisors' behaviors that had made them feel comfortable confiding in them. When Blumberg and Jonas analyzed these data, three macro categories and ten subthemes emerged. These are summarized below (ibid.:60–61):

> 1. The supervisor's task-oriented approach toward the teacher
>   A. The supervisors gave immediate, nonpunitive feedback about the teaching.

    B. The supervisors took a collaborative approach to problem solving.

    C. The supervisors made teachers feel they were the experts on teaching.

    D. The supervisors were genuine in their relationship with teachers.

    E. The supervisors made the teachers feel that they were intelligent.

  2. The supervisor's interpersonal set toward the teacher

    A. The supervisors made the teachers feel that they were always available to them.

    B. The supervisors made the teachers feel that they were being listened to.

    C. The supervisors were open about what they knew or didn't know.

    D. The supervisors made teachers feel they were interested in them as people.

    E. The supervisors made the teachers' interests their interests.

  3. The supervisor's own competence as an educator

From the teachers' descriptions, Blumberg and Jonas concluded that granting access to their work by supervisors was "both gratifying and rare enough to be memorable for the teachers" (ibid.:61). They say that such communication with a trusted supervisor "seems to be an antidote for the loneliness that often accompanies teaching" (ibid.).

The best and the worst in supervisory practices

Zepeda and Ponticell's (1998:71–72) research on effective supervision elicited 114 teachers' perceptions of supervision by having them write two essays. In the first, the teachers answered the question, "What have been your 'best' and 'worst' experiences with supervision?" In the second essay, the teachers were given the following three prompts: What do you believe teachers get from supervision? What do you believe teachers need and want from supervision? What leadership characteristics do you believe administrators need to demonstrate to support teacher growth and development? The respondents were in-service elementary and secondary teachers taking a course on teacher supervision.

A content analysis of the essays revealed several patterns in the teachers' "best" and "worst" supervisory experiences. Table 13.2 provides the data about these categories.

These data reflect teachers' ambivalence about supervision. For instance, nearly identical percentages of the teachers referred to supervision as validation and as a "dog and pony show." It is worrisome that

Table 13.2 *Number and percentage of teachers responding with examples within subcategories describing supervision (Zepeda and Ponticell, 1998:71–72)*

Subcategories	Total (n = 114)
Supervision at its best	
Validation	101 (89%)
Empowerment	68 (60%)
Visible Presence	64 (56%)
Coaching	53 (46%)
Professionalism	44 (39%)
Supervision at its worst	
Dog and Pony Show	103 (90%)
Weapon	85 (75%)
Meaningless / Invisible Routine	79 (69%)
Fix-It List	55 (48%)
Unwelcome Intervention	33 (29%)

(A "dog and pony show" is something done only for appearances.)

three-fourths of the teachers perceived supervision as a weapon and that more than two-thirds saw it as a meaningless or invisible routine.

Four supervisory styles

Fifteen in-service teachers were interviewed by Okeafor and Poole (1992) about their supervisors. The teachers all had more than four years of teaching experience and were employed in the United States at elementary, middle, or secondary schools in general education. The individual interviews covered 23 open-ended questions about the relationship between the teachers and a supervisor (often a school principal). The interviews were audio-recorded and then transcribed. Four prevalent supervisory styles emerged in the transcripts.

Okeafor and Poole called the first style *backstage supervisors* because their interactions with teachers tended to occur "before the start of school, between classes, or after school hours" (1992:389) and were usually "initiated by teachers in reaction to events that occurred 'on stage' (i.e., in the classroom or while on duty on the playground, cafeteria, or hallway)" (ibid.). These principals were unlikely "to come 'on stage' unless they were invited by teachers" (ibid.) or when they had to conduct evaluations. These authors say, "backstage supervisors were perceived to facilitate, rather than direct, the performance of teachers" (ibid.).

The second supervisory style Okeafor and Poole labeled *surly supervisors*. Teachers said these supervisors did not consistently "show respect for teachers, avoided close supervision of instructional work, and overlooked instructional errors" (ibid.:389). The teachers felt the supervisors didn't have time for them and gave low priority to teachers' classroom issues. The conclusion was that "instead of using their time to provide support for teachers' classroom concerns, surly supervisors engaged in activities more visible to their superordinates" (ibid.).

The third supervisory style, the *imperial supervisor*, was seen as supervising teachers closely because she distrusted them: "Her classroom visits were perceived as disrespectful because she did not act friendly or engage in face-to-face interactions with teachers prior to or after classroom observations unless she observed problems with teachers' performance" (ibid.). In this case it apparently wasn't the checking that disturbed one teacher who was interviewed, but rather the principal's failure to talk to her personally (ibid.).

The *collaborative supervisors*, the fourth supervisory style, were perceived as being "highly confident in teachers and frequently interacting with them" (ibid.). The principals engaged in regular, friendly, task-relevant interactions rather than staying away from classrooms:

> Principals and teachers in this pattern jointly engaged in problem finding, problem solving, and trying new procedures, programs, and curriculums. Collaborative supervisors seemed to have educational expertise, view teaching as complex work, and openly discuss the work and how it was done to facilitate effective performance. (ibid.)

Collaborative supervisors showed respect for teachers "by employing tact and choosing the right time and place to discuss problems . . . to help in the corrective process" (ibid.:389–390).

Figure 13.2 shows the four supervisory styles arranged along two axes. One axis represents low to high respect for the teachers. The other

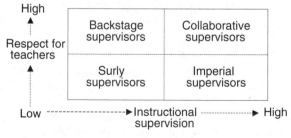

Figure 13.2 Types of supervisory styles (Okeafor and Poole, 1992:388)

287

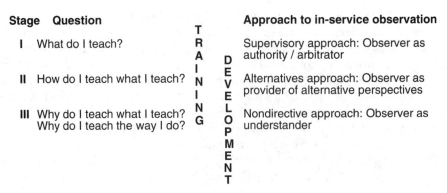

Stage	Question			Approach to in-service observation
I	What do I teach?	T R A I N I N G	D E V E L O P M E N T	Supervisory approach: Observer as authority / arbitrator
II	How do I teach what I teach?			Alternatives approach: Observer as provider of alternative perspectives
III	Why do I teach what I teach? Why do I teach the way I do?			Nondirective approach: Observer as understander

Figure 13.3 The hierarchy of teachers' needs (Freeman, 1982:27)

represents low to high degrees of instructional supervision (i.e., the supervisors' visibility and frequency of discussions with the teachers).

This model shares some similarities with the situational leadership concept, but these supervisorial styles emerged from the data rather than being suggested by a theoretical stance. The model identifies two key variables to monitor: the observable evidence of supervisors' respect for teachers, and supervisors' presence in the instructional process.

How do Okeafor and Poole's four supervisory styles relate to scaffolding, affordances, and the zone of proximal development? The surly supervisors and imperial supervisors make no effort to scaffold teachers' learning or to understand or to identify the teachers' zones of proximal development. Both backstage and collaborative supervisors, however, provide teachers with affordances, allowing them to utilize supervisors' input at their own pace.

Training, development, and supervisor effectiveness

In Chapter 3 we considered Freeman's (1982) ideas about training and development. Freeman has suggested that teachers ask different questions about their work at different points in their professional lives. Their changing needs and foci also call for flexible training and development strategies from supervisors, as depicted in Figure 13.3.

Freeman (1982) says these three approaches are appropriate at different stages in a teacher's career. The supervisory approach, in which the supervisor gives teachers direct advice, is appropriate for novices and those concerned with *what* they teach. Later, when teachers are examining *how* they teach, the alternatives approach is useful. And when teachers address more philosophical questions, the nondirective approach is more appropriate.

Of course, some less experienced teachers may address *why* questions, and with them the nondirective approach may work. Likewise, with a marginal teacher who needs guidance or an experienced teacher in a new job, the nondirective approach may not work well. Gebhard's (1984) creative approach allows supervisors to combine different options in any given post-observation conference. The point is that supervisors must assess the in-service teachers' needs and choose an approach to meet them, rather than assuming that "one size fits all."

The concepts of training and development and the different phases of a teacher's career can be connected to sociocultural theory. In their review of adult learners and sociocultural theory, Bonk and Kim (1998:74) say "the lockstep factory model of education is out of sync with the prevailing view that learning is fundamentally social and derived from membership and engagement with others in a learning community." For supervisors working with in-service language teachers, this position suggests that for individual teachers and their peers, the supervisor is only one part of a complex constellation of learning opportunities and resources. How the supervisor relates to the in-service teachers will influence their receptivity (or resistance) to professional development. Research on adult learning argues for "teaching techniques that dignify and respect adult learners with self-directed learning opportunities wherein learners take as much control as possible over the design, process, and evaluation of their learning" (ibid.). If we apply these ideas to training and development in teacher learning, we necessarily return to the concept of autonomy. In terms of Okeafor and Poole's (1992) analysis, research on adult learners suggests that teachers work best with backstage supervisors or collaborative supervisors.

Concluding comments

This chapter examined the interesting challenges inherent in supervising in-service teachers. We considered Beerens's (2000) distinctions between beginning teachers, experienced teachers, and marginal teachers and noted that the period of the induction years is a particularly sensitive time for teachers. We saw that the stimulated recall procedure can be used to study teachers' decision making. Next we examined key attitudinal factors, including resistance, burnout, and fulfillment. We saw that supervisors' efforts to foster faculty development can be a positive influence in the delicate balance between discouragement and professionalism.

Finally, we considered what the research evidence has to say about effective supervisory practices in the in-service context. We revisited Freeman's (1982) model of training and development to see what sorts of support in-service teachers might need, given their own increasing experience and the changing contexts in which they work.

The following questions are based on the case presented in this chapter. I hope the material covered here and these activities will lead you to further thought and research on supervising in-service teachers.

Case discussion

1. What are your main goals for the first in-service workshop, which will occur in two weeks? List three goals you hope to accomplish as a result of the training day.
2. What steps must you take now to address those goals? (Assume the room has been reserved, lunch ordered, the teachers notified, etc.) How can you utilize the teachers' expertise? List three ways you could involve (some of) the teachers in giving the workshop.
3. Look back at Blumberg's (1980) list of conditions under which a person feels fulfilled in his or her work. Think of one way to build each condition into the design of your workshop.
4. What would you avoid doing at the workshop? What activities would be inappropriate? List three things you do *not* want to do in the in-service training.
5. Given the goals you identified, use the following chart to draft a plan for the training day.

8:00 A.M.	12:30
8:30	1:00
9:00	1:30
9:30	2:00
10:00	2:30
10:30	3:00
11:00	3:30
11:30	4:00
12:00 P.M.	4:30

6. How could you use the framework in Table 13.1 to collect data about the teachers' implementation of the curriculum? What questions could you ask after your first workshop and eight months later to gain useful information?
7. What constituent(s) of teaching are you probably dealing with here: awareness, attitude, knowledge, and / or skills (Freeman, 1989a)? What are the implications of your answer for how you will work with these teachers through the academic year?

8. Look back at Rinvolucri's (1981) advice for overcoming resistance to in-service training. List three ways you could incorporate his advice in your workshops.

9. What data could you collect after the workshop to determine its impact on the teachers' practice? It's possible that the workshop might influence the teachers' attitudes and awareness in unobservable ways. How could you learn about those changes?

Tasks and discussion

1. Think about a particular job in which you had a supervisor. Which factors in Table 13.2 were operative in that relationship? Which of those patterns do you (or would you) apply regularly? Which would you like to continue, and which would you like to change?

2. The following questions were posed by Rinvolucri (1981:48): "When you meet a whole new set of ideas in a teaching area you think you know something about, how do you react? Think back to the last time this happened. When was it? Where was it? How did you feel about the person introducing you to the ideas (the writer, friend, seminar leader)? Did you experience resistance? If so, how did you later come to terms with it?"

3. In the past when you have observed teachers, how did they respond to your presence? What were the observable manifestations of the teachers' attitudes? Did you sense resistance on the part of the teachers? If so, what made you feel the teachers were resistant?

4. When your teaching has been observed, what were your attitudes about being observed? Did you exhibit those attitudes? Does your attitude about being observed vary, depending on the observer? For example, would you feel the same about being visited by a novice teacher and by your supervisor? In which instances is resistance a likely response?

5. Rinvolucri wrote, "Blessed is the conservative, shape-giving principle within the trainee, the immune system, the evaluative resistance" (1981:52). Is there a positive value in teachers' resistance? Give examples based on your experience.

6. Review the case about the French teacher at the beginning of Chapter 7. How would Beerens (2000) characterize that teacher? Which of the attitudinal concepts discussed in this chapter might apply to that teacher? Explain your reasoning.

7. Alfonso et al. stated that "occasional supervisory visits to classrooms merely highlight for teachers the episodic character of supervision" (1984:16). In the context in which you teach (or hope to teach), how often should a supervisor observe a teacher (e.g., in a 15-week semester)? Do your answers vary if you think about observing a novice

teacher, as opposed to a teacher in the induction years or a very experienced teacher?

8. The ESL and EFL teachers in Pennington and Ho's (1995) research on burnout experienced less emotional exhaustion, less depersonalization, and a greater sense of personal accomplishment than did other people in the service professions that Maslach (1982) studied. Why do you think this is so?

Suggestions for further reading

Maslach and Jackson (1986) developed an instrument for measuring burnout. Maslach's (1982) burnout research influenced Pennington and Ho's (1995) study of EFL / ESL teachers and Byrne's (1994) research on elementary, intermediate, and secondary school teachers in Canada. Soppelsa (1997) discusses faculty empowerment as a way to combat burnout.

Woods (1996) studied teachers' decision making. Johnson (1992a, 1992b) used stimulated recall to investigate the in-class decision making of preservice ESL teachers.

Nolan and Hillkirk's (1991) study on coaching for veteran teachers has implications for supervisors. See also Brundage (1996).

For more information about teachers in the induction years, see Borko (1986), Fox and Singletary (1986), and Tisher (1984).

14 Supervising non-native-speaking teachers

Teacher supervision can be tricky under any conditions. Language teacher supervision is even more complicated because of our subject matter: language. When our work involves teaching culture as well, the situation becomes even more complex. Who can lay claim to the appropriate linguistic and cultural knowledge to be an effective language teacher?

The early teacher education literature in our field often focused on teachers' linguistic abilities. It featured many discussions about how to bring non-native-speaking (NNS) teachers' target language skills up to the desired level. (See, for example, Buch and de Bagheera, 1978; Diaz Zubieta, Torrano Jessurun, and Adams, 1978; Greis, 1985; Sukwiwat and Smith, 1981; and Taska, 1975.) Arguments abound as to what that ideal proficiency level may be in various circumstances, and the native speaker has often been held up as a model. But in fact, these days it is no longer clear what exactly is meant by the term *native speaker*.

There are instances, however, when teachers' target language proficiency is an issue of concern. As a supervisor, you will be called upon to assess non-native-speaking teachers' language skills and sometimes to help them improve proficiency. The case in this chapter presents such a situation.

Case for analysis: Working with less-than-proficient language teachers

You are a new supervisor in a large foreign language program with a staff of 50 teachers, including both native and non-native speakers. Most of the non-native speakers are very proficient in the target language. However, two teachers make serious grammar errors, their vocabulary is limited, and their pronunciation is sometimes unintelligible to you (even though you are familiar with their first language).

Neither teacher has lived or traveled in the countries where the target language is spoken. They themselves are graduates of this particular foreign language program, and their contact with the target language and culture has been entirely in the foreign language context. Fortunately, both teachers have the training and experience required to teach in this program, and both exhibit competence and

---

creativity as teachers. In addition, they are both eager to improve, as teachers and as speakers of the target language. Your only concern is about their proficiency.

Because these teachers are in the first year of their three-year contracts, they have been assigned to the lower levels. (This is company policy for all new teachers.) Because they are just starting, you feel you have the time (as well as the responsibility) to help them improve.

You have observed both teachers twice. With their permission, you videotaped the second observation of their classes. You also took notes during their lessons.

Nativeness in the broader context

There is a widespread assumption that native speakers of any language make the best teachers of that language. This position may have had some merit in times past, when international communication and travel were not so quick and easy. And there are still advantages today for the teacher who is a native speaker of the target language. Whether there are advantages for the language learners is another question.

The issue of nativeness is far more complex than folkloric beliefs make it seem. Political, professional, and technological developments have influenced language teaching greatly since the 1940s. These changes have caused language teaching professionals to rethink the potential contributions of both native and non-native-speaking teachers. But as Amin has noted with regard to English, "the 'native speaker of English' is such a powerful construct, one so embedded in myth, that it is daunting to attempt to disentangle fact from fable" (2001:90).

Arguments about native-speakerhood

In EFL teaching, Medgyes says that it is difficult to delineate who should be considered a non-native English-speaking teacher (non-NEST). He says that typically "a non-NEST may be defined as a teacher...for whom English is a second or foreign language; who works in an EFL environment; whose students are monolingual groups of learners; and who speaks the same native language as his or her students" (Medgyes, 2001:433). He adds that this definition is only partially applicable to non-native teachers who work in second language contexts.

The idealized concept of the native speaker has been questioned in recent years. Second language acquisition researchers and sociolinguists have come to view "nativeness" as a continuum of lesser to greater proficiency, rather than a dichotomy of native versus non-native speakers.

Murphy O'Dwyer asked, "What exactly is a native speaker of a language? It soon emerges, if you pursue the idea, that this is a political rather than a linguistic label" (1996:21).

Arguments about target language models

Sociolinguistic research has demonstrated that languages typically do not have a single geographic and social standard that can be identified as the thing native speakers speak. In the past, according to Lowenberg, *standard English* was defined as "the linguistic forms which are the accepted models for official, business, journalistic, and academic writing, and for public speaking before an audience or on radio or television" (1990:157). The English used by educated native speakers is often assumed to be "the universal target for classroom instruction, and the benchmark for attained proficiency in Standard English around the world" (ibid.), but Lowenberg says "such an assumption is no longer sociolinguistically valid" (ibid.). Instead there are different native speaker norms that provide the target models for language learners, and in some instances, learners may have a choice of models (Goldstein, 1987).

In the past, people assumed there were clear-cut standard languages and dialects of those more prestigious standard languages. Dialects were viewed as regionally defined, and dialectology was an important specialization for linguists. Historically, dialectology involved describing and comparing the phonological, morphological, semantic, and syntactic characteristics of regional varieties. However, as people moved from rural to urban areas or from one part of a country to another, and as massive social changes occurred in the 1800s and 1900s (e.g., the Industrial Revolution and the U.S. civil rights movement), linguists began to study socially determined language varieties, which were not entirely geographically defined.

Arguments about nativized varieties

In the late twentieth century, the issue of "nativized varieties" began to receive serious attention. Nativized varieties (such as Indian English) have developed stable new features of phonology, morphology, syntax, semantics, and discourse "that are so systematic, wide-spread, and accepted among their users that we can say that new varieties . . . have evolved, distinct from the more 'established' native speaker varieties" (Lowenberg, 1990:158). Such varieties often occur where a formerly dominant (often colonial) language is used by "substantial numbers of non-native speakers as a second, often official language in a broad range of *intra*national domains" (ibid.:157). As a result of postcolonial linguistic developments, the multicountry languages (such as French, Spanish, Portuguese, and

English) may have hundreds of regional and social varieties. Regardless of the status of nativized languages, these days language teacher supervisors are called on to work with teachers from a wide variety of linguistic and cultural backgrounds.

Thus, it is an oversimplification to talk about hiring only native speakers of a particular target language (see Flynn and Gulikers, 2001). In fact, doing so is to subscribe to "the native speaker fallacy" (Braine, 1999a, 1999b) – the unquestioned assumption that "the ideal English teacher is a native speaker" (Braine, 1999a:23). Canagarajah (1999b:79) has called this notion "linguistically anachronistic" and said that "it creates a disjunction between research awareness and professional practice" (see also Phillipson, 1992).

Arguments about which variety to teach

Deciding which variety will be taught has become increasingly complicated. Once the major purpose for studying a language was to be able to read its literature. Given that goal, issues of which variety to teach arose less often than they do today. But with recent advances in global transportation and communication, speaking and listening skills have become central goals for language learners, who often use the language to communicate with other non-native speakers rather than with native speakers. As early as 1981, Smith noted,

> English is being used by non-native speakers to communicate with other non-native speakers. The countries of ASEAN (Association of South East Asian Nations) use English in their official meetings to represent themselves and their cultures. Japanese businessmen use English in [Malaysia] to represent their company's policy. Singaporeans use English to tell others about their "way of life." New literatures in English have appeared from India, the Philippines, and the South Pacific as well as Africa – literature written in English by non-native speakers intended for a world audience – not just a native-speaking audience. (Smith in Sukwiwat and Smith, 1981:13)

As a result of these developments, many non-native teachers have had to increase their own speaking and listening skills to address their language students' changing needs.

Furthermore, it is no longer sufficient to have declarative knowledge about the target language. "Declarative knowledge includes all of the things we know and can articulate about language" (Nunan, 1999a:3). To be effective language teachers, however, we must have procedural knowledge as well. In our field, procedural knowledge involves knowing how to teach, how to use target language, and how to behave in the target culture. Native- and non-native-speaking teachers may face different challenges in these regards.

Some language programs intentionally provide a particular variety as the target language model taught in class. Learners can enroll in EFL programs to learn British or American or Australian English (though each of these varieties has many identifiable subvarieties). In other cases, the program policy may be to hire teachers who represent a variety of target norms themselves. For example, when I worked at the Chinese University of Hong Kong, the EFL faculty there included teachers whose first language was Mandarin or Cantonese, as well as speakers of Australian, Canadian, British, Sri Lankan, Indian, and American English. But even these national labels are too simplistic to characterize the varieties spoken by our team. Many of the Cantonese teachers had studied in the United Kingdom, the American varieties ranged from California to Mississippi, and one of the Sri Lankan teachers had studied in Texas and worked in Alabama. This rich diversity of varieties among the teachers was entirely appropriate because it mirrored the multiplicity of the Englishes used in Hong Kong by tourists, businesspeople, and local people. Thus it represented the diversity our students would encounter, both immediately and in their futures, as educated members of a fluid international society.

Issues in working with non-native teachers

You may supervise teachers who are not native speakers of the target language and whose linguistic skills fall short of expectations. There are several issues to keep in mind in working with teachers whose proficiency is deemed lacking.

First, it is easier to talk about target language problems in a climate of trust and open inquiry rather than in one of defensiveness. As the supervisor, you will have a powerful influence on the atmosphere in the working context. If you yourself are open to positive, candid discussions about language and teaching, it will be easier for the teachers to be open too. So, for instance, if you are an EFL teacher supervisor and are learning the language of the country where you work, you can ask the local teachers for help with structures, pragmatics, and vocabulary. If you initiate such conversations, the teachers will see that you too are open to learning.

If you already speak the local or target language proficiently, you can ask other teachers (both native and non-native speakers) for their best ideas about how to teach tricky points. Whether you are a native or a non-native speaker and whether or not you are working in your home culture, the teachers you supervise will be more open to learning if you are obviously working on your own professional development, including your language skills.

Some language teachers use the target language fluently but with many errors, whereas others are accurate but not fluent. Supervisors should be aware of when the problems occur. Do the types and number of errors vary depending on the context? For example, do the errors differ when the teachers are focusing on form rather than meaning? Do the majority of errors occur in speech rather than in writing? If so, it might be worthwhile to talk with the teachers about speech versus writing, or the contrast of focus on form versus focus on meaning, as a means of coming up with some strategies for *optimal monitor use* (Krashen and Terrell, 1983: 142–143).

Krashen (1981, 1982) described three types of learners: the "under-users," the "over-users," and the "optimal users" of what he calls "the monitor." By *monitor*, he means the ability to apply target language rules to edit our output (whether in speech or in writing). Krashen and Terrell (1983:143) maintain that monitor "under-users either cannot (or make no effort to) use knowledge which is learned." In contrast, monitor over-users' reliance on rules "interferes with both their attempts to communicate and with the acquisition process itself" (ibid.). Successful monitor use varies widely from one person to another. People with a "background in grammar study in their native language are often able to monitor more successfully than those with little such experience" (ibid.:142–143). Sometimes, non-native teachers become monitor over-users. As a result, their spoken fluency in the target language can be hampered.

The strategies for helping teachers improve their proficiency will be determined, to a large extent, by the nature of the problems. It follows that the first step is to diagnose the problems or get the teachers themselves to do so. If fluency is an issue, different strategies are called for from those that would be helpful to teachers trying to improve their accuracy.

Strategies for supporting non-native-speaking language teachers

Many strategies can be used to support non-native-speaking teachers in developing their target language skills. Here we will consider three that a supervisor can promote: team teaching, immersion experiences, and using authentic materials.

Team teaching

Team teaching pairs can consist of non-native and native speakers. This model was followed in the JET (Japan Exchange and Teaching) Program.

Native speakers of English (often young Canadian, British, Australian, or American college graduates) were paired with Japanese EFL teachers to try to increase the pupils' exposure to English. However, in some situations this plan did not work very well. Some Japanese teachers were worried about their own English proficiency. (See Sturman, 1992, and Tajino and Tajino, 2000.) In other cases, many of the young English speakers had little or no interest in teaching English as a profession. Some pairings succeeded, but in others there were cross-cultural communication difficulties.

Polio and Wilson-Duffy (1998) discuss the importance of team-teaching arrangements in the practicum. These authors say, "We believe that the pairing of NSs [native speakers] and NNSs [non-native speakers] is essential for international MA students to take on an English course in a new culture" (p. 27). Both parties benefit from this arrangement in that "the NNS always has a NS practicum student in the room who could address linguistic or cultural matters unknown to the NNS" (ibid.). The native-speaking teaching partner could also help with idiomatic expressions or slang that might arise. The NNS teachers, on the other hand, "had a better sense of the ESL students' background knowledge of U.S. culture" (ibid.).

In setting up team-teaching arrangements, it is important that teachers choose their own partners rather than be forced into any particular partnership (see Bailey, Dale, and Squire, 1992; Bailey et al., 2001). As Sturman notes, the essential components of successful team teaching are "mutual personal and professional respect, adaptability, and good humor" (1992:145). Medgyes suggests that such collaboration can benefit the language learners in a program: "Given a favorable mix, various forms of collaboration are possible, and learners can only gain from such cross-fertilization" (2001:441). However, in cases where the partnership is forced or unhappy, the students may suffer as a result (see, e.g., Johnson, 1999).

Immersion experiences

Supervisors can also promote staff development opportunities in which teachers who want to improve their language skills are funded for study or travel opportunities (e.g., to conferences, to a country where the target language is spoken, to take an advanced course in the target language, etc.). There may be possible partnerships where the school would cover some expenses and the teachers themselves would cover others. The professional associations, such as IATEFL and TESOL, have competitive scholarship programs to help teachers attend conferences and workshops. Many organizations, such as the International Rotary and the Fulbright Association, also promote teacher exchanges.

Please keep in mind the central premise of this chapter: Both native and non-native teachers have varied strengths and weaknesses. Both have contributions to make. Teachers who are native speakers also benefit from further education and can learn a great deal about teaching, the target language, and language acquisition. Native speakers can continue their own professional development by learning the language(s) of their students (Tinker Sachs, 2002), traveling in cultures where they don't speak the language, taking courses in other languages, and participating in shock language lessons (see Bailey et al., 2001).

Using authentic materials

You and the teachers can also find ways to use both authentic and pedagogical materials that give the students target language samples. Authentic materials are "oral and written texts that occur naturally in the target language environment and that have not been created expressly for language learners" (Larimer and Schleicher, 1999: v).

Authentic speech samples offer voices other than the teacher's, to which the students may be accustomed. Utilizing authentic speech samples that provide new accents and speech at different rates is a valuable practice for native-speaking teachers of the target language as well. As the supervisor, you can help the staff build a program library of tape recordings, videos, magazines, Web site addresses, and the like that would be the source of native and proficient non-native models – both of speech and of writing – for all the teachers to use in their classes.

The use of authentic speech and writing samples should be helpful for non-native teachers' language development as well. In seeking out and using such materials, teachers increase their own target language input and hence the opportunity for improved intake. Learning to use authentic materials may enhance non-native teachers' procedural skills, both in terms of teaching and of their own language proficiency.

Defining language proficiency standards for teachers

It is important to keep your short-term and long-term goals in mind when dealing with the issue of teachers' target-language proficiency. In some cases a short-term, or local, goal would be to make sure the teachers are providing their current students with sociolinguistically appropriate and (nearly) error-free examples of the target language in their lessons and materials. In contrast, a long-term goal would be to help the teachers improve their target language skills and develop their own strategies for continuing to improve their skills. Another long-term goal would be to establish standards and define the hiring criteria to ensure that teachers hired in your program have effective target-language skills to begin with, before they ever enter a classroom.

This last point about teachers' entry-level proficiency involves a very difficult question: How good is good enough? How advanced must a non-native-speaking teacher's language skills actually be for that person to function well in a language program?

These questions are only partly linguistic in nature. They are also social and educational concerns. Some time ago, Saraswathi (1991:75) described a situation in India, where people may have gone into teaching not because they wanted to but because they had limited career options:

> While the brighter learners enroll for coveted courses like Engineering, Medicine, or Business Management, the weaker learners are left with no other option but to become teachers.... [A] teacher of English in the Indian school need not necessarily be a graduate in English language and literature. The weaker learner-turned-teacher is now asked to do the impossible – to teach the English language, which he himself has not mastered.

Saraswathi noted the face-threatening implications of this situation: "Most teachers are not aware of the fact that their own English is of a very poor standard and that they provide very bad models for their own learners" (Saraswathi, 1991:77). It is easy to see how language teachers might feel resistance in this context.

Thus the proficiency level needed by teachers is often an issue of supply and demand. Where the need for teachers outweighs the availability of trained and proficient teachers, people with limited target-language proficiency and / or little or no training will be employed as language teachers. Where there is an ample supply of trained and proficient language teachers, the job market may fragment into conditions of short-term contracts and part-time employment.

Research on standard setting

Many years ago, Livingston studied these issues with regard to ESL and bilingual (Spanish and English) teachers in New Jersey. The research had to do with using expert judgment to set standards. A standard is "simply an answer to the question 'How good is good enough?'" (1978:257). Livingston adds that answers to this question necessarily involve judgment. For this reason, standard-setting must answer four key questions: "(1) What type of judgments will enter into the standard-setting process? (2) Who will make those judgments? (3) How will the judgments be collected? and (4) How will the judgments be issued to determine the standard?" (ibid.). Livingston's research was designed to determine acceptable language standards in three contexts: (1) the ESL teachers' English proficiency, (2) the bilingual education teachers' English speaking proficiency, and (3) the bilingual education teachers' Spanish proficiency (ibid.:259).

Livingston wanted to know, "Given a candidate's interview score, what is the probability that the candidate's actual speaking proficiency would be judged acceptable?" Teacher candidates were interviewed with the Language Proficiency Interview (LPI), which is rated on a scale of zero to five points, with plus factors between rating levels (0, 0+, 1, 1+, 2, 2+, etc.). Livingston eliminated the data rated as 0, 0+, or 5, thinking there would be little disagreement in evaluating these levels. The 30 judges "were all experienced teachers (and in many cases also supervisors of teachers), of ESL or Spanish-English bilingual classes" (ibid.:258). These judges evaluated three interviews that had been rated between 1 and 4+ on the LPI. (For the 4+ level there were only two speech samples for rating.) The ESL rating data are summarized in Figure 14.1, in which each dot represents a particular speech sample.

The speakers whose English proficiency was rated at 2 or below on the five-point scale were judged to be unacceptable. Those rated at 3+ or higher were deemed acceptable. The problem arises in the middle of the scale, where teachers rated at 2+ or 3 were seen as acceptable by some judges but unacceptable by others. For instance, one speaker rated as 2+ was judged unacceptable by all the raters, whereas another was considered entirely acceptable.

Livingston's study provides eight key steps for standard-settings (1978:269–270; underscoring in the original).

1. Determine the measure of performance for which the standard is to be set. In general terms we can call this measure the *test score*. . . .
2. Determine the type of performance that will serve as the basis for judging a person's proficiency as adequate or inadequate. . . . We would call this performance the *criterion performance*. . . .
3. Identify a population of persons qualified to judge examples of the criterion performance as adequate or inadequate. Select a sample . . . to serve as *judges*.
4. Identify the population of persons . . . for which a standard is to be set and obtain their test scores. Select a sample of these *examinees*, making sure the range of their test scores is broad enough to include both the lowest and the highest scores that might conceivably be selected as the standard.
5. Obtain *judgments* of the examinees' . . . performances by the judges.

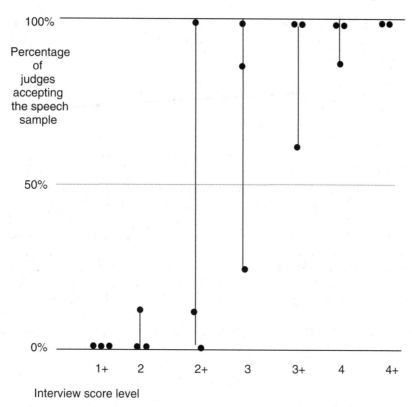

Figure 14.1 Acceptability judgments for English as a second language (Livingston, 1978:262)

6. Analyze the data provided by these judgments to estimate the *probability* that an examinee's criterion performance will be judged adequate.
7. Determine the *relative seriousness* of the two types of possible errors: passing an examinee whose criterion performance is inadequate and failing an examinee whose criterion performance is adequate.
8. Set the *standard* at the test score level that results in an equal risk of the two types of possible errors, weighted by their seriousness in the particular decision-making situation for which a standard is to be set.

Provided the criterion measure is a valid and reliable test, people can be identified with certain competence levels, as measured by that test.

Qualified judges can then evaluate data from people representing those levels, to determine which levels are appropriate.

Components of the spoken language

Figure 14.2 (van Lier, 1995) can help us determine the areas in which non-native-speaking teachers' problems may occur in speaking.

In this pyramid, the smallest linguistic units are pictured at the top. Phonology, the study of the sound system, focuses on distinctive features, the phonemes, and the morphemes of that language, including what constitutes a syllable. Morphology examines both free morphemes (words) and bound morphemes (prefixes, infixes, and suffixes that do not appear independent of words). Syntax includes the rules of word order in units ranging from the phrase, the clause, and the sentence to utterances in speech and to the level of texts (stretches of language made up of multiple utterances or sentences). The study of discourse works with the larger units – clauses, utterances, and texts. When we focus on speaking and listening, we must also consider stress, rhythm, and intonation. (These suprasegmental phonemes are realized in texts by punctuation or typographical conventions such as boldface, capitalization, or underscoring.)

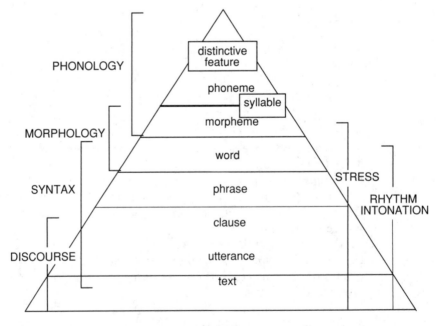

Figure 14.2 Units of language (van Lier, 1995:15)

Van Lier's pyramid depicts the complex interplay among the levels of language that teachers must be able to explain (part of their declarative knowledge). It also represents the procedural knowledge that teachers must master to speak the target language well. Of course, teachers can often explain aspects of language that are difficult for them to produce, but non-native teachers and their supervisors can use this model as a tool for analyzing difficulties.

It is probably important for supervisors to help teachers identify specific language components to work on in cases where improvement is needed. Otherwise the job of developing one's language skills can seem unmanageable and overwhelming.

Contextual factors, training, and teachers' proficiency

The question for language teacher supervisors then becomes, How proficient must teachers be in the target language in order to teach? But even this question is oversimplified. We must examine local needs and constraints and ask, How proficient must language teachers be in order to teach effectively in this program? In multilevel programs, we might even ask about the proficiency needed to teach at particular levels of the curriculum.

Talking about native versus non-native speakers as teachers overlooks some very important issues. The teacher's language proficiency is only one element of professionalism. Another concern is whether the person has the appropriate preparation to be a teacher. The intersection of these two issues is shown in Figure 14.3.

First, we must remember that a key distinction is not whether a teacher is a native or a non-native speaker of the target language, but rather

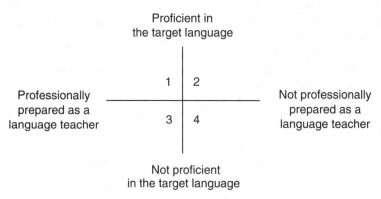

Figure 14.3 Continua of target language proficiency and professional preparation

whether he or she is proficient in that language. *Proficiency* is "knowledge, competence, or ability in the use of a language, irrespective of how, where, or under what conditions it has been acquired" (Bachman, 1990:16). Whether a person has professional training in language teaching is a second key issue.

The combination of these two factors has been a huge source of justified frustration for well-prepared, highly proficient non-native-speaking teachers over the years. In many countries in Asia, for example, the blue-eyed, blond backpacker who runs out of money and looks for work may have better luck getting a position to teach English than will a local teacher with a master's degree or advanced diploma in TESOL. There is no justification for this practice other than the folk belief that native-speaking teachers are somehow inherently superior.

Many people have questioned the assumption that native speakers are automatically better language teachers. For example, Shaw says that native-speaking teachers may lack "the kinds of insight necessary for an English language teacher to prepare and execute his classes" (1979:12). He also notes that "non-native speaker teachers are typically better able ... to control the complexity of their speech in an elementary class" (ibid.). The assumption "that the native speaker has automatic advantages" as a language teacher has also been questioned by Murphy O'Dwyer (1996:21), who asks whether all native speakers are the same:

> Are they all equally competent in their native language? A moment's reflection tells us that they are certainly not.... [N]ative speakers are very different in the range of language competencies they possess. Just because you are a native speaker of English doesn't mean that you can write poetry or novels.

She also says that "native speakers have just as much to learn (and in many cases much more) than nonnative speakers" (ibid.). For example, non-native-speaking teachers who studied the target language formally often have better insights into its structure and use than do untrained native speakers with little or no explicit declarative knowledge of their first language. Furthermore, Murphy O'Dwyer claims, non-native-speaking teachers have a distinct advantage over monolingual native speakers in that "they already have a successful language learning experience behind them, which they can draw on to inform their teaching" (ibid.).

Language teachers' perceptions

Some studies have been conducted on teachers' perceptions of the relative strengths of native and non-native-speaking teachers. It appears that many non-native-speaking teachers are very concerned about their own proficiency levels. For example, an in-service training program for Hong Kong teachers in English medium secondary schools has been described by Hoare and Kong (1994). The teachers they worked with (native speakers of Cantonese who teach academic subjects in English) "believe that an improvement in their language proficiency will lead to the most immediate and significant improvement in their ability to teach through English" (pp. 21–22). Medgyes (2001) would concur with these teachers' opinion. He states that "the most important professional duty that non-NESTs have to perform is to make linguistic improvements in their English" (p. 440). However, Hoare and Kong also note that the "level of proficiency regarded as necessary is a complex and probably controversial matter" (1994:22).

Medgyes conducted research on language teachers' perceptions. He began by delineating four specific assumptions (2001:434): "(1) NESTs and non-NESTs differ in terms of their language proficiency; (2) they differ in terms of their teaching behavior; (3) the discrepancy in language proficiency accounts for most of the differences found in their teaching behavior; and (4) they can be equally good teachers on their own terms." To investigate these assumptions, Medgyes surveyed 325 teachers from 11 countries. The majority (86 percent) were non-native speakers of English. According to Medgyes, "Many non-NESTs participating in the survey commented about their inferiority complex caused by the defects in their English-language proficiency and about some kind of cognitive dissonance due to the double role they played as both teachers and learners of the same subject" (ibid.).

Medgyes says (ibid.) the advantage perceived by the native speakers was their spontaneous ability to use the language in diverse communicative contexts:

> Non-NESTs, on the whole, are well aware of their linguistic deficiencies and of the all-pervasive nature of their handicap. In no area of English-language proficiency can they emulate NESTs: survey participants viewed themselves as poorer listeners, speakers, readers, and writers. True enough, long stays in English-speaking countries, hard work and dedication might help narrow the gap, but very few non-NESTs are ever able to catch up with their native colleagues.

Respondents felt the main difficulty was "vocabulary, together with idiomatic and appropriate use of English" (ibid.). Next came problems with speaking and fluency, pronunciation, and listening. Medgyes notes, "Grammar featured to a far lesser extent and so did writing skills, whereas reading skills and cultural knowledge were not even mentioned" (ibid.).

Based on his survey, Medgyes documented several differences between native- and non-native-speaking teachers' perceptions. The respondents felt that in terms of the teachers' own use of English (the target language), native speakers speak better English, use real language, and use English more confidently. In contrast, they felt the non-native teachers speak poorer English, use "bookish" language, and use English less confidently (ibid.:435).

In terms of their general attitude, Medgyes' research suggests that native-speaking teachers adopt a more flexible approach, are more innovative and less empathetic, attend to perceived needs, have unrealistic expectations, are frequently more casual, and are sometimes less committed to teaching. In contrast, non-native-speaking teachers adopt a more guided approach, are more cautious, are more empathetic to the students, attend to real needs, and have realistic expectations. It appears they are also stricter and are more committed to teaching (ibid.).

Medgyes's data suggest that native speakers often focus on fluency, meaning, language in use, oral skills, and colloquial registers. They will teach items in context, prefer free activities, favor group work or pair work, and use a variety of materials. Compared to non-native-speaking teachers, they also tolerate errors and give fewer tests. They use less of the students' first language, resort to translation less often, and assign less homework.

This finding is supported by the error gravity research (in which people rate the impact of particular written or spoken errors on the learner's reader or interlocutor). Across several studies of different languages, one pattern that has emerged is that teachers are typically more critical of language learners' errors than are nonteachers. Furthermore, non-native teachers are typically more critical than native-speaking teachers. (See Ludwig, 1982, and Medgyes, 2001.)

Medgyes's research shows that non-native-speaking teachers tend to focus on accuracy, including attention to grammar rules. They emphasize the printed word and formal registers and often teach items in isolation. They prefer using controlled, teacher-centered activities and may rely on a single textbook. They also seem to give more tests. Non-native speakers use more of the students' first language and resort to translation more often during lessons. Medgyes says they also assign more homework than do their native-speaking counterparts. Finally, and not surprisingly, with regard to teaching culture, native speakers supply more cultural information than non-native-speaking teachers (ibid.:435).

Medgyes notes an intriguing interaction between non-native English teachers' target language confidence and their classroom practices:

> Preoccupied with their own language difficulties, they are reluctant to loosen their grip over the class. As group work and

pair work often create unpredictable situations full of linguistic traps, non-NESTs favor more secure forms of classwork, such as lock-step activities. Similar reasons were claimed to account for the non-NEST's preference for standard coursebooks, which by their very nature provide security. (ibid.)

He concludes that "non-NESTs are inclined to adopt a more controlled and pedagogic approach" for the same reason (ibid.).

One questionnaire item asked whether native or non-native speakers were the better teachers. Medgyes writes, "While an approximately equal number of votes went for either option (27 percent for NESTs and 29 percent for non-NESTs), 44 percent of the respondents inserted 'both,' an alternative which had not even been supplied in the questionnaire" (2001:436). These respondents documented six areas in which they felt non-native-speaking teachers are better equipped than most native speakers: They can "(1) provide a better learner model; (2) teach language-learning strategies more effectively; (3) supply more information about the English language; (4) better anticipate and prevent language difficulties; (5) be more sensitive to their students; and (6) benefit from their ability to use their students' mother tongue" (ibid.).

A study by Kamhi-Stein, Aagard, Ching, Paik, and Sasser (2001) investigated the perceptions of native- and non-native-speaking teachers working in the K–12 context in California. A survey of 55 native speakers and 32 non-native speakers revealed that the former viewed their own English skills "as being between 'very good' and 'excellent,'" while "[non-native English-speaking teachers] perceive their overall English language skills as being between 'good' and 'very good')" (p. 78). For these groups, the highest self-ratings were in reading for the natives and listening for the non-native teachers. In contrast, their lowest self-ratings were grammar for the natives and pronunciation for the non-natives.

Kamhi-Stein et al. say non-native-speaking teachers may

1. face isolation and separation from their ethnic group culture.
2. experience teacher bashing and the media's distrust of public education.
3. be expected to advocate for their ethnic group and solve emerging problems ... [and] be relied on to communicate with parents, especially when language is a factor.
4. "burn out" trying to meet the needs of bilingual programs while working under the stigma of teaching in a "bilingual" rather than a "regular" program.
5. feel they were hired to fill a quota and provide a minority presence, thus making them feel conspicuous and out-of-place. (ibid.:78)

Supervisors should be aware of these issues and be prepared to support non-native-speaking teachers as they cope with these additional pressures.

The fact is that both native- and non-native-speaking language teachers have perceptions about the benefits of nativeness, as does the public at large. As supervisors, we must look beyond the labels and see teachers as individuals, with particular strengths and areas for improvement.

Concluding comments

In this chapter we have considered issues about defining non-native speakers and what varieties of languages should be taught. We also examined some ideas about setting target-language standards and helping non-native teachers improve their proficiency.

Given the field's shifting understanding of what constitutes native-speaker status, which international varieties may be emerging as target models, and whether standard languages can be identified, it behooves us to be very respectful of the varieties spoken by the language teachers we supervise. This perspective is not so black-and-white as was the earlier view of trying to improve NNS teachers' proficiency in the target language. Let us conclude our discussion by examining the case presented in this chapter, in which the teachers involved fit Medgyes's (2001) definition of non-native-speaking teachers.

Case discussion

1. Given the information in the case, how would you characterize these two teachers in terms of their psychological readiness and job readiness?
2. Using Freeman's (1989a) four constituents of language teaching – awareness, attitude, knowledge and skills – which of the four areas need to be addressed with these two non-native-speaking teachers? What are your goals and concerns as you plan individual post-observation conferences with each teacher?
3. Assume that one of these teachers seems to be a monitor over-user, whose accuracy improves with concentration but whose speech then becomes very hesitant. The other, whose speech is fluent but inaccurate, appears to be a consistent monitor under-user. What specific strategies for improvement will you suggest or do you hope the two individuals will suggest?
4. What helping strategies are available to you as the supervisor? List the possible ways you could help these teachers improve their target-language proficiency or could motivate them to do so. Which of the

strategies you listed are appropriate and which are inappropriate to undertake? For example, should you commit to having a "language lunch" with the two teachers every week? Should you offer workshops for the entire faculty? Or should you leave these teachers to improve their own language skills? What factors will influence your decision making about the strategies you select?

5. Does your position on these issues shift if you think of yourself as a native speaker of the target language or a proficient non-native speaker? If your perspective would change, how are your options affected?

6. If you were one of the teachers described in the case study, what activities and learning strategies would you personally want to utilize to increase your target-language proficiency?

7. You want to send these two teachers to a language teaching conference to be held in a country where the target language is spoken and in a city where you yourself have some close colleagues who are willing to welcome these teachers into their classes. You feel you can put together a beneficial immersion experience for these teachers, including participation in the conference and classroom observations before and after the conference.

   You plan to ask your director for funds to send these teachers to the conference. They will pay for their own food and incidental expenses, but you want the director to pay for their conference registration, their hotel rooms for 10 days, and their international airfare. List four or five benefits to the teachers and to the program that would provide convincing evidence to the director that the trip is worth funding.

Tasks and discussion

1. Thinking of yourself as a language teacher, look at Figure 14.3. Locate yourself in one of the four quadrants relative to each language with which you have a working familiarity.

2. Now think of yourself in the role of supervisor in a program with which you are familiar. Which quadrant(s) best describe(s) the teachers in that program?

3. Your supervisorial strategies for working with teachers in these four quadrants may vary. List two or three appropriate developmental strategies to use with each of the following types of teachers: quadrant 1: proficient *and* professionally prepared; quadrant 2: proficient *but not* professionally prepared; quadrant 3: *not* proficient but professionally prepared; and quadrant 4: *neither* proficient *nor* professionally prepared. Compare your list with those of your classmates or colleagues.

4. For each statement below (Medgyes, 2001:436), circle the number that best indicates your own position: 1 equals strongly disagree, 2 equals disagree, 3 equals neutral or no opinion, 4 equals agree, and 5 equals strongly agree. Compared to native-speaking teachers, non-native-speaking teachers

A. provide a better learner model.	1	2	3	4	5
B. teach language-learning strategies more effectively.	1	2	3	4	5
C. supply more information about the English language.	1	2	3	4	5
D. better anticipate and prevent language difficulties.	1	2	3	4	5
E. are more sensitive to their students.	1	2	3	4	5
F. benefit from their ability to use the students' mother tongue.	1	2	3	4	5

If you are working with a group, compare your ratings with others' and compute the average ratings and standard deviations, to see where the greatest disagreement lies.

5. Think about your own efforts to learn a language other than your mother tongue. Were you typically a monitor under-user, over-user, or optimal user? How did your use of the monitor influence your language learning?

6. List three experiences that have been helpful in increasing your proficiency in a new language. How do your ideas relate to the difficulties of teachers you may supervise?

7. Refer to van Lier's (1995) pyramid in Figure 14.2. If you are a non-native speaker of the target language, use yourself in this task. If you are a native speaker, think of a non-native-speaking colleague or employee. Identify the key linguistic difficulties of the person in question. At which level(s) of the pyramid do the problems occur? Think of three specific steps to generate improvement.

8. Team-teach a language lesson with a non-native-speaking teacher (if you are a native speaker), or with a native speaker (if you are a non-native speaker). What contributions do you both bring to planning and conducting the lesson? Which contributions are related to language proficiency, and which to other kinds of knowledge and skills?

9. Contact the administrators of two language programs and ask whether there is a policy about employing non-native speakers or about teaching a particular variety of the language.

Suggestions for further reading

Braine (1999b) edited a collection of articles about the experience of being a non-native teacher. Anyone who will train or supervise non-native-speaking teachers should read this book. Another useful resource is the 2001 *CATESOL Journal* (Kamhi-Stein, 2001), which addresses the theme of non-native-speaking teachers.

Bailey et al. (2001) includes a chapter on how teachers can utilize language learning experiences for their own professional development. (See also Tinker Sachs, 2002.) Bailey et al. (2001) interviewed two preservice teachers (a native and a non-native speaker) about the pros and cons of team teaching. For more information on team teaching and collaboration between natives and non-natives, see Bailey et al. (1992), Carvalho de Oliveira and Richardson (2001), Matsuda and Matsuda (2001), Nunan (1992b), and Head and Taylor (1997: 192–194). Ruth Johnson (1999) has written an article about a team-teaching experience that failed partly because of cross-cultural misunderstandings.

Larimer and Schleicher (1999) edited a book of 45 different ideas for using authentic materials. The ideas were submitted by practicing language teachers.

Matsuda (1999) and Murphy O'Dwyer (1996) published short articles in *TESOL Matters* about the advantages non-native-speaking teachers bring to the classroom. Medgyes's (2001) survey is an excellent place to start reading about non-native teachers' perceptions.

If you are planning a language improvement course for teachers, the articles by Hoare and Kong (1994), Johnson (1990), and Milk (1990) should be helpful.

Articles about non-native-speaking teachers-in-training have been written by England and Roberts (1989), Lee and Lew (2001), D. Liu (1999), Master (1990), Medgyes (1999), and Samimy and Brutt-Griffler (1999).

J. Liu (1999) has written an interesting data-based article that examines the power of professional labeling. See also Thomas (1999).

15 Professionalism, paradigm shifts, and language teacher supervision

This book began with some definitions of language teacher supervision and an overview of the roles supervisors take. You may agree that "supervision has a rather undistinguished history, a variety of sometimes incompatible definitions, a very low level of popular acceptance, and many perplexing and challenging problems" (Anderson, 1982:181). Nevertheless, I hope that you will also agree that language teacher supervision can be a career path worth pursuing.

In Chapter 1 we examined a partial inventory of professional supervisors' roles and skills. In Chapter 2 we considered attitude and awareness in teacher-supervisor relationships. Next, in Chapter 3 we investigated autonomy and authority as these constructs relate to supervision. In Chapter 4 we first asked whether supervisors should observe teachers, and if so, whether they should collect data during observations. We then examined manual and electronic data collection in Chapters 5 and 6, respectively. In Chapter 7 we considered the post-observation conference in general, and then in Chapter 8 we focused on mitigation in supervisory discourse. In Chapter 9 we reviewed language teacher evaluation, which formed the backdrop to our discussion of criteria for teacher evaluation in Chapter 10. Finally, in Chapters 11 to 14, we discussed the challenges and rewards of language teacher supervisors' work with four groups: preservice teachers, teaching assistants, in-service teachers, and non-native-speaking teachers.

We will now examine the concept of professionalism and consider some alternatives to traditional, hierarchical teacher-supervisor relationships in the context of a paradigm shift in education. This final chapter may raise more questions than it answers, but I hope it will help you review key concepts covered earlier and pull those ideas together into a coherent vision of the kind of supervisor you would like to be. Anderson says that "supervision is after all a form of teaching, and it calls for making such situational adjustments and adaptations as will call forth the best that teachers have to offer" (1982:188). It is with this positive view that I wish to end this book, and the final case was designed with that goal in mind.

This case involves the supervision of preservice and in-service teachers, who are both native and non-native speakers of their various target languages. The issues here draw upon concepts discussed throughout the book, so you may find it helpful to review earlier chapters. In addition, the case involves a very realistic element of time management, which I have found to be a serious challenge for many language teacher supervisors.

Case for analysis: Exploring our options

You are a teacher supervisor in a large program that offers instruction in six different languages. The curriculum includes language classes for immigrants and international students who have recently arrived in the country. The curriculum also provides foreign language classes for local people who wish to travel, study, or conduct business in other countries. Students served include adults, university students, and elementary and secondary school pupils. Thus, it is a comprehensive program offering a diversified language curriculum to a broad audience.

Here is your calendar for the second week of the term. *T(s)* stands for teacher(s), *S(s)* for student(s), and *obs'n* for observation. Gray boxes indicate times when you don't want any appointments, and white boxes indicate possible times for meetings. There are several teacher observations scheduled this week, because the program policy states that teachers on probation will be observed at the beginning, middle, and end of the term.

You oversee and support the work of 50 teachers; 10 teach the local language and 40 teach the five foreign languages in this program. The teachers represent various first languages and levels of experiences. The teaching positions are highly competitive because the salary, benefits, and working conditions are all excellent, and the program has a very good reputation.

The program includes a rigorous teacher evaluation system. Students' evaluations are formally collected every term. Teachers judged to be successful are retained, where success is determined by a combination of student evaluations, supervisory reports, peer evaluation, and self-assessment. Those who are considered less than successful are given three months of probationary status. They are then reevaluated and either retained or released. At this time there are six teachers on probation. It is your responsibility to help each of these teachers develop an action plan that will enable him or her to continue teaching in the program. Here are brief profiles of the six teachers:

Mari is an experienced native-speaking teacher. She has a master's degree and has worked at the school for 12 years. Her teaching has received solid rather than inspired ratings over time. Lately she has

---

Time	Day 1	Day 2	Day 3	Day 4	Day 5
8:00 A.M.	Welcome new late-arriving Ss in auditorium, give placement test.		Meet with Han to discuss obs'n.	Work on field notes of Ahmed's class.	Work on field notes from obs'ns of all 4 student teachers.
8:30		Meet with Simon to discuss obs'n.	Work on follow-up reports of obs's and discussions with Mari, Simon, Han, and Angelique.	Meet with Ahmed to discuss obs'n.	
9:00 A.M.	Help curriculum coordinator score tests and place late-arriving Ss.	Work on field notes from obs'n of Angelique's class.		Observe student teacher (Joseph).	Work on field notes of Kim's class.
9:30					Meet with all 4 student teachers to discuss observations.
10:00 A.M.	Observe Mari's class.	Meet with Mari to discuss obs'n.	Observe student teacher (Marga).	Work on field notes from obs'n of Joseph's class.	
10:30		Meet with 4 cooperating teachers who will work with the 4 student teachers.		Prepare for tomorrow's staff meeting.	View videotape of Juana's class with her.
11:00 A.M.	Work on field notes from Mari's class observation.		Work on field notes of Marga's class.		
11:30			Attend Ss' international luncheon and talent show.	Meet with language student representatives.	Work on follow-up report re: Juana.
Noon	Meet director for lunch to discuss evaluation plan for 6 teachers on probation.				
12:30					
1:00 P.M.		Observe Han's class.	Observe student teacher (Alex).		
1:30					
2:00 P.M.	Observe Simon's class.	Work on field notes from obs'n of Han's class.	Work on field notes of Alex's class.	Judge speech competition for advanced level Ss in the second language course.	Meet with Juana to discuss video.
2:30		Meet with 4 student teachers about their roles & responsibilities here.	Meeting with administrative hierarchy (director, curric. coordinator, bursar) to review budget.		Monthly staff meeting with all teachers (except the student teachers).
3:00 P.M.	Work on field notes from obs'n of Simon's class.				
3:30					
4:00 P.M.	Write letters nominating 2 teachers for teaching awards in your region.			Stay for awards ceremony.	Work on follow-up report re: Ahmed.
4:30				Observe student teacher (Kim).	Meet with university-based practicum instructor re: 4 student teachers.
5:00 P.M.					
5:30					
6:00 P.M.		Meet with Angelique to discuss obs'n.			
6:30					
7:00 P.M.	Observe Angelique's class.		Observe Ahmed's class.		
7:30					

Figure 15.1 Calendar for the second week of the term

seemed uninterested, and her lessons have been repetitive. Some students have complained to you that Mari doesn't like them.

Simon is a proficient non-native speaker of the language he teaches. His background is in elementary education. His teaching evaluations have been very good when he teaches children's classes. But recently, because of shifting enrollments, he has been teaching teenagers and adults. Their evaluations of his work have been less than enthusiastic. His lessons apparently are not challenging or interesting to these older students.

Angelique is a non-native speaker of the language she teaches. She came to this country as a teenager. She has been successful in teaching immigrant and refugee adults, but lately these courses have been undersubscribed, so she has been teaching university-bound students. The students have criticized her lessons as being "simplistic" and "nonacademic."

Han is in his second year at the school, having begun teaching here just after his training. Han is hard-working but apparently overwhelmed by the workload. Students complain that he doesn't return their papers or tests in a timely fashion and that his classes are fun but disorganized. Some say they aren't learning anything from him.

Juana is a proficient non-native speaker of the language she teaches. She has worked at the school for a year and is now attending a teacher training college to complete her advanced certification. Juana's teaching receives average ratings from her students. It seems that she sticks closely to the book, her lessons are boring, and there are too many tests in her courses.

Ahmed is a native speaker who was initially hired because there were no qualified teachers of his language available. The program has grown, and there are now seven other teachers of his language. Ahmed has seniority, but the students evaluate him lower than the other teachers. He sometimes arrives late and dismisses class early. When you ask him about this practice he tells you the class often finishes the material ahead of schedule. However, several students have complained that they are not getting the instruction they paid for.

You are also responsible for observing four student teachers from the nearby teacher training college. The preservice training program there has contracted with your school to serve as a practicum site, which generates additional revenue for your school.

Two of the student teachers, **Marga** and **Alex**, are non-native speakers of their target languages. You judge their proficiency to be upper-intermediate, and you place them with experienced cooperating teachers in lower-level classes. The two native speakers, **Kim**

and **Joseph**, are harder to place. Neither has any teaching experience. Kim seems terrified about dealing with students, and Joseph
appears to be sublimely overconfident. They have very little declarative knowledge and are just beginning a pedagogical grammar course
at their college.

At the end of the new three-month term you must file a data-based
report on each of the six employees, which is a key component of the
summative evaluation process. (Students' evaluations and the teachers' self-evaluations are also utilized, and each teacher may invite
peer appraisals as well.) You must also write a summative evaluation
for each student teacher.

Teacher professionalism and language teacher supervision

Beginning in the mid-1980s there was a groundswell of interest in professional development. Lange (1990:250) defined teacher development
as "a process of continual intellectual, experiential, and attitude growth
of teachers... some of which is generated in preprofessional and professional in-service programs." He distinguishes this term "from training and preparation, as encompassing more and allowing for continued
growth both before and throughout a career" (ibid.). Lange notes that
teachers evolve during their professional lives and that teacher education
programs wish to promote continued professional development (ibid.).
This sort of teacher development is clearly a goal of language teacher
supervision as well.

In Chapter 3 we noted a gradual change toward autonomy in language education during the last quarter of the twentieth century. Negotiated syllabi, student-centered teaching, and self-assessment procedures
are all products of and driving forces in this change. Supervision has also
been changing, particularly in terms of how we view language teacher
development.

During the same period, reflective teaching and action research were
both emphasized as avenues for individual teachers' professional development. Mentoring and coaching were also discussed as ways teachers could work together on professional development goals. What these
four concepts have in common is that teachers – not supervisors – both
take the responsibility for improving their teaching and decide how such
improvements are made.

These developments took place in the context of broad educational
change. We will now briefly consider the paradigm shifts that both contributed to and resulted from this change. Then we will discuss reflective
teaching, before examining action research, mentoring, and coaching as

they relate to teachers' professional development and language teacher supervision.

Changing paradigms in professional development and supervision

A paradigm is "a pattern, example or mental model that guides thought or behavior" (Duffy, 1999:125). Barker defines a paradigm as "a set of rules and regulations (written and unwritten) that does two things: (1) it establishes or defines boundaries; and (2) it tells you how to behave inside the boundaries in order to be successful" (1992:32). So a paradigm is a patterned way of doing things and talking about them, which becomes recognized and codified.

In Chapter 1 we examined two distinct ways of doing supervision: the classic prescriptive approach and the classic collaborative approach (Wallace, 1991). We can think of these models as paradigms of supervision. Although the prescriptive model can be useful (e.g., with novice teachers who need unambiguous direction, or in cases of incompetence or misconduct), the historical trend has been to move toward the collaborative model.

Clinical supervision is closer to the collaborative end of the spectrum than the prescriptive end because it necessarily entails "rapport between supervisee and supervisor, trust in each participant's direction of rates and intensities, and perhaps most importantly, a primary focus on the teacher's agenda" (Tracy and MacNaughton, 1989:246). In fact, Bowers and Flinders say that clinical supervision was "motivated by a desire to move away from past images that portrayed the supervisor as an 'inspector,' whose job was to maintain unilateral control over the transmission of a particular sociopolitical belief system" (1990:200).

When education, including language education, experienced a paradigm shift in the latter part of the twentieth century, teacher supervision was influenced as well. There was a decline in research and articles about the technical aspects of supervision (such as observation schedules) and more emphasis on hoped-for teacher development, in terms of both process and product. The change of attitude is indicated in titles of recent publications on teacher supervision: "The Transformative Practice of Supervision" (Holland, 1989b); *Supervision in Transition* (Glickman, 1992); "Freeing the Teacher: A Supervisory Process" (Gebhard, 1990b); "Teacher Supervision: Moving Towards an Interactive Approach" (Stoller, 1996); and "Nurturing the Reflective Practitioner Through Instructional Supervision" (Nolan and Huber, 1989). Hamid and Azman (1991) wrote about using a "person-centered, non-prescriptive, humanistic approach to supervision" (p. 880). (Once again, we must acknowledge that much of this literature was published in North

America and that the supposed shift toward democratization in teaching is certainly not universal. Some would suggest that the current standards movement and changes in many countries' school-leaving exams represent less freedom for teachers, rather than more.)

Clinical supervision in the paradigm shift

"The spirit of the clinical supervision model reflects the democratic human resources perspective of supervision," according to McFaul and Cooper (1984:5). Writing in general education, these authors say clinical supervision "respects the integrity and individuality of teachers" (ibid.) and is built on "the concepts of collegiality, collaboration, skilled service, and ethical conduct" (ibid.). The word *clinical* emphasizes that this model "deals with the reality of daily school life, not with simulated settings; it illuminates practices in the real world" (ibid.).

There are five key steps in clinical supervision: a pre-observation conference, the observation itself, analysis of the data, the post-observation conference, and the post-conference analysis of the process (Goldhammer, 1969). The pre-observation conference is a crucial element in which "the teacher is an equal partner with the supervisor in determining the focus and the extent of the supervisory process" (Tracy and MacNaughton, 1989:247).

The supervisor is "the central link between what an educational authority intends to happen and what actually takes place in the classroom," write Gaies and Bowers (1990:170). These authors articulate five principles of clinical supervision based on their own experiences with teacher training in Egypt and in the former Yugoslavia:

1. There should be a balance between theory and practice, between the "educational" and the "training" functions.
2. The feasibility of proposals for change in teacher performance should be judged against the real constraints of the teaching context.
3. The personal sensitivity essential to effective counseling and training is best developed within the security of a system or "paradigm" of counselor-teacher interaction.
4. Observation should be systematic and focused, with evaluation based on evidence available to the teacher.
5. Counseling should guide the teacher toward specified, measurable, and moderate changes in behavior. (ibid.:174)

Gaies and Bowers say supervisors play "a crucial role in educating teachers to implement changes in the classroom" (ibid.:170). We will return to this theme when we consider the factors that influence changes in classroom practice. (See also Pennington, 1995.)

Tracy and MacNaughton describe two versions of clinical supervision that have emerged. One group they refer to as *neo-progressives* "because many concepts of clinical supervision have roots in the older progressive movement" in U.S. education (1989:247). In fact, clinical supervision originally developed as a reaction to the inspector role. Those who promoted clinical supervision embraced Dewey's idea that evaluation should be rejected as a supervisory function (ibid.:248). In this view,

> clinical supervision provide[s] for a teacher-directed supervision process that focuses on expressed teacher concerns. . . . The variables of interest cannot be specified before entry into the research situation; they are specified by the teacher and supervisor during the clinical supervision process. (Nolan and Huber, 1989:135)

However, the second school of practice is called the *neo-traditionalists*. In this approach, supervisors focus on "teaching strategies as they relate to learning theory and effective-teaching research" (Tracey and MacNaughton, 1989:248). The term *neo-traditionalists* refers to the fact that this model emphasizes a traditional, technique-oriented approach to supervision, "which is the oldest and most widely used assisting and assessing procedure" (ibid.).

Some neo-traditionalist practices challenge key components of clinical supervision. For example, Hunter (1986) suggested abandoning pre-observation conferences. Table 15.1 summarizes the differences between the neo-progressives and neo-traditionalists. Even within this one model of supervision – some would say the most thoroughly researched model – there are profound differences about how supervision should be done.

Supervisory focus: Individual change versus systemic change

There are two other ways to look at the paradigms that dominate educational supervision (Duffy, 1999:126): "One is primarily espoused in the literature (clinical supervision and variations of it), and the other is primarily practiced in schools (supervision as performance evaluation)." In both the clinical approach and supervision as performance evaluation, educational improvement is seen as a by-product of improving individuals' teaching. This focus has its value: "Clinical supervision is a powerful way to engage individual teachers in conversations about their classroom teaching. The opportunity to have a meaningful dialogue with teachers about teaching must not be abandoned" (ibid.:144). However, Duffy argues that focusing on individual teachers will not change the nature of teaching and learning.

Writing about the United States K–12 context, Duffy describes an approach called Knowledge Work Supervision, in which the focus shifts

Table 15.1 *Contrasts between the neo-progressives and neo-traditionalists in clinical supervision (based on Tracy and MacNaughton, 1989:251–254)*

Category	Neo-progressives	Neo-traditionalists
Specificity of the criteria of good teaching	Criteria are necessarily changing and are generally undefined.	Criteria are consistent and based on quantitative research on teaching and learning.
Locus of criteria determination	Criteria are selected internally based on the needs and experiences of the teacher.	Criteria are selected externally based on research rather than on individual teachers' needs.
Sources of advocacy for the model	Proponents are often academics or teachers' groups.	Proponents are often administrators with supervisory responsibilities.
Role of assessment and evaluation	Teacher evaluation and assessment are rejected as proper roles for the clinical supervisor.	Supervisors and administrators assist teachers but also evaluate them as part of clinical supervision.

"from an examination of teaching behavior of individual teachers" (ibid.:123–124) to an examination of school district variables. Duffy discusses *social architecture,* which includes "organization culture and design, critical job skills, and communication structure and processes" (ibid.:124). Knowledge Work Supervision uses procedures from the business world to promote change in K–12 school districts. Duffy describes four phases in detail: building support for innovation, redesigning for high performance, achieving stability and diffusion, and sustaining school improvement.

To carry out this broad-scale systemic change, Duffy says that "five key players empower Knowledge Work Supervision" (ibid.:134). These are, first, the members of the *strategic leadership team,* which includes the superintendent of schools (and a few of his or her assistants) and representatives of each level of schooling, appointed by their colleagues. Another unit is the *cluster improvement team,* which is a "set of interconnected schools often configured as a single high school and all the middle and elementary schools feeding into it" (ibid.). *Site improvement teams* "create innovative ideas for redesigning what happens inside their buildings while taking into account that their buildings are part of a K–12 instructional program" (ibid.:135). The person in this system who most closely resembles what we have considered to be the supervisor is called the *knowledge work coordinator*. This individual is "a teacher, supervisor, or administrator retrained to provide tactical leadership for systemic school improvement" (ibid.:134). He or she serves an integrating function and "works on the boundary between a cluster and the broader school district" (ibid.).

Another structure is what Duffy calls *communities of practice*. (See also Freeman and Johnson, 1998; Lave and Wenger, 1991; and Wenger, 1998.) These can be formalized, ongoing work teams or "informal groups of like-minded practitioners who collaborate to explore an issue or topic" (ibid.:135). Such groups play a pivotal role in generating "district-wide professional knowledge" (ibid.) by disseminating what they learn. Thus a *community of practice* is "a small group of practitioners collaborating to learn how to do their jobs better" (ibid.:140). The development of such groups is not limited to schools practicing Knowledge Work Supervision. It happens when an organization changes "from a bureaucratic design to a participative design" (ibid.:136). For example, Grimmett (1996) describes teacher research teams in British Columbia that engaged in self-selected investigations in a period of educational reform. He says one outcome was a "community of inquirers" (p. 48).

The hierarchy of interrelating subsystems

The management of change in English language teaching contexts has been discussed by Kennedy (1988). Although his approach is different, his key point is similar to Duffy's. That is, any and all changes at the classroom level are influenced by a hierarchy of interrelating subsystems that surround our classroom worlds. These subsystems are depicted in Figure 15.2.

Kennedy was writing primarily about curricular changes, but this model has implications for language teacher supervision as well. For instance, classroom innovations are directly influenced by institutional factors. How long are the class periods? How many students are in the classes? What is the physical setup of the room? Are there ample supplies and other resources? These concerns are related to the institutional issues of the particular school or program.

The program exists within a certain educational philosophy that influences its actors. Are the students all expected to succeed, or simply to pass? Is education a normative function, producing good citizens, or a broadening function, promoting creative thinking? Although both are

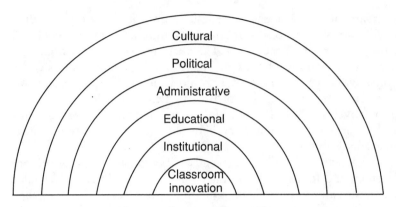

Figure 15.2 The hierarchy of interrelating subsystems in which an innovation has to operate (Kennedy, 1988:332)

significant, the former values conformity, whereas the latter promotes individualism.

At the administrative level, what are the structures that promote or hinder classroom innovations? For example, are textbooks chosen by a centralized ministry of education, the district superintendent's office, a curriculum committee, or a team of teachers who work with the same age group or proficiency levels? How tightly controlled is decision making? Who has control over resources, and how are such resources accessed by individual teachers?

The political and cultural levels involve a somewhat broader geographic scope. All educational changes take place within political climates that may shape what is possible, or at least what is publicly viewed as desirable. For instance, a particular state, province, or country may adopt a policy of accountability, in which students' scores on standardized exams are used as the main criterion for evaluating teachers. In this context, high-stakes exams will exert a powerful influence on how teachers use classroom time and may inhibit the risk taking needed to promote innovations. Other examples are government commissions or national committees that promote certain types of educational reform, and widescale changes in popular attitudes (e.g., about the social value of bilingual education) that exert pressure on schools.

The cultural level is just as important and highly pervasive. This is the level where broad societal norms influence how people teach and learn. Such norms are often expressed in proverbs. For example, "the nail that sticks up gets hammered down" is often quoted as evidence of conformity in Japanese schools. The saying "kill two birds with one stone" embodies the western value of efficiency. The cultural level influences issues such as the importance of saving face versus the importance of speaking one's opinion. Does society favor decisions made by individuals acting independently or through group processes? All these issues, in fact, all these layers, influence the kinds of changes teachers try to make in their classrooms.

The evenly spaced rings in Kennedy's model seem to suggest that these factors are all of equal importance. However, Kennedy notes that "the influence and impact and the relative weighting of the circles will no doubt vary from situation to situation" (p. 332). For example, when I have worked in training programs for supervisors at U.S. federal language schools, they have consistently felt that the political layer is much bigger in their context, because political issues have a huge impact on their curricula, assessment systems, staffing, and so on.

Whatever the situation, it behooves us as language teacher supervisors to be aware of the contextual factors that influence the teachers with whom we work. Kennedy's model is a useful heuristic tool for identifying those variables that influence classroom change and our own attempts to improve supervisory practice. As Anderson notes, "The contextual framework within which most teachers and supervisors function is, if not actually hostile to effective supervisory arrangements, largely non-supportive" (1982:182). Awareness of this climate is important as we work toward enhanced professionalism for teachers and supervisors alike.

Reflective teaching and language teacher supervision

What is *reflective teaching*? Richards and Lockhart (1994:1) say that in a reflective approach to teaching, "teachers and student teachers collect data about teaching, examine their attitudes, beliefs, assumptions, and teaching practices, and use the information obtained as a basis for critical reflection about teaching." Few supervisors would argue about the benefits of these steps to professional development. Yet often, what supervisors do works against these ideas.

The first component of Richards and Lockhart's definition is that "teachers and student teachers collect data about teaching" (ibid.). In many traditional, hierarchical supervisorial relationships, the data that supervisors collect are apparently the only data that matter (in terms of the focus for change, evaluative reports, and so on). In reflective teaching the choices of what data to collect and how to collect them rest with the individual teacher. For supervisors to promote effective teaching, they must collect data in service of the teachers' foci rather than their own and support teachers' efforts to collect data. This stance is consistent with the view of clinical supervision espoused by the neo-progressives (Tracy and MacNaughton, 1989).

The second component is that teachers "examine their attitudes, beliefs, assumptions, and teaching practices" (Richards and Lockhart, 1994:1). Supervisors can either promote or hinder this process, depending on how they discuss teaching events. Using the nondirective or alternatives approaches could support teachers' reflective endeavors, but taking the prescriptive approach (Freeman, 1982, Gebhard, 1984; Wallace, 1991) could stifle reflective practice.

Finally, reflective teachers "use the information obtained as a basis for critical reflection" (Richards and Lockhart, 1994:1). Again, supervisors can promote this process by providing input but refraining from taking over. To be critical about their teaching, teachers must own and control the process. Reflection can be verbalized and shared, but it is essentially personal – teachers must reflect for themselves. Nolan and Huber (1989) say the reflective practitioner approaches teaching problems

> in a thoughtful, curious manner and believes that one of teaching's main outcomes is a greater understanding of the teaching-learning act. By questioning continually the origins, purposes, and consequences of teaching behavior, the reflective practitioner develops an ever-deepening repertoire of metaphors, analogies, and exemplars that are useful for resolving and understanding practical problems. (pp. 130–131)

This description applies whether the reflective practitioner works as a teacher or supervisor.

Phases of reflective teaching

Stanley (1995, 1998) investigated language teachers practicing reflection. Her data included interviews, teachers' journal entries, and recordings of supervisory conferences. The participants were six experienced teachers, in the United States and elsewhere, who worked in both private and public schools, in programs for immigrants and refugees. Stanley's analysis revealed five phases, or "moments," of reflection. These are not sequenced stages or ordered steps. Instead, they are processes that teachers may experience at any given time.

Stanley explains that *engaging with reflection* is not a straightforward choice. Doing so can be influenced by many personal, professional, and contextual factors: "If a teacher needs to work many hours a week to barely make a living, there may be little time left for reflective thinking or writing" (1998:586). She says that teachers can engage in reflection when they are curious about reflecting on teaching and when personal, professional and contextual factors are stable enough to let them do so.

Thinking reflectively is a skill that some teachers need to develop. Stanley cites the following quote from a teacher's preliminary effort to think reflectively:

> I didn't know where I was heading. And I should have taken that sentence and written it on the blackboard and started from there. But I don't know why I left it. I didn't take advantage of that sentence. Instead I kept on talking. . . . Well, starting from there everything, well I think it was a mess although I tried to sort of organize things later. But again, somehow I felt it was not working. (ibid.)

These remarks indicate the teacher is engaging in reflection, but Stanley raises the following questions about the teacher's comments:

> What had been written on the board? Why did she need to go back to it? How did it connect to the rest of the lesson? What data did she observe in order to come to the conclusion that "it was a mess"? Where are the students and their reactions? How does this lesson fit with a larger whole or syllabus? What possible alternative actions could she have taken in the lesson? What will she do the next time she teaches this particular lesson or this group of students? (ibid.)

Stanley concludes that "these questions and many others would help this teacher develop the skill of thinking reflectively" (ibid.).

In the third phase, *using reflection*, teachers understand what reflection is and how to do it. Then reflection can be employed as a tool. One of the teachers in Stanley's original study (1995) had been writing a reflective journal. In a conversation with her supervisor, Stanley reports (1998:586), the teacher said,

> And it's very important to the activity we are doing now to talk about what happened because I was writing and I wrote things in my notebook last week but somehow I tend to be too polite with myself or sometimes too rude with myself. But talking and listening to you and listening to myself is very important.

This teacher was criticizing her reflective work in the journal and questioning her attitudes in the process. Her conversation with the supervisor contributed to the reflective process.

The next phase, *sustaining reflection*, involves continuing reflective work in the face of adversity. Stanley's research reveals that the "emotional reactions to what is uncovered through the investigation of classroom teaching" (ibid.:587) can be problematic. Teachers may find it difficult to face their personal discoveries. This phase is related to moving from the Hidden Self to the Secret Self in the Johari Window (Luft and Ingram, 1969; see Figure 2.4). It also illustrates Underhill's (1992) "conscious incompetence." In this phase, Stanley notes, teachers may find it easier "to sustain reflection at a more externally oriented level... through readings, workshops, or dialogues with other teachers or professionals" (1998:588). In this regard, a supervisor could help teachers by listening, sharing books and articles, and supporting their attendance at workshops.

In the fifth phase, *practicing reflection*, "reflection becomes an integral part of practice" (ibid.). Stanley cites the importance of "having at least one other person with whom reflective conversations are possible" (ibid.). A supervisor could fill this role, provided he or she was practicing an alternative or a nondirective model of supervision (Freeman, 1982; Gebhard, 1984) rather than directive supervision.

Dewey's influence on reflective teaching

Bartlett (1990) has also written about reflective teaching in language education. Like many other proponents of reflective teaching, he was influenced by the work of Dewey (1933). Bartlett lists ten key principles derived from Dewey's work:

1. The issue on which the teacher reflects must occur in the social context where teaching occurs.
2. The teacher must be interested in the problem to be resolved.
3. The issue must be 'owned' by the teacher – that is, derived from his or her practice.
4. Reflection on the issue involves problem solving from the teaching situation. ...
5. Ownership of the identified issue and its solution is vested in the teacher.
6. Systematic procedures are necessary.
7. Information (observations) about the issue must be derived from the teacher's experience of teaching.
8. The teacher's ideas need to be tested through the practice of teaching.
9. Ideas about teaching, once tested through practice, must lead to some course of action. There is a tension between idea and action which is reflexive; once it is tested the action rebounds back on the idea which informed it.
10. Hence, reflexive action may be transformed into new understandings and redefined practice in teaching. (Bartlett, 1990:207–208)

The concept of ownership is a recurring theme in this list. Reflective teaching necessarily entails teachers carefully taking stock of their own work, and herein lies one of the great challenges of supervision in the twenty-first century. How can language teacher supervisors promote positive change and professional development in others without co-opting (and thereby undermining or appropriating) the process? The answer lies in Wallace's (1991) contrast between the classic prescriptive and the classic collaborative approaches (see Table 1.3). In the former, the supervisor is an authority figure who is the only source of expertise. The prescriptive supervisor talks and the trainee or teacher listens. In collaborative approaches, however, the supervisor is seen as a colleague who considers listening as important as talking. The collaborative supervisor values the teacher's own expertise and tries to promote teacher autonomy through reflection and self-evaluation.

Dewey (1933) identified three key traits that teachers must possess in order to be reflective. These are open-mindedness, responsibility, and wholeheartedness. Building on Dewey's ideas, Zeichner and Liston note that "open-mindedness and responsibility must be central components in the professional life of the reflective teacher" (1996:4). They say that being wholehearted means teachers regularly examine their own beliefs and actions, and maintain the attitude that they can always learn something (ibid.). It is essential that supervisors understand these characteristics and support them.

How might a supervisor's influence work against these positive traits? First, if teachers are put on the defensive by a supervisor's presence, style, or message, it will be difficult for them to remain open-minded. Second, if a supervisor makes the decisions about what and how teachers should change, teachers are left with only limited responsibility – that of carrying out changes selected and defined by someone else. Third, if a supervisor's actions limit teachers' open-mindedness and responsibility, it is unlikely that changes in attitude or awareness will be wholehearted or that possible changes in skills and knowledge will be wholeheartedly pursued.

Dimensions of reflective teaching

What are the dimensions of reflective teaching, and how are they carried out? Table 15.2 (reprinted from Zeichner and Liston, 1996:47) lists five areas to consider.

The first two dimensions, rapid reflection and repair, are both types of *reflection-in-action* (Schön, 1983). They occur during teaching. *Rapid reflection* is the automatic, almost instantaneous response to unfolding events in the classroom. *Repair* entails the online decision making teachers do during interaction with learners. As we saw in Chapter 13, repair

Table 15.2 *Dimensions of reflection (Zeichner and Liston, 1996:47)*

1.	RAPID REFLECTION	Immediate and automatic reflection-in-action
2.	REPAIR	Thoughtful reflection-in-action
3.	REVIEW	Less formal reflection-on-action at a particular point in time
4.	RESEARCH	More systematic reflection-on-action over a period of time
5.	RETHEORIZING and REFORMULATING	Long-term reflection-on-action informed by public academic theories

can lead to decisions to change course during a lesson, and even to depart from the lesson plan entirely.

In contrast, review, research, and retheorizing and reformulating are all dimensions of *reflection-on-action* (Schön, 1983): They are *about* teaching, but they occur after or before teaching sessions. The *review* category consists of thinking about teaching, perhaps in a casual way. Zeichner and Liston point out that review "is often interpersonal and collegial" (1996:46). It includes teachers regularly discussing, thinking about, or writing about their work.

Research is more systematic and sustained than review. In this dimension, "teachers' thinking and observation becomes more systematic and sharply focused" (ibid.) and they systematically collect data over time (e.g., by keeping a journal or videotaping their classes).

The final dimension, *retheorizing and reformulating*, is a long-term process. In this category, "while teachers critically examine their practical theories, they also consider these theories in the light of public academic theories" (ibid.). Here reflective teachers make connections between their own work and that of other professionals. In this dimension, reflective teachers can access publications about the issues they themselves are investigating. If they so choose, they may also contribute to that body of published information.

How might supervisors support language teachers in these five dimensions of reflection? In terms of the first two dimensions, those related to reflection-in-action, it is important that supervisors not interfere in teachers' efforts at rapid reflection and repair. The results of these processes can and should be discussed with teachers after a lesson, but in my opinion a supervisor should not intervene in a lesson unless the teacher requests such input, or unless there is a possibility of bodily or material harm. It is particularly important for supervisors to learn about teachers' reasons for departing from their lesson plans or prolonging parts of them, rather than criticizing them for not finishing.

Supervisors can also help teachers during reflection-on-action. In the review stage, supervisors can serve as sounding boards when teachers want to talk, regardless of whether the discussion follows an observation. In the research phase, supervisors' field notes or other data can be part of the database for teachers examining their work. When teachers are retheorizing or reformulating (see Table 15.2), supervisors can share published materials with them that address their concerns. Supervisors can also respond to papers drafted by teachers, locate funding for teachers to attend conferences and substitute while teachers are thus engaged, and so on.

Supervision as reflective practice

Supervision and reflective teaching need not be antithetical, so long as supervisors are not locked into the classic prescriptive approach. Nolan and Huber (1989) compare supervision that promotes reflective teaching with supervision based on "a technically rational conception of teaching" (p. 127). In this approach, supervisors monitor teachers' practice and help them use research and theory to promote effective and efficient teaching (ibid.). In contrast, those supervisors

> who view teaching as professional, reflective activity believe that the practitioners' first task in resolving the context-bound problems of practice involves reframing the problem to identify goals or purposes that will be attended to and those that will be ignored. (ibid.)

The view of teaching that emerges from this perspective is quite different from one that emphasizes technical rationality (ibid.:128). Nolan and Huber also note that "changing teacher behavior is not the most important goal of the supervisor who sees teaching as reflective practice. The critical task of the supervisor from the perspective of reflective practice is to help teachers engage in reflective behavior more successfully" (ibid.).

In this philosophy, supervision takes on four goals different from those of other supervisory approaches: "(1) engaging the teacher in the process of reflective behavior while (2) fostering critical inquiry into the process of teaching and learning, thereby (3) increasing the teacher's understanding of teaching practice and (4) broadening and deepening the repertoire of images and metaphors the teacher can call on to deal with problems" (ibid).

These goals have implications for the reflective supervisor's behavior as well. Nolan and Huber (ibid.:141) describe five crucial behaviors for encouraging reflective teaching: "(1) reflecting in action by the supervisor, (2) encouraging teacher autonomy, (3) using data as evidence for salient teaching patterns, (4) observing and conferring over time, and (5) helping teachers develop the skills to interpret the data collected on their teaching, and allowing them to play a major role in interpreting the data." These behaviors are not totally different from those of other supervisory models, especially classic collaborative supervision (Wallace, 1991). However, they do require a different attitude toward teachers and supervision.

If we are to engage in reflective practice, according to Sergiovanni, a leading author on supervision in general education, teachers and supervisors must join forces "in trying to make sense of complex situations, in sharing perceptions, and in arriving at 'treatments' and other courses of action together" (1985:16). He stresses that "the teacher is not dependent upon the supervisor" in this approach (ibid.). In fact, the supervisor must have the teacher's involvement to understand the situation. This philosophy is markedly different from the inspector's role (Acheson and Gall, 1997) or traditional directive supervision (Freeman, 1982; Gebhard, 1984).

Alternatives to supervision

With the evolution of language teaching in many parts of the world has come a gradual change in how we look at teacher development and professionalism. The supervisor is no longer seen as the dominant source of expertise. Instead, teachers themselves are recognized as possessing a great deal of procedural and declarative knowledge, including knowledge about what and how to improve in their teaching. Given this backdrop, we will now briefly examine three nonsupervisorial approaches to teacher development: action research, mentoring, and coaching. What these three approaches have in common is that teachers themselves are responsible for developing their professionalism.

Action research for professional development

Action research has been described as a viable avenue for teachers' professional development. (See, e.g., Mingucci, 1999.) *Action research* has been defined as "small scale intervention in the functioning of the real world and a close examination of the effects of such intervention" (van Lier, 1994:32). This research method consists of systematic, iterative cycles of planning, acting, observing, and reflecting.

Action research is a clear repeated cycle of collecting and interpreting data (Bailey, 2001b:490). Kemmis and McTaggart (1982) say that the "linking of the terms 'action' and 'research' highlights the essential feature of the method: trying out ideas in practice as a means of improvement and as a means of increasing knowledge about the curriculum, teaching and learning" (p. 5, as cited in Nunan, 1990:63). These processes are consistent with the goals of teacher development and reflective teaching. In fact, the obligatory action step is what distinguishes action research from reflective teaching.

Action research was started by Lewin (1946) to address social problems. Its social orientation is clear in the definition by Carr and Kemmis, who say action research is "'self-reflective enquiry' undertaken by participants in social situations in order to improve the rationality and justice of their own social or educational practices, as well as their understanding of these practices and the situations in which these practices are carried out" (1985:220; see also Kemmis and Henry, 1989:2). Nunan says action research "represents a particular attitude . . . in which the practitioner is engaged in critical reflection on ideas, the informed application and experimentation of ideas in practice, and the critical evaluation of the outcomes of such application" (1990:63).

In language classrooms, the action research cycle begins when the teacher decides to address a problem, investigate an issue, or pose and answer questions in his or her own context. Then he or she plans an action to initiate the first investigative cycle and this action is carried out – hence, the label *action research*. The teacher systematically collects data, which are used as the basis for reflecting on the outcome of the action. He or she plans a subsequent action, after which the cycle begins again. (See Burns, 2000; Kemmis and McTaggart, 1982, 1988; Nunan, 1993; van Lier, 1994.)

The process is not always so precise and neat, however. As action research proceeds, new concerns often arise. As a result, new goals may be set during the subsequent iterations, as depicted in Figure 15.3.

Action research is indeed a viable approach to empirical research in language education, but here our focus is on how the philosophy and procedures of action research can promote teacher development. In fact, the goals of action research are entirely consistent with the usual goals of language teacher supervision. How can supervisors support teachers who are engaged in action research, in terms of the iterative stages of action research?

Supervisors can assist language teachers in *planning* the action to be taken. Whether that action is based on a problem (identified by the teacher or the supervisor) or on an interesting puzzle, the supervisor may be able to contribute ideas about how to approach the problem or puzzle. The alternative approach (Freeman, 1982; Gebhard, 1984) can be particularly useful in helping teachers consider their options and then determine what action to take.

In the second stage, *taking action*, the supervisor has several possible roles, ranging from being present in the classroom as the action is carried

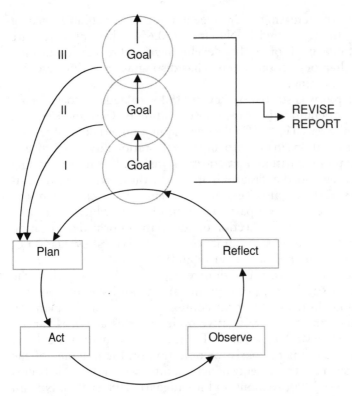

Figure 15.3 Cycles of action research (van Lier, 1994:34)

out to staying out of the way entirely. Enright (1981) describes a case where the supervisor actually taught the class at the teacher's request so the teacher could experience the lesson with the students.

In the third stage, *observing*, supervisors can help teachers monitor their actions by observing the action in person or by reviewing videotapes or audiotapes of lessons. However, it is important that these observations be developmental in focus rather than evaluative.

The fourth stage, *reflection*, is partly a private enterprise and partly social. Reflection in this context refers to analyzing and interpreting the data collected during and after the action step. It is probably worthwhile for a supervisor to be available to respond to reflections if the teacher requests input. A sympathetic and well-informed supervisor can be very helpful, for instance, in viewing videotapes with teachers, using the stimulated recall procedure, or in sharing field notes about the students' response to the action step.

By definition, action research is done by participants in the social context of the investigation. Although collaborative action research is a very useful model (see, e.g., Burns, 1998; Oja and Smulyan, 1989), it is important that the process not be co-opted by outsiders. The control of the project must rest squarely with the teacher. To the extent that a supervisor participates in an action research investigation, it must be in service of the teacher's goals.

Mentoring language teachers

Mentoring is an approach to teacher development that removes evaluative supervision from the teacher-mentor relationship (Wagner, 1985). The rationale is expressed by Fox and Singletary (1986:12–13), who say novice teachers can be

> reluctant to discuss problems or concerns that they are experiencing in their classrooms for fear of receiving low assessments and jeopardizing their jobs. This basic fear can be reduced by creating a situation that allows them to express themselves openly and without fear of external evaluation. This can be accomplished by using personnel not connected with the district's evaluation.

In formal teacher-mentoring, a teacher is paired with someone skillful in those areas that the teacher wishes to improve. Though the teacher being mentored is often a novice or someone in the induction years, this is not always the case. Mentors can also work with experienced teachers who are having difficulty or starting new jobs.

Mentor teachers are selected for their expertise in teaching and their ability to convey those skills to others. They are not part of the chain of command of the teachers whom they support. The philosophy is that teachers will be more forthcoming and proactive about seeking help if they know their efforts to improve are not linked to the evaluation process in any way.

Mentoring was used as a label for one of the supervisory roles discussed in Chapter 1, but there it referred to supervisors stressing their helping responsibilities over their evaluative responsibilities. Here the term is used differently. When we talk about mentoring as a program of sustained developmental support, we are referring to part of the paradigm shift in which the organizational pyramid is intentionally flattened. In mentoring, any evaluative discussion that occurs between the mentor and the teacher is not part of official evaluations.

Malderez and Bodóczky describe five roles that mentors may take among a "bewildering range of interpretations" (1999:4) about what mentoring can be. First they refer to *models* – the type of mentors who inspire teachers and demonstrate effective teaching. Second, they talk about *acculturators*, who help novice teachers learn about the new context in which they are working. Third, mentors can be *sponsors*, who introduce their mentees to the "right people." Fourth, mentors can be *supporters*, who serve as sounding boards in case the mentees need to talk about their teaching or vent their frustrations. Finally, mentors can be *educators*. This type of mentor also acts as a sounding board, but in this case to listen as novice teachers articulate their ideas in pursuing their own professional development. All of these roles are taken by cooperating teachers working with trainees, but mentoring can involve more experienced teachers as well.

Mentors can take on more than one role, as appropriate for the teachers they are helping. In fact, Malderez and Bodóczky note, "most mentors will be involved to a greater or lesser degree in all five roles" (ibid.:4). The situational leadership model (see Chapter 11) suggests that mentors should adapt their leadership style as teachers' needs and readiness levels evolve.

Sometimes the inherently unequal nature of the mentoring relationship is unnecessary. Many teachers benefit greatly from working with peers to improve their teaching. An important model of peer-based professional development is called *coaching*.

Coaching language teachers

Coaching as an approach to teacher development is even less hierarchical than mentoring. In coaching, teachers work together in mutual, collaborative professional development. Benedetti (1997:41) says that in peer coaching "two (or more) teachers meet regularly for problem solving using planning, observation, feedback, and creative skill." Like mentoring, coaching involves no official on-record evaluation. But unlike mentoring, most models of coaching are reciprocal: Both teachers in the partnership are working to improve their teaching. Coaching involves built-in, ongoing peer observation. The coaching partners agree about what they'll work on, observe one another teaching, and give each other feedback.

Coaching as an approach to professional development has three main purposes. First, it is intended "to build communities of teachers who continuously engage in the study of their craft" (Showers, 1985:43). The second goal is to develop "the shared language and set of common understandings necessary for the collegial study of new knowledge and skills" (ibid.:44). Third, "coaching provides a structure for the follow up to training that is essential for acquiring new teaching skills and strategies" (ibid.). Coaching is often used as a follow-on activity after an in-service training program to help teachers implement the ideas and practices from that program. Teams of teachers "study the rationale of the new skills, see them demonstrated, practice them, and learn to provide feedback to one another as they experiment with the skills" (ibid.). All the team members are both coaches and students of teaching, and the feedback "must be accurate, specific and nonevaluative" (ibid.).

Although the coaching model favors peer coaches, Showers notes that there is no *a priori* reason supervisors can't be involved. In fact, she notes that "supervisors and principals can coach effectively" (ibid.:45). The question to be resolved, however, is one of power: "The relationship between coaching and supervision . . . depends on the power of relationship between supervisors and teachers" (ibid.). Coaching and supervision can be compatible in contexts where teachers work in ongoing collegial groups to study their teaching. In situations where the hierarchical structure of a program or the workload do not permit such teams to operate, coaching will not flourish as a means of professional development. The problem is that traditional supervisory roles promote "the imbalance of power by placing administrators and other nonteaching personnel in supervision roles and by combining evaluation with supervision" (ibid.:46–47).

A problem arises if the supervisor is (perceived as) primarily evaluative. Teachers are hesitant to take risks and try new things, because evaluation

> prevents the very climate essential for learning, that of experimentation and permission to fail, revision and trying again while continuously practicing new but awkward skills and procedures. When evaluation is the end product of supervision, those being evaluated will generally put their best foot forward, demonstrate only those well-tested procedures that have been perfected over long periods of use and with which both they and their students are completely familiar. Even if these procedures are patently flawed, they are safer than attempting something new and experimental. (ibid.:47)

Coaching incorporates many practices of good supervision, including observation, feedback, and cooperative planning (of lessons and curricula). However, to play an active role in a coaching partnership, someone whose programmatic function is that of supervisor would have to make changes to be a true coach. He or she would have to teach classes regularly; engage in reciprocal observations – that is, be observed as well as observe others; engage in reciprocal discussions about that teaching; and completely set aside official evaluative responsibilities.

Whether supervisors should participate in coaching is partly a matter of the type of coaching being used. Pierce (1988) describes four models: technical, collegial, challenge, and team coaching.

The first of these, *technical coaching*, refers to "the facilitation of transfer from in-service training to classroom practice" (p. 1). Technical coaching promotes collegiality because teachers engage in professional dialogues and develop "a shared vocabulary for discussing their professional views" (ibid.). This approach focuses on techniques as teachers help one another "transfer a new skill to their teaching" (Benedetti, 1997:41).

Collegial coaching is also concerned with refining teaching practices. Pierce says collegial coaching "helps teachers think more analytically about what they do in the classroom" (1988:1). The coaching partner observes whatever focus the teacher has set. Then the peer helps the teacher analyze and interpret the data and encourages future applications of improved strategies for teaching. In this approach "peers work on skills already present in their teaching repertoire with which they believe they may need help and feedback" (Benedetti, 1997:41).

The third category, *challenge coaching*, is aimed at resolving problems. According to Pierce, "teams, which may include teachers, teacher aides, librarians, or administrators, work together to resolve persistent problems in instructional design or delivery" (1988:1). Challenge coaching "begins with the identification of a persistent problem" (Benedetti, 1997:41) and often includes a formal written plan discussed in advance by all participants.

The fourth type, *team coaching*, is a combination of peer coaching and team teaching. In this model, instead of observing teachers,

> visiting mentors or resource teachers...teach right alongside them. These resource teachers should have considerable expertise in the teaching methodology being used by the teachers they are coaching. Together the coach and teacher plan, teach, and evaluate the lesson as partners. (Pierce, 1988:6)

In describing supervision's future, Anderson says "although teaming has not replaced the self-contained classroom arrangement as rapidly as its advocates would prefer, there is virtual unanimity on the values of professional role definition and sharing" (1982:182). In team coaching such sharing is highly valued. Pierce says the coach should always be a peer: "Otherwise the teachers may perceive coaching as evaluation rather than collaboration" (1988:6).

In Table 15.3 the concepts of coaching, mentoring, and supervision are compared on three dimensions: the peer relationship, reciprocity, and official evaluation.

As Table 15.3 shows, coaching involves reciprocal observations between peers, and the teachers discuss each other's teaching. Part of that discussion intentionally involves evaluation of the targeted techniques, how well the students responded, and so on. Yet these evaluative remarks typically remain within the peer coaching partnership. They are not recorded in teachers' personnel files for evaluative purposes.

Table 15.3 *Peer coaching, mentoring, and supervision compared on three characteristics*

Characteristic	Peer coaching	Mentoring	Supervision
Observation and discussion are carried out with a peer.	+	–	–
Observation and discussion are reciprocal in nature.	+	+/–	–
Observation and discussion are often officially evaluative in nature.	–	–	+

The mentor and the teacher being mentored will certainly discuss how well particular lessons go, but that evaluation remains a private matter between the two. This characteristic is the key to defining mentoring: The teacher may rest assured that no weaknesses or problems shared with the mentor will be documented officially. Although the teacher and the mentor may certainly observe one another teaching, the mentor is not the teacher's peer. By definition, the mentor possesses greater experience and skill than the person being mentored.

Contrasting these approaches can obscure their commonalities. These alternatives to supervision share an emphasis on collaboration. Anderson states, "the future of supervision as well as the future of teaching will depend largely on the willingness and ability of the personnel involved to join forces and to learn from and alongside each other" (1982:183). He emphasizes "the need for embracing colleagueship in supervision and, by extension, the adoption of partnership patterns in both the practice of supervision and the pursuit of further knowledge and expertise" (ibid.:182). It is difficult to see how the classic prescriptive approach could achieve this level of two-way communication.

Indeed, one important feature shared by coaching, mentoring, supervision, and the collaborative model of action research is having someone to talk to about professional concerns: "Because most teachers don't have the opportunity to reflect critically on practice with others, the inadequacy of those practices often remains hidden, and analysis remains fixated at the level of attending to technical problems" (Gitlin and Smyth, 1990:94). Discourse between language teachers and supervisors can provide such an opportunity but only if the supervisors are willing and able to work collaboratively rather than prescriptively. Critical reflection on practice "is more likely to occur when teachers argue about the rightness of practices with other [teachers], rather than submit to habit or remain subservient to the views of those in positions of authority" (ibid.). This

339

kind of ongoing, sustained, professionally focused communication can lead to communities of practice (Duffy, 1999) or communities of inquiry (Grimmett, 1996).

Supervision in service to teaching and learning

One clear message that has emerged in this book is that supervisors can have both negative and positive effects on language teachers. We will now return to this theme.

In describing a future for supervision, Anderson asserts that "supervisory work is among the highest callings available to educated men and women" (1982:189). He adds that "shoddy supervision . . . or the neglect of supervisory services for whatever expedient reasons can have disastrous consequences for children and youth" (ibid.). This is the crux of the matter: The fundamental purpose of supervision is to improve teaching and learning.

Zahorik (1992) defines good teaching as "teaching that is purposeful, consistent, and skillful" (p. 399). By *purposeful* he means that "the teacher has a conception of good teaching that guides his or her classroom behavior" (ibid.). This conception is the teacher's "ideal teaching self" (ibid.) – the professional person that the teacher is "striving to become" (ibid.). Saying that good teaching is *consistent* is a reference to the teacher's actions: "The behaviors must be consistent with the pedagogical purpose . . . a compatible, harmonious set of classroom actions" (ibid.). Finally, good teachers are *skillful*, meaning that they use their chosen set of behaviors "with proficiency and virtuosity . . . in expert ways" (ibid.).

Zahorik's definition of good teaching has implications for teacher supervision. Based on this definition, supervision's goal is "to help teachers find and become proficient in their own ways of teaching" (ibid.:400). He calls this approach *deliberative-collegial supervision* and says it "emphasizes personal frameworks or beliefs as well as practice" (ibid.). It differs from top-down supervision, which does not typically "recognize the personal, thoughtful nature of teaching" (ibid.). Supervision based on this philosophy, Zahorik feels, will "free and encourage the teacher to be his or her own teaching self" (ibid.).

A related concept is the idea that supervisors must be advocates for the students, teachers, and programs they serve. One problem with supervisors taking on an advocacy role is that "all supervisors were once teachers themselves and therefore were socialized into a compliant role before they moved into leadership responsibilities" (Anderson, 1982:189). For many supervisors, serving as advocates will require the development of new skills, including skills related to challenging authority and educating higher level administrators. Anderson states that "anyone with the audacity to participate in helping behaviors, or to pose as teachers of such behaviors, must match that audacity with aggressive advocacy of the roles with which such behaviors are practiced" (ibid.:190). This point brings us back to the metaphor that opened this book – the notion of supervision as the "reluctant profession." Supervisors must answer to the administration, but fundamentally, supervision is meant to support teachers and learners.

In Chapter 1 we reviewed the use of cases for educational purposes. I hope you have found the cases in this book helpful. All these stories are based on actual experiences of supervising teaching and being supervised. Some of these stories had happy endings. Some were not so happy, but I hope you have used the frameworks and the concepts presented here to craft your own resolutions.

Concluding comments

We started this chapter with a case, followed by Lange's (1990) definition of teacher development. We then noted a paradigm shift in language teaching and examined reflective teaching and three alternatives to traditional supervision as routes to professional development: action research, mentoring, and coaching. Finally, we refocused our sights on supervision's key purpose: to enhance teaching and learning.

To close this final chapter, I offer the usual sequence of the Case Discussion, Tasks and Discussion, and Suggestions for Further Reading. However, you will notice that these activities are intended to tie together many themes from the previous chapters.

Case discussion

1. Given the context and the calendar in this case, what are your three main goals for this week? That is, by the end of the week, what three things do you want to have accomplished?
2. What are your main concerns about Mari? What concepts and strategies presented earlier in this book will inform your work with her?
3. What are your main concerns about Ahmed? What concepts and strategies presented earlier in this book will help you develop an action plan with him?
4. What concepts and strategies will inform your work with Angelique and Simon?
5. What are your key concerns about Han? What concepts will guide your work with him?

341

6. What are your main concerns about Joseph? What strategies will you use in helping him? What about Kim? How can you support these novices' cooperating teachers?
7. What are your main concerns about Marga and Alex? What concepts and strategies presented earlier in this book will inform your work with them?
8. Each student teacher works with a cooperating teacher in your program. Each novice will be visited by his or her practicum instructor, but the contract between your program and the college specifies that you will also observe each student teacher three times, once each month that they are working here. What are your main goals for working with each student teacher?
9. When you view the videotape of Juana's class with her, the students appear bored and don't seem to be involved in the lesson. Juana agrees and says that she is worried about her work with this group. How can you use the 10 principles from Dewey's work (reprinted from Bartlett, 1990) in promoting Juana's professional development?
10. This coming weekend you are supposed to give a talk about language teacher evaluation at an important conference. So far you have a sketchy outline, but the presentation needs to be developed with examples. What are your strategies for finalizing that presentation? Given your busy week, how will you use the limited time available to prepare?

Tasks and discussion

1. Look back at Lange's (1990) definition of teacher development in this chapter under the heading Teacher Professionalism and Language Teacher Supervision. If you return to the various supervisorial roles discussed in Chapter 1, which three roles are best suited for promoting teacher development? Are there any roles that might work *against* teacher development? Explain your reasoning to a classmate or colleague.
2. Thinking about the paradigm shift described in this chapter, what connections can you find with the material covered earlier in this book?
3. Thinking of your own experience as a language teacher, try to recall a situation in which you were facing an ongoing problem or puzzle. In that context, which of the following approaches would have been helpful to you and why?

A. Supervision   B. Reflective teaching   C. Action research
D. Mentoring   E. Coaching

Why do you think some of these approaches would have been less helpful?

4. How do each of these five approaches to professional development relate to Freeman's (1989a) components of teaching? Write a comment in each cell of the grid.

	Awareness	Attitude	Knowledge	Skills
Supervision				
Reflective teaching				
Action research				
Mentoring				
Coaching				

5. Turn back to any case in this book that involved an individual teacher. For the case you select, would mentoring, coaching, reflective teaching, or action research be a viable alternative to supervision? Why or why not?

6. Think of a change that you have attempted to bring about in your own teaching (whether it was successful or unsuccessful). Use Kennedy's (1988) model, reprinted as Figure 15.2, to identify the contextual factors that influenced your efforts.

7. Refer to Table 15.2, the dimensions of reflection according to Zeichner and Liston (1996). Think of an example of each phase from your own work as a teacher.

8. Compare Stanley's (1998) phases of reflective teaching with Zeichner and Liston's (1996) dimensions of reflection. How do the two frameworks differ?

9. Based on all you've read and thought about in completing this book, what are four or five aspects of supervision you would definitely want to incorporate in your own work? What are four or five traits you would definitely want to avoid?

Suggestions for further reading

Clinical supervision has been the topic of many books and articles in general education, including Acheson and Gall (1997), Cogan (1973), Garman (1986, 1990), Goldhammer (1969), McFaul and Cooper (1984), McGee and Eaker (1977), Pajak (1993), Retallick (1990), and Sergiovanni (1982, 1984, 1985, 1986, and 1989). The article by Garman, Glickman, Hunter, and Haggerson (1987) presents their conflicting views of clinical supervision. See also Glickman (1985, 1992) and Glickman and Gordon (1987) on developmental supervision.

References on reflective teaching abound in both general education and language education. Some key resources in general education are

Schön (1983, 1987, and 1991) and Zeichner and Liston (1987, 1996). In language teaching, see Bailey (1997), Bailey et al. (2001), Bartlett (1990), Ho and Richards (1993), Kamhi-Stein and Galván (1997), Richards and Lockhart (1994), Stanley (1998), and Yu (2000).

For more information about action research, see Burns (1997), Edge (2001), Kemmis and McTaggart (1982, 1988), Knezedvic (2001), van Lier (1994), McPherson (1997), Nixon (1981), Nunan (1990, 1993), and Wallace (1998).

Mentoring and coaching have received more attention in general education than in second language education. (See, e.g., Wilkin, 1992.) Eisenman and Thornton (1999) have written about using electronic communication in mentoring novice teachers. Seaman, Sweeny, Meadows, and Sweeny (1997) describe a mentoring program for ESL teachers. These authors have also written a mentoring training manual for the ESL context (Lewis, Meadows, Seaman, Sweeny, and Sweeny, 1996). Malderez and Bodóczky (1999) is another key reference on mentoring. Coaching and its development in general education have been described by Showers and Joyce (1996). See also Joyce and Showers (1982, 1987, 1988), Poole (1994), and Showers (1985). For information about coaching in language education, see Benedetti (1997) and Pierce (1988).

Sullivan and Glanz (2000) reviewed many of the same alternatives to supervision discussed here. Holland (1989b) analyzed the themes in 72 stories of supervision collected from her students over the years.

References

Abbott, Suzanne and Ralph M. Carter. 1985. Clinical supervision and the foreign language teacher. *Foreign Language Annals*, 18(1), 25–29.

Abrell, Ronald. 1974. The humanistic supervisor enhances growth and improves instruction. *Educational Leadership*, 32(3), 212–216.

Acheson, Keith A. and Meredith Damien Gall. 1997. *Techniques in the clinical supervision of teachers: Preservice and inservice applications (4th ed.)*. New York: Longman.

Ackerman, Richard, Patricia Maslin-Ostrowski, and Chuck Christensen. 1996. Case stories: Telling tales about school. *Educational Leadership*, 53(6), 21–23.

Alfonso, Robert J. 1977. Will peer supervision work? *Educational Leadership*, 34(8), 594–601.

Alfonso, Robert J., Gerald Firth, and Richard Neville. 1984. The supervisory skill mix. *Educational Leadership*, 41(7), 16–18.

Allan, Margaret S. 1991. Preparing for interactive video. *ELT Journal*, 45(1), 54–60.

Allen, Patrick, Maria Fröhlich, and Nina Spada. 1984. The communicative orientation of language teaching: An observation scheme. In Jean Handscombe, Richard A. Orem, and Barry P. Taylor (eds.), *On TESOL '83: The question of control*. Washington, DC: TESOL, 231–252.

Allwright, Dick. 1988. *Observation in the language classroom*. New York: Longman.

Allwright, Dick and Kathleen M. Bailey. 1991. *Focus on the language classroom: An introduction to classroom research for language teachers*. Cambridge: Cambridge University Press.

Allwright, Richard L. 1980. Turns, topics and tasks: Patterns of participation in language learning and teaching. In Diane Larsen-Freeman (ed.), *Discourse analysis in second language research*. Rowley, MA: Newbury House, 165–187.

Amin, Nuzhat. 2001. Nativism, the native speaker construct, and minority immigrant women teachers of English as a second language. *CATESOL Journal*, 13(1), 89–107.

Anderson, Robert H. 1982. Creating a future for supervision. In Thomas Sergiovanni (ed.), *Supervision of teaching*. Alexander, VA: ASCD, 181–190.

Appel, Gabriela and James P. Lantolf. 1994. Speaking as mediation: A study of L1 and L2 recall tasks. *Modern Language Journal*, 78(4), 437–452.

Appel, Joachim. 1995. *Diary of a language teacher*. Oxford: Heinemann.

Bachman, Lyle F. 1990. *Fundamental considerations in language testing*. Oxford: Oxford University Press.

References

Bailey, Kathleen M. 1984. A typology of teaching assistants. In Kathleen M. Bailey, Frank Pialorsi, and Jean Zukowski Faust (eds.), *Foreign teaching assistants in U.S. universities*. Washington, DC: National Association for Foreign Student Affairs (NAFSA), 110–125.

Bailey, Kathleen M. 1990. The use of diary studies in teacher education programs. In Jack C. Richards and David Nunan (eds.), *Second language teacher education*. New York: Cambridge University Press, 215–226.

Bailey, Kathleen M. 1992. The processes of innovation in language teacher development: What, why and how teachers change. In John Flowerdew, Mark N. Brock, and Sophie Hsia (eds.), *Perspectives on second language teacher development*. Hong Kong: City Polytechnic of Hong Kong, 253–282.

Bailey, Kathleen M. 1996. The best laid plans: Teachers' in-class decisions to depart from their lesson plans. In Kathleen M. Bailey and David Nunan (eds.), *Voices from the language classroom*. Cambridge: Cambridge University Press, 15–40.

Bailey, Kathleen M. 1997. Reflective teaching: Situating our stories. *Asian Journal of English Language Teaching*, 7(1), 1–19.

Bailey, Kathleen M. 2001a. Observation. In David Nunan and Ron Carter (eds.), *The Cambridge guide to teaching English to speakers of other languages*. Cambridge: Cambridge University Press, 114–119.

Bailey, Kathleen M. 2001b. Action research, teacher research, and classroom research in language learning. In Marianne Celce-Murcia (ed.), *Teaching English as a second or foreign language (3rd ed.)*. Boston: Heinle & Heinle, 489–498.

Bailey, Kathleen M., Andy Curtis, and David Nunan. 1998. Undeniable insights: The collaborative use of three professional development practices. *TESOL Quarterly*, 32, 3, 546–556.

Bailey, Kathleen M., Andy Curtis, and David Nunan. 2001. *Pursuing professional development: The self as source*. Boston: Heinle & Heinle.

Bailey, Kathleen M., Ted L. Dale, and Benjamin Squire. 1992. Some reflections on collaborative language teaching. In David Nunan (ed.), *Collaborative language teaching and learning*. Cambridge: Cambridge University Press, 162–178.

Barduhn, Susan. 1989. When the cost of caring is too high. *IATEFL Teacher Development Newsletter*, 11, 1–3.

Barker, J. A. 1992. *Future edge: Discovering new paradigms of success*. New York: William Morrow.

Barnett, Marva A. and Robert Francis Cook. 1992. The seamless web: Developing teaching assistants as professionals. In Joel D. Walz (ed.), *Development and supervision of teaching assistants in foreign languages*. Boston: Heinle & Heinle, 85–111.

Bartlett, Leo. 1990. Teacher development through reflective teaching. In Jack C. Richards and David Nunan (eds.), *Second language teacher education*. New York: Cambridge University Press, 202–214.

Bastidas, Jesús A. 1996. The teaching portfolio: A tool to become a reflective teacher. *English Teaching Forum*, 34, July/October, 24–28.

Bateson, Gregory. 1972. *Steps to an ecology of mind: A revolutionary approach to man's understanding of himself*. New York: Ballantine Books.

Batey, John and David Westgate. 1994. Video action replay. In Antony Peck and David Westgate (eds.), *Language teaching in the mirror*. London: Centre for Information on Language Teaching and Research, 37–41.

Battersby, David. 1984a. The first year of teaching: A grounded theory – part I. *The Australian Journal of Teacher Education*, 9(1), 11–29.

Battersby, David. 1984b. The first year of teaching: A grounded theory – part II. *The Australian Journal of Teacher Education*, 9(2), 76–90.

Beebe, Leslie and Tomoko Takahashi. 1989. Sociolinguistic variation in face-threatening speech acts. Chastisement and disagreement. In Miriam R. Eisenstein (ed.), *The dynamic interlanguage: Empirical studies in second language variation*. New York: Plenum Press, 199–218.

Beerens, Daniel R. 2000. *Evaluating teachers for professional growth: Creating a culture of motivation and learning*. Thousand Oaks, CA: Corwin Press.

Benedetti, Teresa. 1997. Enhancing teaching and teacher education with peer coaching. *TESOL Journal*, 7(1), 41–42.

Benson, Phil and L. Winnie Lor. 1998. *Making sense of autonomous language learning*. English Center Monograph, No. 2. Hong Kong: University of Hong Kong.

Bernard, Janine M. 1979. Supervisor training: A discrimination model. *Counselor Education and Supervision*, 19(1), 60–68.

Biddle, Bruce J. 1964. The integration of teacher effectiveness research. In Bruce J. Biddle and William J. Ellena (eds.), *Contemporary research on teacher effectiveness*. New York: Holt, Rinehart and Winston, 1–40.

Black, Susan. 1993. How teachers are reshaping evaluation procedures. *Educational Leadership*, 51(2), 38–42.

Blase, Jo Roberts and Joseph Blase. 1995. The micro-politics of successful supervisor-teacher interaction in instructional conferences. In David Corson (ed.), *Discourse and power in educational organizations*. Cresskill, NJ: Hampton Press, 55–70.

Bliss, Traci and Joan Mazur. 1998. *Secondary and middle school teachers in the midst of reform: Common thread cases*. Upper Saddle River, NJ: Prentice Hall.

Blue, George and Peter Grundy. 1996. Team evaluation of language teaching and language courses. *English Language Teaching Journal*, 50(3), 244–250.

Blumberg, Arthur. 1980. *Supervisors and teachers: A private cold war (2nd ed.)*. Berkeley: McCutchan Publishing.

Blumberg, Arthur and R. Stevan Jonas. 1987. The teacher's control over supervision. *Educational Leadership*, 44(8), 58–62.

Bodóczky, Caroline and Angi Malderez. 1994. Talking shop: Pre-service teaching experience and the training of supervisors. *English Language Teaching Journal*, 48(1), 66–79.

Bolin, Frances S. 1987. On defining supervision. *Journal of Curriculum and Supervision*, 2, 368–380.

Bolman, Lee G. and Terrence E. Deal. 1997. *Reframing organizations: Artistry, choice, and leadership (2nd ed.)*. San Francisco: Jossey-Bass.

Bolman, Lee G. and Terrence E. Deal. 2002. *Reframing the path to school leadership: A guide for teachers and principals*. Thousand Oaks, CA: Corwin Press.

References

Bonk, C. J. and K. A. Kim. 1998. Extending sociocultural theory to adult learning. In M. Cecil Smith and Thomas Pourchot (eds.), *Adult learning and development: Perspectives from educational psychology*. Mahwah, NJ: Lawrence Erlbaum, 67–88.

Borko, Hilda. 1986. Clinical teacher education: The induction years. In J. V. Hoffman and J. Edwards (eds.), *Reality and reform in teacher education*. New York: Random House.

Boud, David (ed.). 1981. *Developing student autonomy in learning*. London: Kogan Page.

Bowers, C. A. and David J. Flinders. 1990. *Responsive teaching: An ecological approach to classroom patterns of language, culture and thought*. New York: Teachers College Press.

Braine, George. 1999a. From the periphery to the center: One teacher's linguistic journey. In George Braine (ed.), *Non-native educators in English language teaching*. Mahwah, NJ: Lawrence Erlbaum, 15–27.

Braine, George. 1999b. *Non-native educators in English language teaching*. Mahwah, NJ: Lawrence Erlbaum.

Brazer, S. David. 1991. The assistant principal: The search for meaning in teacher evaluation. *Educational Leadership*, 48(6), 82.

Breen, Michael P. and Sarah J. Mann. 1997. Shooting arrows at the sun: Perspectives on a pedagogy for autonomy. In Phil Benson and Peter Voller (eds.), *Autonomy and independence in language learning*. New York: Longman, 132–149.

Briggs, Sarah, Victoria Clark, Carolyn Madden, Rebecca Beal, Sunny Hyon, Patricia Aldridge, and John Swales. 1997. *The international teaching assistant: An annotated critical bibliography (2nd ed.)*. Ann Arbor, MI: The University of Michigan (ELI).

Brinton, Donna and Christine Holten. 1989. What novice teachers focus on: The practicum in TESL. *TESOL Quarterly*, 23(2), 343–350.

Brobeck, Sonja. 1990. Jim – A case study in clinical supervision. *Wingspan*, 21–23.

Brophy, Jere E. and Carolyn M. Everston. 1976. *Learning from teaching: A developmental perspective*. Boston: Allyn and Bacon.

Brophy, Jere E. and Thomas L. Good. 1974. *Teacher-student relations: Causes and consequences*. New York: Holt, Rinehart and Winston.

Brown, James Dean. 1988. *Understanding research in second language learning: A teacher's guide to statistics and research design*. Cambridge: Cambridge University Press.

Brown, James Dean and Kate Wolfe-Quintero. 1997. Teacher portfolios for evaluation: A great idea or a waste of time? *Language Teacher*, 21(1), 28–30.

Brown, Penelope and Stephen C. Levinson. 1987. *Politeness: Some universals in language usage*. Cambridge: Cambridge University Press.

Brundage, Sara. 1996. What kinds of supervision do veteran teachers need? An invitation to expand collegial dialogue and research. *Journal of Curriculum and Supervision*, 12(1), 90–94.

Buch, Georgette and Ivan de Bagheera, 1978. An immersion program for the professional improvement of non-native teachers of E.S.L. In Charles H. Blatchford and Jacquelyn Schachter (eds.), *On TESOL '78 – ESL: Policies, Programs and Practices*. Washington, DC: TESOL, 106–115.

Bunting, Carolyn. 1988. Cooperating teachers and the changing views of teacher candidates. *Journal of Teacher Education*, March/April, 42–46.

Burns, Anne. 1997. Valuing diversity: Action researching disparate learner groups. *TESOL Journal*, 7(1), 6–9.

Burns, Anne. 1998. *Collaborative action research for English language teachers*. Cambridge: Cambridge University Press.

Burns, Anne. 2000. Facilitating collaborative action research: Some insights from the AMEP. *Prospect, A Journal of Australian TESOL*, 15(3), 23–34.

Burton, Jill. 1987. The powers of observation: An investigation of current practice and issues in teacher education. In Bikram K. Das (ed.), *Patterns of classroom interaction in Southeast Asia*. Singapore: SEAMEO Regional Language Center (Anthology Series 17), 153–166.

Burton, Jill. 2000. Learning from teaching practice: A case study approach. *Prospect, A Journal of Australian TESOL*, 15(3), 5–22.

Byrne, Barbara M. 1994. Burnout: Testing for validity, reliability, replication, and invariance of causal structure across elementary, intermediate, and secondary teachers. *American Educational Research Journal*, 31(3), 645–673.

Calzoni, Daniela. 2001. Teacher portfolios. *IATEFL Teacher Development SIG Newsletter*, 1(1), 13–16.

Campbell, Dorothy M., Pamela Bondi Cignetti, Beverly J. Melenyzer, Diane Hood Nettles, and Richard M. Wyman, Jr. 1997. *How to develop a professional portfolio: A manual for teachers*. Boston: Allyn and Bacon.

Canagarajah, A. Suresh. 1999a. On EFL teachers, awareness, and agency. *ELT Journal*, 53(3), 207–213.

Canagarajah, A. Suresh. 1999b. Interrogating the "native speaker fallacy": Non-linguistic roots, non-pedagogical results. In George Braine (ed.), *Non-native educators in English language teaching*. Mahwah, NJ: Lawrence Erlbaum, 77–92.

Carr, Wilfred and Stephen Kemmis. 1985. *Becoming critical: Knowing through action research*. Victoria: Deakin University Press.

Carter, Kathy. 1993. The place of story in the study of teaching and teacher education. *Educational Researcher*, 22(1), 5–12, 18.

Carvalho de Oliveira, Luciana and Sally Richardson. 2001. Collaboration between native and nonnative English-speaking educators. *CATESOL Journal*, 13(1), 123–134.

Casanave, Christine Pearson and Sandra R. Schecter. 1997. *On becoming a language educator: Personal essays on professional development*. Mahwah, NJ: Lawrence Erlbaum.

Celep, Cevat. 2000. The correlation of the factors: The prospective teachers' sense of efficacy and beliefs, and attitudes about student control. National Forum of Teacher Educational Administration and Supervision Journal, 17E, 4 [electronic]. Abstract retrieved July 23, 2002 from ERIC database.

Chamberlin, Carla R. 2000. TESL degree candidates' perceptions of trust in supervisors. *TESOL Quarterly*, 34(4), 653–672.

Chaudron, Craig. 1977. A descriptive model of discourse in the corrective treatment of learners' errors. *Language Learning*, 27(1), 29–46.

Christison, Mary Ann and Fredricka L. Stoller. 1997. Time management principles for language program administrators. In Mary Ann Christison and

Fredricka L. Stoller (eds.), *A handbook for language program administrators*. Burlingame, CA: Alta Book Center Publishers, 235–250.

Clandinin, D. Jean and F. Michael Connelly. 1991. Narrative and story in practice and research. In Donald A. Schön (ed.), *The reflective turn: Case studies in and on educational practice*. New York: Teachers College Press, 258–281.

Clark, Howard M. 1990. Clinical supervision and the alternatives. *Journal of Teaching Practice*, 10(1), 39–58.

Clifton, Rodney A. 1979. Practice teaching: Survival in a marginal situation. *Canadian Journal of Education*, 4(3), 60–74.

Cogan, Morris L. 1973. *Clinical supervision*. Boston: Houghton Mifflin.

Cohn, Marilyn. 1981. A new supervision model for linking theory with practice. *Journal of Teacher Education*, 32(3), 26–30.

Cohn, Marilyn M. and Vivian C. Gellman. 1988. Supervision: A developmental approach for fostering inquiry in pre-service teacher education. *Journal of Teacher Education*, 39(2), 2–8.

Cooper, James M. 1995. *Teachers' problem solving: A casebook of award-winning teaching cases*. Boston: Allyn and Bacon.

Cooper, James M. and E. Seidman. 1969. Helping new teachers focus on behavioral change. *The Clearing House*, 43, 301–306.

Copeland, Willis D. 1980. Affective dispositions of teachers in training toward examples of supervisory behavior. *Journal of Educational Research*, 74(1), 37–42.

Copeland, Willis D. 1982. Student teachers' preference for supervisory approach. *Journal of Teacher Education*, 33(2), 32–36.

Corder, S. Pitt. 1967. The significance of learners' errors. *International Review of Applied Linguistics*, 5, 4, 161–170. Reprinted in Jack C. Richards (ed.), 1974. *Error analysis: Perspectives on second language acquisition*. London: Longman, 19–27.

Corson, David. 1995. Discursive power in educational organizations: An introduction. In David Corson (ed.), *Discourse and power in educational organizations*. Cresskill, NJ: Hampton Press, 3–15.

Cotterall, Sara. 1995. Developing a course strategy for learner autonomy. *English Language Teaching Journal*, 49(3), 219–227.

Crippen, Kent J. and David W. Brooks. 2000. Using personal digital assistants in clinical supervision of student teachers. *Journal of Science Education and Technology*, 9(3), 207–211.

Cross, William K. and Peter J. Murphy. 1990. Teleconferencing in student teacher supervision. *British Journal of Educational Technology*, 21(1), 41–51.

Cullen, Richard. 1991. Video in teacher training: The use of local materials. *English Language Teaching Journal*, 45(1), 33–42.

Curtis, Andy and Liying Cheng. 1998. Video as a source of data in classroom observation. *Thai TESOL Bulletin*, 11(2), 31–38.

Daresh, John C. 2001. *Supervision as proactive leadership (3rd ed.)*. Prospect Heights, IL: Waveland Press.

Darling-Hammond, Linda. 1986. A proposal for evaluation in the teaching profession. *Elementary School Journal*, 86(4), 531–551.

Darling-Hammond, Linda, Arthur E. Wise, and Sara R. Pease. 1983. Teacher evaluation in the organizational context: A review of the literature. *Review of Educational Research*, 53(3), 285–328.

350

Daughtrey, Anne Scott and Betty Roper Ricks. 1989. *Contemporary supervision: Managing people and technology.* New York: McGraw-Hill.

Davis, Hazel. 1964. Evolution of current practices in evaluating teacher competence. In Bruce J. Biddle and William J. Elena (eds.), *Contemporary research on teacher effectiveness.* New York: Holt, Rinehart and Winston, 41–66.

Day, Richard R. 1990. Teacher observation in second language teacher education. In Jack C. Richards and David Nunan (eds.), *Second language teacher education.* New York: Cambridge University Press, 43–61.

Dayan, Yael. 1999. Role perception in fieldwork supervisors of students of early childhood education. Paper presented at the Annual EECERA Conference, Helsinki. Abstract retrieved, July 23, 2002, from ERIC database.

Deal, Nancy. 2000. How the other half work: Student teacher supervision in Kenya. *Action in Teacher Education,* 21(1), 1–9.

Dearden, R. F. 1972. Autonomy and education. In R. F. Dearden, P. F. Hirst, and R. S. Peters (eds.), *Education and the development of reason.* London: Routledge and Kegan Paul.

Denzin, Norman K. 1978. *The research act: A theoretical introduction to sociological methods (2nd ed.)* New York: McGraw-Hill.

Dewey, John. 1933. *How we think.* Chicago: Henry Regnery.

Diaz Zubieta, Marcela, Gloria Torrano Jessurun, and Leslie Adams. 1978. In-service teacher training in a third world country. In Charles H. Blatchford and Jacquelyn Schachter (eds.), *On TESOL '78: ESL policies, programs and practices.* Washington, DC: TESOL, 98–105.

Dickinson, Leslie. 1987. *Self-instruction in language learning.* Cambridge: Cambridge University Press.

Dufficy, Paul. 1993. The pedagogy of pre-service TESOL education. *Journal of Education for Teaching,* 19 (1), 83–96.

Duffy, Francis M. 1999. Reconceptualizing instructional supervision for 3rd millenium school systems. *Journal of Curriculum and Supervision,* 15(2), 123–145.

Ebmeier, Howard and Janice Nicklaus. 1999. The impact of peer and principal collaborative supervision on teachers' trust, commitment, desire for collaboration, and efficacy. *Journal of Curriculum and Supervision,* 14(4), 351–378.

Edge, Julian. 2001. *Action research.* Alexandria, VA: TESOL.

Edge, Julian and Keith Richards. 1993. *Teachers develop teachers research: Papers on classroom research and teacher development.* Oxford: Heinemann.

Edwards, Jane A. and Martin D. Lampert. (1993). *Talking data: Transcription and coding in discourse research.* Hillsdale, NJ: Lawrence Erlbaum.

Eisenman, Gordon and Holly Thornton. (1999). Tele-mentoring: Helping new teachers through the first year. *T.H.E Journal Online,* April.

England, Lizabeth and Cheryl Roberts. 1989. A survey of foreign students in MA-TESOL programs. *TESOL Newsletter,* 23(6), 5.

Enright, Lee. 1981. The diary of a classroom. In Jon Nixon (ed.), *A teacher's guide to action research: Evaluation, enquiry and development in the classroom.* London: Grant McIntyre, 35–51.

EURYDICE European Unit, Brussels. 1999. Supplement to the study on the structures of the education and initial training systems in the European

Union. The situation in Estonia, Latvia, Lithuania, Slovenia and Cyprus. Abstract retrieved July 23, 2002 from ERIC database.

Fanselow, John. 1977. Beyond 'Rashomon' – Conceptualizing and describing the teaching act. *TESOL Quarterly*, 11(1), 17–39.

Fanselow, John. 1987. *Breaking rules: Generating and exploring alternatives in language teaching*. New York: Longman.

Fanselow, John. 1988. "Let's see": Contrasting conversations about teaching. *TESOL Quarterly*, 22, 1, 113–130. Reprinted in Jack C. Richards and David Nunan (eds.), *Second language teacher education*. New York: Cambridge University Press, 182–199.

Flaitz, Jeffra. 1993. Two new observation report formats for teachers in training. *English Teaching Forum*, 31(4), 22–25.

Flanders, Ned. A. 1970. *Analyzing teaching behavior*. Reading, MA: Addison-Wesley.

Flanders, Ned A. 1976. Interaction analysis and clinical supervision. *Journal of Research and Development in Education*, 9, 47–57.

Flowerdew, John, Mark N. Brock, and Sophie Hsia. 1992. *Perspectives on second language teacher development*. Hong Kong: City Polytechnic of Hong Kong.

Flynn, Kathleen and Goedele Gulikers. 2001. Issues in hiring nonnative English speaking professionals to teach English as a second language. *CATESOL Journal*, 13(1), 151–160.

Foucault, Michel. 1980. *Power/knowledge: Selected interviews and other writings, 1971–1977*. New York: Pantheon.

Foucault, Michel. 1981. The order of discourse. In Robert Young (ed.), *Untying the text: A post-structuralist reader*. Boston: Routledge and Kegan Paul, 48–78.

Fox, Sandra M. and Ted J. Singletary. 1986. Deductions about supportive induction. *Journal of Teacher Education*, 37(1), 12–15.

Franck, Marion R. and Fabian A. Samaniego. 1981. The supervision of teaching assistants: A new use of videotape. *Modern Language Journal*, 65(3), 273–280.

Freeman, Donald. 1982. Observing teachers: Three approaches to inservice training and development. *TESOL Quarterly*, 16(1), 21–28.

Freeman, Donald. 1989a. Teacher training, development and decision making: A model of teaching and related strategies for language teacher education. *TESOL Quarterly*, 23(1), 27–45.

Freeman, Donald. 1989b. Learning to teach: Four instructional patterns in language teacher education. *Prospect, A Journal of Australian TESOL*, 4(2), 31–47.

Freeman, Donald. 1990. Intervening in practice teaching. In Jack C. Richards and David Nunan (eds.), *Second language teacher education*. Cambridge: Cambridge University Press, 103–117.

Freeman, Donald. 1994. Knowing into doing: Teacher education and the problem of transfer. In David C. S. Li, Dino Mahoney, and Jack C. Richards (eds.), *Exploring second language teacher development*. Hong Kong: City Polytechnic of Hong Kong, 1–20.

Freeman, Donald. 1996. Renaming experience/reconstructing practice. In Donald Freeman and Jack C. Richards (eds.), *Teacher learning in language teaching*. New York: Cambridge University Press, 221–241.

Freeman, Donald and Karen Johnson. 1998. Reconceptualizing the knowledge base of language teacher education. *TESOL Quarterly*, 32(3), 397–417.

Freeman, Donald and Jack C. Richards. (eds.). 1996. *Teacher learning in language teaching*. Cambridge: Cambridge University Press.

Freiburg, H. Jerome and Hersholt C. Waxman. 1990. Alternative feedback approaches for improving student teachers' classroom instruction. *Journal of Teacher Education*, 39(4), 8–14.

French, John R. P. and Bertram Raven. 1960. The bases of social power. In Dorwin Cartwright and Alvin Zandler (eds.), *Group dynamics: Research and theory (2nd ed.)*. Evanston, IL: Harper & Row, 607–623.

Fröhlich, Maria, Nina Spada, and Patrick Allen. 1985. Differences in the communicative orientation of L2 classrooms. *TESOL Quarterly*, 19(1), 27–57.

Gaies, Stephen and Roger Bowers. 1990. Clinical supervision of language teaching: The supervisor as trainer and educator. In Jack C. Richards and David Nunan (eds.), *Second language teacher education*. New York: Cambridge University Press, 167–181.

Gambrill, Eileen and Theodore J. Stein. 1983. *Supervision: A decision-making approach*. Beverly Hills, CA: Sage Publications.

Garman, Noreen B. 1986. Reflection: The heart of clinical supervision: A modern rationale for professional practice. *Journal of Curriculum and Supervision*, 2(1), 1–24.

Garman, Noreen B. 1990. Theories embedded in the events of clinical supervision: A hermeneutic approach. *Journal of Curriculum and Supervision*, 5(3), 201–213.

Garman, Noreen B., Carl D. Glickman, Madeline Hunter, and Nelson L. Haggerson. 1987. Conflicting conceptions of clinical supervision and the enhancement of professional growth and renewal: Point and counterpoint. *Journal of Curriculum and Supervision*, 2(2), 152–177.

Gass, Susan M. 1997. *Input, interaction and the second language learner*. Mahwah, NJ: Lawrence Erlbaum.

Gass, Susan M. and Alison Mackey. 2000. *Stimulated recall methodology in second language research*. Mahwah, NJ: Lawrence Erlbaum.

Gebhard, Jerry G. 1984. Models of supervision: Choices. *TESOL Quarterly*, 18(3), 501–514. Reprinted in Jack C. Richards and David Nunan (eds., 1990), *Second language teacher education*. New York: Cambridge University Press, 156–166.

Gebhard, Jerry G. 1990a. *The supervision of second and foreign language teachers*. ERIC Digest, ERIC Clearinghouse on Language and Linguistics (EDO-FL-90–06). Washington, DC: Center for Applied Linguistics.

Gebhard, Jerry G. 1990b. Freeing the teacher: A supervisory process. *Foreign Language Annals*, 23(6), 517–525.

Gebhard, Jerry G. 1990c. Interaction in a teaching practicum. In Jack C. Richards and David Nunan (eds.), *Second language teacher education*. Cambridge: Cambridge University Press, 118–131.

Gebhard, Jerry G. 1991. Clinical supervision: Process concerns. *TESOL Quarterly*, 25(4), 738–743.

Gebhard, Jerry G. 1999. Seeing teaching differently through observation. In Jerry Gebhard and Robert Oprandy (eds.), *Language teaching awareness: A guide to exploring beliefs and practices*. Cambridge: Cambridge University Press, 35–58.

References

Gebhard, Jerry G., Mio Hashimoto, Jae-Oke Joe, and Hyunhee Lee. 1999. Micro-teaching and self-observation: Experience in a preservice teacher education program. In Jerry Gebhard and Robert Oprandy (eds.), *Language teaching awareness: A guide to exploring beliefs and practices*. Cambridge: Cambridge University Press, 172–194.

Gebhard, Jerry G. and Agnes Malicka. 1991. Creative behavior in teacher supervision. *Prospect, A Journal of Australian TESOL*, 6(3), 40–49.

Gebhard, Jerry G. and Robert Oprandy. 1999. *Language teaching awareness: A guide to exploring beliefs and practices*. New York: Cambridge University Press.

Geddes, Joann M. and Doris R. Marks. 1997. Personnel matters. In Mary Ann Christison and Fredricka L. Stoller (eds.), *A handbook for language program administrators*. Burlingame, CA: Alta Book Center Publishers, 199–218.

Gitlin, Andrew David and John Smyth. 1990. Toward educative forms of teacher evaluation. *Educational Theory*, 40(1), 83–94.

Glanz, Jeffrey and Richard F. Neville (eds.). 1997. *Educational supervision: Perspectives, issues, and controversies*. Norwood, MA: Christopher-Gordon Publishers.

Glickman, Carl D. 1985. *Supervision and instruction: A developmental approach*. Boston: Allyn and Bacon.

Glickman, Carl D. 1992. *Supervision in transition: The 1992 ASCD yearbook*. http://www.ascd.org/readingroom/books.

Glickman, Carl D. and Stephen P. Gordon. 1987. Clarifying developmental supervision. *Educational Leadership*, 44(8), 64–68.

Glickman, Carl D., Stephen P. Gordon, and Jovita M. Ross-Gordon. 1998. *Supervision of instruction: A developmental approach (4th ed.)*. Boston: Allyn and Bacon.

Goffman, Erving. 1976. *Stigma*. Harmonds-Worth, UK: Penguin.

Goldhammer, Robert. 1969. *Clinical supervision: Special methods for the supervision of teachers*. New York: Holt, Rinehart and Winston.

Goldsberry, Lee. 1988. Three functional methods of supervision. *Action in Teacher Education*, 10(1), 1–10.

Goldstein, Lynn. 1987. Standard English: The only target for nonnative speakers of English? *TESOL Quarterly*, 21(3), 417–436.

Green, James E. and Sheryl O. Smyser. 1996. *The teacher portfolio: A strategy for professional development and evaluation*. Lancaster, PA: Technomic Publishing.

Greis, Naguib. 1985. Toward a better preparation of the non-native ESOL teacher. In Penny Larson, Elliot L. Judd, and Dorothy Messerschmitt (eds.), *On TESOL '84 – A Brave New World for TESOL*. Washington, DC: TESOL, 317–324.

Grimmett, Peter P. 1996. The struggles of teacher research in a context of education reform: Implications for instructional supervision. *Journal of Curriculum and Supervision*, 12(1), 37–65.

Grimmett, Peter P. and E. Patricia Crehan. 1990. Barry: A case study of teacher reflection in clinical supervision. *Journal of Curriculum and Supervision*, 5(3), 214–235.

Gruenhagen, Kathleen, Tom McCracken, and Judy True. 1999. Using distance education technologies for the supervision of student teachers in remote rural schools. *Rural Special Education Quarterly*, 18(3–4), 58–65.

Hackney, Harold L. 1971. Development of a pre-practicum counseling skills model. *Counselor Education and Supervision*, 11(2), 102–109.

Hamid, Bahiyah Abdul and Hazita Azman. 1991. Adapting the six category intervention analysis to promote facilitative type supervisory feedback in teaching practice. In Eugenios Sadtono (ed.), *Language teacher education in a fast-changing world*. Singapore: Regional Language Centre (Anthology Series 29), 88–99.

Hammersley, Martyn and Paul Atkinson. 1983. *Ethnography: Principles in practice*. London: Tavistock Publications.

Hargreaves, Andy. 1994. Development and desire: A postmodern perspective. In Thomas R. Guskey and Michael Huberman (eds.), *Professional development in education: New paradigms and practices*. New York: Teachers College Press, 9–34.

Harrison, Ian. 1996. Look who's talking now: Listening to voices in curriculum renewal. In Kathleen M. Bailey and David Nunan (eds.), *Voices from the language classroom*. Cambridge: Cambridge University Press, 283–303.

Hatch, Evelyn. 1992. *Discourse and language education*. New York: Cambridge University Press.

Hatch, Evelyn and Michael H. Long. 1980. Discourse analysis – What's that? In Diane Larsen-Freeman (ed.), *Discourse analysis in second language research*. Rowley, MA: Newbury House, 1–40.

Hayashi, Reiko and Taku Hayashi. 2002. Duality and continuum in indirect talk: Linguistic style and gender in clinical supervision. In David C. S. Li (ed.), *Discourses in search of members: In honor of Ron Scollon*. Lanham, MD: University Press of America, 135–169.

Hazi, Helen M. 1994. The teacher evaluation-supervision dilemma: A case of entanglements and irreconcilable differences. *Journal of Curriculum and Supervision*, 9(2), 195–216.

Head, Katie and Pauline Taylor. 1997. *Readings in teacher development*. Oxford: Heinemann.

Henning, Grant. 1987. *A guide to language testing: Development, evaluation, research*. New York: Newbury House.

Herschensohn, Julia. 1992. Teaching assistant development: A case study. In Joel C. Walz (ed.), *Development and supervision of teaching assistants in foreign languages*. Boston: Heinle & Heinle, 25–45.

Hersey, Paul. 1984. *The situational leader*. New York: Warner Books.

Hersey, Paul and Kenneth H. Blanchard. 1982. *Management of organizational behavior: Utilizing human resources (4th ed.)*. Englewood Cliffs, NJ: Prentice Hall.

Ho, Belinda and Jack C. Richards. 1993. Reflective thinking through teacher journal writing: Myths and realities. *Prospect, A Journal of Australian TESOL*, 8(3), 7–24.

Hoare, Philip and Stella Kong. 1994. Helping teachers change the language of the classroom: Lessons from in-service teacher education. In David Nunan, Roger Berry, and Vivien Berry (eds.), *Bringing about change in language education: Proceedings of the international language in education conference*. Hong Kong: University of Hong Kong, 21–34.

Hodder, Jaqueline and David, Carter. 1997. The role of new information technologies in facilitating professional reflective practice across the supervisory triad. Paper presented at the Annual Conference of the gasat-IOSTE,

Perth, Australia, December. Abstract retrieved July 24, 2002 from ERIC database.

Holland, Patricia E. 1989a. Implicit assumptions about the supervisory conference: A review and analysis of literature. *Journal of Curriculum and Supervision*, 4(4), 362–379.

Holland, Patricia E. 1989b. Stories of supervision: Tutorials in the transformative power of supervision. *Peabody Journal of Education*, 66(3), 61–77.

Hoy, Wayne K. and Anita E. Woolfolk. 1989. Supervising student teachers. In Anita E. Woolfolk (ed.), *Research perspectives on the graduate preparation of teachers*. Englewood Cliffs, NJ: Prentice Hall, 108–131.

Hsiung, Chao-Ti and Nin-Juin Tan. 1999. A study of creating a distance supervision hot line. Paper presented at the annual meeting of the National Association for Research in Science Teaching, Boston. Abstract retrieved July 23, 2002, from ERIC database.

Hunter, Madeline. 1983. Script-taping: An essential supervisory tool. *Educational Leadership*, 41(3), 43.

Hunter, Madeline. 1984. Knowing, teaching, and supervising. In Philip L. Hosford (ed.), *Using what we know about teaching*. Alexandria, VA: ASCD, 169–192.

Hunter, Madeline. 1986. Let's eliminate the preobservation conference. *Educational Leadership*, March, 69–70.

Jackson, Jane. 1997. Cases in TESOL teacher education: Creating a forum for reflection. *TESL Canada Journal*, 14(2), 1–16.

Jackson, Jane. 1998. Reality-based decision cases in ESP teacher education: Windows on practice. *English for Specific Purposes*, 17(2), 151–166.

Jarvis, G. A. 1968. A behavioral observation system for classroom foreign language skill acquisition activities. *Modern Language Journal*, 52, 335–341.

Jarvis, Jennifer. 1992. Using diaries for teacher reflection on in-service courses. *English Language Teaching Journal*, 46(2), 133–143.

Jesperson, Otto. 1917. Negation in English and other languages, reprinted in Otto Jesperson, 1960, *Selected writings of Otto Jesperson*. London: Allen and Unwin, 3–151.

Johanson, Roger P., Deborah L. Norland, Eric Olson, Les Huth, and Roberta Bodensteiner. 1999. Internet and list-serves to support the student teaching semester. Paper presented at the Annual Meeting of the American Association of Colleges for Teacher Education. Washington, DC, February. Abstract retrieved July 24, 2002 from ERIC database.

Johnson, Karen E. 1992a. The instructional decisions of pre-service English as a second language teachers: New directions for teacher preparation programs. In John Flowerdew, Mark N. Brock, and Sophie Hsia (eds.), *Perspectives on second language teacher development*. Hong Kong: City Polytechnic of Hong Kong, 115–134.

Johnson, Karen E. 1992b. Learning to teach: Instructional actions and decisions of preservice ESL teachers. *TESOL Quarterly*, 26(3), 507–535.

Johnson, Karen E. 1996a. Portfolio assessment in second language teacher education. *TESOL Journal*, 6(2), 11–14.

Johnson, Karen E. 1996b. Cognitive apprenticeship in second language teacher education. In Gertrude Tinker Sachs, Mark N. Brock, and Regina Lo (eds.), *Directions in second language teacher education*. Hong Kong: City University of Hong Kong, 23–36.

Johnson, Karen E. 1996c. The vision versus the reality: The tensions of the TESOL practicum. In Donald Freeman and Jack C. Richards (eds.), *Teacher learning in language teaching*. Cambridge: Cambridge University Press, 30–49.

Johnson, Karen E. (ed.). 2000. *Teacher education*. Alexandria, VA: TESOL.

Johnson, Robert Keith. 1990. Developing teachers' language resources. In Jack C. Richards and David Nunan (eds.), *Second language teacher education*, Cambridge: Cambridge University Press, 269–281.

Johnson, Ruth. 1999. Cross-cultural misunderstanding in a team teaching situation. *TESOL Matters* 9(1), 16.

Joyce, Bruce R. and Beverly Showers. 1982. The coaching of teaching. *Educational Leadership*, 40(1), 4–8, 10.

Joyce, Bruce R. and Beverly Showers. 1987. Low-cost arrangements for peer-coaching. *Journal of Staff Development*, 8(1), 22–24.

Joyce, Bruce R. and Beverly Showers. 1988. *Student achievement through staff development*. New York: Longman.

Jyrhama, Riitta. 2001. What are the "right" questions and the "right" answers in teaching practice supervision? Paper presented at the Annual Meeting of the International Study Association on Teachers and Teaching, Portugal. Abstract retrieved July 23, 2002, from ERIC database.

Kamhi-Stein, Lía D. 1999. Preparing non-native professionals in TESOL: Implications for teacher education programs. In George Braine (ed.), *Non-native educators in English language teaching*. Mahwah, NJ: Lawrence Erlbaum, 145–158.

Kamhi-Stein, Lía. 2001. New voices in the classroom: Nonnative English-speaking professionals in the field of teaching English to speakers of other languages. *CATESOL Journal*, 13(1), 47–51.

Kamhi-Stein, Lía D., Annette Aagard, Angelica Ching, Myoung-Soon Ashley Paik, and Linda Sasser. 2001. New voices in the classroom: Nonnative English-speaking professionals in the field of teaching English to speakers of other languages. *CATESOL Journal*, 13(1), 69–88.

Kamhi-Stein, Lía D. and José L. Galván. 1997. EFL teacher development through critical reflection. *TESOL Journal*, 7(1), 12–18.

Kawachi, Paul. 2000. Listening to other teachers – The professional development of university teachers: Case study of a Japanese national university. *Staff and Educational Development International*, 4(1), 65–82.

Kelly, Peter. 1980. From innovation to adaptability: The changing perspective of curriculum development. In Maurice Galton (ed.), *Curriculum change*. Leicester: Leicester University Press, 65–80.

Kemmis, Stephen and Colin Henry. 1989. Action research. *IATEFL Newsletter*, 102, 2–3.

Kemmis, Stephen and Robin McTaggart. 1982. *The action research planner*. Victoria: Deakin University.

Kemmis, Stephen and Robin McTaggart. 1988. *The action research planner (3rd ed.)*. Victoria: Deakin University.

Kennedy, Chris. 1988. Evaluation of the management of change in ELT projects. *Applied Linguistics*, 9(4), 329–342.

Kiesling, Scott Fabius. 1997. Power and the language of men. In Sally Johnson and Ulrike Hanna Meinhof (eds.), *Language and masculinity*. Cambridge, MA: Blackwell Publishers, 65–85.

References

Knezevic, Anné and Mary Scholl. 1996. Learning to teach together: Teaching to learn together. In Donald Freeman and Jack C. Richards (eds.), *Teacher learning in language teaching*. Cambridge: Cambridge University Press, 79–96.

Knezedvic, Bozana. 2001. Action research. *IATEFL Teacher Development SIG Newsletter*, 1(1), 10–12.

Knop, Constance K. 1980. The supervision of foreign language teachers. In Frank M. Grittner (ed.), *Learning a second language: Seventy-ninth Yearbook of The National Society for the Study of Education, Part II*. Chicago: University of Chicago Press, 186–207.

Knowles, Malcolm. 1975. *Self-directed learning: A quick guide for learners and teachers*. Chicago: Follett Publishing.

Korinek, Lori A. 1989. Teacher preferences for training and compensation for field supervision. *Journal of Teacher Education*, 40(6), 46–51.

Krashen, Stephen D. 1981. *Second language acquisition and second language learning*. Oxford: Pergamon Press.

Krashen, Stephen D. 1982. *Principles and practice in second language acquisition*. Oxford: Pergamon Press.

Krashen, Stephen D. and Tracy D. Terrell. 1983. *The natural approach: Language acquisition in the classroom*. Oxford: Pergamon Press.

Kremer-Hayon, Lya. 1986. Supervisors' inner world: Professional perspectives. *European Journal of Teacher Education*, 9(2), 181–187.

Kremer-Hayon, Lya. 1987. The content and nature of dilemmas encountered by student-teachers' supervisors. *European Journal of Teacher Education*, 10(2), 151–161.

Kulick, Katherine M. 1992. Undergraduate teaching assistants: One model. In Joel C. Walz (ed.), *Development and supervision of teaching assistants in foreign languages*. Boston: Heinle & Heinle, 1–23.

Labov, William. 1972. Some principles of linguistic methodology. *Language in Society*, 1, 97–120.

Lange, Dale C. 1990. A blueprint for a teacher development program. In Jack C. Richards and David Nunan (eds.), *Second language teacher education*. Cambridge: Cambridge University Press, 245–268.

Lankshear, Colin. 1994. Afterword: Reclaiming empowerment and rethinking the past. In Miguel Escobar, Alfredo L. Fernández, and Gilberto Guevara-Niebla with Paolo Freire, *Paolo Freire on higher education: A dialogue at the National University of Mexico*. Albany: State University of New York Press, 162–187.

Lantolf, James P. 2000a. Introducing sociocultural theory. In James P. Lantolf (ed.), *Sociocultural theory and second language learning*. Oxford: Oxford University Press, 1–26.

Lantolf, James P. (ed.). 2000b. *Sociocultural theory and second language learning*. Oxford: Oxford University Press.

Larimer, Ruth and Leigh Schleicher (eds.). 1999. *New ways in using authentic materials in the classroom*. Alexandria, VA: TESOL.

Larsen-Freeman, Diane. 1983. Training teachers or educating a teacher. In James E. Alatis, H. H. Stern, and Peter Strevens (eds.), *Georgetown University Round Table on Language and Linguistics: Applied Linguistics and the Preparation of Second Language Teachers: Toward a Rationale*. Washington, DC: Georgetown University Press, 68–81.

Larsen-Freeman, Diane. 1990. On the need for a theory of language teaching. In James Alatis (ed.), *Linguistics, language teaching and language acquisition: The interdependence of theory, practice, and research.* Washington, DC: Georgetown University Press, 261–270.

Lave, Jean and Etienne Wenger. 1991. *Situated learning: Legitimate peripheral participation.* New York: Cambridge University Press.

Lawrence, C. Edward, Myra K. Vachon, Donald O. Leake, and Brenda H. Leake. 2001. *The marginal teacher: A step-by-step guide to fair procedures for identification and dismissal.* Thousand Oaks, CA: Corwin Press.

Laycock, John and Piranya Bunnag. 1991. Developing teacher self-awareness: Feedback and the use of video. *English Language Teaching Journal,* 45(1), 43–53.

Lee, Elis and Loren Lew. 2001. Diary studies: The voices of nonnative English speakers in a master of arts program in teaching English to speakers of other languages. *CATESOL Journal,* 13(1), 135–149.

Leech, Geoffrey N. 1983. *Principles of pragmatics.* New York: Longman.

Leinhart, G. and J. G. Greeno. 1986. The cognitive skill of teaching. *Journal of Educational Psychology,* 78(2), 75–95.

Lemma, Paulette. 1993. The cooperating teacher as supervisor: A case study. *Journal of Curriculum and Supervision,* 8(4), 329–342.

Leontiev, Alexander N. 1978. *Activity, consciousness, personality.* Englewood Cliffs, NJ: Prentice Hall.

Lewin, Kurt. 1946. Action research and minority problems. *Journal of Social Issues,* 2, 34–46.

Lewis, Marcella, Pamela Meadows, Alan Seaman, Barry Sweeny, and Marilyn Sweeny. 1996. *Mentoring for ESL teachers: A mentor training manual.* Wheaton, IL: World Relief DePage.

Lewis, Marilyn. 1998. A study of feedback to language teachers. *Prospect, A Journal of Australian TESOL,* 13(1), 68–83.

Li, David C. S., Dino Mahoney, and Jack C. Richards (eds.). 1994. *Exploring second language teacher development.* Hong Kong: City Polytechnic of Hong Kong.

van Lier, Leo. 1988. *The classroom and the language learner: Ethnography and second language classroom research.* London: Longman.

van Lier, Leo. 1994. Action research. *Sintagma,* 6, 31–37.

van Lier, Leo. 1995. *Introducing language awareness.* London: Penguin Books.

van Lier, Leo. 1996. *Interaction in the language curriculum: Awareness, autonomy, and authenticity.* London: Longman.

van Lier, Leo. 2000. From input to affordance: Social-interactive learning from an ecological perspective. In James P. Lantolf (ed.), *Sociocultural theory and second language learning.* Oxford: Oxford University Press, 245–259.

van Lier, Leo. 2004. *The ecology and semiotics of language learning.* Boston: Kluwer Academic Publishers.

Little, D. 1991. *Learner autonomy 1: Definitions, issues and problems.* Dublin: Authentik.

Liu, Dilin. 1999. Training non-native TESOL students: Challenges for teacher education in the west. In George Braine (ed.), *Non-native educators in English language teaching.* Mahwah, NJ: Lawrence Erlbaum, 197–210.

359

Liu, Dilin. 2000. Multiple-site practicum: Opportunities for diverse learning and teaching experiences. *TESOL Journal*, 9(1), 18–22.

Liu, Jun. 1999. From their own perspectives: The impact of non-native ESL professionals on their students. In George Braine (ed.), *Non-native educators in English language teaching*. Mahwah, NJ: Lawrence Erlbaum, 159–176.

Livingston, Samuel A. 1978. Setting standards of speaking proficiency. In John L. D. Clark (ed.), *Direct testing of speaking proficiency: Theory and application*. Princeton, NJ: Educational Testing Service, 257–270.

Lnenicka, W. J. 1972. Are teaching assistants teachers? *Improving College and University Teaching* 20(2), 97.

Long, Michael H. 1980. Inside the "black box": Methodological issues in research on language teaching and learning. *Language Learning*, 30, 1, 1–42. Reprinted in Herbert W. Seliger and Michael H. Long (eds., 1983), *Classroom oriented research in second language acquisition*. Rowley, MA: Newbury House, 3–36.

Long, Michael H., Leslie Adams, Marilyn McLean, and Fernando Castaños. 1976. Doing things with words: Verbal interaction in lockstep and small group classroom situations. In John Fanselow and Ruth Crymes (eds.), *On TESOL 1976*. Washington, DC: TESOL, 137–153.

Lortie, Dan C. 1975. *Schoolteacher: A sociological study*. Chicago: University of Chicago Press.

Lowenberg, Peter. 1990. Nativization and interlanguage in Standard English: Another look. In James E. Alatis (ed.), *Georgetown University Round Table on languages and linguistics 1990: Linguistics, language teaching and language acquisition: The interdependence of theory, practice and research*. Washington, DC: Georgetown University Press, 157–168.

Ludwig, Jeanette. 1982. Native speaker judgments of second language learners' efforts at communication. *Modern Language Journal*, 66(3), 274–283.

Luft, Joseph and Harry Ingram. 1969. *Of human interaction*. New York: National Press Books.

Lunenberg, Mieke. 1999. New qualifying requirements for the mentoring of student teachers in the Netherlands. *European Journal of Teacher Education*, 22(2–3), 159–171.

Lyons, Nona (ed.). 1998. *With portfolio in hand: Validating the new teacher professionalism*. New York: Teachers College Press.

Malcolm, Ian G. 1991. "All right then, if you don't want to do that . . .": Strategy and counter-strategy in classroom discourse management. *Guidelines: A Periodical for Classroom Language Teachers*, 13(2), 1–17.

Malderez, Angi and Caroline Bodóczky. 1999. *Mentor courses: A resource book for trainer-trainers*. Cambridge: Cambridge University Press.

Mallam, Ugbo. 1994. A national research study on factors influencing faculty turnover at selected Nigerian colleges of technology/polytechnics. *Higher Education*, 27, 2, 229–238. Abstract retrieved July 24 from ERIC database.

Mansour, Wisam. 1993. Towards developmental ELT supervision. *English Teacher Forum*, 31(3), 48–50.

Martinez, Kay. 1998. Supervision in preservice teacher education: Speaking the unspoken. *International Journal of Leadership in Education*, 1(3), 279–296.

Martin-Kniep, Giselle O. 1999. *Capturing the wisdom of practice: Professional portfolios for educators*. Washington, DC: ASCD.

Maslach, Christina. 1982. *Burnout: The cost of caring*. Englewood Cliffs, NJ: Prentice Hall.

Maslach, Christina and S. E. Jackson. 1986. *Maslach burnout inventory manual (2nd ed.)*. Palo Alto, CA: Consulting Psychologists Press.

Master, Peter. 1990. The spoken English proficiency of international graduates from California MATESL programs. *CATESOL Journal*, 3(1), 101–104.

Master, Peter. 1983. The etiquette of observing. *TESOL Quarterly*, 17(3), 497–501.

Matsuda, Aya and Paul Kei Matsuda. 2001. Autonomy and collaboration in teacher education: Journal sharing among native and nonnative English-speaking teachers. *CATESOL Journal*, 13(1), 109–121.

Matsuda, Paul Kei. 1999. Teacher development through native speaker-nonnative speaker collaboration. *TESOL Matters*, 9(6), 1, 10.

Mattingly, Cheryl. 1991. Narrative reflections on practical actions: Two learning experiments in reflective storytelling. In Donald A. Schön (ed.), *The reflective turn: Case studies in and on educational practice*. New York: Teachers College Press, 235–257.

McCabe, Anne. 2002. Narratives: A wellspring for development. In Julian Edge (ed.), *Continuing professional development: Some of our perspectives*. Whitstable, UK: IATEFL, 71–79.

McCafferty, Steven G. 1994. Adult second language learners' use of private speech. *Modern Language Journal*, 78(4), 421–436.

McDonough, Jo. 1994. A teacher looks at teachers' diaries. *English Language Teaching Journal*, 48(1), 57–65.

McFaul, Shirley A. and James M. Cooper. 1984. Peer clinical supervision: Theory vs. reality. *Educational Leadership*, 41(7), 4–9.

McGee, Jerry C. and Robert Eaker. 1977. Clinical supervision and teacher anxiety: A collegial approach to the problem. *Contemporary Education*, 49(1), 24–28.

McGreal, Thomas L. 1988. Evaluation for enhancing instruction: Linking teacher evaluation and staff development. In Sarah J. Stanley and James W. Popham (eds.), *Teacher evaluation: Six prescriptions for success*. ASCD, 1–29.

McLaughlin, Maureen and Mary Ellen Vogt. 1996. *Portfolios in teacher education*. Newark, DE: The International Reading Association.

McPherson, Pam. 1997. Action research: Exploring learner diversity. *Prospect, A Journal of Australian TESOL*, 12(1), 50–62.

Medgyes, Péter. 1999. Language training: A neglected area in teacher education. In George Braine (ed.), *Non-native educators in English language teaching*. Mahwah, NJ: Lawrence Erlbaum, 177–195.

Medgyes, Péter. 2001. When the teacher is a non-native speaker. In Marianne Celce-Murcia (ed.), *Teaching English as a second or foreign language (3rd ed.)*. Boston: Heinle & Heinle, 415–427.

Medley, Donald M. and H. E. Mitzel. 1963. Measuring classroom behavior by systematic observation. In Nathan L. Gage (ed.), *Handbook of research on teaching*. Chicago: Rand McNally, 247–328.

Milk, Robert D. 1990. Preparing ESL and bilingual teachers for changing roles: Immersion for teachers of LEP children. *TESOL Quarterly*, 24, 3, 407–425.

Mingucci, M. 1999. Action research in ESL staff development. *TESOL Matters*, 9(2), 16.

References

Mosher, Ralph L. and David E. Purpel. 1972. *Supervision: The reluctant profession*. New York: Houghton Mifflin.

Moskowitz, Gertrude. 1966. Toward human relations in supervision. *Bulletin of the National Association of Secondary School Principals*, 50(314), 98–114.

Moskowitz, Gertrude. 1968. The effects of training foreign language teachers in Interaction Analysis. *Foreign Language Annals*, 1(3), 218–235.

Moskowitz, Gertrude. 1971. Interaction analysis: A modern language for supervisors. *Foreign Language Annals*, 5(2), 211–221.

Munro, Petra M. 1991. Supervision: What's imposition got to do with it? *Journal of Curriculum and Supervision*, 7(1), 77–89.

Murdoch, George. 1998. A progressive teacher evaluation system [Electronic version]. *The English Teaching Forum*, 36(3), 2–11.

Murdoch, George. 2000. Introducing a teacher-supportive evaluation system. *English Language Teaching Journal*, 54(1), 54–64.

Murphey, Tim. 2000. Becoming contributing professionals: Nonnative-English-speaking teachers in an EFL environment. In Karen E. Johnson (ed.), *Teacher education*. Alexandria, VA: TESOL, 105–117.

Murphy, John M. 1992. An etiquette for the nonsupervisory observation of L2 classrooms. *Foreign Language Annals*, 25(3), 215–225.

Murphy-O'Dwyer, Lynette M. 1996. Putting the T in TESOL. *TESOL Matters*, 6(2), 21.

Nerenz, Anne G. and Constance Knop. 1982. A time-based approach to the study of teacher effectiveness. *Modern Language Journal*, 66(3), 243–254.

Nixon, Jon (ed.). 1981. *A teacher's guide to action research: Evaluation, enquiry and development in the classroom*. London: Grant McIntyre, 35–51.

Nolan, James F. and Keith Hillkirk. 1991. The effects of a reflective coaching project for veteran teachers. *Journal of Curriculum and Supervision*, 7(1), 62–76.

Nolan, Jim, Brent Hawkes, and Pam Francis. 1993. Case studies: Windows onto clinical supervision. *Educational Leadership*, 51(2), 52–56.

Nolan, Jim and Tania Huber. 1989. Nurturing the reflective practitioner through instructional supervision: A review of the literature. *Journal of Curriculum and Supervision*, 4(2), 126–145.

Numrich, Carol. 1996. On becoming a language teacher: Insights from diary studies. *TESOL Quarterly*, 30(1), 131–151.

Nunan, David. 1988. *The learner-centred curriculum*. Cambridge: Cambridge University Press.

Nunan, David. 1990. Action research in the language classroom. In Jack C. Richards and David Nunan (eds.), *Second language teacher education*. New York: Cambridge University Press, 62–81.

Nunan, David. 1992a. The teacher as decision-maker. In John Flowerdew, Mark N. Brock, and Sophie Hsia (eds.), *Perspectives on second language teacher education*. Hong Kong: City Polytechnic of Hong Kong, 133–165.

Nunan, David (ed.). 1992b. *Collaborative language learning and teaching*. Cambridge: Cambridge University Press.

Nunan, David. 1993. Action research in language education. In Julian Edge and Keith Richards (eds.), *Teachers develop teachers research: Papers on classroom research and teacher development*. Oxford: Heinemann, 39–50.

Nunan, David. 1996. Hidden voices: Insider's perspectives on classroom inter-action. In Kathleen M. Bailey and David Nunan (eds.), *Voices from the language classroom*. Cambridge: Cambridge University Press, 41–56.

Nunan, David. 1999a. So you think that language teaching is a profession? (Part 1). *TESOL Matters*, 9(4), 3.

Nunan, David. 1999b. So you think that language teaching is a profession? (Part 2). *TESOL Matters*, 9(3), 3.

Nunan, David and Clarice Lamb. 1996. *The self-directed teacher: Managing the learning process*. Cambridge: Cambridge University Press.

Nyikos, Martha and Reiko Hashimoto. 1997. Constructivist theory applied to collaborative learning in teacher education: In search of ZPD. *Modern Language Journal*, 81(4), 506–517.

Oates, J. C. 1990. Excerpts from a journal: July 1989. *Georgia Review*, 44(1 & 2), 121–134.

Ohta, Amy Snyder. 2000. Rethinking interaction in SLA: Developmentally appropriate assistance in the zone of proximal development and the acquisition of L2 grammar. In James P. Lantolf (ed.), *Sociocultural theory and second language learning*. Oxford: Oxford University Press, 51–78.

Oja, Sharon Nodie and Lisa Smulyan. 1989. *Collaborative action research: A developmental approach*. London: The Falmer Press.

Okeafor, Karen R. and Marybeth G. Poole. 1992. Instructional supervision and the avoidance process. *Journal of Curriculum and Supervision*, 7(4), 372–392.

Olshtain, Elite and Irit Kupferberg. 1998. Reflective-narrative discourse of FL teachers exhibits professional knowledge. *Language Teaching Research*, 2(3), 185–202.

Olson, J. K. 1982. Dilemmas of supervision: Teacher perspectives. *Teacher Education*, 20(1), 74–81.

Olson, M. W. 1991. Portfolios: Educational tools (research into practice). *Reading Psychology*, 12(1), 73–80.

Omaggio, Alice C. 1982. The relationship between personalized classroom talk and teacher effectiveness ratings: Some research results. *Foreign Language Annals*, 14(4), 255–269.

O'Neal, S. 1983. *Supervision of student teachers: Feedback and evaluation*. *Report no. 9047*. Clinical teacher education – pre-service. Austin: University of Texas.

Oprandy, Robert. 1999. Exploring with a supervisor. In Jerry G. Gebhard and Robert Oprandy (eds.), *Language teaching awareness: A guide to exploring beliefs and practices*. Cambridge: Cambridge University Press, 99–121.

Osburne, Andrea G. 1989. Situational leadership and teacher education. *System*, 17(3), 409–420.

Osunde, Edgerton O. 1999. *Understanding student teaching: Case studies of experience and suggestions for survival*. Lanham, MD: University Press of America.

Pajak, Edward. 1990. Dimensions of supervision. *Educational Leadership*, 48(1), 78–81.

Pajak, Edward. 1993. *Approaches to clinical supervision: Alternatives for improving instruction*. Norwood, MA: Christopher-Gordon Publishers.

Pennington, Martha C. 1989. Directions for faculty evaluation in language education. *Language, Culture and Curriculum*, 2(3), 167–193.

363

References

Pennington, Martha C. 1990. A professional development focus for the language teaching practicum. In Jack C. Richards and David Nunan (eds.), *Second language teacher education*. Cambridge: Cambridge University Press, 132–151.

Pennington, Martha C. 1995. The teacher change cycle. *TESOL Quarterly*, 29(4), 705–731.

Pennington, Martha C. 1996. When input becomes intake. In Donald Freeman and Jack Richards (eds.), *Teacher learning in language teaching*. New York: Cambridge University Press, 320–348.

Pennington, Martha C. and Belinda Ho. 1995. Do ESL educators suffer from burnout? *Prospect, A Journal of Australian TESOL*, 10(1), 4–53.

Pennington, Martha C. and Jack C. Richards. 1997. Reorienting the teaching universe: The experience of five first-year English teachers in Hong Kong. *Language Teaching Research*, 1(2), 149–178.

Pennington, Martha C. and Aileen L. Young. 1989. Approaches to faculty evaluation for ESL. *TESOL Quarterly*, 23(4), 619–646.

Pennycook, Alastair. 1997. Cultural alternatives and autonomy. In Phil Benson and Peter Voller (eds.), *Autonomy and independence in language learning*. London: Longman, 35–53.

Peterson, Penelope L. and Christopher M. Clark. 1978. Teachers' reports of their cognitive processes. *American Educational Research Journal*, 15(4), 555–565.

Pfeffer, Jeffrey. 1992. *Managing with power: Politics and influence in organizations*. Boston: Harvard Business School Press.

Phillipson, Robert 1992. *Linguistic imperialism*. Oxford: Oxford University Press.

Pierce, Lorraine Valdez. 1988. Peer coaching: An innovative approach to staff development. *NCBE Forum*, 11(3), 1, 6.

Pike, Graham and David Selby. 1988. *Global teacher, global learner*. London: Hodder & Stoughton.

Plaister, Ted. 1993. *ESOL case studies: The real world of L2 teaching and administration*. Englewood Cliffs, NJ: Regents/Prentice Hall.

Plakans, Barbara S. 1997. Undergraduates' experiences with and attitudes toward international teaching assistants. *TESOL Quarterly*, 31(1), 95–119.

Polio, Charlene and Carol Wilson-Duffy. 1998. Teaching ESL in an unfamiliar context: International students in a North American MA TESOL practicum. *TESOL Journal*, 7(4), 24–29.

Politzer, Robert L. 1970. Some reflections on "good" and "bad" language teaching behaviors. *Language Learning*, 20, 31–43.

Politzer, Robert L. and L. Weiss. 1970. *The successful foreign language teacher*. Philadelphia: The Center for Curriculum Development.

Poole, Wendy L. 1994. Removing the "super" from supervision. *Journal of Curriculum and Supervision*, 9(3), 284–309.

Popham, W. James. 1988. The dysfunctional marriage of formative and summative teacher evaluation. *Journal of Personnel Evaluation in Education*, 1, 269–273.

Porter, Carol and Janell Cleland. 1995. *The portfolio as a learning strategy*. Portsmouth, NH: Boynton/Cook Publishers.

Powell, Garry. 1999. How to avoid being the fly on the wall. *The Teacher Trainer*, 13(1), 3–4.

Pugh, S. L. 1996. Critical reading and reasoning in the content areas. Unpublished course syllabus, Indiana University.

Quirke, Phil. 1996. Using unseen observations for an IST development program. *The Teacher Trainer*, 10(1), 18–20.

Reeser, Clayton. 1973. *Management: Functions and modern concepts*. Chicago: Scott, Foresman.

Reichelt, Melinda. 2000. Case studies in L2 teacher education. *ELT Journal*, 54(4), 346–353.

Retallick, J. 1990. Clinical supervision and the structure of communication. *Education Action*, 1(2), 14–32.

Rhodes, Nancy C. and Audrey L. Heining-Boynton. 1993. Teacher training with a twist: A collaborative project in North Carolina. *Foreign Language Annals*, 26(2), 155–170.

Richards, Jack C. 1990a. *The language teaching matrix*. Cambridge: Cambridge University Press, 118–143.

Richards, Jack C. 1990b. The dilemma of teacher education in second language teaching. In Jack C. Richards and David Nunan (eds.), *Second language teacher education*. Cambridge: Cambridge University Press, 3–15.

Richards, Jack C. (ed.). 1998. *Teaching in action: Case studies from second language classrooms*. Alexandria, VA: TESOL.

Richards, Jack C. and Graham Crookes. 1988. The practicum in TESOL. *TESOL Quarterly*, 22(1), 9–27.

Richards, Jack C. and Charles Lockhart. 1994. *Reflective teaching in second language classrooms*. Cambridge: Cambridge University Press.

Richards, Jack C. and David Nunan. 1990. *Second language teacher education*. New York: Cambridge University Press.

Richards, Keith. 2002. TRUST: A management perspective on CPD. In Julian Edge (ed.), *Continuing professional development: Some of our perspectives*. Whitstable, UK: IATEFL, 71–79.

Rinvolucri, Mario. 1981. Resistance to change on in-service teacher training courses. *Recherches et Echanges*, 6(1), 45–52.

Rogers, Carmen Villegas. 1987. Improving the performance of teaching assistants in the multi-section classroom. *Foreign Language Annals*, 20(5), 403–410.

Rokeach, Milton. 1971. *Beliefs, attitudes, and values: A theory of organization and change*. San Francisco: Jossey Bass.

Rooney, Joanne. 1993. Teacher evaluation: No more "super"vision. *Educational Leadership*, 51(2), 43–44.

Rosencranz, Howard A. and Bruce J. Biddle. 1964. The role approach to teacher competence. In Bruce J. Biddle and William J. Ellena (eds.), *Contemporary research on teacher effectiveness*. New York: Holt, Rinehart and Winston, 232–263.

Rosenshine, Barak V. 1971. New directions for research on teaching. In *How teachers make a difference*. U.S. Department of Health, Education, and Welfare, Catalogue number HE 5.258: 58044, 69–95.

Rosenshine, Barak V. and Norma Furst. 1973. The use of direct observation to study teaching. In Robert M. W. Travers (ed.), *Handbook of research on teaching (2nd ed.)*. Chicago: Rand McNally, 122–183.

Rounds, Patricia L. 1987. Characterizing successful classroom discourse for NNS teaching assistant training. *TESOL Quarterly*, 21(4), 643–671.

Rowley, James B. and Patricia M. Hart. 1996. How video case studies can promote reflective dialogue. *Educational Leadership*, 53(6), 28–29.

Rueda, Robert. 1998. *Standards for professional development: A sociocultural perspective.* (Research Brief No. 2). Santa Cruz, CA: University of California, Center for Research on Education, Diversity and Excellence.

Samimy, Keiko K. and Janina Brutt-Griffler. 1999. To be a native or a non-native speaker: Perceptions of "non-native" students in a graduate TESOL program. In George Braine (ed.), *Non-native educators in English language teaching.* Mahwah, NJ: Lawrence Erlbaum, 127–144.

Saraswathi, V. 1991. Coping with teacher resistance: Insights from INSET programmes. In Eugenius Sadtono (ed.), *Language teacher education in a fast changing world.* Singapore: Regional Language Centre (Anthology Series 29), 75–87.

Savage, Deborah A. and Paul L. Robertson. 1999. The maintenance of professional authority: The case of physicians and hospitals in the United States. In Paul L. Robertson (ed.), *Authority and control in modern industry: Theoretical and empirical perspectives.* London: Routledge, 155–172.

Schmidt, Richard. 1995. Consciousness and foreign language learning: A tutorial on the role of attention and awareness in learning. In Richard Schmidt (ed.), *Attention and awareness in foreign language learning* (Technical Report #9). Honolulu, HI: University of Hawaii Second Language Teaching and Curriculum Center, 1–63.

Schmidt, Richard and Sylvia Nagem Frota. 1986. Developing conversational ability in a second language: A case study of an adult learner of Portuguese. In Richard R. Day (ed.), *Talking to learn: Conversation in second language acquisition.* Rowley, MA: Newbury House, 237–326.

Schön, Donald A. 1983. *The reflective practitioner: How professionals think in action.* New York: Basic Books.

Schön, Donald A. 1987. *Educating the reflective practitioner: Toward a new design for teaching and learning in the professions.* San Francisco: Jossey-Bass.

Schön, Donald A. (ed.). 1991. Introduction. In Donald A. Schön (ed.), *The reflective turn: Case studies in and on educational practice.* New York: Teachers College Press, 1–11.

Schwebel, Sara L., David C. Schwebel, Bernice L. Schwebel, and Carol R. Schwebel. 2002. *The student teacher's handbook (4th ed.).* Mahwah, NJ: Lawrence Erlbaum.

Seaman, Alan, Barry Sweeny, Pamela Meadows, and Marilyn Sweeny. 1997. Collaboration, reflection, and professional growth: A mentoring program for adult ESL teachers. *TESOL Journal*, 7(1), 31–34.

Sergiovanni, Thomas J. 1977. Reforming teacher evaluation: Naturalistic alternatives. *Educational Leadership*, 34(8), 602–607.

Sergiovanni, Thomas J. 1982. Toward a theory of supervisory practice: Integrating scientific, clinical, and artistic views. In Thomas J. Sergiovanni (ed.), *Supervision of teaching.* Alexandria, VA: ASCD, 67–80.

Sergiovanni, Thomas J. 1984. Expanding conceptions of inquiry and practice in supervision and evaluation. *Educational Evaluation and Policy Analysis*, 6(4), 355–365.

Sergiovanni, Thomas J. 1985. Landscapes, mindscapes, and reflective practice in supervision. *Journal of Curriculum and Supervision*, 1(1), 5–17.

Sergiovanni, Thomas J. 1986. A theory of practice for clinical supervision. In W. John Smyth (ed.), *Learning about teaching through clinical supervision.* London: Croom Helm, 37–58.

Sergiovanni, Thomas J. 1989. Science and scientism in supervision and teaching. *Journal of Curriculum and Supervision,* 4(2), 93–105.

Shapiro, Phyllis P. and Agnes Teresa Sheehan. 1986. The supervision of student teachers: A new diagnostic tool. *Journal of Teacher Education,* 37(6), 35–39.

Shavelson, Richard. 1973. *The basic teaching skill: Decision making.* R & D Memorandum No. 104, Stanford, CA: Stanford University, School of Education.

Shaw, Peter A. 1979. Handling a language component in a teacher training course. In Susan Holden (ed.), *Teacher Training* (special issue No. 3 of *Modern English Teacher*). London: Modern English Publications, 12–15.

Shea, Catherine and Carolyn Babione. 2001. The electronic enhancement of supervision project (EESP). In *Growing partnerships for rural special education: Conference proceedings.* San Diego, CA. Abstract retrieved July 24, 2002 from ERIC database.

Sheal, Peter. 1989. Classroom observation: Training the observers. *English Language Teaching Journal,* 43(2), 92–103.

Showers, Beverly. 1985. Teachers coaching teachers. *Educational Leadership,* 42 (7), 43–48.

Showers, Beverly and Bruce R. Joyce. 1996. The evolution of peer coaching. *Educational Leadership,* 53(6), 12–16.

Shrigley, Robert L. and Ronald A. Walker. 1981. Positive verbal response patterns: A model for successful supervisor-teacher conferences. *School, Science and Mathematics,* 81(7), 560–562.

Shulman, Lee S. 1992. Toward a pedagogy of cases. In Judith H. Shulman (ed.), *Case methods in teacher education.* New York: Teachers College Press, 1–30.

Slimani, Assia. 1987. The teaching/learning relationship: Learning opportunities and the problem of uptake – an Algerian case study. Unpublished doctoral dissertation, University of Lancaster, UK.

Smith, Jan, Nancy Stenson, and K. A. Winkler. 1980. Toward more effective teacher observation and evaluation. Paper presented at the 1980 TESOL Convention, San Francisco.

Soppelsa, Elizabeth F. 1997. Empowerment of faculty. In Mary Ann Christison and Fredricka L. Stoller (eds.), *A handbook for language program administrators.* Burlingame, CA: Alta Book Center Publishers, 123–141.

Stanley, Claire. 1995. Teacher supervision and reflectivity: A relational and interactional process. Unpublished doctoral dissertation, Lesley College, Cambridge, MA.

Stanley, Claire. 1998. A framework for teacher reflectivity. *TESOL Quarterly,* 32(3), 584–591.

Stenson, Nancy, Jan Smith, and William Perry. 1979. Videotape and the training and evaluation of language teachers. Paper presented at the 1979 TESOL Convention, Boston, MA.

Stodolsky, Susan S. 1984. Teacher evaluation: The limits of looking. *Educational Researcher,* 13, 11–22.

Stoller, Fredricka L. 1996. Teacher supervision: Moving towards an interactive approach. *English Teacher Forum*, 34, 2–9.

Stones, Edgar. 1987. Teaching practice supervision: Bridge between theory and practice. *European Journal of Teacher Education*, 10(1), 67–79.

Strevens, Peter. 1989. The achievement of excellence in language teaching. In John H. Esling (ed.), *Multicultural education and policy: ESL in the 1990's*. Toronto: Ontario Institute for Studies in Education, 73–87.

Stronge, James H. (ed.). 1997. *Evaluating teaching: A guide to current thinking and best practice*. Thousand Oaks, CA: Corwin Press.

Sturman, Peter. 1992. Team teaching: A case study from Japan. In David Nunan (ed.), *Collaborative language learning and teaching*. Cambridge: Cambridge University Press, 141–161.

Sukwiwat, Mayuri and Larry E. Smith. 1981. TESOL and training non-native English speakers: Are M.A. teacher education programs getting the job done? In Janet C. Fisher, Mark A. Clarke, and Jacquelyn Schachter (eds.), *On TESOL '80 – Building bridges: Research and practice in teaching English as a second language*. Washington, DC: TESOL, 3–14.

Sullivan, Susan and Jeffrey Glanz. 2000. *Supervision that improves teaching: Strategies and techniques*. Thousand Oaks, CA: Corwin Press.

Swan, June. 1993. Metaphor in action: The observation schedule in a reflective approach to teacher education. *English Language Teaching Journal*, 47(3), 242–249.

Tajino, Akira and Yasuko Tajino. 2000. Native and non-native: What can they offer? Lessons from team-teaching in Japan. *English Language Teaching Journal*, 54(1), 3–11.

Tanner, R., D. Longayroux, D. Beijaard, and N. Verloop. 2000. Piloting portfolios: Using portfolios in pre-service teacher education. *ELT Journal*, 54(1), 20–30.

Taska, Betty K. 1975. Teacher training for the non-native speaker in francophone Africa. In Ruth Crymes and William E. Norris (eds.), *On TESOL '74*. Washington, DC: TESOL, 67–72.

Telatnik, Mary Ann. 1978. The intensive journal as self-evaluative instrument. Paper presented at the 1978 Annual TESOL Convention, Mexico City.

Terry, Robert M. 1992. Improving inter-rater reliability in scoring tests in multisection courses. In Joel C. Walz (ed.), *Development and supervision of teaching assistants in foreign languages*. Boston: Heinle & Heinle, 229–262.

Thomas, Jacinta. 1999. Voices from the periphery: Non-native teachers and issues of credibility. In George Braine (ed.), *Non-native educators in English language teaching*. Mahwah, NJ: Lawrence Erlbaum, 5–13.

Thomson, W. Scott and Parmalee P. Hawk. 1996. Project dist-ed: Teleconferencing as a means of supporting and assisting beginning teachers. *Action in Teacher Education*, 17(4), 9–17.

Tinker Sachs, Gertrude. 2002. Learning Cantonese: Reflections of an EFL teacher educator. In David C. S. Li (ed.), *Discourses in search of members: In honor of Ron Scollon*. Lanham, MD: University Press of America, 509–540.

Tinker Sachs, Gertrude, Mark N. Brock, and Regina Lo. 1996. *Directions in second language teacher education*. Hong Kong: City University of Hong Kong.

Tinker Sachs, Gertrude, Julia Cheung, Dorothy Pang, and Mary Wong. 1998. Transforming the supervision of English language teachers in Hong Kong. *Asia Pacific Journal of Language in Education*, 1(2), 102–128.

Tisher, Richard P. 1984. Teacher induction: An international perspective on provisions and research. In Lillian G. Katz and James D. Roths (eds.), *Advances in teacher education, Volume 1*. Norwood, NJ: Ablex, 113–123.

Tracy, Saundra J. and Robert H. MacNaughton. 1989. Clinical supervision and the emerging conflict between the neo-traditionalists and the neo-progressives. *Journal of Curriculum and Supervision* 4(3), 246–256.

Underhill, Adrian. 1992. The role of groups in developing teacher self-awareness. *ELT Journal*, 46(1), 71–80.

Van den Berg, Rudolf, Peter Sleegers, and Femke Geijsel. 2001. Teachers' concerns about adaptive teaching: Evaluation of a support program. *Journal of Curriculum and Supervision*, 16(3), 245–258.

Van Wagenen, Linda and K. Michael Hibbard. 1998. Building teacher portfolios. *Educational Leadership*, 55(5), 26–29.

Venn, Martha L., Larry R. Moore, and Philip L. Gunter, 2000–2001. Using audio/video conferencing to observe field-based practices of rural teachers. *Rural Educator*, 22(2), 24–27.

Verity, Deryn P. 2000. Side affects: The strategic development of professional satisfaction. In James P. Lantolf (ed.), *Sociocultural theory and second language learning*. Oxford: Oxford University Press, 179–197.

Vigil, N. A. and J. W. Oller. 1976. Rule fossilization: A tentative model. *Language Learning*, 26, 281–295.

Vygotsky, Lev S. 1978. *Mind in society: The development of higher psychological processes*. Cambridge: Harvard University Press.

Wagner, Laura A. 1985. Ambiguities and possibilities in California's mentor teacher program. *Educational Leadership*, 43, 23–29.

Waite, Duncan. 1992a. Supervisors' talk: Making sense of conferences from an anthropological linguistic perspective. *Journal of Curriculum and Supervision*, 7(4), 349–371.

Waite, Duncan. 1992b. Instructional supervision from a situational perspective. *Teaching & Teacher Education*, 8(4), 319–332.

Waite, Duncan. 1993. Teachers in conference: A qualitative study of teacher-supervisor face-to-face interactions. *American Educational Research Journal*, 30(4), 675–702.

Waite, Duncan. 1995. Teacher resistance in a supervision conference. In David Corson (ed.), *Discourse and power in educational organizations*. Cresskill, NJ: Hampton Press, 71–86.

Wajnryb, Ruth. 1986. Learning to teach – The place of self-evaluation. *TESL Reporter*, 19(4), 69–73.

Wajnryb, Ruth. 1992. The lightbulb has to want to change: Supervision as a collaborative process. *TESOL in Context*, 2(1), 6–8.

Wajnryb, Ruth. 1994a. The pragmatics of feedback: A study of mitigation in the supervisory discourse of TESOL teacher educators. Unpublished doctoral dissertation, Macquarie University, Sydney, NSW, Australia.

Wajnryb, Ruth. 1994b. Pragmatics and supervisory discourse: Matching method and purpose. *Prospect, A Journal of Australian TESOL*, 9(1), 29–38.

References

Wajnryb, Ruth. 1995a. Teachers' perceptions of mitigation in supervisory discourse: A report of a pilot study. *South Pacific Journal of Teacher Education*, 23(1), 71–82.

Wajnryb, Ruth. 1995b. The perception of criticism: One trainee's experience. *ELICOS Association Journal*, 13(1), 54–68.

Wajnryb, Ruth. 1998. Telling it like it isn't – exploring an instance of pragmatic ambivalence in supervisory discourse. *Journal of Pragmatics*, 29, 531–544.

Walen, Elizabeth and Mimi DeRose. 1993. The power of peer appraisals. *Educational Leadership*, 51(2), 45–48.

Wallace, Michael J. 1979. *Microteaching and the teaching of English as a second or foreign language in teacher training institutions*. Edinburgh: Scottish Centre of Education Overseas.

Wallace, Michael J. 1981. The use of video in EFL teacher training. *ELT documents 110 – Focus on the teacher: Communicative approaches to teacher training*. London: The British Council, 7–21.

Wallace, Michael J. 1991. *Training foreign language teachers: A reflective approach*. Cambridge: Cambridge University Press.

Wallace, Michael J. 1998. *Action research for language teachers*. Cambridge: Cambridge University Press.

Wallace, Michael J. 2000. The case for case studies. *IATEFL Research SIG and Teacher Development SIG Newsletter: Special Joint Issue*. June, 12–18.

Wallace, Michael and David Woolger. 1991. Improving the ELT supervisory dialogue: The Sri Lanka experience. *English Language Teaching Journal*, 45(4), 320–327.

Walz, Garry R. and Edward C. Roeber. 1962. Supervisors' reactions to a counseling interview. *Counselor Education and Supervision*, 2(1), 2–7.

Walz, Joel D. (ed.). 1992. *Development and supervision of teaching assistants in foreign languages*. Boston: Heinle & Heinle.

Watson-Gegeo, Karen. 1988. Ethnography in ESL: Defining the essentials. *TESOL Quarterly*, 22(4), 575–592.

Weinstein, Carol Simon. 1989. Case studies of extended teacher preparation. In Anita E. Woolfolk (ed.), *Research perspectives on the graduate preparation of teachers*. Englewood Cliffs, NJ: Prentice Hall, 30–50.

Welskopp, Thomas. 1999. Class structures and the firm: The interplay of workplace and industrial relations in large capitalist enterprises. Paul L. Robertson (ed.), *Authority and control in modern industry: Theoretical and empirical perspectives*. London: Routledge, 73–119.

Wenger, Etienne. 1998. *Communities of practice: Learning, meaning and identity*. New York: Cambridge University Press.

Wenzlaff, Terri L. and Katherine E. Cummings. 1996. The portfolio as metaphor for teacher reflection. *Contemporary Education*, 67(2), 109–112.

Wertsch, James V. 1991. *Voices of the mind: A sociocultural approach to mediated action*. Cambridge: Harvard University Press.

Wertsch, James V., Pablo del Río, and Amelia Alvarez (eds.). 1995. *Sociocultural studies of mind*. Cambridge: Cambridge University Press.

Westerman, Delores. 1991. Expert and novice teacher decision making. *Journal of Teacher Education*, 42(4), 292–305.

Wheeless, L. R. and J. Grotz, 1977. The measurement of trust and its relationship to self-disclosure. *Human Communication Research*, 4, 143–157.

White, Ron, Mervyn Martin, Mike Stimpson, and Robert Hodge. 1991. *Management in English language teaching*. New York: Cambridge University Press.

Wiles, Kimball. 1967. *Supervision for better schools (final ed.)*. Englewood Cliffs, NJ: Prentice-Hall.

Wilkin, Margaret. 1992. On the cusp – from supervision to mentoring in initial teacher training. *Cambridge Journal of Education*, 22(1), 79–90.

Williams, Marion. 1989. A developmental view of classroom observation. *English Language Teaching Journal*, 43(2), 85–91.

Winer, Lise. 1992. Spinach to chocolate: Changing awareness and attitudes in ESL writing teachers. *TESOL Quarterly*, 26(1), 57–80.

Wise, Arthur E., Linda Darling-Hammond, Milbrey W. McLaughlin, and Harriet T. Bernstein. 1984. *Case studies for teacher evaluation: A study of effective practices*. Santa Monica, CA: Rand Corporation.

Wolf, Kenneth. 1996. Developing an effective teaching portfolio. *Educational Leadership*, 53(6), 34–37.

Wolfe-Quintero, Kate and James Dean Brown. 1998. Teacher portfolios. *TESOL Journal*, 7(6), 24–27.

Woods, Devon. 1989. Studying ESL teachers' decision-making: Rationale, methodological issues, and initial results. *Carleton Papers in Applied Language Studies*. Ottawa: Carleton University.

Woods, Devon. 1996. *Teacher cognition in language teaching: Beliefs, decision-making, and classroom practice*. Cambridge: Cambridge University Press.

Yeung, Ka Wah and David Watkins. 1998. Assessing student teachers' professional self-esteem: A Hong Kong construct validation study. Unpublished PhD thesis, University of Hong Kong. Abstract retrieved July 23, 2002, from ERIC database.

Yu, Ren Dong. 2000. Learning to see diverse students through reflective teaching portfolios. In Karen E. Johnson (ed.), *Teacher education*. Alexandria, VA: TESOL, 137–153.

Zahorik, John A. 1988. The observing-conferencing role of university supervisors. *Journal of Teacher Education*, 39(2), 9–16.

Zahorik, John A. 1992. Perspectives and imperatives: Good teaching and supervision. *Journal of Curriculum and Supervision*, 7(4), 393–404.

Zeichner, Kenneth M. and Daniel P. Liston. 1985. Varieties of discourse in supervisory conferences. *Teaching and Teacher Education*, 1(2), 155–174.

Zeichner, Kenneth M. and Daniel P. Liston. 1987. Teaching student teachers to reflect. *Harvard Educational Review*, 57(1), 23–47.

Zeichner, Kenneth M. and Daniel P. Liston. 1996. *Reflective teaching: An introduction*. Mahwah, NJ: Lawrence Erlbaum.

Zepeda, Sally J. and Judith A. Ponticell. 1998. At cross-purposes: What do teachers need, want, and get from supervision? *Journal of Curriculum and Supervision*, 14(1), 68–87.

Zuck, Joyce Gilmour. 1984. Comments on Peter Master's "the etiquette of observing." *TESOL Quarterly*, 17(4), 337–341.

Author index

373

Author index

374

Subject index

account behavior, 155–156
accuracy, 298
action meeting, 188, 339
action research, 76, 318, 332–335, 341–344
action-taking, 60, 68–69, 71–72, 76, 220
activating, 36–37
activity theory, 43
administrative supervision, 11, 30
adversarial role, 145–146, 167, 179–180
affective issues, 20–21, 29
affiliation related behavior, 156–157, 159
affordance, 44, 288
alertness, 36
alternatives option, 13–15, 22, 28–30, 51,
    118, 136, 154, 180, 195, 273, 288,
    326, 328
anxiety, 38, 87, 88, 116, 182
applied science model, 150–153, 241
apprenticeship of observation, 279
artifacts, 194, 196, 203
asides, 170, 174–176
aspect shift, 170–172
attention, 36, 40, 114, 128–129, 167, 253
attestations, 196, 203
attitude(s), 19, 20, 27, 29, 34–35, 37–38,
    40–41, 44, 46–48, 50–53, 65, 67–68,
    78, 96, 118, 136–137, 142, 144, 157,
    169, 208, 216, 223, 247, 256, 264,
    276–277, 289–291, 308, 310, 314,
    318–319, 325–326, 333, 343
audiolingual method, 66, 112, 209
audiotape recording, 87, 90, 99–101,
    121–124, 127–129, 132, 135–138,
    145, 180, 192, 224, 229, 236, 270,
    272, 274, 286, 300, 326, 334
authentic materials, 298, 300, 313
authored case studies, 24
authority, 19–20, 27, 29, 45, 54, 56,
    58, 60–61, 68, 73–78, 80, 129,
    146–148, 158, 167, 185, 314, 320,
    329, 339–340
  charismatic, 73
  delegated, 73–74, 77
  functional, 74
  genuine, 73–74, 77, 79
  legal, 73
  traditional, 73

autonomy, 27, 45, 54–57, 59–61, 63, 68, 71,
    73, 76–78, 80, 126, 158, 194, 269, 289,
    314, 318, 329, 331
awareness, 27, 34–41, 44–53, 62, 65–67, 75,
    78, 96, 118, 124–126, 135–137, 141,
    143, 157, 211, 223, 236, 247, 264, 271,
    290–291, 310, 314, 343
  focal, 36, 50
  subsidiary, 36, 50
  peripheral, 36
awareness hypothesis, 34, 52

backstage supervisors, 286–289
beginning teacher(s), 267, 276–277, 289
beliefs, 40–41, 83, 86, 101, 115, 144, 147,
    196, 208, 223, 239, 270, 280, 325–326
blind self, 38–39, 128, 137
burnout, 267, 277, 281–284, 289, 292

case, 2, 22–25, 32–33
case approach, 2, 22
casebooks, 23
case materials, 23, 32, 135
case report, 23–24, 32, 33
case study, 22–24, 32, 33, 204, 236, 249, 270
casual supervision, 11, 30
change, 15, 18, 35, 37, 40, 44–45, 52, 56,
    65–66, 72, 76, 79–80, 125–127, 137,
    141, 143–144, 146, 158–159, 185, 233,
    274, 277, 280, 318, 320–325, 329, 343
classic collaborative approach, 16, 19, 30,
    76, 319, 329, 332
classic prescriptive approach, 16, 19, 30, 56,
    60, 72, 75–76, 192, 319, 329, 331, 339
clause structure, 170–171, 173
clerical supervision, 11–12, 30, 194, 201
clinical supervision, 12–13, 15, 29–30, 92,
    144, 250, 319–322, 326, 343
cluster improvement team, 322
coach, 12, 30, 194, 337
coaching, 239, 292, 318, 332, 336–344
  technical, 337–38
  collegial, 337–338
  challenge, 337–338
  team, 337–338
cognitive apprenticeship, 231
collaborative role, 145–146, 179–180

379

Subject index